Play Therapy

Basics and Beyond

TERRY KOTTMAN

JEFFREY S. ASHBY

American
Counseling
Association

counseling.org

American Counseling Association
2461 Eisenhower Avenue, Suite 300
Alexandria, Viriginia 22314

Published in the United States of America

Publisher's Cataloging-in-Publication Data

Names: Kottman, Terry, author. | Ashby, Jeffrey S., author.
Title: Play therapy : basics and beyond / Terry Kottman and Jeffrey S. Ashby.
    -- 3rd ed.
Description: Alexandria, VA : American Counseling Association, [2024] |
    Includes bibliographical references and index.
Identifiers: LCCN 2024934614 ISBN 9781556204210 (paperback)
Subjects: LCSH Play therapy | Psychotherapy
Classification: LCC RJ505.P6 K643 2024 | DDC 616.89'1653--dc23
LC record available at https://lccn.loc.gov/2024934614

To Rick and Jacob—my two favorite people in the universe.
—Hugs, Terry

To Lucy, Samuel, John and Emily, Eliza, and Isaac.
—Always, Jeff

Contents

Preface i

Acknowledgements v

Basic Concepts

1. Introduction to Play Therapy 3

2. History of Play Therapy 35

3. Theoretical Approaches to Play Therapy 49

Basic Skills

4. Logistical Aspects of Play Therapy 107

5. Tracking 133

6. Restating Content 143

7. Reflecting Feelings 157

8. Setting Limits 175

9. Returning Responsibility to the Child 199

10. Dealing with Questions 217

11. Integration of Basic Skills 235

Advanced Skills and Concepts

12. Recognizing and Communicating Through Metaphors 255

13. Advanced Play Therapy Skills 281

14. Assessing Themes and Patterns in the Child's Play 311

15. Working With Parents, Caregivers, and Teachers................................ 325

16. Professional Issues in Play Therapy..347

    References.. 375

    Appendix A 415

    Appendix B 429

    Appendix C 451

    Index 453

Preface

Over the past 35 years, the demand for mental health professionals and school counselors who have training and expertise in using play as a therapeutic modality in working with children has increased tremendously. There has been a commensurate demand for trained play therapists. I (TK) designed the first edition of *Play Therapy: Basics and Beyond* to provide an introduction to the different skills used in play therapy combined with an atheoretical orientation to the basic concepts involved in play therapy. It was a practical introduction to play therapy concepts and skills. The book stressed the application of various play therapy strategies across a wide range of theoretical orientations. The second edition contained updated references, new developments in the field of play therapy, along with expanded information about professional issues and multicultural applications of play therapy. Building upon the second edition, this third edition has expanded the clinical examples, exercises, and questions for readers to consider. We have also added an extra chapter to this edition on assessing themes and patterns in the child's play.

The book has been widely used to teach introductory play therapy and child counseling courses, and its primary intended audience is students enrolled in these courses. Because the book provides information about many different theoretical orientations, it can be helpful no matter the theoretical orientation of the professor, the program, or the student. The book is also for clinicians who want to have more knowledge and understanding of play therapy but do not have access to formal training in the field.

With these two audiences in mind, we have made some assumptions about the backgrounds of those using the book as their entry to the world of play therapy. We assumed that the reader has some basic background in counseling, psychology, social work, or some other related field—many of the terms and concepts used in this book are borrowed from other mental health-related areas. We also assume that the reader has some knowledge and exposure to children and at least a general understanding of child development.

Plan of the Book

Chapters 1 through 3 compose *Part 1, Basic Concepts*. In Chapter 1, "Introduction to Play Therapy," we provide an explanation of the paradigm shift necessary to move from talk as therapy to play as therapy, several definitions and rationales for play therapy, descriptions of the therapeutic powers of play, information about appropriate clients for play therapy, and descriptions of characteristics and experiences needed by therapists who want to use play as a treatment modality. In Chapter 2, "History of Play Therapy," the reader will learn about the evolution of play therapy. Chapter 3, "Theoretical Approaches to Play Therapy," contains expanded descriptions of nine selected contemporary approaches to play therapy, focusing on the theoretical constructs, the stages of play therapy, the role of the therapist, goals of therapy, approaches to working with parents, and distinctive features of each approach. We have also added information about several "burgeoning" new approaches to play therapy to expand the theoretical orientation options.

Chapters 4 through 11 compose *Part 2, Basic Skills*. In Chapter 4, "Logistical Aspects of Play Therapy," the reader will learn about setting up a space for play therapy, choosing and arranging toys, explaining the play therapy process to parents and children, handling the initial session, assessing children's play behavior, dealing with paperwork, ending a session, and terminating the therapy process. Several basic play therapy skills are used in most approaches to play therapy: (a) tracking behavior, (b) restating content, (c) reflecting feelings, (d) limiting, (e) returning responsibility to the child, and (f) dealing with questions. The application of these skills varies depending on the therapist's theoretical orientation and the therapy stage, but most play therapists use them at one time or another. In Chapters 5 through 10, we define each of these skills, delineate the purpose for their use in the play therapy process, and explain how they can be applied in various situations in play therapy. To make each skill more concrete and accessible to the reader, we provide examples of the application of the skill and invite the reader to practice it using exercises tailored to demonstrate various situations in which the skills would be appropriate. At the end of each chapter, the reader will find practice exercises designed to hone the application of the specific skill. We believe that all play therapists need to look at their own thoughts, feelings, attitudes, and personal issues to become truly skillful in working with children. The "Questions to Ponder" at the end of each chapter are our attempt to facilitate this self-examination process. In Chapter 5, "Tracking," the reader will learn about using tracking to establish a relationship with the child. Building rapport is also the focus of Chapter 6, "Restating Content." The reader can explore strategies for reflecting feelings to help the child learn to understand their emotions in Chapter 7, "Reflecting Feelings." In Chapter 8, "Setting Limits," we provide the reader with several different techniques for limiting inappropriate behavior in the playroom. In Chapter 9, "Returning Responsibility to the Child," a rationale and description of methods for returning responsibility to the child will help the reader explore this important skill. Because all children in the playroom ask questions, the reader will learn how to understand possible meanings and how to handle queries in Chapter 10, "Dealing with Questions." In Chapter 11, "Integration of Basic Skills: The Art of Play Therapy," we provide an explanation of and practice in methods for deciding which skill to use when and for integrating different skills to create a combined intervention that works more smoothly and more efficaciously than an isolated skill would. The reader will also explore the need to blend the therapist's personality and interactional style with play therapy skills to present a more natural flow of interaction with the child.

Chapters 12 through 16 compose *Part 3, Advanced Skills and Concepts*. Much of the communication that takes place in play therapy comes in the form of metaphors. Chapter 12, "Recognizing and Communicating Through Metaphors," contains descriptions of strategies and practice exercises for learning to understand possible meanings of children's metaphors. The reader will also learn and practice ways to use metaphors created by children to facilitate communication with them in their own natural language. In this chapter there is also information on designing therapeutic metaphors and other storytelling techniques that can be used in play therapy. Chapter 13, "Advanced Play Therapy Skills," includes information on using metacommunication, visualization strategies, art techniques, sand tray play therapy, and role playing/playing with children in play therapy. In this chapter, the reader will find examples of the application of each of these advanced skills and exercises that provide guided practice in their use. Chapter 14, "Assessing Themes and Patterns in the Child's Play," is a new chapter we added based on requests from other professionals who have used the book in the past as a cross-theoretical guide for helping play therapists explore the themes present in children's play. In the years since the previous two editions of this book, the research in the field has suggested that one of the main factors that increase the efficacy of play therapy is working with parents. There have also been some suggestions in the literature that consulting with teachers of children who are struggling in school can also enhance the efficacy of play therapy. Chapter 15, "Working with Parents and Teachers," is an overview of the information available concerning filial therapy, Kinder Training, Parent-Child Interaction Therapy, Familial Encouraging Connection Therapy, and Adlerian parent and teacher consultation. Because play therapy is an emerging profession, it is essential that individuals interested in the field stay informed about professional issues that can have an impact on the field. To facilitate this process, in Chapter 16, "Professional Issues in Play Therapy," we include information on the following issues: (a) legal and ethical issues, (b) cultural competence and cultural humility, (c) inclusion of aggressive toys in the playroom, (d) technology in the play-room, and (e) advice to new play therapists from experts in the field.

Becoming a Trained Play Therapist

Reading this book will not transform the reader into a trained play therapist. To become a play therapist, it is essential to thoroughly study the concepts and information in this text, explore specific the-oretical approaches in more depth, learn more about both beginning and advanced-level play therapy skills, and gain experience working with children using play therapy interventions under the supervision of a play therapy professional. We believe that an introductory play therapy class should require the students to conduct multiple play therapy sessions for which they receive feedback from experienced play therapists before venturing to conduct other play therapy sessions (also under the supervision of a trained and experienced play therapy supervisor). We also believe that an individual who wishes to become a play therapist must continue to work on their own personal issues. Several organizations (e.g., Association for Play Therapy, Canadian Association for Child and Play Therapy, British Association of Play Therapy) have provided guidelines for the training and supervised clinical experience necessary to become a trained play therapist.

Acknowledgements

Thanks to my students and my clients over the past 40 years (Yikes!!) of doing play therapy—you help me learn more about play therapy every time I have the pleasure and privilege of hanging out with you.

Thanks to the baristas (and bakers) at Cup of Joe in Cedar Falls, Iowa, who have kept me supplied with single tall iced gingerbread lattes, smoothies, and muffins for months while I worked semi-diligently on this book. Dawn, Leah, Lex, Megan, Vanessa, Xandra, Toby, Monica, Caleb, Indo, Amy, Nora, Isaac, Sue, and Rae, you have kept me going.

Terry

Thanks to play therapy and adventure therapy students at Georgia State over the (many) years. I have learned from you, been inspired by you, and am honored to know you.

Jeff

Basic Concepts

Introduction to Play Therapy

Kendrick walks into a room in which there is an assortment of toys on the shelves and the floor—puppets, a dollhouse and dolls, cars, trucks, a wooden stove and refrigerator, plastic snakes and spiders, figures of animals and superheroes, and many other play materials. He looks around the room and chooses several different figures for play—a tiger, a wolf, a dinosaur, and a family of deer. He starts telling a story about the smallest deer getting "bullied" by the tiger, wolf, and dinosaur. He tries to tell the bigger deer that this is happening to the smallest, but the bigger deer ignores him. A man who is sitting with him talks to him about his play, acknowledging what is happening in the story, reflecting the feelings of the smallest deer, and making comments about what is happening between the smallest deer, the other members of the deer family, and the other animals.

This is play therapy.

• • •

Ginny and her parents come into a room that has some large pillows on the floor. A woman is sitting on the floor next to the pillows. Ginny's parents go to sit on chairs in the corner with a man who talks to them. The woman on the floor is excited that Ginny is there and announces that they are going to have such fun together. The woman brings out several different hats. As she and Ginny try on hats and make faces in a mirror, the man with her parents explains what the woman and Ginny are doing and why, telling the parents that they will soon join in the fun.

This is play therapy.

● ● ●

Bae-Hoon enters a room with a table in the middle. On the table are a dollhouse, some doll furniture (including a bathtub), some family figures (two parents and three children), and a sand tray figure of a tornado. A person sitting at a table in the room suggests that Bae-Hoon show what happened when he and his family were huddled in their bathtub for safety while a tornado destroyed their house. Bae-Hoon and the person at the table use some blocks to build a house, which Bae-Hoon knocks down several times while crying.

This is play therapy.

● ● ●

Play therapy is an approach to counseling young children in which the counselor uses toys, art supplies, games, and other play media to communicate with clients using the "language" of children—the language of play. Because children under age 12 have relatively limited ability to verbalize their feelings and thoughts and to use abstract thinking and verbal reasoning, most lack the ability to come into a counseling session, sit down, and use words to tell the therapist about their problems. (Imagine a child coming into a therapist's office, sitting down on the couch, and saying, "I've just been feeling out of sorts lately." Not likely.) Children tend to lack the introspective and interactional skills required to take full advantage of the "talking cure" in traditional therapy. In play therapy, children can come into a session and use toys, art, stories, and other play tools to communicate with the therapist.

This ability to use play as a natural form of reasoning and communication makes play an appropriate modality for therapeutic intervention with young children (Landreth, 2024). In play therapy, the play can be a means for (a) establishing rapport with children; (b) helping therapists understand children and their interactions and relationships; (c) helping children reveal feelings that they have not been able to verbalize; (d) allowing children to constructively act out feelings of anxiety, tension, or hostility; (e) teaching socialization skills; and (f) providing an environment in which children can test limits, gain insight about their own behavior and motivation, explore alternatives, and learn about consequences (Thompson & Henderson, 2016).

Therapeutic Powers of Play

The Association for Play Therapy has defined *play therapy* as "the systematic use of a theoretical model to establish an interpersonal process wherein trained play therapists use the therapeutic powers of play to help clients prevent or resolve psychosocial difficulties and achieve optimal growth and development" (Association for Play Therapy, n.d., para. 1). While that definition is a mouthful, at its core is the notion that play therapy is an approach to counseling clients using the "therapeutic powers of play" (Reddy et al., 2005, p. 4). Schaefer (1993) and Schaefer and Drewes (2009, 2014) generated lists of therapeutic powers of play, suggesting that each of these powers, or factors, has specific beneficial outcomes for clients. Some of these therapeutic factors are self-expression, access to the unconscious, direct and indirect teaching, catharsis, abreaction, positive emotion, counterconditioning fears, stress inoculation, stress management, therapeutic relationship, attachment, social competence, empathy, creative problem-solving, resiliency, moral development, accelerated psychological development, self-regulation, and self-esteem. Not all play therapy approaches activate all of these therapeutic factors, but the list offers a framework for understanding how play therapy brings about positive change for the child. When play therapy is effective, these therapeutic factors are the mechanisms of change.

Self-Expression

Because young children lack the language skills, vocabulary, and abstract thinking abilities of older children and adults, they may have difficulty expressing themselves with words. As explained by Schaefer and Drewes (2009), "In play, children are able to express their conscious thoughts and feelings better through play activities than by words alone" (p. 5). Because play is the usual mode of communication for the child, using play as a therapeutic modality facilitates the child's capacity for self-expression. The child can use play materials to indirectly communicate thoughts, feelings, and experiences that they cannot express in words or that might be too threatening to communicate directly. In addition, as a counselor your willingness and ability to speak in the child's language can convey a respect for the child that they might never have experienced. By watching how the child plays, what toys they choose, and when they switch from one activity to another, you can receive multifaceted messages from the child.

The following scenario illustrates how the child can use play for self-expression:

> The parents of Levi (age 6) are excited because they are receiving a 6-month-old baby boy as a foster child. They are a little worried because Levi has not expressed any interest, curiosity, or enthusiasm about having a brother. Levi comes into the playroom, picks up a baby doll, and puts it in the trash can. He then proceeds to take all of the other "baby things"—the bottles, the doll clothes, the doll blanket—and stuffs them all into the trash can. He looks around for other items connected with the baby doll, doesn't see anything else, looks rather nervously at you, and goes over and begins to play with some blocks.

Access to the Unconscious

Children are often not aware of unconscious conflicts and issues (which are, after all, unconscious). Because the toys and play objects in the playroom are chosen as neutral vehicles on which the child can project meaning, they can be used by the child to reveal unconscious material "into concrete form" (Gil, 2013, p. 53). In the relationship with the play therapist, the child can use the toys to bring unconscious desires and impulses into consciousness and to express them symbolically.

The following scenario illustrates how the child can use play to access the unconscious:

> Niamh (age 8) was physically abused by her father, who is now in jail. She plays with a doll that looks like an adult male, moving its limbs and then suddenly twisting its head off before she puts it in a jail. She initially appears startled, then she smiles at you and says, "I guess that took care of him. I didn't even know I wanted to do that, but I did."

Direct and Indirect Teaching

Many children lack the skills that they need to survive in the world. One method of teaching social skills, problem-solving skills, negotiation skills, coping skills, and assertiveness skills to children is to use toys, art, and play materials to provide them with direct instruction and allow them to practice these skills in a fun way that optimizes their learning (Kottman & Meany-Walen, 2016, 2018).

Metaphoric/indirect teaching is a method of using storytelling and play narratives to expose clients to new insights, perspectives, and coping strategies without evoking defensive reactions. It also allows clients to address issues indirectly without having to overtly acknowledge situations or issues that might feel threatening or overwhelming. By using stories, interactive play, and artwork to explore issues and present different ways of looking at situations, the play therapist can subtly help children examine their cognitive and affective patterns and teach them new skills and attitudes.

The following scenario illustrates how you could use play to metaphorically teach problem-solving skills:

> Jamar (age 6) and Journey (age 4) are playing in the sandbox with several plastic dinosaurs. Jamar's dinosaur tells Journey's dinosaur to dig a hole to bury his treasure in. Journey uses one of the bigger dinosaurs to hit Jamar's dinosaur, saying, "I don't have to do what you tell me to do." Jamar's dinosaur starts to hit Journey and the dinosaur she is holding. You stop Jamar's dinosaur from hitting Journey and her dinosaur by reminding them, "It's against the playroom rules to hit anyone. Remember, everyone needs to be safe in our playroom." Then you say to Journey's dinosaur, "You need to work out a way to let the other dinosaurs know you don't like it when they tell you what to do," and then you say to Jamar's dinosaur, "I bet you can think of another way to respectfully ask Journey's dinosaur to help you dig the hole for your treasure."

Catharsis

Catharsis involves the expression of powerful feelings, resulting in emotional release or completion of previously denied, inhibited, or interrupted affect (Ayling, 2019). Because the play therapist is a caring and empathic adult who will continue to accept children no matter what emotions they express, many children take advantage of the freedom of the play therapy setting to express strong emotions (both positive and negative) that they might not ordinarily be willing or able to communicate. The sense of release that follows the expression of powerful feelings, especially those that might not be acceptable to many others, can be a growing experience for children.

The following scenario illustrates how the play therapy process can facilitate catharsis:

> Lilliana (age 8) reports that she has again gotten into a fight on the playground of her school. She grabs a plastic sword and starts hitting the dragon puppet, yelling, "I hate her! I hate her! I hate her!" She dissolves into tears, crying and saying, "She doesn't like me just because I'm Mexican! She thinks my hair is too straight and my skin is too brown! She says she doesn't understand me just because I have an accent. I hate her. And the teachers on the playground say I am the bad one. She is the one who is being mean, and I am the one who gets into trouble. It's not fair! I hate all the teachers too."

Abreaction

Abreaction allows children to symbolically relive stressful or traumatic events and reexperience the feelings associated with those events. The purpose of abreaction is to provide children with a vehicle through which they can release some of the negative thoughts and emotions attached to painful experiences. In play therapy, children can reenact "bad stuff" over and over again if necessary. This process helps them gain a sense of mastery over their own negative experiences and interactions, which may assist them with "working through and resolving certain aspects of trauma" (Locatelli, 2020, p. 37).

The following scenario illustrates how play therapy can trigger and facilitate a child's abreactive response:

> During the pandemic, Derrick's (age 4) beloved grandmother became sick with COVID-19 and was admitted to the health center at the retirement community where she lived. Because of the pandemic restrictions on visitation, Derrick and his mother were not allowed to go into the health center to be with his grandmother, but

they often went there to wave at her through the window and show "get well" signs. During one of these visits, Derrick's grandmother went into cardiac arrest and died. Although Derrick's mother quickly moved him away from the window, he witnessed the nurses rush to his grandmother and start to "beat on her chest." He started having nightmares about this experience, waking up crying and screaming, "Grammy! We need to help my Grammy! They are hurting her!" In play therapy, after pandemic restrictions on in-person sessions were lifted, Derrick would take an older-looking female figure and have several other adult figures beat on her body, sobbing and crying as he did this. Although Derrick continued this playroom activity for several sessions, the intensity of his emotional reaction gradually diminished. After a time, he could say how much he missed seeing his grandmother and wished she would come over to their house for dinner like she used to do.

Positive Emotion

Playing together is fun and play therapy can provide children with an experience of laughing and having a good time in an accepting environment. There is preliminary evidence that fostering positive emotions can improve cognitive performance, creativity, problem-solving, and self-regulation (e.g., Stifter et al., 2019). Because many of the children who come to play therapy have not had the opportunity to experience or express positive emotions, the play therapy process can be a revelation to them and significantly enhance their well-being (Kottman, 2014).

The following scenario illustrates how play can promote positive feelings in the therapeutic relationship:

Bonnie (age 6) puts on a puppet show for you. With the puppets, she tells a joke, giggling, and rolling around on the floor of the playroom. She tells you, "I love being here with you. I never want to leave. Nobody else thinks I am funny. You always laugh at my jokes. And you always listen to me like I'm important or something."

Counterconditioning Fears

As a natural function of growing up, children experience certain fears—of the dark, of being alone, and so forth. In certain cultures, there are objects or concepts that typically evoke anxiety in individuals (e.g., several Native American tribes, such as the Navajo, believe that they must not speak of the dead for fear that evil spirits or witches will harm them; Prue-Owens, 2021). For some children, the circumstances in their lives may have created situations in which they feel fearful. In play therapy, children can express and sometimes master these fears by interacting with the toys, art supplies, and play media in a way that lets them experience fear and recognize that they have the skills for coping with fear and taking care of themselves. Schaefer and Drewes (2009) suggested that play therapy can facilitate the counterconditioning of fears because "two mutually exclusive internal states are not able to simultaneously co-exist, such as anxiety and relaxation or depression and playfulness" (p. 7).

The following scenario illustrates how play therapy can help children learn to express and cope with their fears:

> Dakota (age 8) starts to shake when he sees your newly acquired, Halloween-themed plastic severed hand that has blood on the wrist. Looking nervous, he uses the lion puppet to push it off the shelf and toward the door of the playroom. You say, "You seem really scared about that and want it out of the room." In a whisper, you ask, "What do you want to happen next?" Without acknowledging the question, Dakota hands you the lion puppet and whispers, "I wish someone would get rid of it." Because you know that in Dakota's Navajo culture, a person might be considered contaminated by touching a dead person or parts of a dead person, you use the lion puppet to pick up the severed hand, put it in the trash can, and put a lid on the trash can. You turn to Dakota and ask, "How is that?" He says, "Can we put it and the lion puppet out in the hall? I don't think they will hurt anyone out there as long as the lid is on the trash can." As soon as the trash can is out in the hall, you say, "We got rid of that without anybody having to touch it." Dakota smiles shyly without looking at you and says, "We needed it to be gone, but we didn't want it to hurt anyone else either. Now we are safe."

Stress Inoculation

Stress inoculation allows play therapy clients to anticipate and learn to manage stressful feelings (Cavett, 2014). Often children become anxious in anticipation of stressful events in their lives, such as starting a new school year, moving, going to the dentist, or having a medical procedure. Before these stressful events, children can reduce their anxiety if they play out the event as a way to learn what to expect and to become more comfortable with what is going to happen (Wohl & Hightower, 2001).

The following scenario illustrates how play can be useful in inoculating a child to a stressful situation:

> Camila (age 9) uses a courtroom diorama to depict her upcoming testimony about her uncle sexually abusing her. Initially, when she engages in this play, she is very tense and agitated, almost tearful. As she plays through what she has been told will happen in the courtroom, she seems to gradually become more relaxed, even smiling as she repeats comments made by her foster parents, the lawyer representing her, and her court-appointed advocate about how the experience will go.

Stress Management

Stress is a nearly universal experience for children and adults and the "effect of stress on our emotional and physical health can be devastating" (Fink, 2017, p. 1). In addition to stressors directly experienced by children (e.g., changes in parenting structure due to divorce, pressure to perform in school), children are also exposed to indirect "crossover" stress that can occur when stress experienced by one family member leads to stress for another family member, such as when a parent's work stress undermines parenting, communication, and anger management (Liu & Doan, 2020). Several authors (e.g., Razak et al., 2018) have identified the value of play as a stress-management resource, and Ray (2011) noted that "all children use play therapeutically as a way of dealing with stress" (p. 11). Stress management in play therapy can include the process of children discharging the tensions of their daily lives and/or learning and practicing stress management techniques (e.g., controlled breathing and mindfulness).

The following scenario illustrates how play can be useful in helping a child learn strategies or techniques to deal with the unpleasant aspects of stress:

> Alicia (age 10) has developed test anxiety and has "meltdowns" at school whenever she has to take a test, even when she is fully prepared for it. You teach her several anxiety management techniques, such as deep breathing and muscle relaxation. You also ask her to help a stuffed bear learn to manage her stress about climbing a tree by using some of the same anxiety management techniques you want Alicia to learn and practice.

Therapeutic Relationship

The therapeutic relationship between the play therapy client and the therapist allows the client to express themselves in the natural language of play (Post et al., 2019). You can foster this positive relationship through empathy, acceptance, establishing safety, acceptance, and witnessing the child client's experience (e.g., Bent et al., 2022; Winburn et al., 2020). While providing a foundation for specific play therapy interventions, this positive relationship also fosters resilience (Post et al., 2019). Numerous authors have identified the therapeutic relationship as one of the common factors across various play therapy approaches that facilitate change (e.g., Mora et al., 2018).

The following scenario illustrates the therapeutic relationship in play therapy:

> You know that Dequan (age 8) loves to play Plants vs. Zombies on his Nintendo Switch. You ask him if he would rather draw some of the zombies from the game on the whiteboard or practice walking like a zombie around the playroom. You and he start walking around the playroom, taking turns deciding which zombie you are going to imitate. He laughs and says, "No other grown-up will play like this with me."

Attachment

Some children who come to play therapy have limited attachment to other human beings. The process of play therapy provides several avenues for increasing these children's connectedness to others. Play therapy can provide a corrective relationship with a secure adult that allows children to change in attachment over time (Pleines, 2019). Through shared fun, children frequently grow to feel affection and a sense of connection to the therapist. Using role play and fantasy play, the therapist can begin to build a child's empathic responses, which can generalize to a stronger sense of connection to other people. It is sometimes helpful to include the parents or an additional child in several play therapy sessions or involve the child in a group to maximize the sense of connection with peers. The play therapist can also work with parents to help them learn strategies for forming attachments with their children.

The following scenario illustrates how the play therapy process can be used to set the stage for the formation of an attachment between the therapist and a child:

> Isla (age 5) has been in several foster families, moving three times in the past year. Two of these moves were triggered by her own inappropriate behavior, and the third one was necessitated by the foster family's inability to care for her special medical needs. She is referred to play therapy because she does not seem willing to connect with her current foster family. You ask her foster parents to attend sessions with her, inviting them to play with you and Isla, suggesting simple games like "Simon Says," "red light, green light," "pitch and catch," "Mother, May I?", memory-matching games, and Chutes and Ladders. You use tracking, restating content, and reflecting feelings to let Isla know you are paying attention to what is important to her, and you coach her foster parents to do the same. Isla gradually begins to smile more and make eye contact with her foster parents. After 10 sessions of doing this, at the end of the session, Isla gives her foster mother and father a big hug and says, "I love you both!"

Social Competence

Social competence is an umbrella term that describes a constellation of social skills, including empathy, cooperation, conversational proficiency, and having fun (Nash, 2014). Social competence is foundational to academic and social success in children (Denham et al., 2012) and can be a protective factor against behavioral problems, such as violence and aggression, as well as functional impairment (Blalock et al., 2019). Many children referred for play therapy lack social competence and have not experienced success in building relationships with others. Because the play therapist consistently demonstrates a caring, supportive attitude toward them, play therapy clients begin to believe that they may be worthy of love and positive attention. The play therapy relationship allows the client to see social competence practiced by the therapist and provides a context for developing and practicing social skills. Some play therapists (Knell, 2009a, 2016; Kottman & Meany-Walen, 2016) have taught social skills and other strategies for building positive social relationships, either in group or individual modalities.

The following scenario illustrates using play to enhance social competence in play therapy:

> Keefer (age 7) comes to his first four sessions bossing you around, correcting you, and generally being rude. You reflect feelings, restate content, track his behavior, return responsibility, and make encouraging comments. Keefer starts his fifth session by saying, "You look fat today. Fatty, fatty, fatty!" You respond (in a neutral voice), "When you say things like that, my feelings get hurt. I am guessing that if you say things like that to other people, it probably hurts their feelings, and they might not want to be around you." He says, "Lots of kids don't want to play with me at school." You ask, "It sounds pretty lonely. Might you want to learn some other ways to talk to people so they want to play with you?" When he replies in the affirmative, you ask if he wants to use the puppets to practice talking to people so that they will want to be friends with him, and he agrees to try it. (You may also have to deal with your own countertransference about him being rude and calling you names that can easily evoke emotional reactions—even from therapists.)

Empathy

Empathy, the ability to understand the feelings and perspectives of others, is an important social skill that many children who come to play therapy lack. Empathy is important for successful relationships, and deficits in empathy are related to a variety of presenting issues in play therapy (e.g., oppositional defiant disorder, conduct disorder, attention-deficit/hyperactivity disorder [ADHD]; Fantozzi et al., 2021). In the cooperative engagement that often occurs in play therapy, children develop empathy by taking on different roles and learning to identify and understand the affective and cognitive perspectives of others.

The following scenario illustrates how play can increase a child's empathy and ability to take on the perspectives of others:

> AhnJong (age 10) is having difficulty making friends at school. She is in the gifted program and tends to be dismissive of her classmates' feelings. She is unwilling to consider the possibility that their opinions and feelings could be valid. After you have worked hard to establish a relationship with her, you tell her you would like to do a puppet show, and she says, "If you have to, I guess I can sit here and be bored." You do a puppet show in which you have a peacock puppet tell the various other animal puppets that they are "stupid," they don't know anything, their opinions don't matter, and so forth. You have the other puppets give the peacock puppet feedback, talking to the peacock about their feelings and responses to her comments. As she watches, she goes from appearing disinterested to paying close attention. At the end of the puppet show, she says, "You aren't as dumb as I thought you were. Maybe I can be nicer to the other kids at school if that's the way they feel."

Creative Problem-Solving

The ability to see problems from different angles and generate multiple solutions is significantly related to well-being (e.g., Tan et al., 2019). Since play is a creative process in and of itself, play therapy can effectively facilitate the development of creative problem-solving. To play, children must generate ideas from their imaginations to fuel the action. In play therapy, children continually use creative thinking to solve problems in innovative and constructive ways. By not making decisions for the child, not providing solutions to difficult situations, and not telling the child how to play, you consistently return responsibility to the child and encourage creative thought and problem-solving.

The following scenario illustrates how you can use play as a method to encourage a child to solve problems creatively:

> Presley (age 5) is frustrated because some cars that he had used to play "chase" in his session last week were broken by another boy who comes to the playroom. Presley throws the cars on the floor and says, "There's nothing in here I want to play with. I only wanted to play chase—nothing else." You reply, "I know you are disappointed, and I bet you can figure out something else you could use to play chase." Presley looks around the room, grabs some blocks, and says, "These can be my cars. I invented these for playing chase. They will be much better than those old things I played with last week."

Resiliency

Play therapy clients have often faced significant life stressors and numerous adverse experiences (Ray et al., 2021). Through play, clients can develop a greater sense of resiliency in the face of adversity. In play therapy, you can provide opportunities for children to "bounce back" from setbacks and develop protective factors that will buffer the negative effects of stressors. You can encourage children to try activities that they would not usually try, taking care to point out children's efforts in these endeavors. By acknowledging children when they are working hard and when they are making progress, rather than waiting for them to be 100% successful, you will help build their sense of competence and resiliency (Kottman & Meany-Walen, 2015). This process is also reinforced by not doing things for play therapy clients that they can do for themselves. By returning the responsibility for making decisions and getting things done in the playroom to children, you can help reinforce qualities of resilience.

The following scenario illustrates how the play therapist can use play to foster resiliency:

> Cassandra (age 8) begins to get frustrated when she cannot get the toy cash register to stay closed. She starts to throw it on the floor, but then she looks at you and puts it back on the shelf, saying, "I hate that dumb thing. I didn't want to play store anyway." Knowing that she has played store for the past six sessions, you reflect her feelings by saying, "You're feeling really frustrated by the cash register not working the way you want it to work. I know you like playing with the cash register even though you are saying you don't. What else could you try to make it work the way you want it to work?" If she replies, "I hate stuff that doesn't work. I am just giving up," you might say, "You just want to quit trying to make it work. Can I tell you something another kid tried to get it to work that seemed to help?" If she answers in the affirmative, you could give her several suggestions for getting the cash register to close (and hope she is willing to try one of them, and that it works).

Moral Development

Play therapy provides an opportunity for social interaction that can act as an avenue for moral development (Li & Tomasello, 2022). For instance, "gameplay experiences help children move beyond the early stage of moral realism, in which rules are seen as external restrictions arbitrarily imposed by adults in authority, to the concept of morality that is based on the principles of cooperation and consent among equals" (Schaefer & Drewes, 2009, p. 8). Cooperative play and playing games both allow children to enhance their social skills, increase communication strategies, and practice rule-governed behavior through behavior rehearsal. This is true whether children are playing a casual game of pitch and catch, a simple game based on luck, such as Chutes and Ladders, or a highly structured game that requires advanced skill, such as chess or checkers. Specially designed therapeutic games, such as Feelings Bingo and the Talking, Feeling, and Doing Game (R. Gardner, 1973), can provide children with these opportunities and also expand their skills and insights in other ways related to their particular therapeutic goals.

The following scenario illustrates how you can use gameplay to help a child elevate moral judgment, practice social skills, and reinforce rule-governed behavior:

> Morris (age 9) does not follow the rules at school. He gets angry with his teacher because "he keeps telling me what to do. He has no right." He has very few friends because he is unwilling to compromise with his peers about what to play and how to play on the playground. You suggest playing one of the games available in the playroom to help Morris explore his ideas about rules and reasons for having rules. Morris chooses the game Jenga. Having never played the game, Morris wants to stack up the pieces and knock them down. Explaining the rules, you tell him that to play and win the game, players must take turns, with both players paying attention to the arrangement of the pieces as they try to remove them in order to avoid making the entire structure collapse. As the two of you take turns pulling and pushing the Jenga pieces out of the stack, Morris protests "you are just making these rules up, and I don't have to follow them." You invite him to make up his own rules about how to play, so he takes the pieces, stacks them up, and knocks them down. After several times doing this, he says, "It isn't much fun without you too. Will you play with me?" You go back to playing with the original rules and after a time, he says, "This is much more fun. I get it now. We have to take turns for this game to work, and I have to pay attention to what you are doing and what I am doing."

Accelerated Psychological Development

Play is widely viewed as a primary factor in supporting psychological development in children (e.g., Holmes et al., 2019). As a result, play therapy can be an important factor in bringing a child's delayed development closer to a normal range. Specifically, play therapy can facilitate cognitive development (e.g., Etemadzadeh et al., 2023), language development (Rezaee Rezvan et al., 2022), and social-emotional development (Schottelkorb et al., 2020). Through the therapeutic relationship and specific play activities chosen by the play therapist, the child's psychological development can be accelerated.

The following scenario illustrates how the play therapist can use play to foster accelerated psychological development:

Izzy (age 8) is known in her school as an "angry" child. She even introduces herself to new adults by saying, "Hi! My name is Izzy. I have anger management problems." She tends to go from 0–60 with angry reactions with very little provocation, and she likes to blame others for her behavior. She uses the excuse, "I'm just not in control of my feelings and reactions. I am just like Mei from the movie *Turning Red*." You invite her to roleplay the role of Mei, suggesting that what Mei needed to learn in the movie was to "calibrate" her feelings—that there were lots of choices between not being angry and exploding with rage. You work with her to brainstorm a list of words related to anger (e.g., disgruntled, irritated, enraged, annoyed, frustrated, miffed, furious, peeved, fuming, livid, aggravated, exasperated). Over several sessions, using one 3 × 5 card for each word you generate, you collaborate with Izzy on creating drawings to illustrate the intensity of each of these angry feelings and then arrange them in the order of intensity, asking her to use her body to express each word. You invite her to practice using the words for each level of intensity to express her feelings and work on calibrating her reaction's strength.

Self-Regulation

Self-regulation is the modulation and management of emotions, thoughts, and actions to behave deliberately (Bailey & Jones, 2019), and poor self-regulation is considered a transdiagnostic aspect of a range of internalizing and externalizing disorders in children and adolescents (Eadeh et al., 2021). Play therapists can use a variety of techniques to help clients identify and name a range of emotions, both positive and negative. Play therapy can also help clients develop self-control of maladaptive impulses, which is the core of self-regulation in children (Robson et al., 2020), using a variety of interventions, including familiar games like freeze tag, "Simon Says," and "Mother, May I?" (Yaeger & Yaeger, 2014).

The following scenario illustrates how the play therapist can use play to foster self-regulation:

Liam (age 4) is a new foster child, having recently moved in with a foster family when his mother's parental rights were terminated. He is having difficulty settling down in his new home, is having trouble sleeping, experiences nightmares every night, and has two or three 20- to 30-minute temper tantrums every day. His foster parents ask you to give them some ideas on how to help him settle into their family. You sense that they are anxious and frustrated with this process and suggest several books to help them learn to coregulate with him, which will help him begin to self-regulate. These books include *Goodnight Love: A Bedtime Meditation Story* (Kim, 2023), *Bellies to the Sky: A Bedtime Breathwork Book* (Canning, 2021), *Sleepy Time Nighty-Night* (Park, 2023), and *Listening to My Body* (Garcia, 2017). In your sessions, you use bibliotherapy to introduce Liam to several ways of dealing with his emotional reactions: *Amaya's Anger: A Mindful Understanding of Strong Emotions* (Garcia, 2021), *Feelings Ninja* (Nhin, 2021), *Great Big Breath* (Long, 2023), and *A Little Spot of Anger* (Alber, 2019). You work with Liam using puppets, figures, and role-playing to act out the self-regulation techniques described in these books.

Self-Esteem

Self-esteem involves feelings of self-acceptance and self-respect (Orth & Robins, 2014). Because of a variety of adverse experiences, play therapy clients often lack these core feelings (Ray et al., 2021). Many children who come to play therapy lack a sense of competence, which negatively affects the development of positive self-esteem. They frequently feel as though they are not capable people. One of the jobs of a play therapist is to provide opportunities for children to prove to themselves that they have the potential to be successful. Play is an excellent avenue for helping children practice doing things that they can do well. They can also explore their own thoughts, feelings, and behaviors and project themselves into a number of different experiences, both real and imaginary. Because play therapists offer unconditional acceptance of clients, they have the freedom to experiment with who they are and who they want to be.

The following scenario illustrates how the play therapist can help a child to think for herself, make decisions for herself, and discover herself:

> Ebony (age 10) is extremely shy and anxious. She never makes eye contact, seldom smiles, has difficulty making decisions, insists that her mother choose the clothes she wears, and complains that she has no friends either in her neighborhood or at school. In the playroom, she continually asks you to tell her what to do, what color to paint, how she should dress the dolls, and so forth. She also asks you to take care of her by asking her to bring her toys, tie her shoes, draw pictures that she "can't" draw, and so on. You consistently return responsibility to Ebony, never making any decisions for her or doing things for her that she can do for herself. Although she expresses frustration with this process, over the course of several sessions Ebony begins to make her own decisions and take care of herself in ways she had not before. After 6 weeks of this, she says, "I can do things for myself. I am actually pretty smart. I really like doing things for myself. I never knew that before now."

Personal Qualities of a Play Therapist

We've explained what play therapy is and some of the therapeutic factors at work in play therapy, but who makes a good play therapist? The therapist's personal characteristics and personality traits are key elements in the play therapy process (Landreth, 2024; Nalavany et al., 2005; Nash & Schaefer, 2011). Numerous authors and professional organizations have identified these key personal characteristics. For instance, the British Association of Play Therapists (2022) has indicated that play therapists should have the following personal qualities: empathic, sincere, honest, respectful, ethical, knowledgeable, self-aware, self-responsible, congruent, compassionate, committed to professional development, and committed to personal development.

Nalavany et al. (2005) used concept mapping to identify the qualities, competencies, and skills needed to be a good play therapist. Analyzing participant responses to their question, "Name three qualities of a 'good' (i.e., competent) play therapist," the researchers found seven clusters of qualities: being attuned to and reflecting the child's verbal and nonverbal behavior and feelings; being sensitive to the child; being warm, empathic, genuine, and accepting of the child; being open to personal awareness and growth; having the skills for working with parents and families; having a theoretical understanding of the process of child therapy; and having a structured, intentional approach to the therapeutic process.

In a study designed to identify the key qualities of effective play therapists, Purswell et al. (2021) analyzed published literature related to play therapist qualities. After analyzing 15 relevant articles and book chapters published between 2009 and 2018, the researchers identified 10 themes: attunement to the child, attunement to self, composure/demeanor, acceptance of the child, authenticity, acceptance of self, being child-focused, willingness/commitment, commitment to creating a safe place, and receptivity. The researchers noted that although some of these characteristics might be more relevant to particular theoretical approaches in play therapy, few were conclusively associated with a particular approach.

Finally, in a study designed to establish play therapy competencies, Turner et al. (2020) identified cultural humility as a *metacompetency*, or personal characteristic, for play therapy and noted that play therapists should practice through a lens of cultural humility. Hook et al. (2017) defined cultural humility as "an awareness of one's limitations to understand a client's cultural background and experience . . . [and] an interpersonal stance that is other oriented rather than self-focused in regard to the cultural background of the client" (p. 9).

Acknowledging the key role of cultural humility in the personal characteristics of effective play therapists, we maintain that effective play therapists should (a) like children and treat them with kindness and respect, (b) have a sense of humor and be willing to laugh at themselves, (c) be playful and fun-loving, (d) be self-confident rather than dependent on the positive regard of others for a sense of self-worth, (e) be open and honest, (f) be flexible and able to deal with a certain level of ambiguity, (g) be accepting of others' perceptions of reality without feeling threatened or judgmental, (h) be willing to use play and metaphors to communicate, (i) be comfortable with and have experience interacting with children, (j) be able to firmly and kindly set limits and maintain personal boundaries, and (k) be self-aware and open to taking interpersonal risks and exploring their own personal issues.

Personality and personal history will have a tremendous influence on play therapists' interaction with children in the playroom. As part of the process of learning more about play therapy, you will need to learn more about yourself—your own personal characteristics, your strengths and weaknesses, your likes and dislikes, and your own psychological and emotional issues. This knowledge can help you to understand your own reactions to children in the playroom and to avoid letting your own personality or issues interfere with your ability to interact effectively with children.

Appropriate Clients for Play Therapy

Although there are play therapists who work with adults (e.g., Frey, 2015; Kaduson, 2016; Olson-Morrison, 2017; Schaefer, 2003), most clients in play therapy are children between the ages of 3 and 11. However, play therapy's suitability depends on the client's developmental level and abstract verbal-reasoning skills. The play therapy age range has recently expanded to include infants and toddlers (e.g., Courtney, 2020; Kohlhoff et al., 2021; Schaefer et al., 2008), and adolescents (Gallo-Lopez & Schaefer, 2010; B. J. Gardner, 2015; Green & Myrick, 2014; Shen, 2017; Thomas & Morris, 2020). With many preadolescent and younger adolescent children, it is appropriate to ask whether they would be more comfortable sitting and talking to the therapist or playing with the toys and art materials. By adding toys aimed at older children, such as craft supplies, stickers, office supplies, board games and cards, streaming music, musical instruments, a digital camera, and sporting equipment, the therapist can often extend the usual age range of play therapy (Kottman & Meany-Walen, 2018; Milgrom, 2005).

Another important consideration in the question of appropriate clients for play therapy is whether play therapy will be effective. Although play therapy may not be suitable or effective for every child client, there is considerable evidence for its efficacy in treating a wide array of presenting issues. For instance, several meta-analyses, a statistical procedure used to synthesize the results of several studies using different measures (Borenstein et al., 2021), have offered evidence for the overall effectiveness of play therapy. In an early meta-analysis of 42 play therapy studies with children, LeBlanc and Ritchie (2001) reported an overall effect size similar to that found for adult psychotherapy (M. L. Smith & Glass, 1977), suggesting that the average play therapy client in the reviewed studies was better off than roughly 75% of the untreated children. LeBlanc and Ritchie also found that the duration of play therapy was related to outcome, with the strongest effects between 20 and 30 sessions, and that parent involvement was linked to better outcomes. In an additional meta-analysis of 93 studies, Bratton et al. (2005) found a similar effect size to LeBlanc and Ritchie and concluded that "play therapy appeared equally effective across age, gender, and presenting issue" (p. 376). Lin and Bratton (2015) completed another meta-analysis of 52 controlled studies of child-centered play therapy (CCPT) completed between 1995 and 2010. They reported a slightly smaller overall effect size for CCPT and noted that their finding "provides support for the overall effectiveness of child-counseling interventions using CCPT methodology" (Lin & Bratton, 2015, p. 49). Finally, in a more recent systematic review of individual play therapy, Drisko et al. (2020) reviewed 180 studies and concluded that "across most concerns, play therapy was affirmed as an empirically supported therapy" (p. 715).

While these meta-analyses and systematic reviews provide evidence supporting a combination of play therapy modalities and presenting problems, there is also evidence for play therapy's effectiveness in addressing specific concerns. Drisko et al. (2020) noted that the strongest evidence for the effectiveness of play therapy, with a variety of effect sizes, was for externalizing behaviors (e.g., Meany-Walen et al., 2014), internalizing behaviors (Schumann, 2010), anxiety (Blanco et al., 2015), aggression (e.g., Bratton et al., 2013), trauma symptoms (e.g., Schottelkorb et al., 2012), and ADHD (e.g., Zakershoshtari & Bozorgi, 2016). In addition, there is recent evidence for play therapy's effectiveness in enhancing social-emotional strengths and reducing the problem behaviors associated with adverse childhood experiences, including abuse/neglect, family violence, natural disasters, and other potential stressors/traumas (Parker et al., 2021; Ray et al., 2021).

On the basis of anecdotal case studies and limited empirical research, play therapy also seems to be an effective treatment for children with numerous other presenting issues, including selective mutism (Fernandez & Sugay, 2016; Wonders, 2020), grief (Gonzalez & Bell, 2016; Salinas, 2021), social skills deficits (Blalock et al., 2019; Schottelkorb et al., 2020), issues related to parental divorce (Chen et al., 2021; Haas & Ray, 2020), and maladaptive perfectionism (Akay & Bratton, 2017; Evans, 2021). In addition, many authors have highlighted ways play therapy can be combined with other treatment modalities (e.g., medication, occupational therapy) in the treatment of autism (e.g., H. Hillman, 2018; Müller & Donley, 2019), ADHD (e.g., Hashemi et al., 2018), learning disabilities (e.g., Esmaili et al., 2019), developmental delays (e.g., Garofano-Brown, 2010), intellectual disability (Astramovich et al., 2015), fetal alcohol syndrome (Denny et al., 2017), and developmental language disorders (Loeb et al., 2021).

No matter the child's presenting problem, therapists must clearly define their goals for play therapy with a child and communicate these goals to parents. For instance, although play therapy does not reduce impulsivity and distractibility in children with ADHD, it can help them deal with feelings of discouragement, failure, and low self-esteem. Depending on their theoretical orientation, the play therapist may decide that children with ADHD should learn needed skills (e.g., social skills, anger management tactics) in play therapy. For children with more severe pathology or problems with organic components, play therapy will not eliminate symptoms. However, it may help them with quality-of-life concerns. An essential task of the play therapist is to be clear with parents about specific goals and what play therapy can and cannot do.

Although there is evidence for play therapy's wide applicability and efficacy, it will still be helpful for you to have a structured method for considering whether specific clients are appropriate for intervention through play therapy. One such method involves considering questions related to the child and you as the therapist. First, you would consider the following questions related to the child:

1. Can the child tolerate/form/utilize a relationship with an adult?
2. Can the child tolerate/accept a protective environment?
3. Does the child have the capacity to learn new methods of dealing with the presenting problem?
4. Does the child have the capacity for insight into their behavior and motivation and into the behavior and motivation of others?
5. Does the child have the capacity for sufficient attention and/or cognitive organization to engage in therapeutic activities?
6. Is play therapy an effective/efficient way to address this child's problems?
7. Are there conditions in the child's environment over which you will not have control that will negatively impact the therapy process?

If the answers to Questions 1 through 6 are "no," then play therapy may not be the optimal intervention strategy for this particular child. If the answer to Question 7 is "no," you should consider how detrimental the conditions that might negatively impact the therapeutic process. If you believe these obstacles will effectively sabotage the process, play therapy will probably not be the best intervention for this child.

The decision whether to use play therapy with a specific child should also be influenced by the answers to the following questions you should ask yourself:

1. Do I have the necessary skills to work with this child? Is there consultation or supervision available if I need it?

2. Can I effectively treat this child in my current practice setting (e.g., appropriate space, funding issues, length of treatment allowed)?

3. If effective therapy for this child involves working with other professionals, can I work within the necessary framework?

4. Is my current energy/stress level such that I can fully commit to working with this particular child?

5. Have I resolved any personal issues that will interfere with my capacity to work with this child and their family?

6. If the answer to any of these questions is "no," you should seriously consider avoiding play therapy as an intervention strategy for that particular child.

Paradigm Shift From Talk to Play

If you wish to learn how to provide play therapy, you will need to make a cognitive leap across a chasm. On one side of the canyon is the practice of using conversation, verbal skills, and the "talking cure" as the primary vehicle for communication and change in the therapy process. (We think of this as the "home turf" of therapy because most therapists are trained in the basics of talk therapy and naturally default to these skills and the talk therapy paradigm.) On the other side of the canyon is the practice of using play, toys, metaphor, and art as the primary vehicle for communication and change in the process of therapy.

On the face of it, this change seems simple to make—just stop focusing on words as communication and start focusing on play. In reality, the transition from talk therapy to play therapy involves an extremely complex conceptual paradigm shift that, while natural for children, can be difficult for adults to make. As a play therapist, you will learn to look at yourself, your clients, and the world from a different perspective than when you do talk therapy. If you decide you want to be a play therapist, before you can begin to acquire the skills involved in using play to communicate with clients, you must learn a completely different way of understanding communication. You must learn to think of communication as a symbolic, action-oriented world where the actions of puppets and animal figures are important pieces of information and where a shrug, a smile, or a turned back can be an entire "conversation." You will need to learn to think differently about the therapeutic process, looking "underneath" the child's actions in the playroom to discern what the play means. (We know this is a lot to ask of you, but we promise it will be worth it when you get the hugs and brilliant smiles from children who finally feel heard and understood because you are willing to speak their language.)

There are some therapists who call what they do play therapy but have not actually made the paradigm shift into thinking about the doing and the playing as the actual communication. These therapists use toys and play to trick clients into answering questions rather than using toys and play as the vehicle for communication. For example, they might write questions on Jenga blocks and require children to answer the questions on their turn, or they might play the Talking, Feeling, and Doing Game in which children are asked to talk about their feelings and experiences and receive chips as rewards for participating. We tend to call this "talk therapy in the playroom." There isn't anything inherently wrong with this practice, but this isn't play therapy as we define it.

Play Therapy Dimensions Model

Throughout this book, there are references to play therapy approaches being directive or nondirective. This refers to a traditional method of conceptualizing play therapy approaches on a continuum from very *nondirective* (e.g., the child always leads, making decisions about what and how to play, and the therapist consistently follows the child's lead) to very *directive* (e.g., the therapist leads by choosing the play materials and making decisions about what and how to play). Although play therapists often discuss this continuum, little in the current professional literature provides an in-depth understanding of it. Play therapists Lorri Yasenik and Ken Gardner provide such an understanding with their play therapy dimensions model, which integrates various models, approaches, and theories applied to play therapy (Yasenik & Gardner, 2018, 2024; K. Gardner & Yasenik, 2008).

The play therapy dimensions model posits two dimensions: Directiveness and Consciousness (see Figure 1; Yasenik & Gardner, 2024). The Directiveness dimension includes the degree of immersion in the play by the therapist and the level of the therapist's interpretations. Immersion signifies how often and to what degree the therapist joins in and directs the play. The lowest level of Directiveness involves the therapist using tracking based on their observation of the play. At that level, the therapist does not actively involve themselves in the play. At the highest level, the therapist joins in the play as co-facilitator and actively elaborates on and extends the play. (Yasenik & Gardner, 2024).

The various approaches to play therapy described in Chapters 2 and 3 occupy different places on the directiveness continuum. Child-centered, psychodynamic, and Jungian analytical play therapy all fall on the nondirective side of the continuum. Cognitive-behavioral play therapy, ecosystemic play therapy, experiential play therapy, narrative play therapy, and Theraplay all fall on the directive side of the continuum. Gestalt play therapy is usually conducted in a directive fashion but may also involve some nondirective components, depending on the child and the therapist. Adlerian play therapists start as nondirective and become more directive as the relationship with the child is established. Prescriptive play therapists are sometimes directive and sometimes nondirective, depending on their conceptualization of the particular client and the course of their therapeutic process.

The Consciousness dimension of the model (see Figure 1) is represented by the child's play activities and verbalizations. Many children feel a need to create emotional distance from their issues. Sometimes, there is a process where they move up and down in this dimension, going from an increased level of consciousness to a decreased level of consciousness. When children are playing in a direct and literal manner, combined with verbalizations, they are usually working within a higher level of consciousness. When they need distance and protection from disturbing thoughts or feelings, they may use pretend play in a more symbolic and out-of-awareness way (Yasenik & Gardner, 2024). Children working in the higher range of consciousness express thoughts, feelings, and behaviors related to presenting problems or other issues directly, without needing to resort to metaphoric communication. Children working in the range of unconsciousness use the play and play materials in symbolic, metaphorical ways, communicating indirectly about their life through imaginary rather than actual situations.

All play therapists are committed to being respectful of and supportive of children. However, some maintain that it is essential to match children's level of consciousness, whereas others believe it is important to help the child move from an unconscious to a more conscious process. Several theoretical approaches to play therapy (e.g., child-centered, Gestalt, Jungian analytical, narrative, psychodynamic) are grounded in the belief that children can remain totally immersed in the unconscious realm, moving toward healing without needing the therapist to invite them to begin dealing with their issues in a direct, conscious way. Play therapists who ascribe to these approaches seldom use interpretations, and when they do, their interpretations are "soft" and can be ignored or denied by clients. Other approaches (e.g., cognitive-behavioral, ecosystemic, Theraplay) are based on the premise that change happens when children can move out of a need to deal with problems in an indirect or unconscious way toward a willingness to deal with problems consciously and directly. Play therapists who use these theories often make interpretations designed to bring issues outside of a client's awareness into sharp focus for them. In Adlerian play therapy, the play therapist decides on an individual basis whether it is appropriate to make interpretations designed to shift a client from an unconscious process to a conscious awareness. The decision can depend on many factors, such as the child's developmental level and the therapy phase.

According to Yasenik and Gardner (2018, 2024), the intersection of the two dimensions (Directiveness and Consciousness) creates four quadrants resting on a foundation of preimaginative play (see Figure 1). These four quadrants are:

I. Active Utilization (nondirective/conscious). The therapist follows the child's lead but occasionally makes interpretive comments designed to trigger conscious responses from the child.

II. Open Discussion and Exploration (directive/conscious). The therapist is immersed in the play, providing structure and direction as well as openly and directly discussing issues and making interpretations with the purpose of inviting the child to consciously process material that might have been less consciously available to the child previously.

III. Nonintrusive Responding (nondirective/unconscious). The therapist maintains a stance of nonevaluative acceptance and serves as a nonintrusive witness who follows the child's lead while the child initiates and directs the play.

IV. Cofacilitation (directive/unconscious). The therapist shares the power with the child in an egalitarian relationship, serving as a cofacilitator of the play, playing with the child, and deliberately staying in the child's metaphor with interpretations and directions.

Figure 1

Full Play Therapy Dimensions Model Diagram

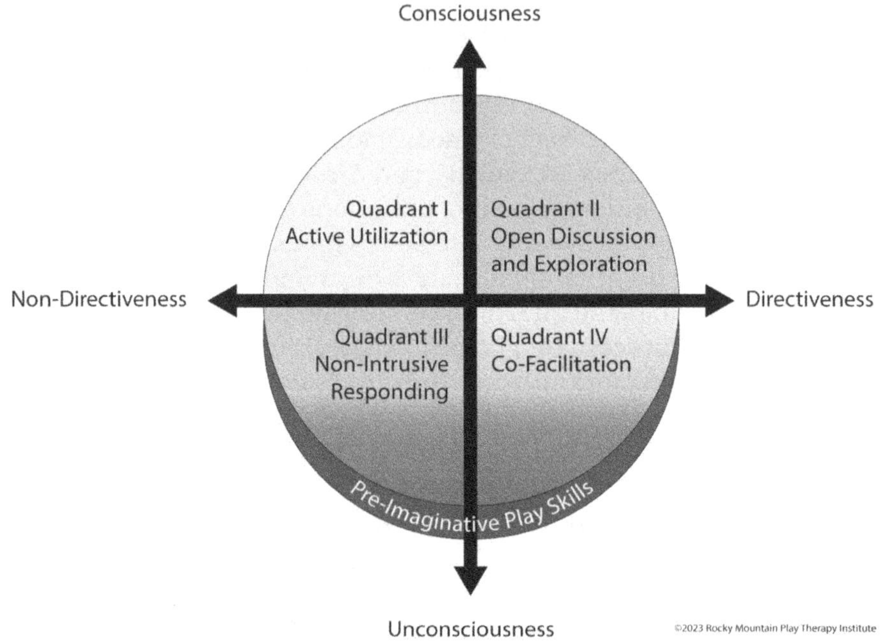

Note. Yasenik & Gardner, 2024

In addition to showing the four quadrants, the model in Figure 1 depicts a "cradle" of preimaginative play skills that support the lower half of the circle. Some children, as a result of developmental issues, neurodiversity considerations, and/or trauma, may not have mastered the discrete play skills needed for pretend or metaphoric play. These children "present with limited ability to use play materials, which means that the play therapy would work differently and not expect that a child may drive and direct metaphorical complex play in a play therapy setting" (Yasenik & Gardner, 2024, p. 49). Children who have not yet mastered preimaginative play skills will need extra scaffolding from the play therapist to develop those skills before moving to the consciousness part of the model.

In some approaches to play therapy, you would steadfastly remain in a single quadrant (e.g., child-centered play therapists stay in the nonintrusive responding quadrant; see Figure 1); in other approaches to play therapy, you would move from quadrant to quadrant, depending on a variety of factors (e.g., Adlerian play therapy, prescriptive play therapy). The play therapy dimensions model is an invaluable tool for play therapists who want to understand the various theoretical approaches and have a tool for making decisions about the unfolding process of play therapy. However, an in-depth description of the play therapy dimensions model is beyond the scope of this book. For more information about the model, we recommend that you read *Play Therapy Dimensions Model: New Insights for Integrative Play Therapists* (Yasenik & Gardner, 2024), and *Turning Points in Play Therapy and the Emergence of Self: Applications of the Play Therapy Dimensions Model* (Yasenik & Gardner, 2018).

Skills, Strategies, and Techniques (Oh My!)

We see differences among play therapy skills, strategies, and techniques. *Play therapy skills* are basic relational tools used by most play therapists across approaches to play therapy throughout the play therapy process. Skills include tracking, restating content, reflecting feelings, returning responsibility to the child, encouraging, and setting limits. These are mostly the "things you say" in the playroom. (Skills are what this book is all about—it's a primer on play therapy skills, with some strategies and techniques thrown in for good measure.) *Play therapy strategies* represent broad areas of expertise that can be applied in every part of the play therapy process—some approaches to play therapy use them, and some do not. We designate the following strategies: adventure therapy, storytelling, and therapeutic metaphors; movement, dance, and music experiences; sand tray activities; art techniques; and structured play. You may need additional training, experience, and supervision to master these strategies, even after you have completed basic play therapy training (which will almost always focus on skills rather than strategies and techniques). *Play therapy techniques* are activities the play therapist can use as assessment and intervention tools throughout the therapy process; techniques are the "things that you do" in the playroom (e.g., Kinetic Family Drawing technique, Pocket Palsart technique, Trust Walk activities) (Kottman & Meany-Walen, 2018). Some approaches to play therapy (e.g., Adlerian and Gestalt) advocate using techniques, and others (e.g., child-centered, Jungian) do not.

Issues to Consider

Making the paradigm shift from talk to play as the primary tool for communication in therapy can be a difficult process (and we have confidence that you can do it!). To begin this transformation, consider the following issues:

1. What do you believe about how people communicate their thoughts and attitudes? What do you believe about how people communicate their feelings?

2. What do you believe about how children communicate their thoughts and attitudes? What do you belie ve about how children communicate their feelings? What are the differences between how children and adults communicate? What do you believe is the best way to communicate with children?

3. How do you build rapport with adults? How do you express yourself to adults?

4. What are your strengths in communicating with adults? What are the weak areas in the way you communicate with adults?

5. How do you usually build rapport with children? How would this fit into the play therapy modality?

6. How do you usually express yourself to children? How do children usually express themselves to you?

7. What are the strengths in the way you communicate with children? What are the weak areas in the way you communicate with children?

8. Consider how you could shift from thinking about talk as communication to thinking about play as communication. What do you think would be involved for you to begin to make this paradigm shift?

9. Begin to observe how children naturally relate to others, both peers and adults. What do you notice about patterns in how they interact and express their thoughts, attitudes, and feelings?

10. As you observe children, focus on the potential for play being metaphoric. What have you observed about the metaphors present in children's play and communication?

11. What do you think about the possibility of doing play therapy with adolescents? If you were to do play therapy with adolescents, what do you think you would do differently from the way you would do play therapy with younger children?

12. What do you think about the possibility of doing play therapy with adults? If you were to do play therapy with adults, what do you think you would do differently from the way you would do play therapy with younger children or adolescents?

Questions to Ponder (Because We Know You're a Thoughtful Person)

1. As you think about the therapeutic powers of play described in this chapter, which are valuable to you? Which have you observed in the lives of other adults and children?

2. Which of these therapeutic powers of play do you think would be most helpful with clients? Why?

3. With which of the therapeutic powers of play do you think you would be most comfortable? Why?

4. With which of the therapeutic powers of play do you think you would be uncomfortable? What would the sources of that discomfort be?

5. As you think about children with whom you have worked in the past and other children of your acquaintance, are there certain problem situations or diagnoses with which you think you would want to work? What are they? What draws you to these children?

6. As you think about children with whom you have worked in the past and other children of your acquaintance, are there certain problem situations or diagnoses with which you think you would not want to work? What are they? What are the sources of your discomfort?

7. How would you describe the process of play therapy to a friend or a colleague?

8. Which of the play therapy dimensions model quadrants do you think will be the most comfortable for you?

9. Which of the play therapy dimensions model quadrants do you anticipate you might want to avoid?

10. How comfortable do you think you will be in moving from quadrant to quadrant in the play therapy dimensions model?

2

History of Play Therapy

The historical evolution of play therapy, in many ways, parallels the history of the development of psychology and reflects the zeitgeist of contemporary society. Many approaches to play therapy evolved nearly simultaneously, making it difficult to place them in chronological order.

In this chapter, we briefly describe the evolution of various approaches to play therapy, beginning with the work of Sigmund Freud and continuing to present-day trends. Those approaches more likely to be practiced, cited, or named as significant by the play therapy profession are discussed in more detail in Chapter 3 along with newer approaches (e.g., AutPlay, FirstPlay, StoryPlay) that were designed for use with specific populations of clients.

We encourage you to explore the various theoretical orientations described in this chapter by reading the original works of the experts who pioneered them.

Psychoanalytic or Psychodynamic Play Therapy

The first report in the professional literature of play as having a role in a psychological intervention described Sigmund Freud's (1909/1955) treatment of "Little Hans," a child who was experiencing a phobic reaction. Freud did not work directly with Hans, but he had Hans's father describe the child's play. On the basis of the information he gathered from Hans's father, Freud provided interpretations of the underlying conflicts and suggested how the father could intervene directly with Hans. Freud believed that play is a repetition of unconscious concerns and conflicts. He suggested that play has a role in the process of mastery and abreaction.

Hermine Hug-Hellmuth (1921) was the first psychoanalytic therapist to directly use play with children in therapy (Johnson, 2016). She visited children's homes and watched and participated in their natural play without directing it in any way. Although no specific play techniques are mentioned in her writings, Hug-Hellmuth maintained that the therapist can use the material present in the child's play to understand the child, much like fantasies and dreams are used in adult analysis. She saw play as a vehicle for bridging the communication gap between the therapist and the child (Plastow, 2011).

Anna Freud (1928, 1946) also worked directly with children. She used the observation of children's play as a tool for building a relationship with these clients. Although she suggested that play was an appropriate way for establishing communication with children, Freud did not actually use the play in a therapeutic way because she did not believe behaviors in play were necessarily symbolic or metaphoric. After she had used the play to establish rapport, she switched to the more traditional forms of therapeutic dialogue, such as history taking, dream interpretation, free association, and drawing (Johnson, 2016).

Melanie Klein (1932), who was also a psychodynamic therapist, had a totally different understanding of the function that play can serve in therapy. She maintained that play is children's natural medium of expression and should be considered as a direct substitute for the verbal expression that takes place in adult therapy. Klein suggested that spontaneous play is the equivalent of free association in adults, full of important information about subconscious processes. Rather than simply storing the information gathered through the play and making interpretations to parents or crafting a conceptualization of the client for the sole purpose of the therapist's understanding, Klein advocated interpreting play behavior using psychodynamic concepts to the children themselves (Johnson, 2016).

Margaret Lowenfeld (1935/2008) studied the work of Piaget and Montessori and was inspired by H.G. Wells's book *Floor Games*, which described Wells sitting on the floor and using miniatures and other small objects to play with his children. Lowenfeld began to gather small toys and other materials to use in her work with children, developing the *world technique* in which children are invited to put miniatures in a tray of sand to create a world. Lowenfeld advocated observing and following the play without making interpretations or offering suggestions for what the children should do in their play (Hutton, 2004).

Structured Play Therapy

Based on psychodynamic conceptualizations of clients combined with a more structured, goal-oriented practice of interacting with children, *structured play therapy* stems from a belief in the cathartic value of play (Jones et al., 2003; Leggett & Boswell, 2016). In all the structured approaches to play therapy, the therapist plays an active role in determining the focus and goals of therapy and the activities introduced in play therapy sessions. David Levy (1938), Joseph Solomon (1938), and Gove Hambridge (1955) were well-known practitioners of structured play therapy.

Levy (1938; Kaduson, 2015) developed *release therapy* to treat children under the age of 10 years who had experienced a specific trauma incident. He provided specially chosen toys that he said would facilitate clients' focus on the traumatic event. He did not direct them to play with the toys in a certain way, nor did he interpret their play. Building on Sigmund Freud's concept of repetition compulsion theory, Levy maintained that clients could resolve problems through catharsis if given the appropriate setting and toys. Levy suggested that children might act out various scenarios so that painful memories, thoughts, and emotions could be discharged and no longer threaten their emotional or mental well-being.

Solomon (1938) developed active play therapy to work with impulsive, acting-out children. On the basis of Sigmund Freud's concept of abreactive effect, he advocated encouraging children to express their negative feelings, inappropriate impulses, and regressive tendencies in play therapy sessions, where the children would not receive the usual negative or judgmental "adult" reaction from the therapist. Solomon maintained that children experiencing a nonjudgmental, accepting attitude from an adult, even when they were expressing themselves in ways that usually evoked negative reactions, could be transformational for them. By externalizing their impulses and releasing their frustrations in the play therapy process, children could let go of their need to act out in other situations and relationships, leaving room for experimenting with more socially appropriate behaviors (Johnson, 2016).

Hambridge (1955), building on the ideas of Levy (1938), used an even more directive approach to play therapy. After having established a relationship with children, he asked them to play out specific situations similar to stressful experiences or relationships in their lives. On the basis of the idea that repetition would first provide a cathartic experience and then help the children resolve any issues connected with the trauma, Hambridge maintained that by exactly reenacting a traumatic experience, children would learn to cope more effectively with any aftermath that lingered subsequent to the event.

Relationship Play Therapy

In a shift away from psychodynamic ideas about psychology, Rank (1936) suggested that the relationship between the therapist and the client in the here and now was the primary vehicle for change in clients. Jessie Taft (1933), Frederick Allen (1942), and Clark Moustakas (1959) each based their work with children on this concept.

Taft (1933) maintained that the essence of therapy with children was the examination of the real relationship between the therapist and the client and of the client's functioning in the here and now. She emphasized the process of building a relationship with the child and the use of time in therapy. Because she believed that the ending of each therapy session and the final termination of therapy are parallel to the process of birth—with the trauma experienced being similar—Taft set the date for termination at the beginning of therapy. Taft made a connection between successful separation from the therapist and successful resolution of the trauma resulting from the original separation from the child's mother.

Allen (1942) also focused on the child-therapist relationship, with an emphasis on the autonomy and self-actualizing ability of the child. Allen maintained that the primary task in therapy is for the child to learn to function in relationships and everyday life. He wanted to create an experience in which children were accepted exactly as they were, without any expectations for them to change.

Moustakas (1959, 1997) focused on using a secure therapeutic relationship as the basis for the child to explore interpersonal interactions and move toward individuation. He emphasized the need for the growth process to be mutual, asserting that the therapist must continue to grow with the child in both self-awareness and awareness of others. The therapist also must convey unconditional acceptance and faith in the child's ability to move in a positive direction without guidance or interference. The emphasis in the interaction with the child is on the child's feelings, without interpretation on the therapist's part. Moustakas also believed that the therapist must be an active participant in the play if invited by the child to do so.

A more contemporary approach to play therapy based primarily on the curative powers of the child-therapist relationship is *experiential play therapy* (Norton & Norton, 2006, 2008). A foundational premise for experiential play therapy is the belief that children "encounter their world in an experiential style as opposed to a cognitive one. That is, children do not think about their encounters; rather, they involve their senses as a means of incorporating information from their environment" (Norton & Norton, 2006, p. 29). Norton and Norton (2008) supported the idea that through the relationship with the play therapist, the child gains a sense of empowerment over their native emotionality.

Child-Centered Play Therapy

Virginia Axline (1947, 1969, 1971) combined Carl Rogers's (1951) client-centered therapy for adults with many of the ideas from relationship play therapy when she developed nondirective, child-centered play therapy. She maintained that children naturally move toward positive growth if they are provided with a relationship in which they experience unconditional acceptance and safety (Axline, 1947). Axline (1969) postulated that change in the child occurs as a result of the relationship with the therapist, not as a result of the application of specific techniques. She suggested that it is not appropriate to interpret the child's play or to praise their behavior.

As time marched on, Axline's (1947, 1969) work was expanded upon by a number of play therapists (e.g., Cochran et al., 2022; L. Guerney, 2001; Landreth, 2024; Ray, 2011; VanFleet et al., 2010; K. Wilson & Ryan, 2005). Some combined Axline's ideas with concepts from others who emphasized the therapeutic relationship with children (Ginott, 1959; Moustakas, 1959) in the nondirective child-centered approach to play therapy. In child-centered play therapy, the therapist creates a therapeutic relationship in which they unconditionally accept and empathize with the child. Through this relationship, the child begins to actuate their innate potential for development and growth. Landreth (2024) suggested that the therapist must serve primarily as a mirror for the child and the child's feelings.

Bernard Guerney (1964) and Louise Guerney (1997) adapted many of the concepts and strategies of nondirective, child-centered play therapy to teach parents to work directly with their children using filial therapy. In *filial therapy*, parents are trained in nondirective play therapy techniques they can use in specifically designated "play sessions" intended to build the parent-child relationship and enhance children's self-esteem (L. Guerney, 2015; VanFleet, 2009, 2013). Landreth and Bratton (2020) have developed their own 10-session version of filial therapy they call *Child-Parent Relationship Therapy*. The primary techniques taught in filial therapy training are tracking, restating content, reflecting feelings, and setting limits.

Limit-Setting Therapy

Bixler (1949) and Ginott (1959) contended that the development and enforcement of limits are the primary vehicles of change in therapy sessions. Bixler (1949) stated bluntly that "limits are therapy" (p. 1). He maintained that the therapist must set limits in the playroom to maintain an unconditionally accepting attitude toward clients and to establish that this relationship is different from other relationships. Bixler contended that setting limits in the playroom communicates to the child that the relationship is grounded in a sense of integrity and responsibility. He defined the basic types of limits necessary in play therapy as those that ensure the safety of people, property, and play materials.

Ginott (1959) maintained that limits are a key component in play therapy with children who have experienced inconsistent reactions from adults and consequently feel that they must continually test their relationships with adults with acting-out behavior. He suggested that the therapist, by carefully and consistently applying limits, could reestablish these children's views of themselves as people who are protected and supported by adults. According to Ginott, by setting limits on aggressive or acting-out behavior, the therapist is much more likely to maintain a positive attitude toward children in therapy.

Following Bixler's (1949) and Ginott's (1959) works on limit setting, not much happened in play therapy in the 1960s and early '70s. We believe this may have been because of many other things going on in the world during this era. Johnson (2016) suggested that during this time period, parental problems were thought to be the cause of children's struggles, so most therapists focused on working directly with parents and not children.

Theories for Working With Children Who Have Attachment Issues

In the late 1970s, play therapy again began to evolve as interest grew in helping children who were struggling with attachment. Jernberg (1979) developed Theraplay, and Brody (1978) designed developmental play therapy. Later, as more information emerged about attachment and how to work with children with attachment problems, Benedict (2006; Benedict & Hastings, 2002; Patton & Benedict, 2015) developed object relations/attachment-based play therapy as a strategy for using play to work with this population.

Theraplay

Theraplay therapists use directive methods to duplicate the interactions typically present in parent-infant interactions and to improve impaired parent-child relationships (Booth & Jernberg, 2010; Booth & Winstead, 2016; Norris & Lender, 2020; Norris & Rodwell, 2017; Tucker & Smith-Adcock, 2017). They design each of a limited number of sessions to support four dimensions: structure, challenge, engagement, and nurture. In traditional Theraplay, a child has one therapist who focuses on working with them, while another focuses on working with the parent or caregiver in another part of the treatment room, first explaining what is happening with the children and then helping the parent or caregiver to integrate themselves into the session as co-therapists. The ultimate goal in Theraplay is to enhance the ability of parents and caregivers to continue to foster positive connection with their children through modeling and coaching.

Developmental Play Therapy

In *developmental play therapy,* another directive approach designed to improve attachment in parent-child relationships, the emphasis is on the developmental processes (Brody, 1978, 1997; Short, 2008). Practitioners of developmental play therapy evaluate the developmental stage of the child, adapting the therapeutic approach to provide the elements of nurturing missed by the child in their early attachment to their parents. Brody stressed the need for children to experience touching as they grow in order to adequately attach to parental figures. In developmental play therapy, the therapist holds, strokes, and rocks the child in an attempt to provide them with experiences vital to the development of infants, in the hope that this remedial nurturing will help the child move forward in the developmental process (Johnson, 2016; Stammers, 2017). Although developmental play therapy is still practiced, those interested in this approach should consult the *Paper on Touch: Clinical, Professional & Ethical Issues* (Association for Play Therapy, 2022a) and *Touch in Child Counseling and Play Therapy: An Ethical and Clinical Guide* (Courtney & Nolan, 2017).

Object Relations/Attachment-Based Play Therapy

Object relations/attachment-based play therapy is based on object relations theory and is especially effective for children with attachment disorders (Benedict, 2006; Benedict & Mongoven, 1997; Patton & Benedict, 2015). In object relations/attachment-based play therapy, the therapist first works to establish a trusting relationship with the child. By providing a totally different experience in play therapy than any previous experiences the child has had, the therapist begins to modify the way the child conceptualizes the world, shifting the child's internal working model of the world and relationships. When the child's worldview has changed enough for them to believe that some people can be trusted, the therapist works to teach the child how to discern between those who are trustworthy and those who are not.

Approaches Based on Theories for Work With Adults

One recent trend in play therapy is for practitioners to develop approaches to play therapy derived from theoretical orientations that have traditionally placed an emphasis on understanding and working with adult clients. These approaches include Adlerian play therapy, cognitive-behavioral play therapy, Gestalt play therapy, Jungian play therapy, and narrative play therapy.

Adlerian Play Therapy

Adlerian play therapy, our favorite approach, combines the theoretical principles and strategies of individual psychology (Ansbacher & Ansbacher, 1956) with the treatment modality of play therapy (Kottman, 1993; Kottman & Ashby, 2015; Kottman & Meany-Walen, 2016, 2017; Meany-Walen, 2018).

Using this approach, therapists integrate nondirective and directive interaction with clients, depending on the needs of the individual client and the unfolding of the process of play therapy. Adlerian play therapists use structured and unstructured play, art, storytelling, sand tray, music, dance, movement, adventure therapy, and other active interventions to build the relationship with the child, explore the child's intrapersonal and interpersonal dynamics, help the child gain insight, and provide a context in which the child can learn and practice more constructive ways of thinking, feeling, and behaving. In Adlerian play therapy, therapists work with parents to help them shift how they perceive their children, learn additional parenting strategies, and (when appropriate) work with teachers to help them learn new ways of interacting with children to reduce emotional and behavioral problems that can interfere with learning.

Cognitive-Behavioral Play Therapy

Drawing from the work of cognitive behaviorists (A. Beck, 1976; J. Beck, 1995), Susan Knell incorporated cognitive and behavioral interventions within a play therapy paradigm in cognitive-behavioral play therapy (Dasari & Knell, 2015; Knell, 1993, 2009a, 2009b, 2016). This approach is structured, directive, and goal-oriented. Cognitive-behavioral play therapists use behavioral techniques and cognitive strategies couched in play to teach children new ways of thinking about themselves, relationships, and problem situations. They set up play scenarios that parallel the behavioral and emotional dilemmas experienced by children to help them learn and practice new coping skills and alternative appropriate behaviors.

Gestalt Play Therapy

Oaklander (1978/1992, 1993, 2006) based her conceptualization of child clients and her work in the playroom on the ideas of Fritz Perls (1973), founder of Gestalt therapy. She focused on the relationship between therapists and children, the concept of organismic self-regulation, children's boundaries and sense of self, and the therapeutic role of awareness, experience, and resistance. Gestalt play therapy combines elements of directive and nondirective play therapy approaches, using all of the play therapy strategies to help children increase their sense of contact with their environment and other people. At times, the therapist controls the session by asking a child to participate in experiences and experiments; at other times, the therapist follows the lead of the child in the playroom (Blom, 2006; Carroll, 2009; Fried & McKenna, 2020; Mortola, 2014).

Jungian Analytical Play Therapy

Several therapists based their approach to play therapy and sand tray play therapy on Jungian principles. Kalff (1971) expanded on Lowenfeld's world technique, with the therapist choosing special miniatures for each client and asking the client to arrange the miniatures in a sand tray and develop a narrative that described the scene. Bradway (1979) used the sand tray and miniatures without encouraging a great deal of verbalization on the part of the child. She photographed each sand tray scenario to look for patterns and themes in the child's worldview. Carey (1990, 1999), in her work with sand tray therapy, suggested that the most important element of the play is the exploration of the child's expression of the collective unconscious, in both the verbal and the nonverbal communication of the child.

Allan (1988, 1997) applied Jung's concepts and techniques to working with children in Jungian analytical play therapy. In addition to sand tray work, Jungian analytic play therapists use art and other play strategies to help children explore the ego, the self, and the collective unconscious. By establishing a nondirective relationship with the child, the therapist provides an environment in which the child can feel safe to do the work needed to move along the natural path of individuation and healing (Green, 2009, 2011, 2014; Lilly, 2015; Lilly & Heiko, 2019; Punnett, 2016).

Narrative Play Therapy

Narrative play therapy (Cattanach, 2006, 2008a, 2008b) is based on Michael White's narrative therapy (White, 2007; White & Epstein, 1990). In narrative play therapy, the therapeutic process focuses on telling and retelling children's problem-saturated stories to create new choices for their stories. By using narrative and storytelling as the vehicle for the therapeutic relationship and exploration of the children's lives, histories, and problems, the play therapist co-constructs a space where children can externalize and create a sense of distance from their problems. This distance can allow children to imagine new stories about themselves and their problems. Listening to children's stories and telling them stories with little or no interpretation comprises the bulk of the interaction in narrative play therapy.

Approaches Integrating Different Theories

Another trend that has developed in the past several decades is the evolution of approaches to play therapy that have integrated multiple theoretical conceptualizations and therapeutic strategies usually used with adults and families. These approaches to play therapy include ecosystemic play therapy and family play therapy.

Ecosystemic Play Therapy

In *ecosystemic play therapy*, O'Connor (1994, 2000, 2016) proposed that play therapists shift their focus away from the individual facets of children's lives and consider the multiple spheres of the many subsystems that affect them. These subsystems include the family, the school, and the peer group. According to this approach, the therapist can truly understand clients and their struggles only by considering the impact of each system in which children take part.

The ecosystemic play therapist uses evaluative tools in a systematic fashion to assess the developmental level of children in each of the following areas: cognitive, physical, social, emotional, and processing of life experiences (O'Connor, 2000, 2016). On the basis of this assessment, the therapist plans therapeutic experiences designed to remediate the deficits in children's development, either in a group or in an individual context. The therapy process is structured and directive, with the therapist controlling the setting, the materials, and the activities. Ecosystemic play therapy uses a minimalist playroom setup, with an empty room into which the play therapist brings the materials to use with children for that specific session.

Family Play Therapy

Similar to the process in family therapy, the family play therapist must make a paradigm shift to conceptualize difficulties as system problems rather than as a specific individual's problems. Instead of focusing on an identified client who needs help, the family play therapist thinks of the entire family as the client (Czyszczon et al., 2015; Daley et al., 2018; Gil, 2015; Lyles, 2021; Chen et al., 2021; Spooner, 2020). By combining elements of various play therapy techniques with family therapy strategies and conceptualizations, the practitioner of family play therapy acts as an educator, play facilitator, role model, and directive therapist to help parents and children make changes in the way they see themselves and one another and in the way they interact with one another.

Harvey (2006, 2016) integrated family therapy, expressive arts therapies (e.g., art, dance, drama), and play therapy into *dynamic play therapy,* a form of family play therapy that may include movement, dramatic play, art, and video expression. Harvey suggested the therapist use the play process to identify family interactive patterns and metaphors. The therapist uses the understanding of these themes and metaphors to develop and prescribe the creation of new family metaphors and to coach the family in practicing more appropriate ways of interacting with one another and resolving conflicts.

Short-Term, Time-Limited, Solution-Focused Play Therapy

Given the current focus on brief therapy in the field of mental health, it is not surprising that there is a trend toward developing short-term, time-limited, solution-focused approaches to play therapy (Kaduson & Schaefer, 2015). One early version of a time-limited model of play therapy, developed by Sloves and Peterlin (1993, 1994), is based on a psychodynamic conceptualization of a client's problems with a central theme used to organize the therapy process. In this model, the time-limited play therapist uses a highly structured, directive method of interacting with a child to help them work toward the resolution of this central theme, which is a reenactment of the separation-individuation process. The therapist works to maximize the child's development of a positive transference and a sense of mastery while attempting to minimize regression, dependency, and feelings of helplessness. The time-limited play therapist (a) assesses whether the client and the client's family are appropriate for this approach; (b) works to establish positive transference; (c) helps the child move toward understanding and resolving the central theme of separation-individuation; and (d) helps the child to "internalize the therapist as a positive replacement or substitute for earlier ambivalent objects, thereby making separation a genuine maturational event" (Sloves & Peterlin, 1994, p. 54). The therapist also works with the child's family in several family sessions to help them learn new ways of supporting the child's separation-individuation process in other relationships outside of the therapy process.

Other practitioners have described short-term play therapy applications with individual children using cognitive-behavioral play therapy (Dasari & Knell, 2015), Gestalt play therapy (Oaklander, 2015), and child-centered play therapy (Ritzi et al., 2017). There are short-term, solution-focused play therapy interventions for specific populations, such as children with posttraumatic stress disorder (Kaduson, 2015), disruptive behavior disorders (Riviere, 2015), ADHD (Leben, 2015), or serious health concerns (E. Taylor, 2019). VanFleet (2015) described a short-term intervention using filial therapy with adoptive families.

Prescriptive or Integrative Play Therapy

Another recent trend is *prescriptive* or *integrative* play therapy. Beckley-Forest and Monaco (2021), Gil et al. (2015), Schaefer and Drewes (2016), and Kaduson et al. (2020) have suggested that there is an increased interest in integrating approaches to play therapy and their therapeutic practices. These authors maintain that the most appropriate method for working with children is for the play therapist to choose from various theories and techniques based on the individual client and their presenting problems, specific personality traits, and particular situations. Tailoring treatment to the individual client and family, they contend, makes play therapy much more effective and best serves clients, even though it requires therapists to have training and experience in many different treatment modalities and ways of conceptualizing problems.

Questions to Ponder

1. What are your thoughts about how the zeitgeist of society influences psychology/play therapy? How is the current situation in society affecting the profession? What changes do you project for the next 20 years?

2. What is your reaction to Sigmund Freud's technique of using the reports of Hans's father as the basis for his intervention with Hans? What would be the advantages of working directly with the parents and not with the child? What would be the disadvantages?

3. Hug-Hellmuth's method of working with children in their homes rather than in an office is similar to the practice of in-home therapy. What is your reaction to that way of delivering play therapy services?

4. What is your reaction to Klein's strategy of making psychodynamic interpretations directly to children as a way of helping them gain insight into their issues?

5. If you were going to conduct play sessions using a structured play therapy approach, would you prefer Levy's method of providing children with the toys they would need to reenact a traumatic event or Hambridge's method of directing children to reenact a traumatic event? Explain your reasoning.

6. What is your reaction to Taft's idea that it is more therapeutic for children to enter therapy with the termination date already set? How would this practice affect the process of therapy?

7. What is your reaction to Moustakas's assertion that the therapist must be an active participant in the play if invited by the child to do so?

8. What is your reaction to Axline's contention that children will naturally move toward positive growth if they are provided with a relationship in which they experience unconditional acceptance and safety? Do you believe that the provision of these core conditions is sufficient to move children toward adequate functioning and resolution of their problems? Explain your reasoning.

9. What is your reaction to Bixler's contention that "limits are therapy"?

10. What is your reaction to Brody's contention that children must be physically touched for therapy to be effective?

11. What do you think about the Adlerian play therapy practice of combining directive and nondirective play therapy interactions with clients?

12. What is your reaction to the contention of family play therapy practitioners that the entire family system, not just the child, is the client?

13. What is your reaction to the concept of short-term, time-limited play therapy?

14. If you were going to practice prescriptive or integrative play therapy, how would you go about preparing yourself to respond to the needs of a wide range of clients? What factors would limit your ability to practice prescriptive or integrative play therapy?

15. If you were going to integrate several different approaches to play therapy, what would you want to include in your integration (recognizing that you might not know much about them yet)?

16. Which of the newer approaches to play therapy appeal to you? Which do you want to explore more thoroughly in the future?

3

Theoretical Approaches to Play Therapy

In this chapter, we describe and compare nine established theoretical approaches to play therapy that practitioners currently use: Adlerian play therapy, child-centered play therapy, cognitive-behavioral play therapy, ecosystemic play therapy, Gestalt play therapy, Jungian analytical play therapy, psychodynamic play therapy, Theraplay, and prescriptive play therapy. We also briefly describe and compare six emerging approaches: AutPlay Therapy, FirstPlay, Reality Play Therapy, StoryPlay, Synergetic Play Therapy, and TraumaPlay.

Our choice of approaches to present was based on three factors: (a) surveys of practitioners regarding their theoretical orientation toward play therapy (Kranz et al., 1998; Menassa, 2009; Phillips & Landreth, 1995), (b) the predominance of certain theories in recent play therapy literature (e.g., articles, books, book chapters), (c) the number of presentations at play therapy conferences devoted to particular orientations, and (d) a list of historically significant approaches to play therapy compiled by the Association for Play Therapy (2023).

For eight of the nine established approaches discussed in this chapter, we provide a brief synopsis of the following topics: (a) important theoretical constructs, (b) phases of the counseling process, (c) role of the therapist, (d) goals of therapy, (e) approach to working with parents and teachers, and (f) distinctive features. Our discussion of the ninth approach, prescriptive play therapy, focuses on tenets and core practices therapists can apply when selecting the interventions that best meet the needs of individual clients. At the end of this chapter, we offer a set of reflective questions (Kottman & Meany-Walen, 2018) for you to use to determine which theoretical approach to play therapy might work best for you.

Because our discussion is intended to be introductory, we suggest you seek more in-depth coverage of the orientations that interest you. (See Appendix A for a list of recommended readings.)

Adlerian Play Therapy

Adlerian play therapy (Kottman, 1993, 1994; Kottman et al., 2021; Kottman & Meany-Walen, 2016; Meany-Walen & Kottman, 2017) combines the concepts and strategies of individual psychology with the skills, strategies, and techniques drawn from play therapy. We—Terry Kottman, who developed Adlerian play therapy, and Jeff Ashby, who practices from that theoretical model—have each found this approach best for our practices. However, neither of us believes it is necessarily "the best" approach to play therapy, and in this book, we try to offer an unbiased presentation of all of the theories.

In Adlerian play therapy, the therapist conceptualizes clients from an Adlerian perspective while using toys and play materials to communicate with them. Adlerian play therapy can be used with a variety of clients and works particularly well with clients who have power and control issues, externalizing behavior problems, anxiety, depression, attention-deficit/hyperactivity disorder (ADHD), grief and loss issues, maladaptive perfectionistic tendencies, and self-image problems (Kottman & Meany-Walen, 2016). It also works well with children who are struggling with behavioral or academic difficulties at school and children whose families are experiencing problems such as divorce, family violence, abuse and neglect, or parental alcoholism. It is not the treatment of choice for children with reactive attachment disorder, limited cognitive functioning, or psychosis.

Important Theoretical Constructs

Adlerian theory is practical and optimistic, with an emphasis on the creativity of all people (Ansbacher & Ansbacher, 1956; Kottman & Meany-Walen, 2016; T. Sweeney, 2019). Adlerians believe that people are unique, social, goal-directed beings who perceive and interpret their experiences through a subjective filter that can be positive or discouraged. During play therapy, Adlerian play therapists look for each child's special qualities and assets so that they can celebrate the uniqueness and creativity inherent in each individual. Because Adlerians posit that people re-prove what they already believe to be true, an essential part of the approach is exploring how clients see themselves, others, and the world. As they make changes in how they see themselves, others, and the world, clients can make new choices about their patterns of thinking, feeling, and behaving; attitudes; usual methods of building and maintaining relationships; and strategies for solving problems.

According to Adlerian theory, people are born with an innate capacity to connect with others (social interest) but must learn how to make those connections in constructive and useful ways (Ansbacher & Ansbacher, 1956; Kottman & Meany-Walen, 2016; Sperry & Binensztok, 2019). Teaching children to value connection with other people and learn the skills for building relationships and fostering social interest is an integral part of the process of Adlerian play therapy (Kottman & Meany-Walen, 2016). The relationship between the therapist and the child is considered the foundation of the process of Adlerian play therapy, with everything else that happens in the therapeutic process built upon that foundation. By creating this experience of connection, the therapist can demonstrate to the child that connecting can be positive. The therapist then works to encourage the child to develop positive relationships with other people, starting with the family.

Alfred Adler (Ansbacher & Ansbacher, 1956) noticed that young children may interpret the fact that they are not as strong, knowledgeable, or competent as the other (older) people in their lives as evidence that they are weak, inferior, and incompetent—that they are not "enough." He posited that, because of these feelings, people are always striving to move away from this position of inferiority to a position of confidence. In dealing with inferiority feelings, some people overcompensate and move toward a superiority complex, trying to outdo others to prove that they are better than others. Other people become so disheartened by their feelings of inferiority that they are overpowered by a sense of discouragement and despair, and they give up trying to gain a sense of competence. Still more use their feelings of inferiority as a motivation to work hard to achieve all they can—to get stronger, more knowledgeable, and more competent—without needing to outdo others. In Adlerian play therapy, it is the therapist's responsibility to explore clients' feelings of inferiority and help them let go of overcompensation and discouragement and move toward healthy coping strategies for dealing with their inferiority feelings.

Adlerians believe that all behavior is purposeful (Sweeney, 2019). Adlerian play therapists continually look for the purposes of all behavior, both inside and outside the playroom. Dreikurs and Soltz (1964) suggested that there are four basic goals involved in children's misbehavior: attention, power, revenge, and proof of inadequacy. In considering which goal of misbehavior toward which a child might be striving, the therapist considers (a) the behavior, (b) the child's thinking and feeling that undergirds the behavior, (c) the need the child is fulfilling with the misbehavior, (d) adults' reactions and feelings when confronted with the child's behaviors, and (e) the child's response when they are corrected for that behavior. When the play therapist discovers the goal of a child's misbehavior, they help them to gain insight into that goal, explore whether they want to continue their current patterns, and shift toward more appropriate goals. Lew and Bettner (2000) delineated several positive goals, known as the *Crucial Cs*, toward which the therapist can help clients move: feeling Connected, feeling Capable, feeling like they Count, and developing Courage. Kottman and Meany-Walen (2016, 2018) suggested several different methods for helping children move toward enhancing their Crucial Cs in play therapy.

An important theoretical construct in Adlerian theory is *lifestyle*, which is an individual's unique approach to life (Ansbacher & Ansbacher, 1956; Kottman & Meany-Walen, 2016; Sweeney, 2019). Adlerians maintain that the family constellation (the psychological birth order of the children in the family) and the family atmosphere (the affective tone of the family) are important factors in the formation of a person's lifestyle. Each individual develops their lifestyle before the age of 8 years based on observations of others, their interactions and relationships, their treatment by others, and so forth. From these observations, the individual formulates perceptions of self, others, and the world, and their behavior is predicated on the idea that these perceptions are accurate. Children tend to excel at observing others but may misinterpret situations and relationships. Thus, their perceptions and conclusions may be inaccurate. If you are an Adlerian play therapist, your job, then, is to gather enough information in the therapy process to understand what the client's lifestyle is; to learn about the conclusions the client drew at an early age; to begin to explore the accuracy and efficacy of these conclusions; and to help the client make new decisions about self, others, and the world and formulate new strategies for approaching problems and interacting with others. One of the wonderful things about play therapy with young children is that you will have many opportunities to positively influence how the child sees self, the world, and others.

Phases of the Counseling Process

Adlerian play therapy has four phases: (a) building an egalitarian relationship with the client, (b) exploring the client's lifestyle, (c) helping the client gain insight into their lifestyle, and (d) providing reorientation and reeducation for the client when necessary (Kottman & Ashby, in press; Kottman & Meany-Walen, 2016). In the first phase, building an egalitarian relationship, the play therapist tracks, restates content, reflects feelings, returns responsibility to the child, encourages, sets limits, answers questions, asks questions, and engages the child in cleaning the room together to build a partnership with the child. In the second phase, exploring the client's lifestyle, the therapist uses observation of the child's behavior (both in the playroom and in the waiting area); drawing techniques; questioning strategies (asking questions of the child, the parent, and sometimes the child's teacher); investigation of goals of behavior, Crucial Cs, family constellation, and family atmosphere; and solicitation of early recollections to gather enough information to be able to formulate hypotheses about the child's lifestyle. During the third phase, helping the client gain insight, the Adlerian therapist uses metacommunication, drawing techniques, metaphors, storytelling, and "spitting in the client's soup" (a technique of pointing out situations in which the child is acting as if self-defeating beliefs about self, others, and the world are true; Sweeney, 2019) to help the child gain a better understanding of their lifestyle and decide whether to begin making changes in parts of it. The fourth phase, reorientation and reeducation, involves teaching the child new skills and attitudes and helping them practice those new skills so that they will be useful in relationships and situations outside the play therapy setting. Encouragement and direct and indirect teaching are crucial skills used in this phase.

The boundaries between the four phases are not rigid. For instance, Adlerian play therapists are constantly working on the relationship, and they may decide to help a child gain insight into part of their lifestyle before they finish exploring the child's views on self, others, and the world.

Role of the Therapist

Adlerians are "technically eclectic" in that they are free to choose a variety of techniques to achieve their ends. This encourages a flexibility in Adlerian play therapy similar to that in prescriptive play therapy. In Adlerian play therapy, the role of the therapist shifts according to the phase of counseling, the therapist's personal preferences and experience, and the child's needs (Dillman Taylor et al., 2022; Kottman et al., 2021; Kottman & Meany-Walen, 2016). Adlerian play therapists consistently conceptualize clients in a systematic way, but they adjust the process of what they do in the playroom according to the needs of the individual child. There are certain skills that they use with every child and other skills that they use only with specific children (Kottman et al., 2021). The therapist's role changes at least partly in response to the phase of therapy.

If you are an Adlerian play therapist, you will be both partner and encourager in the first phase. You will usually be relatively nondirective, sharing power in most sessions with the client. During this phase, one aspect of your job will be to use encouragement to help the client gain self-confidence and a sense of competence.

During the second phase, you would be an active, relatively directive detective, ferreting out information about the child's attitudes, perceptions, thinking processes, feelings, and so forth. This process is important because all subsequent interventions depend on your formulation of lifestyle hypotheses based on the data gathered during the investigation in the second phase.

In the third phase, the therapist's role is again as a partner, but one with essential information to communicate. At times, you would be nondirective and supportive. At other times, you would challenge clients' long-held, self-defeating, or mistaken beliefs about self, others, and the world. This is also when you would deliver the initial invitation for the child to decide to make some changes in their perceptions, attitudes, emotions, thinking patterns, and behavior. During this phase, there is a special emphasis on helping the child gain access to their unconscious processes, using the Adlerian conceptualization of the unconscious as information and understanding that has been out of the client's awareness.

The reorientation and reeducation phase will require you to be an active teacher and encourager, helping the child learn and practice new skills and incorporate new perceptions, attitudes, emotions, and thinking patterns into their way of looking at self, others, and life. To help the child change their behavior, you could provide training and experience in assertiveness skills, negotiation skills, social skills, or other useful strategies for getting along with others and coping with problem situations.

Goals of Therapy

The goals of Adlerian play therapy are parallel to the phases of the process. The first goal is for the child to develop a relationship with the therapist, sharing power and working together as partners (Kottman & Meany-Walen, 2016). The second goal is for the therapist to understand the child's lifestyle well enough to comprehend the underlying issues related to the presenting problem. The third goal is for the child to gain a developmentally appropriate awareness and understanding of their lifestyle and to decide to make necessary changes—emotional, attitudinal, cognitive, and behavioral. The fourth goal is to help the child experiment with these changes and practice them, both in and out of the playroom. The fifth goal is to help the child learn any new skills necessary to effect these changes outside the playroom. As part of this process, the therapist hopes to move the child from destructive goals and misbehavior toward constructive goals; foster Crucial Cs; increase the child's social interest; adjust any self-defeating beliefs about self, others, and the world; reduce discouragement; and help the child to acknowledge their personal assets.

Approach to Working With Parents and Teachers

In Adlerian play therapy, there is a special emphasis on working with parents and teachers (Kottman & Meany-Walen, 2016). Because Adlerians believe that all people are socially embedded and cannot be understood without comprehending their social system (which starts with the family), they work conjointly with children and their parents whenever possible. Most Adlerians divide their sessions between play therapy with the child and consultation with the parents or caregivers; others do family therapy for at least part of the process. It is often helpful to introduce parents and caregivers to familial encouraging connect therapy (FECT) as a tool to teach them to use nondirective play therapy skills to enhance their relationship with their children and introduce them to Adlerian concepts as a vehicle for gaining a better understanding of their children (Kottman, 2023a, 2023b). If the child is struggling with school-related issues, Adlerian play therapists also frequently work with teachers.

In parent or caregiver consultations, the process goes through phases very similar to those in play therapy (Kottman & Meany-Walen, 2016). First, as an Adlerian play therapist, you will use basic counseling skills to build a relationship with the parents and caregivers. Next, you will use Adlerian exploration strategies to gain insight into parents and caregivers and their relationships with their children. You will gather information from them about their own lifestyles, social interests, goals of behavior, and so forth, and those of their child. On the basis of your understanding of the parents' or caregivers' personality priorities and other aspects of their lifestyles, you will customize your suggestions so as to avoid evoking defensive responses (Dickinson & Daly, 2020; Kottman & Meany-Walen, 2016). In the third phase, you will work to help the parents or caregivers gain insight into themselves and their child so that they will have a better basis for making decisions about which parenting strategies to use and how to implement them. Teaching parenting skills is one of the essential components of the fourth phase with parents and can be accomplished using Adlerian parenting resources such as *Honey, I Wrecked the Kids: When yelling, screaming, threats, bribes, time-outs, sticker charts and removing privileges all don't work* (Schafer, 2009); *Ain't misbehavin': Tactics for tantrums, meltdowns, bedtime blues, and other perfectly normal kid behaviors* (Schafer, 2011); *A Parent's Guide to Understanding and Motivating Children* (Lew & Bettner, 2000); and *Positive Discipline for Today's Busy (and Overwhelmed) Parent: How to balance work, parenting, and self for lasting well-being* (Nelson et al., 2018).

The process for consulting with teachers follows this same pattern, building the relationship with the teacher, exploring the teacher's lifestyle and classroom management style, exploring the teacher's attitudes toward and perception of the child and their lifestyle, helping the teacher learn more about the child's lifestyle, and helping the teacher gain insight into their own lifestyle and the interaction with the child's lifestyle. With many teachers, this process is enough to make a shift in how they relate to the client. As an Adlerian play therapist, you may need to teach Adlerian skills to teachers, such as encouragement, identification of goals of misbehavior, assessment of Crucial Cs, dynamics of personality priorities, and logical consequences.

Distinctive Features

Adlerians are nondirective or directive depending on the phase of the therapy and the lifestyle of the child. The decision of whether to be nondirective or directive is both fluid and systematic. This flexibility is one of the distinctive features of Adlerian play therapy.

Adlerians set limits using a four-step process in which the therapist, rather than redirecting the child's behavior, engages the child in redirecting their own behavior (Kottman & Meany-Walen, 2016). They also set up logical consequences as an integral part of the limiting process. (See Chapter 8 for more on Adlerian limit setting.)

The emphasis on gathering information is stronger in Adlerian play therapy than in most other approaches to play therapy because the unfolding of the therapeutic process depends on the conceptualization that the therapist formulates as a result of the exploration. The therapist aims to customize the therapeutic intervention by understanding how the child makes decisions and incorporates perceptions into their lifestyle. The therapist asks questions, observes play, and engages the child in art, puppetry, and storytelling activities designed to gather information about family constellation, family atmosphere, goals of misbehavior, Crucial Cs, personality priorities, and mistaken beliefs. The therapist may also ask the child to draw or describe a series of early memories, providing clues about the child's lifestyle.

The process of cleaning the room as a team (Kottman & Meany-Walen, 2016) seems to be unique in the play therapy literature. Although other play therapists ask children to pick up toys and materials, the Adlerian approach to this task is structured, specific, and designed to promote teamwork. (For more on the logistical aspects of play therapy, see Chapter 4.)

Whereas other approaches to play therapy may emphasize encouragement, Adlerian play therapists consider encouragement an essential part of the therapy process (Kottman & Meany-Walen, 2016). They use strategies designed to point out children's assets and focus on effort and improvement to improve children's sense of self-efficacy and reduce discouragement.

Child-Centered Play Therapy

Virginia Axline (1947, 1969, 1971) applied the basic concepts of client-centered therapy (Rogers, 1951) to work with children when she developed nondirective, child-centered play therapy. Contemporary experts, such as Garry Landreth (2024), Dee Ray (2011; Ray & Landreth, 2015), Risë VanFleet (VanFleet et al., 2010), and Kate Wilson and Virginia Ryan (2005) have continued to refine the ideas and strategies of child-centered play therapy in their work with children. According to Cochran et al. (2022), child-centered therapy is

> an approach applicable across the helping professions and settings with wide-ranging child difficulties, from depression, conduct disorder, attachment problems, physical and sexual abuse, and other trauma to grief and other more normally occurring concerns. It can

> be extraordinarily helpful when applied singularly or within sets of
> services at schools, agencies, and private practice (p. xii).

Important Theoretical Constructs

Child-centered play therapists adhere to the belief that the human personality structure consists of the person, the phenomenological field, and the self (Glover & Landreth, 2016; Rogers, 1951). The *person* consists of the individual's thoughts, feelings, behaviors, and physical being, all constantly changing and developing. The person is a balanced system, so when one aspect of the person changes, the other aspects also change, moving toward actualizing the self (Glover & Landreth, 2016). This faith that all people have an innate tendency to move in a positive direction, striving toward self-actualization and constructive growth, is a key concept in child-centered play therapy.

As part of this process toward self-actualization, each person must attempt to satisfy their needs as experienced in the *phenomenological field*, which is the sum total of all the person's experiences (Glover & Landreth, 2016). Each individual's perception of their experiences is the reality of that person. Because of the phenomenological view of reality, the child-centered play therapist must try to understand each child client from that child's perspective (Landreth, 2024).

As children grow up, they begin to organize some of their perceptions into a concept of "me"—the *self*. Initially, these perceptions are filtered through the child's organismic valuing system, an innate process in which the child attaches positive significance to experiences seen as self-enhancing and negative significance to experiences seen as threatening or self-defeating (Glover & Landreth, 2016; Rogers, 1951).

As time passes, however, on the basis of children's experience of being conditionally accepted and judged by others, children begin to introject the ideas and evaluations of others and discount their own organismic valuing (Glover & Landreth, 2016; Landreth, 2024; Rogers, 1951). Children incorporate these experiences into their perceptions of the self, resulting in feelings of self-doubt and insecurity. They may also begin to distort how they interpret the phenomenological field and experience reality in ways inconsistent with their own true perceptions. A gap may appear between their *real self*—the self based on their organismic valuing—and their ideal self—the self based on their introjection of the attitudes and values of others. This incongruity frequently leads to maladjustment.

To remedy this problem and restore children to the path toward self-actualization, Axline (1969) outlined eight basic principles of non-directive, child-centered play therapy:

1. The therapist must build a warm, friendly, genuine relationship with the child client that will facilitate a strong therapeutic rapport.

2. The therapist must be completely accepting of the child without desiring the child to change in any way.

3. The therapist must develop and maintain an environment of permissiveness so the child can feel free to explore and express their feelings completely.

4. The therapist must pay constant attention to the child's feelings and reflect them in a manner that encourages the child to gain insight and enhance their understanding of self.

5. The therapist must always be respectful of the child's capacity for solving their own problems if given the opportunity and resources necessary. The child must be solely responsible for their own decisions and be able to freely choose whether and when to make changes.

6. The therapist must not take the lead in therapy. This responsibility and privilege belong to the child. The therapist always follows the lead of the child.

7. The therapist must never attempt to hasten the course of therapy. Play therapy is a slow and gradual process dependent on the child's pace, not the therapist's.

8. The therapist must set only those limits essential for anchoring therapy to reality and return responsibility to the child for their role in the therapeutic process.

Carl Rogers (1957) identified six necessary and sufficient conditions for therapeutic change:

1. Two people are in psychological contact.
2. The first person (the client) is in a state of incongruence, feeling vulnerable or anxious.
3. The second person (the therapist) is congruent or integrated in the context of the relationship.
4. The therapist feels unconditional positive regard for the client.

5. The therapist has an empathic understanding of the client's internal frame of reference and works to convey this understanding to the client.

6. The therapist communicates this unconditional positive regard and empathic understanding to the client.

Phases of the Counseling Process

Some child-centered play therapy experts (e.g., Landreth, Ray, Geraldine Glover) subscribe to the stages posited by Clark Moustakas (1959, as cited in Glover & Landreth, 2016). Moustakas suggested that the therapy process in child-centered play therapy has five distinct stages. The descriptions of these stages focus on the child's feelings and attitudes rather than the child's behavior or the interaction between the therapist and the child. In Moustakas's model, during the first stage, children express diffuse negative feelings in every aspect of their play. In the second stage, they primarily manifest ambivalent feelings, usually anxiety or hostility. The third stage again features mostly negative feelings, but in this stage, these feelings are expressed directly toward parents, siblings, or the therapist or are expressed through regressive behaviors. In the fourth stage, ambivalent feelings (positive and negative) resurface but are focused on parents, siblings, the therapist, and others. In the final stage of play therapy, children express primarily positive feelings, with realistic negative attitudes expressed appropriately and without ambivalence.

Other child-centered play therapy experts (e.g., Nordling, VanFleet) adhere to a different model of the stages originally posited by William Nordling and Louise Guerney (1999): (a) warm-up/exploratory, (b) aggressive, (c) regressive, and (d) mastery (Cochran et al., 2022). Because the emphasis in this model is on the child's behavior, what happens in each stage is fairly self-evident. During the warm-up/exploratory stage, the child explores the room and begins to build rapport with the therapist. As the child experiences the unconditional positive regard that is essential in child-centered play therapy, the child feels more comfortable revealing their aggression and regressive tendencies in the next two stages. Because the child feels accepted, they can work through their aggression and regression and move on to demonstrating competence in the mastery stage.

Role of the Therapist

If you are a child-centered play therapist, you truly believe that the child has within them the power to move to a healthier place, so there is no need to "interfere" with the process. Your job will be to create an atmosphere of safety and acceptance—no small task, actually—so that the child's own resilience and healing abilities can emerge (Landreth, 2024; Ray, 2011; VanFleet et al., 2010). In child-centered play therapy, your primary role is to provide the child with the core conditions of unconditional positive regard, empathic understanding, and genuineness. Child-centered therapists consider these core conditions to be necessary and sufficient for change. By conveying acceptance and communicating belief in the child's ability to solve their own problems and make any changes required for optimal living, the therapist frees the child to grow in positive directions.

As a child-centered play therapist, you will fulfill this role using nondirective skills—tracking, restating content, reflecting feelings, returning responsibility to the child, and setting necessary limits. You would not use skills that involve leading the child in any way, so you will avoid interpreting, designing therapeutic metaphors, or using bibliotherapy and other techniques that take the child somewhere the child would not naturally go.

Goals of Therapy

The goals of child-centered play therapy are broad and general. The therapist does not set specific individual goals for each child but rather works to provide a positive experience in which the child moves in a positive direction and discovers their own personal strengths (Glover & Landreth, 2016; Landreth, 2024). Landreth (2024) listed the following objectives in child-centered play therapy:

1. Help the child enhance their positive self-concept.
2. Help the child move to accepting more responsibility for self.
3. Help the child reach enhanced levels of self-acceptance.
4. Help the child develop more self-reliance.
5. Assist the child in becoming more self-directing.
6. Help the child practice self-determined decision-making.
7. Help the child feel more in control.
8. Help the child increase their awareness of the process of coping.
9. Help the child develop an internal locus of evaluation.
10. Help the child learn to trust themselves more.

Within this framework, the child may choose to work on specific issues or problems (Glover & Landreth, 2016; Landreth, 2024). However, as a child-centered play therapist, you will not lead or direct the child's attention or efforts to particular issues, such as a presenting problem described by parents or teachers. As a child-centered play therapist, you do not try to explore specifically (either through making conversation or making guesses about the meaning of play) what the child wishes to establish as a goal, and you may not even truly know what the child's goals are. Believing in the child's ability to set their own goals and direction, you will lean into your faith that the child is working on whatever they need to be resolved.

Approach to Working With Parents

The most widely acknowledged approach to working with parents among child-centered play therapists is filial therapy (L. Guerney, 1997; Landreth & Bratton, 2020; VanFleet, 2013). *Filial therapy* is a strategy for teaching parents the skills involved in child-centered play therapy. These skills were defined by VanFleet (2013) as (a) structuring skills, (b) empathic listening skills, (c) child-centered imaginary play skills, and (d) limit-setting skills. Through lectures, demonstrations, modeling, role playing, skills exercises, feedback, supervised play sessions, and reinforcement, the filial therapist teaches parents how to use these skills in weekly half-hour sessions with their children. The goals of filial therapy are to reduce problem behaviors in children, help parents learn skills they can apply in daily interactions with their children, and improve parent-child relationships. This training can take place in group situations or individual families. The therapist can deliver the training as a formal structured program or can teach individual skills as needed by specific parents.

Not all child-centered play therapists are trained to use filial therapy, and those who are not generally do not use it. Although parental involvement is desired in child-centered play therapy, "it is not required for effectiveness" (Glover & Landreth, 2016, p. 111). Some child-centered play therapists do not work with parents at all, focusing exclusively on the work with children, individually or in groups. Others often spend a portion of each session consulting with parents about parenting skills, family relationships, and interactional patterns. They may also work with parents on parenting skills, school issues affecting the child, and ways to better understand the child (Ray, 2011).

Distinctive Features

The primary distinctive feature of child-centered play therapy is the absolute faith that children can work out their own problems with minimal intervention or interference from adults. In most other approaches to play therapy (and other kinds of counseling for children), there is an underlying belief that one or more adults must intervene in children's lives to help them get back on track. Play therapists who focus on child-centered therapy do not believe this. Child-centered play therapists subscribe to the belief that each child has the capacity for self-healing and self-actualizing. Their trust in "the child's innate process when provided the conditions for growth" (D. Ray, personal communication, February 2010) is their unique contribution to the world of child therapy.

Cognitive-Behavioral Play Therapy

Developed by Susan Knell (1993, 2009a, 2009b, 2016), *cognitive-behavioral play therapy* incorporates cognitive and behavioral strategies within a play therapy delivery system. It is based on cognitive and behavioral theories of emotional development and psychopathology. Cognitive-behavioral play therapists use interventions derived from these two theories, combining play activities with verbal and nonverbal communication. The presenting problems that seem most amenable to a cognitive-behavioral play therapy intervention are toileting issues, trauma, reactions to divorce, anxiety, fear and phobias, depression, noncompliant behavior, and selective mutism (Dasari & Knell, 2015; Knell, 2003; Razak et al., 2018).

Important Theoretical Constructs

Cognitive-behavioral play therapy integrates ideas from behavior therapy, cognitive therapy, and cognitive-behavioral therapy. Knell (1993, 2009a, 2009b) borrowed constructs from each of these schools of thought in formulating the theoretical basis for cognitive-behavioral play therapy.

From behavior therapy, Knell (1993) took the concept that all behavior is learned. A key component in behavior therapy is discovering factors that reinforce and maintain behavior deemed inappropriate. By changing these factors, the therapist can alter the child's behavior. A cognitive-behavioral play therapist might use behavioral techniques directly with a child client or teach parents and/or teachers behavioral intervention strategies.

Neither cognitive therapy nor cognitive-behavioral therapy has a theory of personality development (Cavett, 2015; Knell, 1993, 2009a, 2009b). Instead, the focus is on psychopathology and the factors that lead to difficulties in emotional development. According to this model of emotional disorders, behavior is mediated through verbal and cognitive processes. The three key ideas in cognitive therapy are (a) thoughts influence emotions and behavior; (b) beliefs and assumptions influence perceptions and interpretations of events; and (c) most individuals with psychological problems have errors in logic, irrational thinking, or cognitive distortions (A. Beck, 1976; Knell, 2009a, 2009b).

Knell (1994) and Cavett (2015) listed six specific properties important to an understanding of cognitive-behavioral play therapy:

1. The child is involved in treatment through the play. The child is an active participant in the therapy process.
2. he therapist deals with the child's thoughts, feelings, fantasies, and environment. The therapy is problem-focused rather than client-focused.
3. The emphasis is on developing new, more adaptive thoughts and behaviors and developing more helpful coping strategies for dealing with problems.
4. The process is structured, directive, and goal-oriented.
5. The therapist uses behavioral and cognitive techniques that have empirical evidence that supports their efficacy.
6. The therapist has many opportunities to empirically examine the effectiveness of specific treatments for specific problems.

Phases of the Counseling Process

The process of cognitive-behavioral play therapy has several distinct stages: (a) assessment, (b) introduction/orientation to play therapy, (c) middle stages, and (d) termination (Knell, 1993, 2009b, 2016). During the assessment stage, the therapist uses various assessment tools to gather information about the child's current level of functioning, the child's development, the presenting problem, the child's perception or understanding of the problem, and the parents' perspective on the child and the problem. The therapist can use parent-report inventories, clinical interviews, play observation, formal cognitive/developmental instruments, projective tests, drawings, and therapist-created measures to gather information about the child and their thoughts, feelings, attitudes, perceptions, and behaviors.

During the introduction/orientation to play therapy, the therapist and/or parents need to give children a clear, nonjudgmental explanation of their perception of the presenting problem and a description of the play therapy process. During this stage, the therapist meets with the child's parents to give feedback on the initial evaluation of the child and to develop a treatment plan, including treatment modality and goals for the therapy. Deciding on the role of the parents in the process is one part of this.

In the middle stages of therapy, the therapist focuses on using specific cognitive and behavioral intervention strategies to teach children new adaptive responses to cope with specific situations, problems, issues, or stressors (Knell, 1993, 2016). Behavioral interventions can include modeling, positive reinforcement or shaping, systematic desensitization, stimulus fading, differential reinforcement of other behaviors leading to extinction, time-outs, self-monitoring, and activity scheduling (Knell, 2016). Cognitive interventions can include recording dysfunctional thoughts, countering irrational beliefs, developing coping self-statements, and using books for bibliotherapy. The therapist also tries to help children transfer what they have learned in the playroom with the therapist to other situations and settings. Built into their interactions during this stage are interventions designed to teach children coping strategies for avoiding relapses after therapy is finished.

During the final stage, the therapist prepares children for the termination stage by gradually phasing therapy out over a period of time (Knell, 2009a, 2009b, 2016). During this stage, the therapist and the child talk about the child's plans for handling situations after termination. The therapist reinforces changes the child has made in thoughts, feelings, and behaviors and arranges for practice in generalizing learning from the play therapy setting to other settings.

Role of the Therapist

The therapist's role in cognitive-behavioral play therapy is active and directive (Knell, 2009b, 2016). If you are a cognitive-behavioral play therapist, you will use formal and informal instruments to assess the current functioning of both the child and their parents. After completing this baseline assessment, you will actively engage the parents (and sometimes the child, depending on cognitive ability and developmental age) in generating a treatment plan with concrete, measurable goals for changes in behavior, feelings, attitudes, and beliefs. This includes considering a wide variety of available cognitive and behavioral intervention techniques and deciding which might prove most effective with this child and their specific difficulties. You would then implement the plan, usually using some form of modeling, role playing, or behavioral contingency to implement changes in the child (Knell, 1993, 2016). Interventions can be used directly with the child or taught to teachers and/or parents who will use them with the child. You would constantly monitor change, comparing current functioning with the functioning at the beginning of the therapy process and checking for the attainment of the goals delineated during the initial stage of therapy. The extent to which goals have been attained is a major consideration in the decision to terminate.

Goals of Therapy

In cognitive-behavioral play therapy, there are global goals in addition to specific goals for each child and their family (Knell, 2009a, 2009b, 2016). In general, the therapist tries to increase the child's ability to cope with problem situations and stressors; help the child master tasks that have been difficult; decrease the child's irrational, faulty thinking patterns; and/or assist the child in meeting developmental milestones that have been stalled for some reason.

Specifically, each child has behavioral and cognitive goals to work toward that are tailored to their particular situation. These goals may include increasing the child's ability to express feelings, decreasing maladaptive thoughts and perceptions, increasing adaptive and realistic assessments of relationships, increasing positive self-talk, increasing appropriate use of problem-solving skills, and so forth. The child's parents may also have specific goals designed especially for them, usually related to parenting issues or personal issues that interfere with their ability to parent optimally.

Approach to Working With Parents

In cognitive-behavioral play therapy, there is a clear mandate to involve parents in the process, whether as active participants in change or as helpers in supporting change in children (Knell, 1993, 2009b, 2016). Parents are always active partners in the development of the treatment plan. Part of the process of developing this plan is deciding whether the therapy involves cognitive-behavioral play therapy with the child, direct work with the parents, or some combination thereof. If the child needs only minimal help implementing a treatment plan outside of therapy, the primary focus is on working directly with the child. If the parents need a lot of work changing their interactions and relationship with the child, the emphasis is on working mostly with the parents. If the child needs a great deal of help implementing a treatment plan outside of therapy, the focus is on working with both the child and the parents. When a child is noncompliant in the play therapy sessions, the cognitive-behavioral play therapist may shift away from working directly with the child to focus solely on working with the parents.

Cognitive-behavioral work with parents usually takes the form of parent consultation. The therapist may work with parents on parenting skills and discipline strategies, family dynamics, school issues, or personal or marital issues that might interfere with parents' ability to interact positively with their children (Knell, 2016). Using strategies similar to those used with children, the cognitive play therapist may use modeling, role playing, self-monitoring, cognitive change strategies, positive-coping self-statements, bibliotherapy, or contingency management (e.g., positive reinforcement, shaping, stimulus fading, extinction and differential reinforcement of other behavior, time-out).

Even if parents do not need a lot of help, the cognitive-behavioral play therapist must still meet with them on a regular basis (Knell, 2009b). The therapist uses these meetings to gather information about the child, monitor the interaction between the parents and the child, help parents learn new skills to support the child, and provide reinforcement for the parents' efforts.

Distinctive Features

Most interventions in cognitive-behavioral play therapy are delivered (a) through modeling, such as by using a puppet, stuffed animal, or doll to demonstrate the desired behavior to the child; (b) through role playing with the child to practice specific behaviors within the session; or (c) through behavioral contingencies, such as by providing rewards to the child for acquiring new skills. The cognitive-behavioral therapist has a wide range of behavioral and cognitive strategies available for use in the play therapy process (Knell, 1993, 2009b, 2016). Depending on the child's developmental level, these tactics can be adapted to rely more on verbal communication or on toys and play media.

One other unique aspect of cognitive-behavioral play therapy is the emphasis on gathering empirical data for specific intervention strategies and cognitive-behavioral play therapy in general (Knell, 2009b, 2016; Razak et al., 2018). The beginning baseline assessment process encourages the play therapist to gather concrete information about current functioning, and the specifically delineated treatment goals allow for close monitoring of progress and change.

Ecosystemic Play Therapy

The ecosystemic play therapy approach developed by Kevin O'Connor (1994) is a hybrid model that "derives from an integration of biological science concepts, multiple models of child psychotherapy, and developmental theory" (p. 61).

O'Connor and Vega (2019) proposed that children, unlike adults, are largely dependent on the "systems in which they are embedded" (p. 32) and so must rely on others to get their needs met. Ecosystemic play therapy addresses these differences between children and adults, they wrote, by drawing on multiple theories, including psychoanalytic, object relations, attachment, cognitive, behavioral, family systems, and developmental, as well as therapy models such as reality therapy and Theraplay.

Rather than focusing primarily on the functioning of the child, the ecosystemic play therapist tries to actively consider the context of the child's ecosystem in optimizing the child's functioning (O'Connor, 1994, 2000, 2016; O'Connor & Ammen, 2013; O'Connor & Vega, 2019. The therapy is structured and directive, with the therapist making many of the decisions about the materials and activities used in any one session. O'Connor (2016) suggested that ecosystemic play therapy can be used effectively to help any child with any presenting problem.

Important Theoretical Constructs

Ecosystemic play therapy is based on an "integrative metatheory" (O'Connor, 2016, p. 196). In describing this, O'Connor (2000, 2009) differentiated between *structure* elements of the approach, which are consistent and stable across practitioners, and *fill* elements of the approach, which vary among individual practitioners. Since many of the diverse theories that make up this integrative metatheory

> contain elements that directly contradict one another, ecosystemic theory is tasked with providing a rationale for integrating them. [Ecosystemic play therapy] does, in fact, provide therapists with a rationale for selecting one theoretical element over another, as well as a solid model upon which to base case conceptualizations and to develop, implement, and evaluate treatment plans (O'Connor, 2016, p. 196).

Because O'Connor purposely kept the structure elements to a minimum to optimize theoretical adaptability and flexibility, using his model, it is difficult to describe the "typical" method of conceptualizing clients or doing play therapy. Each ecosystemic play therapist develops their own fill elements to complete the theory.

The most important of these fill elements is integrating theories that fit the therapist's experiences and view of the world. O'Connor (2000, 2009, 2016) contended that the actual content of the therapist's personal theory is unimportant because there is no evidence that any one theory is more helpful than any other theory. However, it is essential that the theory is internally consistent. The therapist must understand their integration of theory well enough to use it as a vehicle for clearly and consistently developing and communicating an understanding of each client's functioning and transactions with the world.

Given this context, there are still several theoretical constructs that could help gain an understanding of ecosystemic play therapy. These constructs include the ecosystemic model and O'Connor's (1994, 2000, 2016) personal theory of psychotherapy.

Ecosystemic model. Probably the most important theoretical concept in ecosystemic play therapy is the ecosystem and its function in the theory (O'Connor, 2000, 2009, 2016; O'Connor & Ammen, 2013). To understand what is happening with any particular child, the therapist must consider all the various levels of the ecosystem that can simultaneously affect that child and their world.

If you are an ecosystemic play therapist, you will always use an ecosystemic view to conceptualize the difficulties children are experiencing, to anticipate the support and interference each system will generate as the child begins to change with treatment, and to facilitate the generalization and maintenance of those changes over time. At the same time, you are committed to preserving and valuing differences whenever and wherever possible. (O'Connor, 1994, 2016). You also consider children's developmental level in all stages of the therapeutic process (O'Connor, 2016).

Personal theory. O'Connor (1994, 2000, 2009) maintained that people are motivated by biological drives that move them to seek rewards and maximize their gratification while simultaneously seeking to avoid punishment. Initially, the behavior generated by these drives is extremely egocentric, but as the individual matures, their behavior is tempered by interaction with others and becomes more social and less egocentric. According to O'Connor's personal theory, personality is a result of the interaction between the individual's experience and developmental progress (e.g., social, emotional, behavioral).

In ecosystemic play therapy, psychopathology can derive from three different sources (O'Connor, 1994, 2000, 2009; O'Connor & Vega, 2019) as follows:

- *The individual.* The origin of pathology may be genetic, biological, neurological, cognitive, or even constitutional in nature.
- *Interactions between individuals.* Neither the individuals involved nor the environment is specifically triggering the pathology. Instead, the psychopathology seems to be rooted in the interaction of those specific individuals in that particular environment.
- *A pathological or pathogenic system.* The environment is triggering the pathology.

No matter what the origin, in this theory, psychopathology is viewed as the individual's best attempt to cope with their internal or external situation rather than as a deviant response or an irretrievable flaw. O'Connor (1994) and O'Connor and Ammen (2013) suggested that children and parents who come to play therapy are stuck in their negative behavior patterns and cannot engage in appropriate problem-solving to consider alternative behaviors. Your function if you are an ecosystemic play therapist is to help them see themselves and their world in a new light and to help them begin to engage in problem-solving and consideration of new behaviors.

Phases of the Counseling Process

O'Connor (2016) described the stages of ecosystemic play therapy as (a) introduction and exploration, (b) tentative acceptance, (c) negative reaction, (d) growing and trusting, and (e) termination. In the introduction and exploration stage, the therapist conducts an extensive assessment of the child and uses the assessment data to develop a treatment contract with both the parents and the child. As the play therapist and the child move into the exploration stage, interactions consist of activities such as explaining the play therapy process and exploring its parameters. Children tentatively explore the playroom and play materials and interact with the play therapist. They gradually become more active and may gently test limits. During this time, they are mainly gathering information about what happens in the playroom and what the therapist does.

The stage of tentative acceptance is when children begin to feel more relaxed in the playroom and in the company of the play therapist. They may temporarily yield to the therapist's control and tentatively believe that the playroom is a safe place.

If you are an ecosystemic play therapist, you will maintain tight control during sessions. Many of the children who come to play therapy use control to get their needs met. When these children experience the loss of control necessitated by the directive nature of ecosystemic play therapy, they frequently have negative reactions as they try to continue the behavior they have used in the past to get their needs met. During the negative reaction phase, children may decide that they do not like you, the playroom, or other aspects of the therapy.

As children realize that you (as an ecosystemic play therapist) use your control only to ensure their welfare, they move toward the growing and trusting phase of play therapy. Through the corrective experiences of the play therapy process, children become less stuck in their way of looking at themselves and their world. By gaining a better understanding of their experiences, they can begin experimenting with new, more appropriate behaviors.

When the changes that evolve during the growing and trusting phase of therapy are consolidated, and the learning is transferred to other situations and relationships, children are ready to terminate play therapy. During the termination stage, many children reexperience the issues and problems that originally brought them to therapy. You would help them once again gain an understanding of what is happening and how to meet their own needs without infringing on the rights of others. An important part of the termination stage is the deliberate work to help the child generalize the gains they have made in therapy.

Role of the Therapist

The role of the therapist in ecosystemic play therapy is active and directive (O'Connor, 1994, 2000, 2009, 2016; O'Connor & Ammen, 2013). If you are an ecosystemic play therapist, you choose the toys to use during a particular session and decide on the activities and their sequence. As explained by O'Connor and Vega (2019), the therapist's primary function in a session would be to

> assume responsibility for managing the child's level of arousal during each session and throughout treatment. Further, because the amount of arousal each child finds optimal varies dramatically, as does each child's ability to self-regulate, the therapist intervenes and structures

> the session only when, and as much as necessary, to promote the
> child's ongoing growth and development. (p. 32)

Once you have established the child's arousal level within the appropriate range for learning, you engage the child in problem-solving by (a) involving the child in alternative/corrective experiences or (b) providing the child with new cognitive insight for specific problems or situations in which the child currently feels stuck. You could choose among six broad categories of play: physical (gross and fine motor), challenge/mastery, creative/constructive, language/communication, pretend/imaginative, and games with rules (O'Connor & Vega, 2019). You might also serve as an advocate for the child in the various systems within the child's ecosystem.

Alternative/corrective experiences can occur in the context of the play session or the child's interactions outside the play session. They may be (a) symbolically experienced, such as through pretend play in which the child uses puppets or dolls to act out problem situations with new, more appropriate resolutions, or (b) actually experienced, such as through effectively resolving real situations and conflicts in the relationship with the play therapist.

The therapist can bring about alternate cognitive understandings of specific problems through the problem-solving process or the use of interpretations. O'Connor (2000) presented a five-stage model of interpretations used in ecosystemic play therapy: (a) reflection, (b) pattern, (c) simple dynamic, (d) generalized dynamic, and (e) genetic. A reflection occurs when the therapist interprets a thought, feeling, or motive the child has not expressed directly. A pattern interpretation is when the therapist points out similarities or consistencies that have occurred over a period of time in the child's behavior. In a simple dynamic interpretation, the therapist identifies a relationship connecting the child's unexpressed thoughts, feelings, or motives with patterns in their behavior. A generalized dynamic interpretation involves the therapist pointing out how this pattern is transferred across various settings and interactions. In a genetic interpretation, the therapist attempts to identify the historical source for this pattern, stressing the differences between the source event and current situations that seem to trigger the behavior. The purpose of using interpretations is to help the child begin to see situations and relationships differently and to help them learn new behavioral responses to getting their needs met.

Goals of Therapy

There are three primary goals in ecosystemic play therapy: (a) to help children get their needs met effectively and appropriately, (b) to maximize children's attachment to others in their environment, and (c) to help children resume normal development as the energy that was supporting symptoms becomes available to them and promote optimal development in physical, cognitive, emotional, and social areas (O'Connor, 2016). To accomplish these goals, the ecosystemic therapist must achieve several intermediate individualized goals structured for the particular child, including (a) gathering information to facilitate an understanding of the origins of the child's psychopathology, (b) making a treatment plan based on this understanding, (c) executing the treatment plan, and (d) evaluating the effectiveness of the treatment plan (O'Connor, 2009).

As an ecosystemic play therapist, you will develop specific treatment objectives for each child based on an assessment that includes interviews with the child and their parents, standardized instruments, developmental assessment tools, behavior rating instruments, projective assessment tools, observation of play, and play interviews (O'Connor & Ammen, 2013). Based on the gathered data, you would summarize the child's functioning in the areas of cognition, emotions, behavior, physical and motor development, family, and social interactions. Using this summary, you would develop hypotheses about the child's psychopathology—which of the child's needs are not being met, ineffective response repertoires, etiological factors in the development of pathology, ecosystemic factors related to the pathology, and so forth. From these hypotheses, you would decide on specific goals and plan treatment objectives and treatment modalities. The treatment plan should specify stage goals (based on the stage of therapy), materials needed, experiential components, verbal components, and collaborative components (advocacy, consultation, education, and evaluation).

Approach to Working With Parents

O'Connor (2000, 2009, 2016) stressed the importance of working with parents as part of ecosystemic play therapy. Typical ecosystemic interactions with parents may include (a) information exchange so that the therapist can incorporate data about what is happening in the child's life into sessions, (b) consultation about behavior management strategies or general parenting skills, and (c) problem-solving sessions to devise ways parents can support the changes their child might be making. In ecosystemic play therapy, the session is usually divided between the parents and the child, with parents meeting the therapist for about 20 minutes and the child playing for about 30 minutes.

In some cases, the therapist may wish to teach the parents play therapy techniques they can use outside the sessions to facilitate the parent-child relationship. In other cases, it might be helpful to conduct conjoint parent-child sessions that allow the therapist to observe parent-child interactions and to model appropriate boundary setting and other important concepts. Sometimes it may be necessary to refer a parent for individual work on personal issues or to refer both parents for couples counseling.

Distinctive Features

As should be evident from the descriptions of the therapeutic constructs, the role of the therapist, and the goals of the therapeutic process, there are many distinctive features of ecosystemic play therapy. The purposeful limitation of structure elements to the theory is unique. By requiring each therapist to supply the fill elements of the theory, including devising their own personal theory of psychotherapy, O'Connor increased the flexibility of this approach and made each individual application of ecosystemic play therapy different from all others.

The ecosystemic therapist's role is more narrowly defined and more individual than in other approaches. The therapist has a certain framework within which to operate that sets strict parameters on the amount of control and structure that they must provide in this approach. However, within that structure, each therapist has the freedom to choose how to work with children and their families. The therapist must adhere to the philosophical framework and focus on the ecosystem of each child and on helping the child get their needs met in more appropriate ways. As long as these conditions are met, the therapist can actuate their role in any way that fits their personality or setting.

The complexity of the steps necessary for attaining therapy goals is also a unique feature of ecosystemic play therapy. The data gathering in this theory is extensive, partly because of the therapist's need to understand the various elements of each child's ecosystem. It is also a result of the underlying belief that, to be able to help a child, the therapist must understand the child's psychopathology as a basis for conceptualizing the child and formulating a treatment plan.

The treatment plans in ecosystemic play therapy are much more intricate and thorough than in any other approach to play therapy. Each session is planned out in detail to specify what the therapist wishes to accomplish, how those wishes fit into the client's overall conceptualization, the particular materials and activities to be used, possible interpretations that might be helpful, and so forth. The level of detail and intention in the design of intervention strategies differs from that in other approaches to play therapy.

Gestalt Play Therapy

Gestalt play therapy is based on concepts from Gestalt therapy, a humanistic, process-oriented approach to therapy that is concerned with the healthy functioning of the total organism, including senses, body, emotions, and intellect (Carroll, 2009; Carroll & Orozco, 2019; Oaklander, 1978/1992, 1993, 2006, 2015). Gestalt play therapy works especially well with children who have problems with anxiety, depression, elimination disorders, family transitions, grief and loss, anger and aggression, trauma and abuse, posttraumatic stress disorder, defiance, social isolation, somatic complaints, and illness (Blom, 2006; Fried & McKenna, 2020; Mortola, 2014).

Important Theoretical Constructs

The important theoretical constructs of Gestalt play therapy are the I-Thou relationship, organismic self-regulation, contact-boundary disturbances, and awareness and experience (Carroll, 2009; Carroll & Orozco, 2019; Oaklander, 1978/1992, 2006). All these theoretical constructs originated in Gestalt therapy with adults but have special importance in work with children.

I-Thou relationship. The I-Thou relationship involves a meeting of two individuals who are equal in power and entitlement. In Gestalt play therapy, the I-Thou relationship is characterized by both parties being willing to fully bring themselves into the interaction with complete honesty and without walls or pretenses (Oaklander, 1992, 2006, 2015). The relationship is filled with mutual honor and respect, genuineness, and congruence. Although therapists may have more knowledge and status than the child client, it is essential that they never see themselves as more important or powerful than the child in this relationship. As part of the therapeutic process, therapists stay in touch with their own boundaries and limitations, not losing themselves in the child's circumstances but not being afraid of them either. Each session is an existential encounter in which therapists may have goals or plans but have no expectations of the child or their behaviors and no need to push the child beyond a place where they are capable or willing to go.

Organismic self-regulation. According to the practitioners of Gestalt therapy, each organism seeks homeostasis as a way to maintain health (Carroll & Orozco, 2019; Oaklander, 2015). As change occurs in the environment and the needs of the organism develop, the organism seeks ways to satisfy needs and achieve equilibrium. Human beings use the organismic self-regulation process to get their needs met and to integrate their experiences. This process results in "learning, growth, and fulfillment of the potentialities of the child" (Carroll & Oaklander, 1997, p. 184).

When children encounter difficulties, such as loss, family problems, or trauma, they react in different ways, trying to get their needs met and maintain homeostasis (Carroll & Orozco, 2019). The coping strategies they choose may not work to restore balance and equilibrium, but they will continue to seek ways to do so.

Contact-boundary disturbances. People make contact with others and their environment at the boundary of the self (Fried & McKenna, 2020; Oaklander, 1978/1992). Many times, people are afraid to make contact. They feel a need to protect themselves from others and from the environment and are afraid that they will not be able to get their needs met if they make contact. In the process of trying to protect themselves, children may inhibit, block, repress, or restrict various aspects of their organism—the senses, the body, the emotions, and/or the intellect.

When children block any aspect of their organism, it causes contact-boundary disturbances, which can lead to the development of adversarial behaviors and/or psychological, emotional, or physical symptoms (Carroll, 2009; Fried & McKenna, 2020; Oaklander, 2015). Contact-boundary disturbances can include (a) retroflection (pulling in energy that should be directed outward, doing to themselves what they would like to do to others), (b) deflection (turning away from feelings of grief or anger), (c) confluence (merging with others to the point of the denial of self and the need for individuation and separation), (d) projection (denying personal experiences and responsibility, projecting personal feelings onto others), and (e) introjection (incorporating negative or conditional messages from others about the self into the self-image).

Although all children tend to suffer from some form of contact-boundary disturbance, those who come to play therapy may have such major disturbances in this area that their sense of self is weak and fragile (Blom, 2006; Oaklander, 1994). In the quest for homeostasis and equilibrium, children may desensitize themselves, restrict their bodily feelings and functions, block their emotions, and/or inhibit their intellect. The Gestalt play therapist seeks to restore the children to their original organismic self-regulation, improve the level of contact with others and their environment, and instill a sense of self that is strong and positive.

Awareness and experience. Children who suffer from a weak sense of self have limited awareness of their own experiences (Blom, 2006; Carroll, 2009; Oaklander, 2015). Through experiences and experiments in the play therapy process, the Gestalt play therapist helps children become more aware of themselves in play sessions, which can increase their general awareness of themselves, others, and the world around them.

Phases of the Counseling Process

The Gestalt play therapy process has no prescribed sequence of steps or stages. However, to work toward the therapeutic goals of Gestalt play therapy, most play therapists strive to (a) develop an I-Thou relationship, (b) evaluate and establish contact, (c) strengthen the child's sense of self and self-support, (d) encourage emotional expression, (e) help the child learn to provide self-nurturing, (f) focus on the child's process, and (g) finalize the therapy (Carroll & Orzoco, 2019; Fried & McKenna, 2020; Oaklander, 1994, 2006).

The first component in Gestalt play therapy is the development of an I-Thou relationship between the therapist and the client (Fried & McKenna, 2020; Oaklander, 1993, 1994). The main vehicle for establishing this relationship is the demonstration of genuine respect and patience. If you are practicing Gestalt play therapy, you would need to let go of all expectations about the relationship and the child, entering into the interaction with a sense of adventure and empathy for the child.

Establishing contact involves making a connection with the environment and with other people (Fried & McKenna, 2020; Oaklander, 1994). In play therapy, this contact means interacting with the play materials and the play therapist. Many children are uncomfortable sustaining contact with others, using contact-boundary disturbances to diminish the "danger" they perceive in contact. During the first several sessions with the child, if you are a Gestalt play therapist, you will evaluate the child's ability to make and maintain contact by observing the child's behavior. With children who have difficulty establishing and sustaining contact, you would plan play and art experiences to encourage the child to begin to establish contact with you and the play therapy environment.

During the first sessions, you would also be evaluating the child's sense of self and ability to provide self-support (Mortola, 2014; Oaklander,

1994). Most children who come to play therapy have a weak sense of self and limited ability to provide self-support. They may be blocking their own emotions, blaming themselves for traumatic experiences, and introjecting negative messages about themselves. To help children strengthen their own sense of self, you would design activities to (a) stimulate the use of their senses, (b) increase their awareness of their own bodies, and (c) help them cognitively define who they are by talking about their attitudes, ideas, and opinions.

The process of encouraging emotional expression involves tapping into aggressive energy and learning to express feelings (Fried & McKenna, 2020; Oaklander, 1994). In Gestalt terms, aggressive energy is the energy it takes to promote action. Most children who come to play therapy are confused about their own aggressive energy. They may use this energy too much, resulting in acting-out behavior or suppressing it altogether, resulting in passivity and fearfulness. By teaching children to tap into their own aggressive energy and use it appropriately, you could help them become comfortable expressing their own inner power. You would also help children learn to express their feelings. By using different kinds of play, storytelling, music, art, body movement, photography, and sensory awareness activities, you could help children become more aware of their own emotions and learn to express them.

Children need to learn to accept the parts of themselves that they do not like (Fried & McKenna, 2020; Oaklander, 1994, 2006). Self-nurturing helps them to achieve this acceptance and teaches them skills for taking care of themselves and treating themselves well. Many children, as they increase their sense of self and their ability to provide self-nurturing, stop exhibiting negative behaviors and other symptoms. Other children continue to use negative behaviors and other symptoms to try to get their needs met. With these children, you would begin to focus on the negative process. Without making judgments or suggesting that they might want to change, you would ask children to pay attention to what they are doing and how they are feeling when they exhibit these behaviors.

Children are usually ready to terminate the current installment of therapy when they have worked through their issues as far as their developmental level will allow (Oaklander, 1994). Through several different sessions, children are invited to review progress, celebrate changes, and express mixed feelings about bringing this important relationship to closure.

Role of the Therapist

The role of the therapist in Gestalt play therapy is twofold—partly non-directive and partly directive (Fried & McKenna, 2020; Oaklander, 1994). In the nondirective component of the therapeutic role, the play therapist works to establish the I-Thou relationship and to encourage the child to maintain contact with them in a session. This is done by conveying acceptance without expectations, simply being together in existential moment after existential moment. The Gestalt play therapist seldom uses the basic play therapy skills of tracking and restating content. These skills are not necessary for establishing an I-Thou relationship and are not particularly helpful in the more directive component of Gestalt play therapy. They do reflect feelings and may return responsibility to the child to help strengthen the self with choice-making.

In the directive component of the therapeutic role, the Gestalt play therapist preselects play media and art materials and designs activities and experiments to provide children with experiences that are different from the experiences they have encountered in other settings and other relationships (Oaklander, 1978/1992, 2006). The therapist directs children to use the materials in the playroom to increase their contact with the environment, enhance their sense of self, express their emotions, and learn self-nurturing skills. When being directive, the Gestalt play therapist uses many advanced play therapy skills, including creative dramatics, role plays, video enactments, mutual storytelling, therapeutic metaphors, art projects, confrontation, guided imagery, and so forth.

Goals of Therapy

Carroll and Orozco (2019) described the goal of Gestalt play therapy as

> integrated aliveness—the networking of all organismic functions so that the child's basic physical, developmental, social, emotional, and intellectual needs/wants are understood and organized. Integration is an emergence that is not easily measured but is experienced. (p. 36).

The general goals of Gestalt play therapy are for the child to (a) restore a sense of self, (b) accept previously unacceptable parts of the self, (c) learn to support the self, and (d) be able and willing to experience pain and discomfort. The therapist must also be willing to work with the various social systems in which the child interacts to enhance system support for the child and their emotional, physical, and intellectual functioning. Related to these general goals and to the components of the therapeutic process, the therapist has goals for each child in therapy. These goals reflect the need to form a therapeutic relationship, restore sensory and motor functioning, develop self-support, organize aggressive energy, express emotions, integrate organismic functioning, and decrease contact-boundary disturbances (Fried & McKenna, 2020; Carroll & Oaklander, 1997).

Approach to Working With Parents

Parents are an integral part of the Gestalt play therapy process (Carroll, 2009). The Gestalt play therapist usually works with parents for at least part of every play therapy session. The therapist educates parents about the therapeutic process and engages them to support the changes the child is making through homework assignments. Parents can also be an important source of information for the therapist about what is happening with the child at home and school. The Gestalt play therapist provides parenting suggestions for them to avoid exacerbating the child's contact-boundary disturbances. By encouraging parents to increase their own level of awareness and to express their emotions, the Gestalt play therapist can optimize parental functioning, which in turn can free a child to set off on their own "rightful, healthy path of growth" (Oaklander, 1994, p. 156).

Distinctive Features

Gestalt play therapy is a unique combination of nondirective and direct elements. Establishing the I-Thou relationship is an extremely nondirective process, using few, if any, play therapy skills to build rapport between the child and the therapist. In contrast, the therapist uses many advanced directive skills in later sessions to facilitate increased sensory awareness and expression of emotions. Many of the theoretical constructs in Gestalt play therapy (e.g., contact, contact-boundaries, boundary disturbances) are unique to this approach to play therapy (Carroll & Orozco, 2019).

Jungian Analytical Play Therapy

Jungian analytical play therapy was developed by John Allan (1988) based on the work of Carl Jung (1963). Jungian play therapists "facilitate children's activation of the self-healing archetype by encouraging creativity and accepting the inexplicable mystery and psychic energy associated with the unconscious symbol" (Green, 2005, p. 76). This approach to play therapy can be used in any setting and with any client population, including adolescents, adults, and individuals with developmental delays (Lilly, 2015). Presenting problems that seem to be most amenable to intervention with Jungian analytical play therapy include trauma and mood disorders and children who have experienced sexual abuse, chronic interpersonal abuse, bereavement, neglect, parental divorce, low self-esteem, or depression (Green, 2011, 2014).

Important Theoretical Constructs

The Jungian analytical play therapist, as described by Lilly and Heiko (2019)

> believes that the therapeutic power of healing and transformation comes directly from within the child, and not from any outside technique/person. The source of that change lies within the unconscious; and healing is manifested symbolically through the process of play. Play is the method by which children are empowered to engage with difficult material. Through play, children make the ineffable distinguishable and audible, and are able to achieve healthy transformation. (p. 40)

In Jungian theory, the psyche is described as the center of an individual's thoughts. It regulates conscious experiences, including behaviors and emotions. It has three parts: the ego, the personal unconscious, and the collective unconscious (Green, 2009; Lilly & Heiko, 2019; Punnett, 2016). The ego is the core of consciousness and contains an awareness of reality, thoughts, feelings, fantasies, and sensations. It functions as a tool for mediation between the demands of the unconscious and the demands of the rest of the world—from parents, teachers, peers, and culture. When a child is born, there is no ego consciousness because the ego is embedded in the self (Green, 2014; Lilly, 2015; Lilly & Heiko, 2019). At birth, the ego deintegrates only to be reintegrated if the child experiences adequate care. As the ego emerges from the unconscious, islands of ego consciousness are created by a process of deintegration and reintegration, creating a sense of self (Punnett, 2016).

The unconscious, in Jungian psychology, is the self and is composed of two components (Lilly & Heiko, 2019). The personal unconscious is similar to the Freudian version of the unconscious—the repository of thoughts, memories, fantasies, wishes, desires, and feelings that have been repressed or forgotten (Green, 2014). The shadow, which exists in the personal unconscious, carries the positive and negative aspects of the personality. The shadow is considered pathological only when it engenders destructive behaviors. Jungians maintain that healing can occur when the individual, through the process of analysis, integrates both the positive and negative aspects of the shadow.

The collective unconscious "consists of universal images that transcend an individual's personal (or conscious) experience . . . a virtual storehouse of archetypes—where images, symbols and myths are transmitted from primordial humans to modern humans" (Green, 2009, pp. 85–86). Archetypes are "universal organizing principles that form the basic structural matrix of the human personality" (Peery, 2003, p. 23). They are represented by symbols or images that have shared meanings across cultures, including the hero, the good mother, the villain, the divine child, the wise old man, and so forth.

When a child experiences positive parenting in which their basic needs are met, they develop positive parental imagoes or introjects, which create a secure attachment. When a child's basic needs are not met, they internalize not-good-enough parental introjects (Allan, 1997). If they cannot count on their parents to meet basic needs, the child creates rigid ego defenses to protect against feelings of abandonment and rejection. They may also decide that they are not good enough to be protected or loved by their parents.

Phases of the Counseling Process

There is no standard designation of phases of the counseling process in Jungian analytical play therapy, partly because the process is cyclical rather than linear. Most practitioners appear to have developed their own labels for the process of therapeutic unfolding. Lilly (personal communication, September 2020) has labeled the stages as (a) acclimation, (b) exploration, (c) working, and (d) resolution. In the *acclimation* stage, the child is adapting to the environment (e.g., place, therapist, toys) and has not begun to focus on the work at hand. During the *exploration* stage, the child begins to relate to the play therapist and the play therapy materials (Lilly & Heiko, 2019). As this relationship develops, the child can switch their attention and energy to the issues related to whatever problems they are experiencing; this process of mending what has been wounded moves the therapeutic process into the *working* stage. With some children, this work is primarily symbolic and metaphorical, and the child works through problems without ever verbalizing concerns or issues to the therapist; with other children, the process may involve conversations with the therapist about particular issues or struggles. The child is always allowed to choose whether to talk about their struggles without prompting from the therapist. During the *resolution* stage, the child has resolved their issues through the process of engagement with the play materials and the therapist, reduced their symptoms, and restored themselves to a healthy level of ego functioning.

Role of the Therapist

If you are a Jungian analytical play therapist, your primary role will be to act as an observer-participant who uses nondirective or semidirective techniques designed to engage the child's creativity through spontaneous drawings, drama play, and/or sand therapy as a means of boosting available ego energies (Green, 2014; Lilly, 2015).

As a Jungian play therapist, you will have three responsibilities: (a) creating safety, welcome, and trust; (b) joining the client as a witness and companion; and (c) making meaning of the play, understanding its significance, and occasionally participating in and interpreting the play (Peery, 2003). By creating a safe, welcoming, and trusting space, you will be providing the child with an experience of temenos, the sacred place where transformation can occur because it is safe there (Lilly, 2015). Within the safety of the temenos, you would establish and maintain limits, stressing the rules connected to personal safety, room integrity, and time. You would demonstrate an ability to tolerate the client's deintegration and create an atmosphere of acceptance in which primitive, frightening, and uncomfortable material can emerge. By joining the client as a witness and companion, you would validate the client's experiences, staying at the "feeling level" of the client without trying to change anything for the client in terms of thinking, feeling, or behaving. While you would be working at making meaning of the play and understanding its significance, you will seldom share those interpretations with the client. When you feel that interpretation might be helpful to the child, you will use soft hypotheses that are key to the child's ego strength and the level of deintegration (Peery, 2003).

In Jungian analytical play therapy, working in the transference is essential (Green, 2014). While Jungians acknowledge the usual definition of *transference* as the client projecting material from past relationships and experiences onto the therapist, they also define transference as "the unique interpersonal field which is generated between therapist and patient, which both experience and to which both contribute" (Peery, 2003, p. 42). As therapists witness the play, they analyze what they perceive is occurring, why it is occurring, and what their internal reactions, or countertransference, can communicate about the internal landscape and worldview of the client.

Goals of Therapy

According to Lilly and Heiko (2019), the goal of Jungian analytical play therapy is

> to assist the child in engaging disturbing material safely so that she can use the symbolic materials (i.e., toys) to activate the archetypal "inner healer" to resolve complex dynamics and tensions responsible for symptomatic behavior. (p. 41)

The therapist honors images so that the child can regulate impulses and maintain equilibrium of the energy flow between their inner and outer worlds. Because of their analytical stance, the Jungian analytical play therapist sees intense conflictual emotions, including rage, as an important part of the play therapy process. The therapist can recognize rage and, through permissiveness, encourage the child to express it through behavior, emotions, and symbols (Green, 2014). The Jungian play therapist "allows the psychic integration of all of the shadowy aspects of children so they may eventually come to accept themselves as unique and complete. Children come to acknowledge the dark side of their personality as being part of their psychological composite, but do not allow it to dominate their composite." (Green, 2010, p. 42)

Approach to Working With Parents

Because most Jungians believe that a child's struggles are often a result of unresolved issues of the parents, they often encourage parents to seek therapy for themselves (Allan, 1997). By working out their own problems, the parents can create a space for the child to optimally continue the process of his or her own individuation.

Many Jungians also advocate consulting with parents about parenting issues. After the initial meeting with the parents, Jungian analytical play therapists meet with them every few sessions to review the child's progress and provide them an opportunity to give the therapist feedback and ask questions (Peery, 2003). Peery (2003) reported using these parent consultation sessions as a way to support, educate, and provide limited counseling to parents for issues stemming from their relationship with their child. Green (2011, 2014) requested that parents or caretakers participate in one filial or family play session every 1 to 2 weeks. He also advocated consulting with a multidisciplinary team of school and community-based professionals who collaborate to provide a comprehensive care network for the child.

Distinctive Features

Jungian analytical play therapy has many distinctive features. The theory itself, which is much more complex than we can describe here, is very rich, with many unique theoretical constructs. The concepts of the collective unconscious and the shadow aspects of the self are two such constructs that do not appear in any other theory. Jungians work with the archetypes from the unconscious through sand tray work, storytelling and metaphors, creative drama, and drawing techniques. Although other play therapists may use these same techniques, the emphasis and purpose in Jungian play therapy are different from other approaches. Based on the analytical stance, the Jungian often has ideas about the meaning of the play but frequently does not share those ideas with the client, as would an Adlerian, Gestalt, or cognitive-behavioral play therapist. Although Jungian play therapists are seldom directive in a session, they are free to ask questions about drawings and other artwork, sand trays, and creative dramatics.

Psychodynamic Play Therapy

Although there are several different schools of psychodynamic play therapy (A. Freud, 1968; Klein, 1932; Winnicott, 1971), the work of Anna Freud seems to be the dominant influence in psychodynamic play therapy theory and practice. Therefore, the description in this section focuses on the ideas articulated in Anna Freud's approach to play therapy. Psychodynamic play therapy can be particularly helpful for children who have experienced trauma and children who are struggling with anxiety, depression, encopresis, defiance, self-hatred, poor regulation of anger, poor self-concept, affective dysregulation, phobias, excessive inhibition, and early narcissistic issues (Meersand & Gilmore, 2017; Mordock, 2015).

Important Theoretical Constructs

The origin of all psychodynamic theoretical constructs is in the writings of Sigmund Freud (1938/1995). Because most students studying counseling and psychology have been exposed to a wide range of information related to Freudian theory, we will not discuss the theoretical constructs of this approach in depth.

In brief, however, Sigmund Freud (1938/1995) theorized that human personalities develop from the striving of biological drives toward gratification. He viewed human development as following predictable psychosexual stages: oral, anal, phallic, and genital. Part of this developmental process is aimed at resolving Oedipal feelings and sexual attraction to the opposite-sex parent.

According to A. Lee (2009), Sigmund Freud described several different models of the functions of the mental apparatus. The models that have meaning for psychodynamic play therapy include the structural model (id, ego, and superego), the economic model (movement of instinctual energy toward discharge and attainment of homeostasis), and the dynamic model (movement of awareness from the unconscious to the preconscious to the conscious).

Although Anna Freud incorporated her father's structural model and the psychosexual stages into her work with children, her emphasis was on the functioning of the ego, maintaining that the purpose of analysis was to increase ego control through expanded consciousness (Punnett, 2016). Her particular interests were the working of defense mechanisms, and the ego's striving toward mastery.

Anna Freud (1968) further suggested that children could benefit from analysis when they experience the following:

- Conflicts between and among the id, ego, and superego that limit the energy available for life tasks.
- Unsuitable or inappropriate defenses that limit the efficiency of ego functioning.
- Overwhelming levels of anxiety that limit functioning.
- Fixations of large amounts of sexual energy that prevent appropriate developmental progress.
- Strong repression or denial of aggression that limits the ability to maintain productive levels of activity.

Psychodynamic play therapists also consider psychosexual development, unconscious conflicts, and transference issues (T. Tisdell, personal communication, September 2022).

Phases of the Counseling Process

A. Lee (2009) described the treatment stages in psychodynamic play therapy as (a) introduction/orientation, (b) negative therapeutic reaction, (c) working through, and (d) termination. The *introduction/orientation* phase includes interactions with both the child and the parents. If you are a psychodynamic play therapist, you will outline the schedule of appointments for parents, the need for attendance, and policies for missed sessions. With the child, you will explain the reason for therapy, the rules for conduct in the playroom, and the procedures of the therapist. You might also introduce the child to the "language of therapy" (A. Lee, 2009, p. 63), including feeling vocabulary. During this phase, you will work to establish the therapeutic alliance with the child, using basic play therapy skills such as tracking and restating content.

In the *negative therapeutic reaction* phase, a child may exhibit hostility and resistance to the therapeutic process (A. Lee, 2009). This hostility and resistance can occur in the context of the transference relationship, causing the child to (at least initially) reject you and the play therapy process. As a psychodynamic play therapist, you would acknowledge the child's negative reactions and make interpretations about the underlying dynamics of the hostility and resistance. It will be essential to do this in a gentle, nonconfrontive manner to avoid exacerbating the negative reactions.

During the *working-through* phase of play therapy, you will elaborate and extend your interpretations to different contexts, situations, and directions so that the client "withdraws [their] investment in a particular pattern of mental activity or behavior" (A. Lee, 2009, p. 65). You might have to repeat interpretations repeatedly to help the child let go of defenses and coping strategies that are not currently effective and move on to the next level of development.

Because the loss of love objects is a central issue in psychodynamic theory, *termination* is considered an essential stage in psychodynamic play therapy. As a psychodynamic play therapist, you will concentrate on helping the child resolve any transference ties and acknowledge the impending pain of another loss of an important object—you.

Role of the Therapist

For most psychodynamic play therapists, their role is relatively nondirective. The therapist often follows the behavioral lead of the child, allowing the child to direct the play, choose the toys, and so forth (A. Lee, 2009). The therapist may also provide structure, make interpretations, ask questions, and use some directive activities designed to strengthen adaptive skills and develop healthy defenses (Meersand & Gilmore, 2017; Mordock, 2015). The therapist may use confrontation to point out behavior, play themes, and other important observable phenomena. The purpose of this intervention is to make issues explicit to the child to enhance ego mastery. The therapist may also use clarification in this process, asking detailed questions to clarify various behaviors, to increase the child's awareness of defenses, and to explore related affect (Cangelosi, 1993).

Shifting away from the conscious processes highlighted with confrontation and clarification, the therapist moves toward interpretation of unconscious material (Cangelosi, 1993). Interpretations from a psychodynamic play therapist provide explanations of the source, history, and meaning of defenses and drives. Interpretation is a means to help children become more aware of the defenses they use, resistance, and transference issues (Mordock, 2015). The therapist constantly gauges children's tolerance of interpretation to determine the depth and focus of interpretation.

With many young children, the therapist may also take on educative functions to strengthen ego functioning and encourage ego mastery (Cangelosi, 1993; T. Tisdell, personal communication, September 2022). The therapist may use therapeutic metaphors to help children explore conscious and unconscious concerns and engage in teaching, role playing, or problem-solving to help children replace nonadaptive defenses and behaviors with more appropriate and adaptive ones.

Goals of Therapy

The ultimate goal of psychoanalytic play therapy is

> to explore, understand, and resolve the etiology of the arrests, fixations, regressions, defensive operations and so forth which bind up important sources of psychic energy to aid the resumption of normal development. (A. Lee, 2009, p. 43)

Based on Anna Freud's (1946) description of reasons for children entering analysis, the therapist would help a child accomplish the following:

- Resolve conflicts between and among the id, ego, and superego and increase the energy available for life tasks.
- Eliminate unsuitable or inappropriate defenses that can limit the efficiency of ego functioning, replacing them with more functional defenses.
- Reduce levels of anxiety that interfere with functioning.
- Eliminate fixations of sexual energy and free children to make appropriate developmental progress.
- Acknowledge and appropriately channel aggression to optimize productive levels of activity.

Approach to Working With Parents

Although there seem to be no universal guidelines for working with parents in psychodynamic play, most such therapists seem to favor some collateral work with parents (A. Lee, 2009; Meersand & Gilmore, 2017; Mordock, 2015). This work may include (a) parent consultation to discuss behavior management, (b) information-gathering sessions to solicit data about child development, current functioning, and so forth, and (c) individual therapy sessions to facilitate parents working on their own issues.

Distinctive Features

The description of the therapist's role in the initial stages of psychodynamic play therapy may sound similar to the therapist's role in child-centered therapy; however, the psychodynamic therapist is constantly analyzing and storing impressions about the underlying issues present in the child's play. As the relationship progresses, the therapist shares their ideas about the unconscious dynamics of the child's behavior and motivations with the child. The use of this type of interpretation is unique to the psychodynamic approach to play therapy, as is the emphasis on the analysis of the transference and countertransference issues present in the therapeutic process. The other distinctive feature of psychodynamic play therapy is the willingness to work with children who have psychotic functioning.

Theraplay

Theraplay is an engaging, playful treatment method modeled on the healthy interaction between parents and children (Booth & Winstead, 2015, 2016; Bundy-Myrow & Booth, 2009; Lindaman & Hong, 2021; Norris & Lender, 2020). It is an intensive, short-term approach that actively involves parents—first as observers and later as cotherapists. The goal is to enhance attachment, self-esteem, trust, and joyful engagement and empower parents to continue, on their own, the health-promoting interactions of the treatment sessions. Although Theraplay was originally designed for children with attachment issues, therapists have expanded the scope of practice to include relationship difficulties, behavior disorders, anxiety, depression, insecurity, low self-esteem, lack of trust, withdrawal, trauma, and autism.

Important Theoretical Constructs

Theraplay is based on a model of healthy parent-child interactions in which there is a "sensitive, responsive give-and-take that occurs between parents and their infants and young children" (Booth & Winstead, 2015, p. 142). Practitioners of Theraplay believe that playful, empathic, joyful responses from a child's caretakers result in the child developing a strong sense of self; feelings of self-worth; and strong, secure attachment (Bundy-Myrow & Booth, 2009; Jernberg & Booth, 1999; Norris & Lender, 2020). According to this theory, when a child does not have these elements in interactions with caretakers, the child can be vulnerable to the development of intrapersonal and interpersonal difficulties.

Jernberg (1979) maintained that children learn to soothe and nurture themselves from being soothed and nurtured by their caretakers when they are very young. Children who do not receive this kind of comforting from caretakers grow up to deal poorly with separation, loss, and other situations in which self-comforting would be appropriate.

Jernberg also felt that children who have strong, loving, and empathic relationships with their caretakers develop a view of themselves as being lovable, competent, and capable; a view of others as loving and trustworthy; and a view of the world as a safe and exciting place to explore (Bundy-Myrow & Booth, 2009). Children who do not have these experiences tend to view themselves as unworthy of love, others as untrustworthy and unresponsive, and the world as threatening and negative.

The elements of healthy parent-child interactions Jernberg observed became the Theraplay dimensions used in remediating attachment difficulties for children (Booth & Winstead, 2015, 2016; Norris & Lender, 2020). These dimensions are (a) structure, (b) challenge, (c) engagement, and (d) nurture.

Structure in the parent-child relationship occurs when the parent provides rules and responses to ensure the child's safety and comfort. In Theraplay, the dimension of structure is exhibited through clearly stated rules for safety, experiences with a beginning, a middle, and an end (e.g., singing games), and activities designed to define body boundaries

Challenge in the parent-child relationship occurs when the parent challenges the child to stretch beyond their usual comfort zone. These experiences help the child learn to deal with anxiety-provoking experiences and increase a sense of mastery and competence. In Theraplay, the dimension of challenge is exhibited when the therapist encourages the child to take small age-appropriate risks—to try behaviors that they would not ordinarily try—to build feelings of mastery and self-confidence.

Engagement in the parent-child relationship occurs when the parent does things to draw the child into interaction with others. In Theraplay, the dimension of intrusion/engagement is exhibited when the therapist invites the child to interact in a playful, spontaneous manner. The therapeutic purpose of this dimension is to teach the child that the world is a fun, enjoyable, and exciting place and that others can be both stimulating and trustworthy.

Nurture in the parent-child relationship occurs when the parent does things to soothe, calm, quiet, and reassure the child. The parent engages in activities designed to meet the child's emotional needs. In Theraplay, this dimension is exhibited when the therapist engages in activities designed to soothe, calm, quiet, and reassure the child by meeting their early unsatisfied emotional needs. These experiences can include activities such as feeding, making lotion handprints, or swaddling the child in a blanket.

Phases of the Counseling Process

Theraplay is intensive and short-term. With most children, the beginning interview and assessment with the parents and the initial contract of 8 to 12 Theraplay sessions will bring about enough changes for the family to continue the therapeutic process without outside intervention. These 8 to 12 Theraplay sessions follow a standard format of (a) introduction/ orientation, (b) negative reaction, (c) working through, and (d) termination (Bundy-Myrow & Booth, 2009).

Before work with the child begins, there is an initial interview with the parents and an assessment of the parent-child relationship using the Marschak (1960) interaction method. The next session is a feedback session with the parents in which the therapist explains the Theraplay philosophy, begins to build rapport with the parents, gives feedback from the initial assessment, and proposes a treatment plan. The therapist also explains the logistics of the Theraplay process, including that two therapists may be participating in each session—the Theraplay therapist, who works directly with the child, and the interpreting therapist, who works directly with the parents. During the first four sessions and the first 15 minutes of the second four sessions, the interpreting therapist and the parents watch the session from behind a one-way mirror, with the therapist explaining the therapeutic interaction to the parents. During the second four sessions, in the last 15 minutes of each session, the interpreting therapist and the parents join the child and the Theraplay therapist in the play.

In the first session with the child, rather than explaining the Theraplay process, the therapist communicates the rules, either by demonstration or by explanation. (Booth & Winstead, 2016). These rules are as follows:

- The therapist is in charge of the session.
- Sessions are fun.
- Sessions are active.
- Sessions are structured and predictable.
- Sessions are free from physical hurting.

Part of the first session (and all subsequent sessions) is devoted to exploring the ways the therapist and the child are alike and different (e.g., height, favorite color, eye color). All four Theraplay dimensions come into play in each session with the child.

During the first several sessions of Theraplay (either during or outside of a session), the child might express negative reactions to the therapy process (Bundy-Myrow & Booth, 2009). This negative reaction is considered normal and helpful in the Theraplay process—an opportunity for parents and the therapist to show the child that they will keep working on the relationship and caring for the child even when they express hostility and anger.

In the working-through phase of Theraplay, the child begins to accept the therapist being in control and to enjoy being nurtured and soothed (Bundy-Myrow & Booth, 2009). This process frequently leads to regressive behaviors, with the child acting much younger than their chronological age. These episodes of relaxed and regressive behavior may alternate with lapses into hostile, angry behavior and other forms of negative reaction until the child becomes comfortable trusting adults and feeling more confident and competent.

A significant part of the working-through phase is helping the parents learn to interact appropriately with the child (Booth & Winstead, 2015, 2016). This process involves the parents spending 15 minutes in every session participating in the interactions using the four dimensions modeled by the Theraplay therapist and coached by the interpreting therapist.

As parents gain competence and confidence in their ability to handle the child appropriately, the therapists set a date for termination (Booth & Winstead, 2015, 2016). The therapists schedule several follow-up sessions to ensure parents continue incorporating the four Theraplay dimensions in their interactions with the child. During the follow-up sessions, the therapists provide support and suggestions for continuing to develop a healthy parent-child relationship.

Role of the Therapist

The role of the Theraplay therapist is active and directive (Lindaman & Hong, 2021). If you are a Theraplay therapist, you will not spend much time talking—the doing is the focus of all Theraplay sessions. Before each session begins, you will have a plan for how the session will go, with specific activities and materials chosen to facilitate the various dimensions. Each session would be tailored to the needs of the individual child, with the percentage of time spent on each dimension based on the issues of that particular family. As the session unfolded, you might change or adapt some of the activities, depending on the child's mood and/or the child's reactions to the interaction or activities. You would not use many of the basic play therapy skills, including tracking, restating content, or returning responsibility to the child, nor would you use interpretations, metaphoric storytelling, or art activities.

In some applications of Theraplay, the therapist's role is shared by an interpreting therapist and a Theraplay therapist. If you are the interpreting therapist, you will (a) be verbal and directive in explaining the process unfolding between the child and the Theraplay therapist to the parents, (b) describe different activities that could help the child, (c) elaborate on the need for the various Theraplay dimensions in the parent-child relationship, (d) coach parents as they enter the Theraplay process and participate in activities, and (e) provide support and encouragement for changes the parents make in their interactions with the child.

Goals of Therapy

The goal of Theraplay is "to enhance children's view of themselves and to increase their joy in the world" (Jernberg & Jernberg, 1993, p. 48). Theraplay therapists maintain that the best way to promote children's positive views of themselves, others, and the world is through activities modeled on the healthy attachment-enhancing behaviors between parent and infant. By working toward improving the attachment between parent and child, practitioners of Theraplay believe they can move children toward feeling more trusting, having a higher level of self-worth and self-confidence, and being more willing to let others have control in age-appropriate situations. Their goals are also to guide and support parents in becoming more attuned and responsive to their children, more able to meet the needs of their children, and more able to help their children gain the ability for healthy self-regulation (Lindaman & Hong, 2021; Norris & Lender, 2020).

For each child and their parents, based on the results of the Marshack interaction method, family history information, and observation of parent-child interactions, the Theraplay therapist devises specific goals for the therapy process. These goals usually include forming a more secure attachment, shifting the child's view of self and others from negative to positive, teaching the child self-soothing behaviors, and changing the patterns inherent in the parent-child interactions so that the parents can appropriately provide the four Theraplay dimensions in the relationship outside the therapy sessions. The therapist may also work on school, marital, and sibling issues and any personal issues of one or both parents.

Approach to Working With Parents

As we have mentioned, the approach to working with parents in Theraplay is intensive. Parents are actively involved in every half-hour session. They often have a separate therapist (the interpreting therapist) devoted to explaining the process and involving them. The therapist works with the parents helping them attune to the child's cues and needs, regulate the child, soothe and calm the child when needed, and share in the fun and joy of play at other times.

Distinctive Features

Theraplay has many distinctive features. The therapists seldom use standard play therapy intervention strategies (e.g., tracking, restating content, reflecting feelings, interpreting, role playing, storytelling). Rather, the Theraplay therapist engages the child in playful activities and games using limited materials in an empty room on a mat-covered floor. Sessions are short—usually 30 minutes—and intense. Often, two therapists are actively involved in the process, one with the child and one with the parents.

The extensive involvement of the parents is also unique to Theraplay. Although other play therapy approaches may include parents in the process, a key objective of Theraplay is to teach the parents the skills needed to assume primary responsibility for providing their child with a nurturing relationship.

Prescriptive Play Therapy

Prescriptive play therapy is a therapeutic approach that incorporates a variety of theories and techniques to customize the play intervention to meet the specific and diverse needs of individual clients. The focus is on resolving the specific problems that brought the client into therapy rather than enhancing their general psychological well-being or personal development (Schaefer & Drewes, 2016).

Practitioners of prescriptive play therapy (Gil & Shaw, 2009; Kaduson et al., 2020; Schaefer, 2001, 2003; Schaefer & Drewes, 2014, 2016; Yasenik & Gardner, 2024) individually tailor their interventions for each child. To do this in a theoretically consistent way, they must have a depth of knowledge—both conceptual and practical—about each of the various theoretical orientations. With that knowledge, they can appropriately conceptualize the client and their problems. Prescriptive therapists must also have a great deal of experience working with children and their parents to apply specific intervention strategies with skill.

> They "choose which approach to use with a given client based on the client's unique presentation. The child's symptomatology, diagnosis, developmental needs, and natural leanings are matched first to appropriate treatment goals and then to the most helpful interventions. The interventions, which may run the gamut from nondirective to directive, can then be prescribed at various phases of treatment, for various lengths of time, and in a flexible clinician-informed order." (Goodyear-Brown, 2010, p. xiv)

According to Gil and Shaw (2009), to find the best fit between a child and a proposed course of treatment, prescriptive play therapists must consider three questions: (a) What client and treatment variables and characteristics would be relevant to therapeutic change? (b) What combination of client-treatment qualities best predicts and facilitates a successful outcome? (c) What are the relative contributions of the client, the treatment, the relationship between the therapist and the client, and the matching of the treatment to the client?

Kaduson et al. (2020) proposed five basic tenets and five core practices of prescriptive play therapy. The basic tenets are as follows:

- *Differential therapeutics.* Prescriptive play therapists recognize that some interventions are more effective with specific disorders than others. A client who does not make progress with one approach to play therapy might make more progress with a different approach to play therapy.

- *Eclecticism.* Instead of strictly adhering to a specific theoretical orientation to play therapy, prescriptive play therapists choose a therapeutic strategy from different theories and techniques that they believe would work best for a particular client.

- *Integrative psychotherapy.* Prescriptive play therapists are not confined to a single therapeutic approach, so they frequently combine different theories and techniques to "strengthen and broaden the scope of their intervention" (p. 6). They blend the healing elements from different approaches to play therapy into an integrated treatment for specific clients.

- *Prescriptive matching.* Prescriptive play therapists try to match the most effective play therapy interventions with each specific disorder or presenting problem. The therapist selects the therapeutic change agent deemed most likely to reduce or eliminate the cause of the problem and the symptoms of that problem. Prescriptive play therapists consider which of the therapeutic powers of play will address the underlying changes a particular client needs and choose interventions designed to activate those changes.

- *Individualized treatment.* Prescriptive play therapists believe that each client is unique and that what has worked for one client may not work for another. They always tailor the intervention to meet the specific needs of the individual client, and their goal is to treat both the problem and the person who is manifesting that problem.

The core practices of prescriptive play therapy proposed by Kaduson et al. (2020) are as follows:

- *Comprehensive assessment.* Prescriptive play therapists perform an extensive assessment of the problem before beginning treatment, using multiple sources and assessment methods. Their assessment usually includes (a) multiple informants (including parents, teachers, and the child), (b) multiple methods (e.g., clinical interviews and/or standardized assessment tools, and (c) direct observation of the child and parent-child interactions. Based on this assessment, they develop an individualized case formulation of the client that includes a description of the issues/problems, assets, probable causes of the problems, treatment goals and plans, predicted barriers to progress, and a method for evaluating progress.

- *Monitoring of progress.* Prescriptive play therapists continually monitor any changes in the client's presenting problems to determine whether the symptoms are getting better. If the symptoms improve, they continue with their prescribed treatment plan; if not, the therapists adjust their treatment plan and interventions.
- *Empirically supported treatments.* Prescriptive play therapists seek out treatments with empirically supported efficacy.
- *Treatment selection.* Prescriptive play therapists select a treatment by integrating three primary sources of information: (a) empirically supported treatments for the specific disorder or problem, (b) the needs and preferences of the client, and (c) therapist variables, including therapist expertise and clinical judgment.
- *Role of the therapist.* Prescriptive play therapists must be competent in multiple theoretical orientations and approaches to play therapy. They should be skilled in at least one directive and one non-directive form of play therapy. The role of the prescriptive play therapist varies depending on the specific play therapy interventions selected for the particular client and their problem.

According to Kaduson et al. (1997), the prescriptive play therapist must also

- be familiar with virtually every approach to play therapy, including the theoretical constructs and the main treatment strategies;
- be skilled in the application of this wide range of theoretical constructs and treatment strategies;
- have integrated the numerous philosophical ideas about people, their motivation, the change process, the role of the therapist, and myriad other aspects of psychological theory formation into an internally consistent model of personality development and therapeutic process;
- understand the various psychological and emotional issues related to common childhood disorders;
- know enough about the short- and long-term needs of children with specific diagnoses and presenting problems to be able to formulate treatment plans based on those needs;
- be skilled at discovering the specific biopsychosocial variables unique to individual children; and

- know the research related to each common childhood disorder and presenting problem well enough to evaluate the efficacy of various intervention strategies with specific populations.

One essential element in developing an effective prescriptive approach is to focus on the internal consistency of the underlying theoretical conceptualization of the client (Kottman & Meany-Walen, 2018). This means that the clinician must clearly understand each theory and the philosophical concepts on which the theory is based. Kaduson et al. (1997) advocated *synthetic eclecticism*, which emphasizes applying various theories into "one interactive and coordinated modality of treatment" (p. xi). However, they cautioned against "kitchen-sink" eclecticism, an atheoretical approach in which practitioners haphazardly apply techniques without considering their underlying theories.

The nature of prescriptive play therapy's eclectic approach makes it difficult to summarize in a book chapter concisely. Because theoretical consistency is not particularly important in prescriptive play therapy, every therapist's approach to every child will be unique. That being said, there is a clear mandate for prescriptive play therapists to carefully customize a comprehensive, systematic plan that can efficiently meet the needs of each client.

The play therapy dimensions model (Yasenik & Gardner, 2024) can serve as a guide for this process (see Chapter 1, Figure 1). As a decision-making and treatment-planning tool, the model was designed to help play therapists answer the *who, what, when, why, and how* of the play therapy process. This model can be used as a method for considering the complexities involved in the change mechanisms in play therapy, and it helps therapists to choose among the many possible applications of various theoretical approaches and techniques, allowing them to tailor the intervention to the client.

Emerging Approaches to Play Therapy

In the past 10–15 years, therapists have developed several different approaches to play therapy, including AutPlay Therapy, First-Play, Reality Play Therapy, StoryPlay, Synergetic Play Therapy, and TraumaPlay. Following is a brief description of each. For more information about any of them, you can delve into the resources listed in Appendix A.

AutPlay Therapy

AutPlay Therapy is a behavioral play-based treatment approach to working with children and adolescents with ADHD, dysregulation issues, and other neurodevelopmental disorders (Grant, 2017a, 2023). Developed by Robert Jason Grant, AutPlay Therapy weaves together ideas from the neurodiversity paradigm, the social model of disability, and family systems theory with the therapeutic powers of play therapy. AutPlay Therapy combines nondirective processes and directive play therapy techniques to meet children where they are and help them develop an awareness of their strengths. It is based on the premise that when children can learn to understand and regulate their system, possess awareness of and receive support for the environments in which they are asked to function, and have meaningful relationship connections, they are far less likely to have any type of "behavioral issues" and more likely to successfully maneuver in their day-to-day environment (Grant, 2023, p. 150).

FirstPlay

Developed by Janet Courtney, FirstPlay is based on the premises of developmental play therapy. It is designed to enhance parent/child bonding and attachment through infant massage storytelling and kinesthetic storytelling (Baldwin et al., 2020; Courtney, 2020; Courtney et al., 2017). The practitioners teach parents and caregivers to combine respectful and caring touch with storytelling to help build the connection between themselves and their infants and young children.

Reality Play Therapy

Reality play therapy was created by Diane Stutey and Robert Wubbolding (2018; Stutey et al., 2020) as a way to combine the therapeutic powers of play with the principles and practices of reality therapy. This approach to play therapy involves helping children examine what they want and can control in their lives, which allows them to think about and evaluate their choices. By teaching children to evaluate what they are doing and whether it is working for them and helping them plan for future decisions, therapists who practice reality play therapy can help improve children's quality world and positively impact their behaviors.

StoryPlay

StoryPlay was developed by Joyce Mills based on the principles espoused by Milton Erickson (Erickson & Rossi, 1981). StoryPlay is a transcultural, resiliency-based play therapy model that draws upon the natural inner resources, skills, and strengths of clients to generate healing, growth, and change by using the symptom and all of the other parts of a client's story to help bring about behavioral and emotional change (Mills, 2015; Mills & Crowley, 2014). This indirective approach (designed for clients who have experienced trauma or other forms of adversity) features storytelling, sand tray experiences, music, dance, art, and other expressive arts techniques.

Synergetic Play Therapy

Created by Lisa Dion, Synergetic Play Therapy is a "research-informed model of play therapy combining the therapeutic powers of play with nervous system regulation, interpersonal neurobiology, physics, attachment, mindfulness, and therapist authenticity" (Synergetic Play Therapy Institute, n.d., para. 1). Synergetic Play Therapy (Dion, 2018) incorporates the therapeutic powers of play, the science that governs relationships, and the development of the therapist, capitalizing on the interplay between these three systems that support transformation for therapists and children (Schaad & Dion, 2021). Synergetic Play Therapy is based on the premise that the therapist's authentic ability to engage in mindfulness and model regulation of their own nervous system can serve as a model for clients to learn how to manage their nervous systems.

TraumaPlay

Paris Goodyear-Brown (2019, 2021, 2022) developed the TraumaPlay model (formerly known as flexibly sequential play therapy) as a way to equip practitioners to use a combination of directive and nondirective play therapy techniques to create the space for children to tell their stories while helping them manage emotional, cognitive, and physiological sequelae of traumatic experiences. Under the umbrella of TraumaPlay, play therapists help children by enhancing safety and security, assessing and augmenting their coping skills, soothing their physiology, increasing their emotional literacy, addressing their thoughts, helping them work through the impact of the trauma through posttraumatic play and trauma narratives, and making positive meaning of their posttrauma life. They also learn to support parents in becoming "soothing partners" for their children.

Choosing a Theoretical Orientation or Approach

As a first step in choosing a personal theoretical orientation or approach to play therapy, you may want to consider your perspective on the philosophical assumptions underlying counseling and play therapy theories and your view of how therapy works to help people make changes. Kottman and Meany-Walen (2018, pp. 40–42) proposed 12 essential questions for potential play therapists to consider:

1. What do you believe about the basic nature of people? Are people inherently good (e.g., positive, self-actualizing), bad (e.g., negative, irrational, evil), neutral, or some combination of these? If you believe it is a combination of the three, how would you describe the configuration of these factors?

2. How are personalities formed/constructed?

   a. What factors influence the formation of personality?

   b. What combination of heredity/environment influences the formation of personality?

   c. Which do you believe is more important in the development of personality: nature or nurture? If you were to assign percentages for each (i.e., "50/50"), what would they be?

   d. In relation to what you believe about free will and determinism in the formation of personality, do you believe that people exercise free will in forming their personalities, or are personal qualities determined by outside factors without input from the person? Is there some combination of free will and determinism? What percentages would you assign to each if you believe it is a combination?

   e. What is the relationship between thinking, feeling, and behaving? Is there a linear, causal relationship between thoughts, emotions, and behavior? If so, what causes what? If not, what is the relationship between these factors?

   f. What is the basic motivation for people's behavior? What motivates people to do the things they do in their lives?

   g. What are the basic elements of a person's personality?

3. What is your stance on perception of reality—is it subjective or objective?

4. What do you believe is the role of the therapeutic relationship in counseling? Do you believe the therapeutic relationship is necessary and sufficient (as in, it is the primary and only factor in clients moving toward healthy functioning)? Do you believe the therapeutic relationship is necessary and that it serves as the foundation for helping clients through the creation of opportunities to entertain alternative perspectives, learn new coping skills, learn and practice socially appropriate behaviors, let go of destructive patterns, and so forth?

5. In counseling, do you think you need to help clients extensively explore the past, look at their current issues in the context of their past, or focus only on the "here and now" without considering anything about the past?

6. Do you believe it is important to help clients become more aware of their own motivation and patterns by helping them gain insight/become more conscious? Or do you believe they will get better if they learn better coping skills without becoming more aware of their motivation and patterns? Will clients get better if they experience certain conditions that activate their own self-actualizing tendencies without additional information, practice, or insight?

7. What do you believe should be the primary focus of counseling: creating a relationship with the client or helping the client make changes in personality, feelings, behaviors, attitudes, and/or thoughts? If it is important to help clients make changes, do you believe you should help clients make changes in only one of these factors or some combination of them? If so, which would be the "firing order" you would prioritize?

8. How do you define psychological maladjustment?

9. What do you think should be the goals of counseling?

10. How can you tell if your clients are getting "better"? How will you judge whether or not clients are making progress?

11. Do you imagine your role as a counselor to be more directive or nondirective in your play therapy sessions?

    a. Would you prefer to create the space for the client to grow without making suggestions for in-session activities or homework (allowing the client to play without therapist intervention in play therapy)? Or are you more comfortable intervening by inviting clients to participate in structured techniques and assigning homework?

    b. How comfortable are you with participating in active interactions with the client (by this, we mean *playing* with them)? Do you believe playing with the client in a session is never appropriate? Do you believe playing with a client at the client's invitation is only appropriate? Is it acceptable to initiate playing with a client? If a client invites you to play something, do you think you must play even if you are uncomfortable with what the client wants you to play?

12. When working with a child client, what is your stance on working with parents? Teachers? Do you believe involving parents and/or teachers is always necessary? Do you believe it is not necessary to include these adults in counseling? If you do believe it is necessary, to what degree do you think they should be included?

The comparison tables in Appendix B show the similarities and differences among the various approaches to play therapy discussed in this chapter.

Questions to Ponder

1. What is your reaction to this quote? "Play therapy may be directive in form—that is, the therapist may assume responsibility for guidance and interpretation, or it may be nondirective; the therapist may leave responsibility and direction to the child" (Axline, 1947, p. 9).

2. What do you think about the Adlerian concept that the therapist's role should change depending on the counseling phase or the child's needs?

3. What is your reaction to the child-centered principle that all people have an innate tendency to move in a positive direction, striving toward self-actualization and constructive growth?

4. Do you agree or disagree with the child-centered concept of organismic valuing? Explain your reasoning.

5. What do you think about Axline's principles of play therapy? With which do you agree or disagree? Explain your reasoning.

6. How does the cognitive-behavioral emphasis on developing more adaptive thoughts and behaviors fit into your view of play therapy?

7. How comfortable would you be with an assessment stage, such as the cognitive-behavioral assessment period, in which the

therapist uses formal and informal instruments to assess the current functioning of the child and their parents?

8. If you were doing Gestalt play therapy, how would you deal with the fact that sometimes you would be directive and other times you would be nondirective?

9. In Jungian analytic play therapy, the therapist must have dealt with their own issues so they do not interfere with the process. What issues might you have that would be triggered by the stricture that you must be permissive about emotional, behavioral, and symbolic expression of rage?

10. What would you want to include in the fill for your approach to play therapy (if you were following O'Connor's idea that each individual therapist should provide the bulk of the fill for their approach to play therapy)?

11. What is your reaction to the level of control the ecosystemic play therapist maintains in a session?

12. Theraplay is extremely directive, with the therapist making most of the decisions about what to play. What is your reaction to this?

13. To adequately do prescriptive play therapy, you would have to be educated about all of the different theoretical approaches to play therapy, all of the different treatment techniques, and the research that supports which treatment modality works best with which presenting problems. What is your reaction to this?

14. Which of the newly emerging approaches to play therapy interests you? What is it about the approach(es) that are attractive to you?

15. Which of the approaches described in this chapter do you think might be the best fit for you? Explain your reasoning.

16. How would you answer each of the 12 questions proposed by Kottman & Meany-Walen (2018) cited in this chapter?

17. As you review the tables of historically significant approaches to play therapy in Appendix B, which of the theoretical approaches most closely aligns with your answers to these questions? What is your reaction to this process?

Basic Skills

4

Logistical Aspects of Play Therapy

This chapter covers important logistical aspects of play therapy, including (a) setting up a space for therapy, (b) choosing and arranging toys, (c) explaining the play therapy process (including confidentiality) to parents, children, and teachers (for play therapists who work in schools); (d) handling the initial session; (e) ending each session; (f) children's themes in the playroom; (g) writing session reports; and (h) terminating play therapy. Play therapists may encounter various logistical issues and challenges in planning their play therapy implementation. While each play therapist will have their own unique circumstances to deal with, there are commonalities that can inform their decision-making process.

Many of the descriptions contained in this chapter assume an "ideal" situation that likely will not exist: a large, warmly lit, acoustically tight space in a beautiful child-proof building; all the money you need to buy whatever toys, materials, and furniture you want; intelligent, insightful children with only minor problems who will quickly respond to therapy; optimally cooperative parents; colleagues who understand and support what you are doing; and insurance companies that will provide unlimited reimbursement for your services. As a play therapist, you are unlikely to have even one of these ideal conditions in the real world. Realistically (and sadly), most of the decisions you will make about logistical matters will be based on the practical considerations of your professional position, the clients you serve, available resources, and the setting of your work.

Setting Up a Space for Therapy

Landreth (2024) described an ideal playroom. His specifications included information about the playroom size, location, and accommodations.

- The room should measure approximately 12 by 15 ft, with an area between 150 and 200 sq ft. This will provide children with room to navigate and move around without having so much space that they might feel overwhelmed or evade your attention.
- The room must have privacy so children can feel safe revealing information and feelings without fear of others overhearing. If there is a window in the room, there should be curtains or blinds that children can close if they wish.
- Wall coverings should be washable so children can make messes with impunity. Painting the walls with a neutral color of washable enamel is recommended.
- The floors should be vinyl tile, an easy surface to clean or replace.
- There should be enough shelves to accommodate toys and materials without crowding. Top shelves should be no higher than 38 in. from the floor to ensure that smaller children can reach them. Shelves for toys should be securely attached to walls so that they cannot be toppled, either by accident or on purpose.
- A small sink, cold running water only—hot water presents an injury risk.
- A child-sized desk and chair for doing artwork or "school" work; a countertop space to sort materials and/or spread them out would also be helpful.
- Storage containers and/or a cabinet to store materials such as paint, crayons, paper, clay, and paper.
- A marker board or chalkboard (wall-mounted or on an easel).
- A small bathroom connected to the main room to eliminate the need to escort children to restrooms outside of the office.
- The playroom should be located in an area of the building where noise will not present a problem, either for other building inhabitants or passers-by. If possible, the room's ceiling should be fitted with acoustic tile to reduce noise.

- Furniture (e.g., desks, tables, chairs) should be constructed of wood or molded plastic and designed to accommodate children. If you are working with parents in the playroom, adult-sized furniture should also be available.
- A place for you (the therapist) to sit, such as a chair or a floor pillow that is comfortable without being too relaxing such that it undermines your ability to focus on the child.
- A one-way mirror and equipment for video recording or listening to sessions, which offers the opportunity for supervision, training, and self-monitoring.

This description is for a room where you would do individual play therapy. If you are working with groups or families, the space should be larger, with enough furniture to accommodate all session participants.

There is no prohibition against doing play therapy if you do not have a space that meets the description suggestions. The authors have had their own experiences with different room configurations. Terry has done play therapy in an elementary school closet but now has a custom-designed playroom in her house; due to space limitations, she does not have all the ideal features previously described. Jeff has done play therapy on one side of a multipurpose room in a school (also not ideal) and in a playroom in a university setting designed for training, where conditions were much closer to ideal. Across these settings, the authors have not noticed that the quality of the therapy or the results of their interactions with children have been significantly different.

The most important factor in establishing a place for play therapy is your own personal feeling of comfort—if you feel safe and happy in the space, so will children. Your play therapy setting should fit your interaction style with children and their parents. In designing your setting, consider how you work with children and your own personal preferences for the arrangement of space. For instance, if you like to sit on the floor, it would make sense to have big, soft pillows scattered on the floor; if you feel uncomfortable with clutter, you may prefer to have cabinets, built-in shelves, and bins for toys.

Choosing and Arranging Toys

Although the types of toys best used to attain therapeutic goals may differ according to the therapeutic approach, there are some common ideas about toy selection. Most play therapists would agree with Landreth's (2024) suggestion that toys and play materials used in play therapy should (a) facilitate a wide range of emotional and creative expression by children, (b) engage the interest of children in some way, (c) encourage verbal and nonverbal investigation and expression by children, (d) provide mastery experiences in which children can experience success without having to follow certain rules about how to use them, and (e) be sturdy and safe for children to use in play. Kottman and Meany-Walen (2016) added several other considerations. They proposed that toys and play materials should also (a) provide ways for children to communicate in metaphoric or symbolic ways, (b) be useful to children across a wide range of developmental levels, (c) provide experiences in which children can be successful, and (d) allow for both individual play and interactive play. Ray (2011) recommended that play therapists choosing toys and other play materials for their playrooms should ask the following questions:

1. What therapeutic purpose will these toys or play materials serve for the children who use this room?
2. How will these toys or play materials help children express themselves?
3. How will these toys or play materials help me build a relationship with children?

Play therapists must also consider ethnic and cultural factors when selecting toys for the playroom and choosing dolls and doll families with various racial identities. It is also important to have enough doll family members on hand for families with two fathers, two mothers, a grandfather and grandmother, and so forth—many families are not "one size fits all."

There are many different approaches among play therapists in selecting toys, miniatures, art supplies, and other play materials, but most align with two basic practices. Many play therapists have no or minimal play materials in their playrooms (e.g., Theraplay, eco-systemic play), and those who have a wide variety of materials (e.g., Adlerian, child-centered, cognitive-behavioral, prescriptive, Jungian, narrative, psychodynamic).

Play therapists who use Theraplay or ecosystemic play therapy conduct their sessions in a relatively empty room, introducing only a few play materials selected especially for an individual child, for a specific intervention, or to attain a particular goal (Booth & Winstead, 2016; O'Connor, 2016). For instance, Theraplay therapists might use simple props such as baby powder, lotion, cotton balls, feathers, and old newspapers.

In contrast to this approach, Adlerian, child-centered, cognitive-behavioral, prescriptive, Jungian, narrative, and psychodynamic play therapists tend to have playrooms with extensive inventories of toys to maximize the possibility that they will have the "right" object(s) available for each child. That "right" object appeals to the child enough to encourage them to use it, often holds some symbolic meaning for them, and can be used to help resolve the particular issue they are facing. In these playrooms, children have the freedom and opportunity to choose the toys or play materials they want to use at that particular moment. Some prescriptive play therapists may have both a fully equipped playroom and another room into which they can bring specific materials they plan to use with a particular child (Goodyear-Brown, 2019). Several of the potentially more directive approaches to play therapy (Adlerian and prescriptive) often include games such as Candyland, Don't Break the Ice, Jenga, UNO, and Mancala in their playrooms (Kottman & Meany-Walen, 2016; Stone, 2016; Stone & Schaefer, 2020).

Altvater (2021), Hull (2016, 2020), Kottman and Petersen (2021), Snow et al. (2012), and Stone (2022) have suggested that play therapists consider integrating technology in the form of iPads, video game consoles, and other digital play therapy tools in their playroom as well because "trying to keep technologies out of the therapy setting is unrealistic and will ultimately be counterproductive" (Pykhtina, 2014, p. 4). Altvater (2021) suggested that play therapists considering integrating play therapy digital interventions in their work should (a) personally explore technology, (b) research the use of technology in therapeutic settings, (c) stay aware of technological advances that could be applied in play therapy, (d) establish ground rules, limits, and boundaries around how technology will be used in their sessions, (e) gradually introduce technological applications in play therapy sessions, and (f) engage in ongoing self-reflection about their feelings and reactions to technology in general and in therapeutic practice. Nevertheless, using technology as a tool in play therapy remains a controversial idea in the world of play therapy. Some play therapists embrace technology, while others reject it.

Play therapists who use toys, miniatures, and other play materials should ensure that the placement of these items is predictable and consistent—this is very important. Play materials should be returned to the same place, or as near as possible, after every session. This helps establish the playroom as a place where the child can count on routine and structure where the environment is consistent and predictable. One way to facilitate the return of toys and play materials to their usual spots is to arrange them according to specific categories. In Terry's playroom, for example, the snakes share a shelf, the dinosaurs share another shelf, the transportation toys have their own shelf, and all the puppets go on a puppet tree. This arrangement makes it easier to put the toys back where they belong at the end of a session, making it easier for children to remember where they are. In Terry's playroom, children sometimes say things like, "OK, this is where the snakes go, so that green snake must be somewhere on this shelf."

If you do not have a stationary playroom, instead traveling to different settings to work with clients or do in-home therapy, you can still maintain a consistent and predictable arrangement of the toys. This can be accomplished by placing the toys in a certain order on the floor or on a table in whatever space is currently your "playroom."

Some play therapists have specific categories of toys in their playrooms, while others list specific toys they prefer. For instance, in our playrooms, we use toys and play materials that represent each of five distinct categories: family/nurturing toys, scary toys, aggressive toys, expressive toys, and pretend/fantasy toys (Kottman & Meany-Walen, 2016). Although a variety of toys and play materials are listed for each category, it is not necessary to have every toy listed. It is much more important for you to have representative toys from each category.

Family/nurturing toys in the playroom provide opportunities for children to build relationships with you, explore familial relationships, and represent situations that occur outside the playroom. These toys can include a dollhouse, baby dolls, a cradle, animal families, a soft blanket, people puppets, baby clothes, baby bottles, stuffed toys, sand in a sandbox, several different families of dolls (with removable clothing and bendable bodies if possible), pots, pans, dishes, silverware, empty food containers, and play kitchen appliances (e.g., sink, stove). The dolls and people puppets should represent a broad spectrum of ethnic and racial origins.

The purpose of scary toys is to provide opportunities for children to deal with their fears. These toys can include snakes, rats, plastic monsters, dinosaurs, sharks, insects, dragons, alligators, and "fierce" animal puppets (e.g., wolf, bear, alligator). With children who have experienced a traumatic event, toys that would not normally be considered particularly frightening (e.g., cars, trucks, ambulances) may be scary for children who have been injured in accidents, for example. If you know of events that might have been frightening for particular children, including toys that could represent various aspects of the trauma in the playroom can be helpful.

The purpose of aggressive toys is to provide opportunities for children to symbolically express anger and aggression, to protect themselves from their fears, and to explore control issues. These toys could include a bop bag, toy weapons (e.g., guns, swords, knives), toy soldiers and military vehicles, small pillows for pillow fights, a foam bat, plastic shields, and handcuffs.

The purpose of expressive toys is to provide opportunities for children to express feelings, enhance a sense of mastery, practice problem-solving skills, and express creativity. These materials could include an easel and paints, watercolors, crayons, markers, glue, newsprint, Play-Doh or clay, finger paints, scissors, tape, egg cartons, feathers, and pipe cleaners.

The purpose of pretend/fantasy toys is to provide opportunities for children to express feelings, explore a variety of roles, experiment with different behaviors and attitudes, and act out situations and relationships from outside the playroom. These toys can include masks, costumes, magic wands, hats, jewelry, purses, a doctor kit, telephones, blocks, and other building materials, people figures, zoo and farm animals, puppets and a puppet theater, a sandbox, trucks and construction equipment, kitchen appliances, pots, pans, dishes, silverware, and empty food containers.

Depending on the strategies you use in your play therapy practice, you might need other toys or play materials. For instance, if you want to use bibliotherapy as a form of metaphor and storytelling, you will need appropriate books that can be helpful in therapy (for suggestions, see Ginns-Gruenberg & Bridgman, 2021; Kottman, 2020; Van Hollander, 2022; Ward & Allred, 2023). If you plan to use music and dance as a modality in play therapy, you will need a way to play music or an assortment of musical instruments (Taylor, 2019). For structured play activities, you may need an assortment of tabletop games you can use therapeutically (Petersen & Kottman, 2022); Stone, 2016; Swank & Weaver, 2020). Incorporating dramatic play will require some costumes and maybe puppets as part of the materials in your playroom (Drewes & Schaefer, 2018; Gil & Dias, 2020; Hartwig, 2020). If you want to use sand trays as a play therapy strategy, you should also have a wide selection of miniatures that can be used by both children and adults (D. Sweeney, 2020). According to Homeyer and Sweeney (2023) and Homeyer and Lyles (2022), miniatures should include people (e.g., families, babies, brides and grooms, people in various occupations, soldiers), animals (e.g., domestic animals, pets, wildlife, sea creatures, insects, amphibians), vegetation, fences and signs, buildings, vehicles, household items, natural objects (e.g., rocks, shells, feathers), fantasy figures, mystical/spiritual/religious figures, and assorted other items (e.g., bridges, gates, doors, rivers, windmills, lighthouses, wishing wells, treasure chests).

Explaining the Play Therapy Process

Parents and their children come to play therapy with ideas about the process and what it entails. Some of these ideas are accurate, and some are inaccurate. To provide clarity and a sense of safety, and avoid misunderstandings, you will need to have a plan for communicating important information about play therapy—what it is and what it is not—to parents and children. Before you begin seeing play therapy clients, you will need to consider what you want to discuss with parents and children about the play therapy process and how you will explain the concepts you want them to understand. If you work in a school or collaborate with school personnel, it is essential to consider how you will communicate with teachers, principals, and other faculty and staff about play therapy.

Explaining to Parents and Teachers

Parents will frequently come to your office with a distorted picture of what play therapy is. They often bring in their child dressed in their best clothes—clothes that could be soiled while painting or playing in the sandbox. Parents, and sometimes teachers, might expect a detailed report (either from the child or you) about what happened in the session—what the child played with, what they said, what you said, and so on. These adults often expect you to use a single session to "examine" the child and then present them with a "diagnosis" or explanation of what is "wrong" with them and a plan for "fixing" them. In many cases, their ideas are based on experience with a medical model in a physician's office where the mandate is to "decide what is wrong and fix it as expediently as possible."

This medical model does not work well when applied to play therapy, and it will be necessary for you to explain that. To counteract erroneous preconceptions, you will need to describe how play therapy works and why you have chosen to use play as a modality to help children. You will need to describe your general goals for children in play therapy and your philosophy about working with parents and children.

What play therapy is. You will need to tell parents and teachers that play therapy is usually a relatively slow process of gradual unfolding. It will take time for you, the play therapist, to understand what is going on with the child. Changes in a child's attitudes, perceptions, feelings, and behaviors brought about by play therapy evolve slowly over time. It is essential to explain that the child will probably not be coming to the playroom and verbally spewing information about what is happening in their life—they will be coming in to play! You will need to do your best to communicate that play is exactly what should be happening and that it will help you learn what you need to know about their child to help them change in positive ways.

The following is an example of how you might explain what play therapy is:

> Little kids don't know how to tell us about their problems with words like grown-ups do. They can show us what is happening in their lives in their play. In play therapy, my job is to watch what Claire does and try to figure out how she is feeling and what she is thinking about what is happening in her life. We usually won't do much talking—the main thing that happens in play therapy is playing.

Pitching play therapy. You might want to consider how (and whether) you want to "pitch" or convince parents or teachers of the benefits of play therapy and the consultation process. As Adlerian play therapists, we use personality priorities as a way to understand parents and teachers and to customize our description of the value of play therapy and consultation to them (Dickinson & Daly, 2020; Kottman & Ashby, 1999; Kottman & Meany-Walen, 2016). Using this strategy, you can anticipate the sources of resistance and plan approaches that circumvent or prevent many potential problems of getting them onboard with the process.

Kefir (1981) described four *personality priorities,* or patterns of behavior and reactions based on a person's convictions about how they establish belonging, significance, and a sense of mastery. These personality priorities are pleasing, comfort, control, and superiority. We can only describe these personality priorities in brief here. However, as a play therapist, you may be able to get a sense of a parent's (or teacher's) personality priority by listening to their description of their life, their child, and their presenting problem (Dickinson & Daly, 2020; Kottman & Meany-Walen, 2016). Those whose personality priority is *pleasing* may talk about their attempts to make sure that everyone else is happy. Pleasing parents tend to portray the child as (a) demanding and overpowering, (b) overly aggressive and tyrannical, or (c) extremely anxious, easily overwhelmed, and lacking courage. The primary complaint from those whose personality priority is *comfort* is that "adulting" (including parenting and being a teacher) is too much work. Comfort parents and teachers have a strong need to avoid tension and stress, and parenting or teaching for them is often stressful, uncomfortable, and difficult. Those whose personality priority is *control* will usually describe their world as "out of control." They often radiate anger and fear because it is impossible for them to gain control over the various elements of their lives. They may use words like "disrespectful," "disobedient," "lazy," "uncooperative," "bad-tempered," and "inappropriate" to describe the children who are coming to therapy. Those with the personality priority of *superiority* have high and sometimes unattainable standards for themselves and their children. They are trying to eliminate or avoid their own feelings of inferiority. Their complaints related to the child often stem from the child's inability to live up to these standards in some way (e.g., failing or underachieving in school, being overly anxious socially, not having enough friends). (For more on using personality priorities in play therapy consultation, see Kottman & Meany-Walen, 2016.)

When pitching the benefits of play therapy to parents or teachers, you might consider tailoring your approach to their personality priorities as follows:

- Pleasing parents/teachers. Emphasize that the desired end result of the play therapy process is a happier, more balanced child and a family or classroom whose members experience smoother communication, more cooperation, and reduced tension.

- Comfort parents/teachers. Focus on the potential for things going more smoothly for the child, life becoming less stressful; and parenting or teaching becoming easier, more fun, and more comfortable.

- Controlling parents/teachers. Stress that the process can help them feel more in control of themselves, of how things go with the child, and of their lives.

- Superiority parents/teachers. Accentuate their previous accomplishments and expertise as parents or teachers and suggest that play therapy and parent consultation can help to make them even better.

How long play therapy will take. Parents and teachers often want to know how long the process of play therapy will take. It would be best if you gave them some idea of what to expect about the course of treatment. The number of sessions the process takes will depend on many different factors, including the severity of the presenting problem, the support and cooperation from parents and teachers, the child's desire for things to be different, the willingness of family members to experiment with new patterns of interaction, and many other things. Meta-analyses of the play therapy research suggest that the optimal number of sessions is between 30 and 35 (Bratton et al., 2005; Lin & Bratton, 2015). Theoretical orientation, the presenting problem, and the therapist's personal style will also influence how long the process takes, with more sessions for children with complex problems, serious psychopathology, severe trauma experiences, or difficult family situations. After seeing several clients, you will have more clarity on how long your process usually takes.

What children should wear. On a practical note, there will be less confusion later if you explain that you generally ask that children not wear their best or expensive clothes to play therapy. Instead, they should wear "play clothes" that they can get messy and dirty and not worry about damaging.

Reports about the session. Because you will not want parents or teachers demanding a verbatim report about the session's content from the child, you will need some strategies for explaining this to them. It is sometimes helpful to suggest that children may not act naturally or play in ways that will be optimally helpful if they think they must remember what they have done in the playroom and report it. With some parents and teachers, it can also be helpful to discuss the years of training it has taken for you to learn how to gain meaning from children's behavior in the playroom.

The following is an example of how you might suggest to parents or teachers that they avoid asking children about the specifics of a session:

> I usually ask parents and teachers to avoid asking kids a lot of questions about a session after the session is over. I have found that kids don't usually remember specific details about what happened. Kids who try to concentrate on remembering exactly what happened so they can tell their parents or teachers don't really play the way they would otherwise, which can slow the process down.

Notice that we phrased these requests in general terms, describing what we usually say to both "parents and teachers." This practice is a subtle way of defusing potentially negative reactions. It is difficult for these significant adults to feel defensive when you are simply explaining your usual procedures, which would, of course, also apply to them.

Confidentiality. During this discussion, it is also essential to explain to parents and teachers the child's right to confidentiality. This is a difficult concept to present on two fronts. First, it may be hard to explain why it is important for a child to have privacy if all they are doing is playing. Sometimes, it helps to repeat the explanation that play is equivalent to adult conversation and to equate the child's desire for privacy about the specific details of play with an adult's desire for privacy.

The other difficulty in explaining confidentiality in play therapy is the conflict between ethical guidelines and legal issues (Brooks et al., 2013; Wade, 2015). Although professional codes of ethics clearly state that your first duty is to the client and that the client has the right to confidentiality (except in cases of clear and imminent danger to self or others, child abuse, or a court order), the legal system in the United States does not recognize children as having a right to privacy. You will need to balance the parents' *legal* right to know what is happening in their child's life so they can make appropriate decisions with the child's *ethical* right to confidentiality.

We believe that it is important for children to feel that they can trust us and not tell their parents everything that transpires in the playroom so that they can play out what they need to play out. However, we also want parents to understand what is going on with their children to be able to help them.

The following is an example of explaining confidentiality to parents:

> I won't be reporting everything that Fancy does or says in the playroom to you, but I will talk to you about themes and patterns I see in the playroom. I will also try to use my understanding of Fancy and the situation to help you learn new ways of thinking about her and her behaviors, attitudes, and motivation. I will use the information I gather in the playroom from the play and from my interaction with Fancy to make suggestions about ways you can help and support her. I may also think up some ideas to help solve problems more smoothly in the family.

Based on observations in the playroom, you can ask questions about how the child behaves in specific situations at home. Because a child's behavior is usually relatively consistent across situations and settings, parents' reports about behavior at home (and teachers' reports about behavior at school) can serve as a basis for making suggestions or revealing information about the child without going into detail about interactions in the playroom.

The following is an example of how to use information gathered in the playroom to ask questions about how the child behaves at home:

> Asa is a child who seems to thrive on power struggles. He often gets into power struggles with you in the playroom and frequently acts

out with the animal families and the dolls. Instead of describing this playroom behavior to his mother, you could ask, "How do things go at home when Asa does not get his way?" As Asa's mother describes his behavior, you could make guesses about what is going on and suggest different ways of handling the power struggles based on observations of and interactions with Asa in the playroom without revealing anything that happened in a therapy session.

Explanation handout/introductory book. Some misconceptions may persist even when you explain (sometimes by phone before the first session and again at the first session) these aspects of play therapy to parents or teachers. To eliminate as many of these as possible, it can help to provide them with a brief handout explaining the play therapy process and any requests you have about how you would like parents or teachers to handle the practical aspects of the play therapy process.

Another option is to loan these important adults a book on play therapy written for children (e.g., *When a Donut Goes to Therapy* [Winters, 2021]; *My Book About Play Therapy* [S. Wilson, 2018]) and ask them to read it to the child before the child's first session. These books give a clear and concrete explanation of what play therapy is. Reading either of them may help clarify the play therapy process for both children and adults.

Therapeutic goals. Depending on your approach to play therapy, you may also want to come to consensus with the parents or teachers about therapeutic goals for the child. As you do this, you will need to clarify what play therapy can and cannot do for the child. It is important to work with parents and teachers to generate realistic, concrete, and appropriate goals for change. One helpful method to facilitate this discussion is to ask, "How will we know when we are done? What needs to happen (with the child, with the family, at school, and so forth) before we can begin to terminate the sessions?"

Roles and responsibilities. You may also want to define the roles and responsibilities of the various people involved in the change process. It is helpful to discuss your role and the role of the child. If you expect parents to participate in the process, it is appropriate to discuss the specifics of their participation during your first session with them. You should tell parents how often you want them to come to sessions, what you will discuss with them, and what you expect of them in terms of making specific changes in their behaviors and interactions with the child. If you want others in the family (e.g., siblings, grandparents, stepparents) or teachers to be involved in the process, you should explain the details of their involvement as well.

Information about insurance and managed health care. If you are working with managed health care companies or insurance companies, parents need to understand the procedures and risks involved with this process. It is important for you to explain that their child will have to have a mental health diagnosis to qualify for services. You might also wish to explain to them any potential risks you see in having such a diagnosis on record.

Once the parents have given permission for you to release information to the insurance company or managed health care organization, employees of these companies may ask probing questions about what happened in sessions and the backgrounds of various family members with impunity. You must explain all this to the parents—that when they file a claim and sign a release, they have waived their rights and their child's rights to privacy from the insurance company or managed health care organization (Marshall, 2023).

Other important information. The authors find explaining their theoretical orientation and how they work with children is helpful. We talk to parents about our fundamental beliefs about people and describe how we conceptualize problems. We give them a tour of our playrooms and briefly discuss a typical play therapy session—what a child might do and say and what we might do and say.

We also tell parents, and sometimes teachers, that many children in play therapy get worse before they get better. Because things are changing and change is frightening, children frequently escalate whatever negative behavior they were manifesting before they started therapy, or they invent new ways to maintain the status quo. In alerting parents to this possibility, we make suggestions for handling potential problems and try to normalize any negative reactions in their child. With children who do get worse, we help the parents acquire tools for dealing with problems and establish credibility as someone who knows what we are doing. With children who do not get worse, this warning makes us appear to be wonderful therapists and the child to be a miracle child who responds positively to the therapy process much more quickly than other children. Neither of these perceptions will hurt your relationship with the parents.

Explaining to Children

In explaining confidentiality to children, most play therapists make a comment such as, "I will not tell your parents (or teachers) what you do or say in the playroom unless you tell me that someone is hurting you or that you might hurt yourself or someone else." Whether to explain more of the play therapy process to children depends on the individual therapist's inclination. Most child-centered play therapists seem to keep the explanation of the play therapy process and confidentiality to a minimum (Ray, 2011). The play therapy process is usually described in a short statement at the beginning of the initial session (e.g., "This is the playroom, and in here, you can play in many of the ways you want to play.").

In some other approaches, the therapist may give the child a detailed description of the play therapy process. Different play therapy approaches emphasize specific factors in the play therapy process. For example, a narrative play therapist might emphasize the story aspect of play therapy, saying something like, "Play therapy is a place where we can share stories and make stories up." A Gestalt play therapist might emphasize how using play materials and art can help children feel better about themselves and learn to be fully present with themselves and others and in contact with their world. As Adlerian play therapists, we concretely describe our roles and the process by saying, for example,

> I work with a lot of different children. Sometimes I will get to decide what we are going to do, and sometimes you will get to decide what we are going to do. Some days we will play, some days we will draw and do artwork, some days we will talk, and some days we will do a couple of these things.

Many play therapists also explain logistical details to the child (e.g., when sessions are scheduled, how often the child will come, how long each session lasts, parent consultation, and confidentiality). Theraplay and ecosystemic play therapists do not explain the process at all. In Theraplay, the therapist begins the session and immediately involves the child in the play without describing what will happen or why. They may say something like, "I am Barbara. I am really excited because you and I are going to hop down the hall together. Let's go."

Your Personal Application

As you consider what is important to discuss with parents, teachers, or children, it might help to make two lists of what you want to cover—one for parents or teachers and one for children. Once you have made the lists, you will need to plan strategies for conveying this information in a way that is clear and developmentally appropriate. If you can make the process of play therapy sound useful, interesting, non-threatening, and fun, parents, teachers, and children will be more likely to want to be involved. It is also essential to strike a balance between giving your clients so much information that they feel overwhelmed and giving them so little information that they feel lost.

The Initial Session

Very few children wake up one day and think to themselves, "I need to go see a therapist!" From the first moment you meet the child, you should communicate that even though they may not have wanted to come and not understand what is going to happen, this will be a fun and exciting process. We find it helpful to do this in a way that reveals our own personalities and the way we do therapy. Remember that your first meeting with a child and the initial play therapy session set the tone for all the other sessions.

In individual play therapy, when we introduce ourselves to a child, we greet the child by name, get down to their eye level, establish eye contact, and smile. We tell the child our name and briefly describe the nature of play therapy. When we sense the child is ready, we suggest we go into the playroom. For example, we might say,

> Hi, Zack. My name is Terry [or Jeff], and I am glad you're here. I am the one who is going to be with you in the playroom. We will have a lot of fun. Let's go in and see the playroom. Your grandmother will be waiting for you right here when we are done.

If the child is unwilling to go with us, we usually request that the parent or guardian accompany us to the playroom by saying something like, "Grandma, would you like to come to the playroom with us to scope it out so that Zack can show you all the neat things in there?"

With children who are still reluctant, you may ask the parent to stay and watch part of the session until the child feels safe and secure enough to stay in the playroom without the parent. However, you will eventually want the parent to leave the room—either to return to the waiting room or to sit out in the hall.

It is essential to avoid stating the invitation to the playroom as a question (e.g., "Are you ready to go to the playroom?" or "Do you want to go back to my office now?"), because this is a trap for both you and the child. If you use a question instead of a statement, you imply that the child has a choice. If a child answers that they do not want to go to the playroom, you will either have to honor that choice or communicate (by insisting on going to the playroom) that the child doesn't have a choice right now.

To avoid getting into a power struggle or exacerbating a child's anxiety, we have found that it is helpful to observe the child and their reaction to our greeting and adjust the timing and phrasing of our invitation to the playroom accordingly. With children who avoid eye contact and move closer to their parents as we greet them, we might remain sitting on the floor beside them and initiate some play activities in the waiting room rather than prematurely suggesting that we venture to the playroom. Some children just need a bit of time to get used to a therapist before they are willing to walk together into unknown territory. For example, you may find it helpful to sit down and draw pictures for them or tell them a funny story. Terry may show them the rainbow shoelaces on her sneakers or a pair of mismatched funny earrings she is wearing or comment on something the child is wearing. Jeff might be less informal. In any case, this interaction aims to build rapport with the child so that they can feel comfortable enough with us and who we are to take a risk and come visit "our" playroom.

After entering the playroom sometime during that first session, you should briefly explain the play therapy process and continue establishing a relationship with the child. Depending on your personal approach to play therapy, you will probably use tracking, restatement of content, and reflection of feelings (see Chapters 5, 6, and 7, respectively) during that initial session to gently begin to build rapport and convey the idea that the playroom is a safe place for the child. You might also describe the layout of the playroom and provide any information the child will need to know about the session or the office (e.g., the location of the bathroom or how to close blinds for more privacy) if that seems appropriate.

The first session of individual play therapy can unfold in many different ways. Usually, however, children will begin to familiarize themselves with the toys and you. This exploration may involve touching, picking up, and putting down items in the playroom, putting on a brief puppet show, standing still and looking around the room, interrogating you about your life, or using other strategies for making contact with a place and a person.

In most approaches to play therapy, your primary job during this time is to convey acceptance and warmth without trying too hard to "bond" with the child. Patience is essential in the first session, even with a child who is eager, willing, and excited to be in the playroom. Most play therapists (except those who are very directive) try to avoid communicating, even unintentionally, that the child "should" play or talk to them. To ensure that you do not do this, you can avoid making comments like, "There are a lot of things to do in here," "You might want to check out the sandbox," or "Most kids really like playing with the dart guns." If you cannot think of anything particularly helpful to say, it is often better to smile warmly, make lots of eye contact, and say nothing at all.

Obviously, if you are doing Theraplay, family play therapy, or group play therapy, you will start the session differently. In Theraplay, parents often observe the first few sessions of child play, and in family play therapy, parents and children will be included in sessions together. For group play therapy, you will have already chosen the children who will be a part of your group. The first session will focus on explaining the group rules and allowing participants to get to know one another.

Ending a Session

The primary decision you must make when ending play therapy sessions is whether to have the child participate in picking up the toys. There are two distinct positions on this: the client-centered perspective (Axline, 1969; Landreth, 2024; VanFleet et al., 2010) and the Adlerian perspective (Kottman & Meany-Walen, 2016). Axline (1969) maintained that asking the child to help clean up the room is the detrimental equivalent of asking an adult to "clean up" their words. Kottman and Meany-Walen (2016) suggested that when the therapist and the child collaborate in putting away the toys, it can be helpful to the therapeutic relationship. For each of these two approaches, there is a standard procedure for the end of a session.

Therapist Cleans the Room

If you decide not to engage the child in the picking-up process, 5 minutes before the time for the session expires, you can make an announcement that sounds something like, "In 5 minutes, our time together will be over, and it will be time for us to leave the playroom." When the time is over, you will say, "All right. Our time is up for today."

Therapist and Child Clean the Room Together

If you decide to work collaboratively with the child to pick up the toys 10 minutes before the session ends, you can tell the child, "In 5 minutes, it will be time for us to pick up the room together." When there are 5 minutes left in the session, you stand up and say something like, "It is time for us to pick up the room together. What do you want me to pick up, and what are you going to pick up?" The child is then in charge of delegating the clean-up process.

Most children are perfectly willing to work with the therapist to clean up the room. Some children are a little resistant, and if you decide to pick up the toys and materials collaboratively, you may need to make the procedure more fun by making the picking-up time into a cooperative game (e.g., a race against the clock) or a competitive game (e.g., a race against one another). When this happens, it is important for you to consider the reason for the child's reluctant behavior.

In the rare event that children choose not to participate in the picking-up process, we recommend setting up logical consequences (Kottman & Meany-Walen, 2016) as follows:

1. Tell the child in a friendly, neutral voice, "If you choose not to help pick up, you choose not to be in this playroom (or have all of these toys) next session."

2. If the child continues to choose not to collaborate, say in a friendly, neutral voice, "OK, since you choose not to participate in picking up the toys, next time we will have only a couple of toys that I will choose for us." At this point, even the most resistant children usually decide to participate in the clean-up process.

3. For children who decide not to collaborate on picking up, follow through in the next session by moving the therapy location and bringing several toys chosen from the playroom or removing most of the toys from the playroom. Again, this is done in a friendly tone of voice to avoid the appearance of setting up a punishment for noncompliance.

There are some children and situations for which this strategy is contraindicated (Kottman & Meany-Walen, 2016). With children who are overanxious or overly responsible, having the opportunity to participate in making a mess they do not have to help clean up can be freeing. With children who have power and control issues, asking them to collaborate on any task could be counterproductive to the therapeutic relationship. If the presenting problem is related to messiness or room cleaning, sometimes it is wiser not to replicate an already established power struggle in the playroom. Children with attention-deficit/hyperactivity disorder (ADHD) may feel overwhelmed in a maximalist playroom filled to the brim with toys, and they sometimes opt out of that setting by choosing not to help clean up. In our experience, only children with ADHD have repeatedly chosen to avoid participating in cleaning up. These children often feel more comfortable in a more spartan setting, so a playroom with fewer toys may work better for them anyway—that way, they don't feel the need to call our bluff and force a move to a different setting by refusing to cooperate.

Handling Children Who Do Not Wish to Leave the Room

Most children will comply with the suggestion that it is time to leave the room without any fuss. However, there are some who are reluctant to leave the session, and a strategy for moving them out of the room is essential. In most such cases, simply reflecting their feelings about wanting to stay in the playroom or making a guess about the purpose of their behavior is enough to get them moving. In our practices, we often make leaving the playroom fun by asking the child if they want to race to the waiting room, skip down the hallway to their classroom, or show their parent or teacher something they have been playing with in the session. Every once in a while, with children who are resistant to all of these "trick" ways to get them to leave the playroom, you may have to take more drastic measures, such as turning off the light and walking out or asking their parents to help them exit the room. You should consider your stance on involving parents in this process before you work directly with children in a play therapy situation. It would also be helpful to have a plan for how you want to handle such a situation if it occurs.

Writing Session Reports

Depending on their work setting, most play therapists keep a record of each play therapy session. There are multiple purposes for writing reports of therapy sessions. You will be able to use this record to (a) document what happened between you and the client and between the client and the toys; (b) facilitate recognition of patterns or themes across sessions; (c) refresh your memory of what went on in the previous session or sessions with a particular client before the beginning of a new session; (d) track changes in behavior, feelings, thoughts, and attitude and progress; and/or (e) provide documentation for insurance companies or court cases. A valuable resource in considering what to include in your session reports is *The Guide to Play Therapy Documentation and Parent Consultation* (Homeyer & Bennett, 2023).

It is generally helpful to include demographic data such as the date of the session, your name, the child's name, the parents' names, the child's date of birth and age, the number of the session, the child's physician's name, a list of who was present during the session, and a list of medications the child is taking. Other information that might be helpful includes your assessment (usually using a numerical scale or several word descriptors) of any situational stressor the child is experiencing and a subjective assessment of the child's mood during the session. You may also want to make a note of the sequence of toys the child used during a session, what the child did with the toys, verbalizations the child made during the session, limits that were set, and the child's reaction to the limits. It can be helpful to record any themes or patterns in play or verbalizations observed during the session or across several sessions. If there is a change in the child's behavior—which might include the child doing something they have never done, a shift in the intensity of the child's play or verbalizations, or the discontinuation of play that had occurred several times—you should note this change. Depending on your theoretical approach, both short- and long-term goals for the child and a concrete plan for how to meet those goals should also be incorporated into the record. If you work with parents or teachers on a regular basis, it is important to have a space on the form to record adult interactions.

Some play therapists restrict their notes to objective information—who, what, when, where, and how—recording as little as possible regarding personal opinion or professional speculation. Other therapists include much more detailed information and may range into theories about the underlying causes and factors in the child's problem. This practice is riskier because it is not based on data. If you have to testify in court or make a case for your treatment with a third-party payer, you will need to explain and justify your thoughts and speculations (Homeyer & Bennett, 2023).

Termination

There are many issues related to termination in play therapy (Gil & Crenshaw, 2016). These include consideration of (a) when to terminate, (b) who makes the termination decision, (c) how to handle the termination process, and (d) how the child will react to the termination.

When to Terminate

In deciding when to terminate therapy, you should consider factors related to the presenting problem and the child's behavior in the play therapy sessions. You will be looking for positive changes in both of these areas.

The primary questions related to the presenting problem are "Have the child's attitudes, relationships, and/or behaviors at home or school that were creating difficulties changed in a positive direction?" and "Has the child met the therapeutic treatment goals?" These questions can be answered through reports from family members or teachers or through self-report from the child about the presenting problem. Frequently, the child may volunteer comments like, "I don't need to come here anymore. I get along a lot better with my family now." Another helpful informal assessment involves observation of the child's behavior with family members in the waiting room or family sessions in the playroom and/or with teachers and classmates in the school. Some play therapists (especially ecosystemic and cognitive-behavioral play therapists) use assessment data from more formal instruments.

To determine whether it is time to terminate, you may find it helpful to compare the child's current functioning with the child's initial functioning. You would be looking for general changes in the playroom in the following areas: (a) dependence on you; (b) confusion; (c) ability to directly express needs; (d) ability to focus on self; (e) acceptance of responsibility for personal actions and feelings; (f) self-monitoring and self-control; (g) flexibility; (h) tolerance of situations, self, and others; (i) initiation of activities; (j) manifestation of cooperation, but not conformity; (k) appropriate expression of anger; (l) movement away from negative-sad affect toward positive-happy affect; (m) level of self-acceptance; and (n) shift in play so that play has direction (Landreth, 2024).

You may also consider indications of a change in the intensity of sessions and the willingness of children to use the sessions productively. Children may ask to have fewer sessions, skip several sessions without valid excuses, or express an interest in being somewhere else. They may also act bored, complain that the playroom does not interest them anymore, ask when they will be finished with coming to play therapy or ask to bring in friends or siblings to play.

Who Makes the Termination Decision

There seems to be no consensus among the approaches to therapy about who makes the decision to terminate therapy. Obviously, you should be a key person in the decision-making process, but sometimes you may be excluded (e.g., if parents decide to discontinue the therapy or a managed health care plan will not cover additional sessions). Ideally, you should always collaborate with the child and the parents in making the decision to terminate, with additional input (when appropriate) from teachers, siblings, grandparents, and other interested parties.

How to Handle the Termination Process

Most therapists start the process of termination by bringing up the idea with the parents and the child at least several weeks before they actually wish to terminate. This allows time for a discussion about whether all parties agree that the child is ready and allows time to prepare the child in advance for the eventuality of the final session. After coming to a consensus that the child is ready for termination of play therapy, most therapists begin a kind of countdown toward termination, reminding the child each week of how many sessions are left. It is important to include a time for processing the child's feelings about terminating in those last few sessions. It is also frequently helpful to let the child know how to contact the play therapist if they need to resume sessions or communicate about a specific situation.

Many play therapists develop rituals as a way of handling the termination process. Some therapists have a session where they sit down with the child and look through photographs of sand trays or artwork the child created during their relationship. Other therapists use the last session as an opportunity for a party or celebration and to review their interactions with one another and the progress made in therapy. Writing the child a letter detailing their strengths and accomplishments in therapy and making a photo album or memory book for the child are also strategies for handling termination. Many therapists give the child a small gift or work on a final project with the child so that the child will have a tangible reminder of the therapy process.

In some approaches to play therapy, it is important to prepare parents (or other family members) to take on some of the functions performed by the therapist. For example, filial therapists (L. Guerney, 1997; L. Guerney & Ryan, 2013; VanFleet, 2009, 2013) train parents to use nondirective play therapy techniques, and Theraplay therapists (Booth & Winstead, 2016; Norris & Lender, 2020; Norris & Rodwell, 2017) teach parents to use more directive play therapy techniques with their children at home.

Child Reactions to the Termination Decision

If the decision to terminate is appropriately made, the child's reaction should be predominantly positive. However, because the child will undoubtedly experience a certain amount of anxiety and sadness about the ending of a relationship that has been important to them, they may also express some negative feelings. You must be alert to the whole gamut of feelings and convey empathy and acceptance to all of the emotions expressed by the child.

If the decision to terminate is made prematurely, the child will probably express anger and hostility in addition to anxiety and sadness. One way to tell if this is the case is to watch for the ambivalence usually expressed by children who are ready for termination. If the ambivalence is absent and the child expresses only negative feelings about the termination, it may be appropriate to reopen the discussion about whether to end therapy.

Most children use the last several therapy sessions to recapitulate many of the play therapy themes from earlier sessions. If, after the decision to terminate, children return to old patterns (both at home or school and in the playroom), they may seem to be regressing. This behavior is perfectly normal as long as it does not last for a prolonged time period. Recapitulation becomes a problem, however, if it is pervasive and lasts more than 4 to 6 weeks. It is important to warn parents and teachers of the tendency for children to revert to earlier behavior and interactional patterns so that they do not overreact. By helping parents and teachers generate a plan for dealing with such an eventuality, you can help them feel prepared to cope effectively.

Questions to Ponder

1. What would be your top three priorities among all of the specifications listed by Landreth for designing a playroom?

2. What factors might you want to adjust in your play therapy setting so that the space would fit your style of interacting with children and their families?

3. Would you prefer a large, empty, open space for your play therapy setting or a room with shelves and furniture? Explain.

4. What is your reaction to the suggestion that toys should go back to approximately the same place at the end of every session? Explain your reasoning.

5. Would you tend toward letting children choose toys from a wide selection or toward bringing in toys and materials selected for that particular child on that particular day? Are you a minimalist or a maximalist? Explain your reasoning.

6. Are there certain toys you would definitely want in your playroom? What are they? Explain why these particular toys would be important to include in your playroom.

7. Are there certain categories of toys you would not want to have in your playroom? If so, explain your reasoning.

8. What information do you think would be essential to communicate with parents about the process of play therapy? Why is that information essential?

9. What information do you think would be essential to communicate with children about the process of play therapy? Why is that information essential?

10. How would you deal with the potential conflict between parents' legal right to know what happens in the play therapy session and children's ethical right to confidentiality?

11. How would you explain confidentiality to parents? To children?

12. How would you introduce children to the playroom and the play therapy process?

13. How would you deal with children reluctant to go to your play therapy setting?

14. What is your stance on cleaning up the playroom together at the end of a session? Explain your reasoning.

15. How would you deal with children reluctant to leave the playroom?

16. In making decisions about termination, which of the two main factors do you think is most important—progress on the presenting problem or behavior in the playroom? Explain.

17. Who do you think should be involved in the termination decision? Explain your reasoning.

5

Tracking

Tracking is a basic skill used in many approaches to play therapy. To track is to describe, in a literal and noninterpretive way, what is happening in the playroom—either what the child is doing or what the play objects are doing (Kottman & Meany-Walen, 2016, 2018; Landreth, 2024).

The purpose of tracking is to let the child know that the play therapist is paying attention to what the child is doing and that communication in the play is important to the therapist (Kottman & Meany-Walen, 2016, 2018; Landreth, 2024). This skill is one method of building a relationship with the child. Although there is no direct parallel in adult therapy to tracking, it serves the same purpose as paraphrasing in adult therapy.

How to Track

Tracking can be aimed in either of two "directions": what the *client* is doing or what the *play object* is doing. By tracking the client, you concretely describe what the child is doing. An example of this type of tracking would be saying to the child, "You picked that up." When tracking what the play object is doing, you describe what is happening with the toy. An example of this type of tracking would be, "It is moving up and down." You can also track the toy by talking to it. For example, you could say to a doll that seems to be trying to hide underneath a pillow, "It looks like you are trying to get underneath that." Although the idea of talking to a toy might be somewhat unusual, in our experience, children love it as long as you don't overdo it and stop talking to them.

There is no hard and fast rule governing which method of tracking you should use, and generally, we are opposed to telling you what you "should" do in your sessions. Sometimes, the decision of which tracking method to use stems from issues related to you and the way you choose to do play therapy. In other cases, it stems from issues related to the client, their preference, and their presenting problem. Some therapists arbitrarily mix both methods of tracking in play therapy sessions. Some therapists purposely use more tracking of play objects in early sessions and then move toward tracking the child's behavior in later sessions. Others decide which tracking method to use depending on the individual child's reaction to the intervention.

It is helpful to notice how children react to the different tracking styles. Children who are resistant or defensive when their behavior is tracked may be more open and accepting when the tracking focuses on the play objects. For the most part, these children seem to be relatively indirect in their communication with others. They may also not enjoy being the focus of the therapist's attention. Other children are more responsive to tracking that focuses on their behavior and less interested in tracking that focuses on play objects. These children frequently have a direct communication style and like to be the center of the therapist's attention. Some children will react positively to your tracking by talking to the toy, and others will not like it when you speak to the toy. Many children (maybe even the majority of children) have no preference for the direction of the tracking, so you can use whichever style feels more comfortable to you, or you can mix and match.

You will need to decide whether you will use tracking and, if you do, which method best fits your style. This may be determined by your theoretical approach, your usual mode of communication, your understanding of the child, or some combination of these factors. You will need to consider whether you wish to have a standard tracking method or whether you wish to vary the focus of your tracking based on the reactions of individual children.

Because play therapy is a projective method of therapy, it is essential for the child to impose their own meaning on the objects in the playroom. To facilitate this process, when you track, it is helpful to avoid using *labeling* nouns (e.g., people, places, things) and verbs (i.e., action words). For example, instead of saying, "The cat is climbing up that tree," you could say, "It is going up." By avoiding labeling, you allow the child to decide what the "cat" is, what the "tree" is, what the cat is doing, and what the relationship between the cat and the tree is. By not labeling the nouns, you encourage the child to project their "vision" of what these objects are. By not labeling the verbs, you encourage the child to project their vision of the relationship between the objects and to decide what each of them is doing. This process may be grammatically awkward at times, but it is potentially liberating for the client. Sometimes, it may be difficult to avoid labeling the toys or asking children to tell you what things "are." However, it is much easier for children to let their imaginations flow if we have not told them what the toys are by labeling them. Often, refraining from labeling is among the most difficult play therapy skills for new play therapists to learn, but it is important to keep trying.

If the child has supplied a label for either objects or actions in previous sessions or early in your current session, it is fine to use the child's label. However, you will need to monitor the child's nonverbal reactions and verbal feedback to ensure that the label you are using now is consistent with the child's *current* interpretation of the object and what is happening with it. What was a beanstalk for a giant last week or even 5 minutes ago may now be a dart gun used to shoot a hippopotamus, so you need to be flexible and follow the child's vision. What was "jumping" before may be "stomping" now.

In rare instances, you may decide to ask the child what the objects are and what they are doing. It is important to remember that when you do this, you are putting pressure on the child to take care of your need to know and understand rather than supporting the child's ability to let the identity of things be flexible. When you ask the child to define what something is or what it is doing, make sure you do so to advance the play therapy process or your ability to accurately reflect the meaning of the play rather than simply satisfy your curiosity.

Monitoring Children's Reactions to Tracking

When tracking, it is important to watch for the child's reaction to your tracking statements. Reactions from the child can take the form of direct or indirect feedback and verbal or nonverbal communication. The style of reaction from the client can guide you in deciding on future directions for tracking and which method of tracking will work with this particular child.

Many times, children will directly correct you if the tracking response does not fit with their image of what is happening. They will make comments like "That's not right," "Of course that potato can't jump—potatoes are not alive, and they don't jump," or "Why would you think that was a cow? It is obviously a chicken."

Children may also directly correct you if the tracking response is aimed in the wrong direction. When this happens—for instance, when they want the tracking to focus on their own behavior—they will make comments like, "Why do you always tell me what the toys are doing? I don't care what they do since I make them move anyway." When they want the tracking to focus more on the play objects and not on their own behaviors, they will make comments like, "Don't always talk about what I am doing. It's not me doing stuff in here; it's the toys."

Sometimes children will let the therapist know that the tracking response is aimed in the wrong direction in more subtle, indirect ways. Those children who would be more comfortable with you tracking their behaviors might tell you to switch the focus away from the play objects with comments like "Don't you know anything? Of course, that dog didn't save the girl. I did that." Or they might say something like, "The puppet did not pick that up. I did it." Those who would be more comfortable with tracking play objects might tell you to switch the focus away from them with comments like "I didn't cry when that happened. The baby did." Or they might say, "It wasn't me who knocked all the sand out. It was that truck over there."

Other reactions that might help you gain insight into the child's response to tracking comments are nonverbal. Sometimes, these reactions seem to be deliberate, thought-out responses to your comments—the child makes eye contact with you and nods, stares defiantly, or throws down a toy and goes to the other side of the room to play. This feedback is a direct form of nonverbal communication. In other cases, the feedback can take an indirect form, such as by gradually moving away from you or slowly changing the focus of the play. Indirect nonverbal feedback may also involve an involuntary nonverbal reaction, such as a shrug, nod, or twitch.

With some children, their combined patterns of indirect verbal and nonverbal reactions can clue you on how to proceed. For instance, if Leonard, who always wants your approval, suddenly starts using the same phrases you did in describing an object or action and continually visually checks on your reaction, you may be getting too concrete in your statements, causing him to change his vision to correspond with your interpretations. If Amira, a child who tends to be openly defiant and hostile, constantly corrects everything you say when you track, you may want to use nonspecific and vague descriptions or even stop tracking. In Amira's case, tracking doesn't seem to be serving its purpose of helping build the relationship.

It is advisable to pay close enough attention to these reactions to notice themes and patterns. The feedback you get from tracking can help you gain insight into children's thoughts and feelings and their usual mode of communication with other people. Children who respond to you in a more direct fashion will usually use that style with others, whereas children who respond to you in a more indirect fashion will usually use that style with others.

If you plan on adjusting the focus or direction of your tracking based on children's preferences (when they have them), you will need to watch for patterns in how they respond to tracking. That way, you can decide whether to use tracking of the child or tracking of the play objects according to the preference of the individual. Also, with children who tend to communicate directly, you may wish to tailor your interactions with them to use a more open and concrete communication style yourself. With children who tend to communicate indirectly or nonverbally, you may wish to tailor your interactions with them to use a more subtle, metaphoric style.

Applications in Different Theoretical Orientations

Tracking is a basic skill appropriate for many play therapy approaches. However, there seem to be several trends in how it is applied. With the more nondirective approaches (e.g., child-centered, Jungian), tracking is usually used throughout the play therapy process as an essential primary tool for interacting with children. Nondirective play therapists seem to use tracking more often than other play therapists do. They usually use tracking extensively in the initial sessions of therapy. During the middle and later sessions, they continue to use tracking as a significant interactional skill but less often as the relationship becomes firmly established. In other approaches (e.g., Adlerian, narrative, prescriptive), tracking is usually used more during early sessions when the therapist is establishing a relationship with the client. As time passes, most therapists in these approaches reduce their tracking responses and use other skills for interacting with the client. The use of tracking varies even among individual therapists within the same theoretical orientation. This variance may result from a combination of the individual therapist's personality, interpretation of theory, therapeutic style and comfort with tracking as an intervention, and personal philosophy about modifying a theoretical approach for individual clients.

Examples of Tracking

After each of the following play therapy scenarios, there is an example of possible tracking responses by the therapist.

Example 1

Aurora (age 6) picks up a wolf puppet, approaches the play therapist, and puts the puppet very close to the therapist's face.

> "You're moving that close to me."
>
> "It came really close to my face."
>
> To the wolf puppet, "You are getting very close to my face."

Example 2

Sam (age 4) throws the two small family dolls on the floor and stomps on them.

> "You threw them down."
>
> "Looks like something is happening to them."
>
> To the small doll figures, "Someone is doing something to you."

Example 3

Jada (age 8) sorts the deer family figures into one group and the tiger family figures into another group.

> Pointing to the first group and then the second group, "You put all of those together, and then you put all those together."
>
> "You had an idea of exactly where you wanted them."
>
> "The ones that look kind of alike are with the other ones who look like them."

Example 4

Jasper (age 7) points a gun at the therapist and smiles broadly at her.

> "You decided where you want to point that."
>
> "It is pointing at me."
>
> To the gun, "You are aimed at me."

Example 5

Claudia (age 9) picks up some scarves and wraps them around her torso.

> "You are putting them around your body.""You are putting them around your body."

> "You put those on yourself."

> To the scarves, "You are all around Claudia."

Practice Exercises

Exercise 1

For each of the following scenarios, write five possible tracking responses. If the scenario makes it possible, generate two responses that track what the child is doing, two that track what the play objects are doing, and one that addresses the tracking comment to the play object. Label which responses are directed toward the child, which are about the play objects, and which is to the play object.

1. Nazir (age 5) picks up a grasshopper and has it jump up and down all around the room.
2. Kathy (age 8) gets the mother doll and uses it to hit the baby doll.
3. Griff (age 4) pushes a chair around the room as if it is a wheelchair.
4. Chwan (age 9) puts a hat on her head and makes faces in the mirror.
5. Sam (age 8) throws a ball in the air for several minutes and then drops it on the floor.
6. Nancy (age 5) uses the wolf puppet to bite her own hand.
7. Nancy (age 5), after making the wolf puppet bite her own hand, brings it over and starts to bite your hands and feet with it.
8. Star (age 6) drapes snakes all over her head, torso, arms, and legs.
9. Keshawn (age 7) paints stripes all over a piece of paper.
10. Esther (age 4) puts food into the pots and pans, cooks the food, and brings it over to feed it to you.
11. Gunthur (age 8) purposely knocks over the trash can, spilling out all the trash and staring defiantly at you.
12. Sally (age 7) draws a picture of you, brings it over, and asks if you like it.
13. Emilio (age 4) picks up a book (which he doesn't yet know how to read) and pretends to read it.

14. Candy (age 7) arranges the tiger family with the parents at one end of the sandbox and the children at the other, with a wall of blocks between them.

15. Liam (age 3) sits and smiles at you.

16. Deepa (age 6) arranges the animal figures from largest to smallest.

17. Rick (age 8) puts on a cape, grabs a sword, and comes over and brandishes it at you—far enough away that you know he does not intend to actually threaten or hit you.

18. Jessie (age 5) turns the dollhouse upside down, spilling its contents onto the floor.

19. Abdullah (age 7) carefully constructs a tall tower out of blocks and then knocks it all down.

20. Filomena (age 4) uses the biggest dinosaur to bite all of the smaller dinosaurs, drops the smaller dinosaurs on the floor, and then throws the bigger dinosaur across the room.

Exercise 2

Would tracking be the best way to respond to each of the following scenarios? Explain your reasoning. For those scenarios where tracking is the appropriate response, what would you say?

1. Gloria (age 5) says, "I like you."

2. Santiago (age 9) hands you a doll and says, "Hold this."

3. Garry (age 5) tells you, "My grandmother spanked me last night and I didn't do anything wrong."

4. Aika (age 8) asks you, "What is your favorite TV program?"

5. Tim (age 4) moves the train car back and forth on the table.

6. Lyn (age 6) smiles at you.

7. Liam (age 9) walks into your playroom, looking down and away from you, and then says, "I got in trouble at school today."

8. Takako (age 7) picks up a doll with no clothes on, puts it back in the doll house, then turns away and plays the toy drum.

9. Jake (age 5) buries a baby doll in the sand, looks up at you, and says, "Got rid of him."

10. Kira (age 8) enters the play area, then sits and puts her head on the table.

Questions to Ponder

1. What was the easiest part of tracking for you when doing the practice exercises?

2. What was the most difficult part of tracking for you when doing the practice exercises?

3. What was it like to have to decide whether tracking was the best response for specific child behaviors or comments in the practice exercises?

4. What are your views on the advantages and disadvantages of using tracking in play therapy?

5. Are you likely to use tracking in your play therapy? What is your reasoning for using or not using it?

6. If you are going to use tracking, how will the amount of tracking vary over the course of your work with a child?

7. What do you think about the distinction between tracking the child, tracking the play objects or materials, and tracking to the toy? Are you likely to use this distinction in your work? What is your reasoning?

8. If you decide to make this distinction, how will you decide when to track the child, when to track what the play materials are doing, and when to track to the play materials? What is your reasoning?

9. As you practice tracking with children in sample play sessions, notice whether it is more difficult than you expected, easier than you expected, or about what you expected it to be. Explain.

10. Often, novice play therapists are uncomfortable with the awkwardness of simply telling a child what the child is doing in a session. If this is your experience, how will you deal with your discomfort?

11. Sometimes, children will give you feedback that "you talk weird." What do you think it means when they do this?

12. Sometimes, novice play therapists track too much. Sometimes they track too little. How will you know if you are tracking too much, too little, or just the right amount?

6

Restating Content

Another basic skill used in many approaches to play therapy is restatement of content (Kottman & Meany-Walen, 2016, 2018; Landreth, 2024). When you *restate content,* you paraphrase what the child has just said. Because your intent is to provide the child with a mirror of their remark, your response should be interchangeable with the child's remark without any added meaning or interpretation.

The purpose of restating content is to let the child know that you are listening to what they are saying and hearing their message (Kottman & Meany-Walen, 2016, 2018; Landreth, 2024). Restating content by paraphrasing what the child says is another method of building a relationship with them.

How to Restate Content

Although it sounds relatively simple, effectively restating content in play therapy requires skill and practice. Children tend not to expect adults to listen to them and may initially feel suspicious of an adult who spends so much time and energy conveying the essence of what they said back to them. Many children are sensitive to the possibility that other people, especially those they perceive to be more powerful than they are, might be mocking them. Other children think that an adult who tells them what they just said is "stupid" or "talks funny," and they may reject anything the adult says in restating content.

One way to prevent children from reacting negatively is to convey respect and genuine interest in what they are saying. You can contribute to your child client's feelings of being cared for and respected by making eye contact, getting down at their level as they speak, and presenting a "listening" body posture. This posture is usually taught as leaning forward, with open arms and legs, and making eye contact. We believe the most important element of a listening posture is to be relaxed and comfortable, facing the speaker but not necessarily making eye contact with them, as some children might be uncomfortable.

Another important factor in effective restatement of content in play therapy is to use vocabulary that is age-appropriate without parroting the child's exact words and intonation. By using your own words and not the child's words, you will show the child that you have heard the message and have thought about it enough to be able to translate it into a paraphrase rather than simply repeating what was said. You need to use your own natural intonation rather than mimicking the child's. Otherwise, the restatement of content can sound artificial and make the child suspect you do not truly care about what they say.

When paraphrasing what the child says, it is also important to use words that the child can understand. If you use vocabulary beyond the child's developmental and intellectual grasp, even with the best intentions, they may feel unheard and disrespected. When you are in doubt, it is better to use words that the child is likely to understand than to risk using words that may confuse the child. However, if you choose to use a word the child might not comprehend, you should watch for the child's nonverbal reaction. If the child appears to be struggling with the vocabulary, you can provide a clear explanation.

Focusing Restatements of Content

There are three ways that children talk in play therapy sessions about emotions, situations, interactions, and the other aspects of their world: (a) directly, (b) about the play media, and (c) through the play media. Sometimes children will talk directly to you about events, feelings, relationships, and so forth in their lives (e.g., "My father didn't pick me up this weekend, even though he promised that he would."). Sometimes they will talk about the play media (e.g., "This little boy's daddy didn't pick him up last weekend, even though he said he would."). Sometimes they will talk through the play media (e.g., the child has a doll say to another doll or to the therapist, "My daddy didn't pick me up this weekend, even though he said he would.").

It is important to match the child's method of expression. If the child talks in a direct fashion, the restatement of content should also be direct (e.g., "Your dad promised to pick you up this weekend, but he didn't."). If the child talks about the play media, the restatement should be about the play media (e.g., "That little boy's dad said he would pick him up this weekend, but he didn't do it."). If the child talks through the play media, the restatement should also be through the play media (e.g., use a different doll to restate to the child's doll, "Your dad didn't pick you up this weekend, even though he said that he would."). We do it this way to convey respect to the child and how they are choosing to communicate with you—and to be considerate by sticking to the metaphor if the child is using a metaphor to tell you what is going on in their life rather than communicating directly. [In Chapter 12, we'll talk more about the concept of using metaphors to communicate.]

Influencing by Restating Content

Although most nondirective play therapists would not purposely influence a child's thinking or the direction of a session through restatement, there is a possibility that it may still occur. More directive play therapists sometimes intentionally guide a child to explore specific elements of their experiences, thoughts, or attitudes. By choosing to focus on particular words or concepts in a child's statements or by arranging the order of the words in your response, you can guide the child to explore different aspects of the information in their comments. Play therapists may do this intentionally for a specific therapeutic purpose.

For example, Samantha (age 9) says, "My mother has started dating a new boyfriend. He isn't anything like my father, and I hate him." This statement has many disparate elements, and you would usually not respond to all of them at the same time. If you wanted to be relatively neutral and guide the child to find out more details about the mother's new beau, a response like "Your mom has a new boyfriend" might be most appropriate. If you want to explore the child's thoughts and feelings about her relationship with her father, you might begin the response with an emphasis on Samantha's father by saying something like, "Your father isn't anything like your mother's new boyfriend." If you want to explore the child's attitudes and feelings toward her mother's new boyfriend, it might be appropriate to say something like, "You really don't like this new man your mom's dating," or "Your mom's new boyfriend is nothing like your dad, and it sounds like you don't like that."

Another example would be when Hakim (age 7), while playing with the schoolhouse toy, has one of the doll figures say, "School is so hard. I just can't finish any of my work, and my teacher is always mad at me." If you wanted to simply restate content, you might say to the doll figure, "It sounds like you are not sure you can get all your work done." If you wanted to focus on the child's relationship with his teacher, you could say something like, "That person is thinking his teacher is angry with him because he is behind on his assignments." If you wanted to highlight the child's inability to complete schoolwork, you might address your comment to the child about the doll: "He just can seem to get all his work done." Or if you want to make sure the child feels heard and validated because of his school struggles, you might say to the doll figure, "You feel like school is too difficult." In this case, it might be more helpful to reflect a feeling instead of restating content, though restating content is also a valid response. [In Chapter 11, we'll discuss the integration of play therapy skills.]

You can also change the meaning of your restatement of content by emphasizing certain words, which is another way of potentially leading the client in a specific direction. For instance, Leticia says, "I used to be friends with Cloe, but now she is only friends with Rebecca, the most popular girl in the fifth grade." By emphasizing the word "friends," you are recognizing that Leticia's friendship with Cloe is important in this statement. If you stress the word "now," you are acknowledging that this situation has changed for Letitia. By putting emphasis on the word "only," you are conveying that you hear Letitia saying she feels left out of the relational triangle. Through the emphasis of specific words in your restatement, you can guide the client to a path for the unfolding interaction.

Monitoring Reactions to Restating

Just as in tracking, you will need to observe the child's reactions to restatements of content. Again, feedback from the child can be direct or indirect, verbal or nonverbal. The child's reaction can help you more clearly understand the child and the child's view of their life situation. If you are purposely guiding the conversation in a certain direction, the child's reaction may also help you decide what to explore further.

Direct verbal feedback is usually typified by the child telling you that the restatement of content was inaccurate or accurate. The child will make a straightforward comment such as, "You don't know what you are talking about," or "That's right." In *indirect verbal feedback*, the child will correct the content of the restatement without overtly challenging your grasp of the meaning of their verbalization. The following dialogue illustrates indirect verbal feedback:

> Allison: I have had my new heart for ten weeks now.
>
> Therapist: You have had your new heart for a long time.
>
> Allison: I have had it for only ten weeks.

In this interaction, Allison (age 7) lets the therapist know that his restatement of content is inaccurate by giving him feedback that ten weeks is not a "long time" to her.

Nonverbal feedback is usually more subtle than verbal feedback. *Direct nonverbal feedback* consists of behavior the child exhibits that is an obvious and conscious reaction to something you have said. In the child's response to the restatement of content, direct nonverbal feedback usually consists of the child nodding, shrugging, shaking their head, turning their back to you, or making a face—some kind of action indicating the child's conscious thoughts and feelings about what you said. *Indirect nonverbal feedback* consists of behavior that the child exhibits that is a more subtle reaction to your comments, such as a slight movement of the body, switching of play patterns, and so forth. This form of feedback is usually involuntary or out of the child's awareness. It may, however, be a safe communication vehicle for a child who does not wish to "own" their reaction to your comments.

It will be important for you to practice observing children's reactions to your interventions—many times, these reactions will contain the most important information conveyed in a session. By noticing patterns in reactions, you will begin to understand how the child perceives their place in the world and generally communicates with the other people in their life.

Applications in Different Theoretical Orientations

Restating content is a basic skill that is used in many approaches to play therapy. Like tracking, restating content is generally used more in the nondirective approaches (e.g., child-centered, Jungian, psychodynamic) than in the directive approaches (e.g., Adlerian, cognitive-behavioral, prescriptive, narrative). Restating may be avoided in some directive approaches, such as ecosystemic and Theraplay. In these approaches, acknowledging exactly what a client says is somewhat less important than orientations with other methods for relationship building with the client.

Among therapists who use restatement of content to build a relationship with a client, there is a tendency to restate content more in the beginning stages of therapy, when the therapist is working to establish rapport, and less in the middle and end stages, when the therapist is working on client issues. In prescriptive and Adlerian approaches (the two applications that emphasize custom designing what happens in the playroom for individual clients), the timing of when to use tracking and restating depends on whether the therapist believes the techniques would be helpful to the client at a particular stage of therapy.

Examples of Restating

After each of the following scenarios, we list several possible restatements of content appropriate for that situation. For every example, we have provided several examples of *not leading* or influencing the child's thinking, feelings, attitudes, or behaviors, as well as several examples of *leading* or influencing the client. In some examples of leading, we also explain why the therapist may be doing so.

> As Aurora picks up a wolf puppet, she approaches the play therapist, puts the puppet very close to the therapist's face, and says, "This wolf is going to bite your face off."
>
> 1. "The wolf is going to chew on me." (Not leading)
>
> 2. "That wolf going to bite me." (Not leading)
>
> 3. Speaking to Aurora, "You are letting me know that the wolf is going to bite my whole face off." (not leading)
>
> 4. Speaking to the wolf puppet, "You are moving over to bite my face." (Not leading)
>
> 5. "The wolf is planning on biting me on the face." (By using the word "planning," the therapist might lead the child to think about the purposeful or planful aggression of the wolf.)

6. "That wolf wants to hurt me." (By changing the word "bite" to "hurt," the therapist is trying to convey that Aurora's intent is to intimidate or damage the therapist. The therapist could also change the meaning of the restatement by emphasizing the word "wants," the word "hurt," or the word "me." By emphasizing different words in the same sentence, the therapist can change the direction of the interaction and the statement's meaning, which can lead the child to explore different aspects of their comment.)

As Sam throws the two small family dolls on the floor and stomps on them, he says, "That's what happens to people who try to tell me what to do. They get hurt."

1. "So, people who tell you what to do get hurt." (Not leading)

2. "Folks who try to boss you around get injured." (Not leading)

3. "You are telling me that bad things happen to people who try to tell you what to do." (By generalizing from "get hurt" to "bad things happen," the therapist might influence Sam to consider whether people who cross him can experience more than just physical injuries.)

4. "You want to punish people who try to tell you what to do." (By emphasizing Sam's desire for revenge rather than the actual act of revenge, the therapist may be able to help him become conscious of his unconscious desire for revenge. This response could also guide him to use symbolic means, rather than actual aggression, to punish others.)

5. "You want others to know they can't tell you what to do." (This is more direct, acknowledging Sam's subtle message that the therapist should not try to tell him what to do.)

6. Speaking to the dolls being stomped, "You are getting hurt because you tried to tell Sam what to do." By shifting the focus to the play material while restating the content, the therapist hopes that Sam will elaborate on his complaint by talking to the dolls.

7. To the dolls being stomped, "Sam wants you to know he doesn't like it when you tell him what to do." (By talking to the dolls, the therapist takes the pressure off Sam to worry about the therapist's judgment or disapproval because of the aggression in this interaction, and it still conveys an understanding that Sam doesn't like to be told what to do.)

As Jada sorts the deer family figures into one group and the tiger family figures into another group, she says, "They belong with the other ones that look like them."

1. Pointing to the first group and then the second group, "You wanted me to know that you put all of those together because they look alike, and then you put those all together because they look alike." (Not leading)

2. "You wanted them to be with the other ones that look like them." (Not leading)

3. Pointing, "Those ones moved to be with the others that look like them, and those moved to be in different group with the ones who look like them." (Not leading)

4. Speaking to the animal figures, "You all wanted to be with the other ones who look like you." (Not leading)

5. "It's important to you that they are with others that look like them." (Leading by emphasizing Jada's valuing of homogeneous groups.)

6. Using a growly voice and speaking for the tiger figures, "We only want to be with those who look like we do." (Leading by acknowledging a value that emphasizes excluding those who do not share a similar identity.) [The authors recognize that sometimes you will need to decide whether to restate content that might represent different values than your values.]

7. Using a quavering voice and speaking for the deer figures, "We want to be away from them because they might think we are prey." (Leading by focusing on the relationship between prey and predators, bullies and the bullied.)

Jasper points a plastic gun at the therapist, smiles broadly at her, and says, "If you don't do what I want you to do, I will shoot you."

1. "You are going to shoot me if I don't do what you want me to do." (Not leading)

2. "You want me to know that I should do what you want." (Not leading)

3. "You really want me to follow your directions." (Leading by acknowledging the underlying meaning of the threat.)

4. "It's important to you to make sure I am listening to you and doing what you want." (Leading by acknowledging the underlying meaning and value.)

5. "Pointing that weapon at me is the way you think you can get what you want to happen." (Taking the focus off Jasper's demand for compliance and shifting it to his belief that he needs to threaten someone to get what he wants.)

6. To the gun, "You are the threat Jasper is using to get me to do what he wants." (Shifting the focus to Jasper's means of ensuring that he gets his way.

> This might be used to avoid getting into a power struggle with a child.) [This sequence might also be something you would want to limit in your playroom—we will get to how to do that in Chapter 8. We probably wouldn't limit it if it was a pretend plastic gun that doesn't shoot darts and doesn't have a method of actually causing harm to me or the child. We would use the chance to remind the child that, in the playroom, everybody needs to be safe, and everybody needs to feel safe.]

Claudia picks up some scarves, wraps them around her torso, and says, "Now I am invisible."

1. "Not one single person can see you." (Not leading)

2. "You're not visible." (Not leading)

3. "You don't want anyone to be able to see you." (Focusing on Claudia's underlying motivation for putting the scarves around her, which takes this statement a little deeper than a restatement that doesn't lead anywhere.)

4. "You are so well-hidden that you can't be found." (Emphasizing Claudia's hiding to suggest that hiding is a viable coping skill for her in dealing with certain circumstances in her life.)

5. "You know how to hide so that no one can see where you are." (By stressing Claudia's ability to take care of herself, the therapist could be trying to build her sense of being capable—maybe of keeping herself safe.)

Practice Exercises

In the following two exercises, practice restating content as explained in this chapter.

Exercise 1

For each of the following numbered scenarios, write four possible restatements of content, acknowledging what the client said using phrases like "You wanted me to know . . ." "You're telling me . . . " or "It's important to you for . . .." " If you are commenting about the toys that "spoke," you can say something like "That fox is saying . . ." "The spider wants me to know . . ." or "That one is telling me . . ."). When possible, generate two non-leading responses that simply restate what the child is saying without trying to influence the child's thoughts, feelings, or behavior. Then, generate two leading restatements that could influence the child in a specific direction. For the two influencing restatements, explain how your restatement might affect the child's thoughts, feelings, attitudes, or behaviors. Even if you prefer a nondirective approach, this exercise can help you learn how to weight your restatement and avoid the tendency to lead.

1. Mustafa (age 5) picks up the grasshopper and says, "He really knows how to jump, but he isn't as good at jumping as I am."

2. Dimitri (age 5) picks up the kangaroo and says, "He is a good jumper. I don't know how to jump like that. People from my country are supposed to be good at sports, but I am not."

3. Kathy (age 8) has the mother doll hitting the baby doll and says, "Take that you brat. That will teach you not to talk back to me."

4. Griff (age 4) pours sand from one container to another, saying, "This one has more than that one. That one doesn't have as much as this other one."

5. Katrinka (age 9) puts on a hat, looks in the mirror, and says, "I am ugly. I hate my face."

6. Sam (age 8) throws a ball in the air for several minutes, drops it on the floor, and says, "That ball is stupid. I hate it in here. There is nothing fun to do."

7. Brigitte (age 5) uses the wolf puppet to bite her own hand, saying in a gruff voice, "I am a wolf. I can bite you any time I want and you don't even know how to stop me."

8. After using the wolf puppet to bite her own hand, Brigitte brings it over and starts to bite your hands and feet with it, saying in that same gruff voice, "You can't stop me either. No one can stop me. I can't even stop myself."

9. Bright Star (age 6) drapes snakes all over her head, torso, arms, and legs. She laughs and says, "There are snakes everywhere all over me. They are my friends."

10. Zack (age 7) paints stripes all over a piece of paper. Then he says, "This is a jail like the one where my auntie lives. We go visit her there."

11. Yasmin (age 4) cooks food for you and says in a nurturing voice, "Now you need to eat this food baby. I know that you don't like it, but it is good for you, and you always need to eat food that is good for you."

12. Walter (age 8) purposely spills all the trash from the trash can and says, "This place is a dump. Can't you keep it clean?"

13. Antonia (age 7) draws a picture of you, gives it to you, and says, "Do you like it? My mother never likes the pictures I draw. She says I am not a good artist."

14. Deepak (age 4) has a bunny puppet "read" to an owl puppet, and then the owl says to the bunny, "You didn't read those words right. I don't think you really know how to read. You are just pretending."

15. Olga (age 7) arranges the tiger family with the parents at one end of the sandbox and the children at the other end, with a wall of blocks between them. The mother tiger turns to the father tiger and says, "Well, we got rid of those children. They were more trouble than they were worth anyway. They were just more mouths to feed, and I am so tired."

16. Kali (age 6) arranges the animal figures from the largest to the smallest and says to you, "The biggest ones are the boys, and they are the most important. The little ones are the girls, and they are not important at all."

17. Rick (age 8) puts on a cape, grabs a sword, and says, "Let's have a sword fight. I think I can beat you. I am pretty good with a sword."

18. Jessie (age 5) turns the dollhouse upside down, yelling, "Everybody out. Nobody can stay in there. It just isn't safe."

19. Akihito (age 7) makes a tower and knocks it down, saying, "That wasn't the way it was supposed to be. I have to get it perfect."

20. Emer (age 4) uses the biggest dinosaur to bite the heads off of the smaller dinosaurs and says in a loud, mean voice, "No one can mess with me. I can get every single one of those little ones and bite their heads off."

Exercise 2

For the scenarios in Exercise 1 in which a child is speaking for a toy (1, 2, 3, 7, 8, 14, 15, 16, and 20), write a restatement of content aimed at the toy that spoke. Choose five of your restatements from Exercise 1 and explain how changing the emphasis to specific words in your restatement could change the direction of the interaction.

Questions to Ponder

1. In the practice exercises, what was the most difficult aspect of restating content for you?

2. How will you ensure that you convey respect to the child when you restate content?

3. What are your thoughts or feelings about using the emphasis in restating content to influence or lead a child in a certain direction?

4. Are you likely to use restatements to influence or lead children? What is your reasoning?

5. You can change the meaning of a restatement of content by emphasizing particular words. How do you feel about doing this? If you use this tool, how will you decide which word to emphasize in your restatement?

6. How could mirroring what the child is doing or saying help to build a relationship with the child?

7. In your sample sessions with a child, what has been the easiest aspect of restating content? What has been the most difficult aspect? Explain.

8. In your sample sessions with a child, have you used the emphasis on restating content to influence or lead the child? How has this worked for you? What are your reactions to or feelings about doing this?

9. What are your beliefs about leading the client? How could you unintentionally be leading when you restate content? How would you feel if you discovered you were doing this?

10. If you wish to be nondirective and avoid leading, how can you catch yourself when you unintentionally lead the client? What can you do to prevent this from happening?

Reflecting Feelings

One reason to use play as the medium for communication in therapy is that children do not have the abstract verbal reasoning skills needed to adequately describe their feelings (Cochran et al., 2022; Kottman & Meany-Walen, 2016, 2018; Landreth, 2024; Mellenthin, 2019). This does not mean that children do not have feelings—they do! It does mean, however, that children may not be able to clearly articulate their feelings. Most children can (and do) express their feelings both verbally and nonverbally—in their voices, facial expressions, posture, behavior, play, and stories.

There are several purposes for reflecting children's feelings in the playroom. By making guesses about the feelings children are trying to communicate, you, as a play therapist, can help them learn to use words to express themselves. Because of children's incomplete understanding of affective concepts, they often have a truncated awareness and understanding of their emotions. By making guesses about children's feelings in the process of play therapy, you help children begin to understand the emotions they experience. This assistance in enhancing their awareness and understanding of feelings and their ability to articulate them can be invaluable to children. You can also help children expand the vocabulary they use to express their feelings. Young children tend to know the concepts of sad, mad, glad, and scared. They may know several words they can use to express each of these feelings, but they are usually unsophisticated in their expression of the nuances. The playroom can serve as a setting in which children experiment with their understanding and use of new feeling vocabulary.

How to Reflect Feelings

The skill of reflecting feelings involves making guesses or statements about what you think the client is feeling. You can point out one or more specific feelings that the child is experiencing at that moment (e.g., "You seem really sad right now.") or a pattern of feelings that the child consistently expresses (e.g., "I have noticed that whenever you talk about your grandmother, you smile and act really happy.").

Reflections should be clear and to the point. Although you may want to include a brief attribution or connection of the feeling to an antecedent event or to the child's reasoning, it is inappropriate to give the child complex explanations or interpretations about why they are experiencing that particular feeling (Kottman & Meany-Walen, 2016, 2018).

It is essential to refrain from trying to convince children that certain feelings are inappropriate. People have the right to whatever feelings they experience, and telling someone they should not feel a certain way is incredibly disrespectful. Even if we do not understand why a child feels a particular way, e.g., happy to see a father who beats them, sad because a cartoon show was canceled, we do not have the right to tell the child that their feeling is misplaced or disproportionate. It is also important to avoid asking children how or why they feel certain emotions. Most of the time, they cannot answer these questions and may get frustrated with your insistence that they provide descriptions of their feelings or their causes.

Generally speaking, most play therapists try to avoid the phrase "makes you feel" (Kottman & Meany-Walen, 2016, 2018). Nothing can make a person feel a certain way, and everyone has some control over what they choose to feel and how they express what they feel. Although some children express themselves using the "makes me" configuration (e.g., "My brother always makes me mad, so I hit him." "This makes me very sad."), it is best not to get into a power struggle with them trying to teach them not to use this formula. Modeling that there are other ways to express feelings (e.g., "You feel mad at your brother, and you decided to punch him." "You seem very sad about that.") is usually a better way of handling these situations.

What to Reflect

In deciding what to reflect to a child, it is helpful to consider how children express their feelings and the depth of feelings expressed. You will also need to choose what to reflect when a child expresses more than one feeling simultaneously.

Manner of Expression

In addition to reflecting the feelings verbally expressed in a direct manner by the child, it is important for you to reflect the emotions inherent in the play. This would include reflecting (a) the feelings expressed nonverbally through the child's facial expressions, body language, tone of voice, and so forth, (b) the feelings expressed in the general affective tone of the play, and (c) the feelings expressed in an implicit way in the child's comments. It is also essential to reflect feelings communicated (both verbally and nonverbally) by various play media, such as dolls, puppets, or animal figures. This becomes easier with practice, and once you get the hang of it, you will think through all of these factors quickly and automatically.

Direct verbal expression. Sometimes it is easy to recognize the feeling expressed by a child because they clearly verbalize it in a way that shows they "own" it, e.g., "I am really angry at my mom today." This is the simplest type of feeling expression, and the reflection should be equally simple. You need only mirror the feeling to the child using similar words, e.g., "You are very mad at your mother."

Indirect expression. The indirect types of feeling expression are frequently more difficult to recognize than the direct acknowledgment of emotions. For some children, the *nonverbal expression* of feelings is obvious, and you can begin to make guesses in the first session about the feelings expressed in this manner. However, because nonverbal expression of emotions can be influenced by the child's personality, family, ethnicity, and culture, many times you will need to observe an individual child's facial expressions, voice tone and inflection, speed of speech production, body posture, and proxemics for several sessions to get an idea about how that particular child expresses feelings. It is essential to understand the cultural influences on how the child and their family nonverbally express themselves (Gil & Drewes, 2021; Ray et al., 2022b; Summers & Nelson, 2023).

The same is true for the *affective tone* of the session, expressed in the patterns of what the child says and does and how they emote throughout the session. For instance, both Jacquie and Sam could play in the dollhouse the entire session, saying things like, "This mother really likes the little boy." If Jacquie plays with no animation, speaks in a sad or listless voice, and does not make any eye contact, the affective tone of her session would be significantly different from that of Sam's session if he were to play and speak in a lively manner, smiling, laughing, and making eye contact with the therapist.

The affective tone may also relate to the play themes you observe during a session. By watching what the child plays and noticing consistent patterns in what the play is about, you can draw some conclusions about the affective tone of the session. For instance, if Georgine were to consistently play with dolls or animal figures by having them hit and make negative, disparaging comments to one another, the affective tone of her session would probably seem angry.

At times, children verbally express feelings in subtle, indirect ways because the emotions are *implicit* in what they say. When they do this, they may not openly acknowledge feeling a certain way, but what they say implies an emotional content. For instance, Oscar could say, "Do I have to go in there?" Depending on the nonverbals, the implicit feeling in this question could be anxiety, timidity, or another similar emotion. Alternatively, it could be defiance, hostility, or just simple curiosity.

With all three of these types of indirect communication of feelings—nonverbal expression, the affective tone of the session, and implicit feelings—your reflection of the child's feelings should be tentative rather than definitive. The child may be less willing to acknowledge feelings that have been indirectly expressed, and you may be less sure of your discernment of the feelings expressed. By using tentative hypotheses or guesses in the reflection rather than definitive statements, you can convey the idea that you *believe* this is what is happening with the child on an emotional level, but that corrective input from the child would be welcome and helpful.

Because play therapy depends on the child's play for communication, you will need to pay attention to the emotions expressed by the child through the surrogates—the toys—in the playroom. Dolls, puppets, and animal figures (and, less obviously, toys such as guns, cars, blocks, and so forth) can all "speak"—verbally and nonverbally—for the child about feelings.

When the child chooses to express emotions through such a "spokestoy," you can direct the reflection of feelings either toward the toy (e.g., "So, Mr. Wolf, you are feeling really angry right now.") or toward the child about the toy (e.g., "Mr. Wolf seems to be really angry right now."). Some children are more comfortable with you directly addressing the toy, some are more comfortable with you addressing them and discussing the toy's feelings, and others do not seem to have a preference. You should experiment using both ways with individual children and decide your approach based on the child's reactions.

How you deliver a reflection in situations where toys express the child's feelings should parallel how you deliver it when there is no play intermediary. When a toy directly expresses a feeling, you can directly and simply reflect the feeling. For instance, Siri picks up the ant, bounces it up and down, and says in a squeaky voice, "Hooray, I am excited!" In response, you could say something like, "The ant is really excited." When a toy nonverbally expresses a feeling, you could guess the emotion the toy might be expressing. For example, Sly has the wolf puppet beat up the lamb puppet, and the lamb puppet curls up in a ball and cries. You might say, "Lamb, it seems like you are really sad and scared because you got hurt by the wolf." When an affective tone is typically attributed to a certain toy, you could use a tentative hypothesis about what is going on with that toy. For instance, Pilar has a doll that always seems angry and picks on the other dolls. You could reflect the pattern of feelings associated with that doll by saying, "That doll seems to get mad at the other dolls a lot."

Deeper Feelings

As a play therapist, you should always acknowledge the surface feelings as well as look for deeper, less apparent feelings. Children tend to show feelings with which they are relatively comfortable but may hide other feelings that are unacceptable to them—because of a sense of vulnerability, personal values, or family rules. For instance, James may think it perfectly acceptable to express anger and hostility, but if he has learned that "boys do not cry," he may not express sadness, disappointment, or loneliness. Children may not recognize some feelings. If Lakesha's family has a prohibition against being angry, she might act sad or hurt because she does not recognize that she is feeling anger.

After you get to know the child and their behavior patterns, it may be helpful to make tentative guesses about any underlying feelings you believe are present. It is important to closely watch the child's reaction to gauge the impact of the reflection.

In other situations, you might know enough about the child's life circumstances or culture to be sure that there are underlying feelings present (Gil, 2017). For instance, 9-year-old Lixue's little brother died from a rare disease the previous year. In Lixue's family and her culture, grief is considered to be private and is not openly discussed. For several sessions, she comes into the playroom and has the large giraffe hovering over the baby giraffe. Then she has the larger giraffe scolding the baby giraffe, making comments like "You should not have done that." Knowing that sadness is one of the emotions Lixue is likely feeling, you might choose to acknowledge both the surface and the underlying feelings by saying something like, "That bigger one seems kind of mad at the baby. I am guessing that she may also be worried or sad about something that could happen to the baby." Although you can reflect a variety of feelings in the play session, you should not push the child to acknowledge a feeling that would not be acceptable or appropriate to express in the child's family or culture.

Here-and-Now Versus Patterns of Feelings

Some play therapists focus strictly on feelings in the here-and-now. Others may also look for affective patterns within a session or across sessions. Your decision whether to focus on here-and-now feelings, affective patterns, or some combination of the two may depend on (a) the particular client and their specific issues and therapeutic goals, (b) your theoretical orientation, and (c) your personal style.

The client. Sometimes the choice of whether to focus on the here-and-now, to look for affective patterns, or to integrate elements of both is related to the particular issues or play of certain children and the goals in their therapy. In this case, you will base your decision regarding where to focus reflections of feelings on an assessment of the child's current needs. You might choose to primarily concentrate on reflecting present feelings but occasionally use a reflection of an affective pattern with certain children.

With some children, the affective themes are so obvious and deep that it would seem a waste not to point them out. For example, Achim talks a lot about various people in his life. He is usually a lively, cheerful child who always has a kind word to say about others. However, when he refers to his paternal grandfather, his animation dies, and he seems angry and sad. This pattern occurs for 10 sessions. As his play therapist, you would probably be remiss in not bringing up this pattern in a therapy session.

With other children, the here-and-now is so intense and potentially overwhelming that it is all they can handle. With these children, it is best to stay in the present and not ask them to think about affective patterns. For instance, Henry's adored grandfather has died. Every time Henry brings up a topic or activity even tangentially related to his grandfather or death, he begins to cry. Although this is a pattern, it would probably not be helpful to point this out to Henry. He already knows that he is hurting and sad and that this is a theme for him right now. It would likely be more useful for you to stay in the here-and-now and support him by providing empathy and warmth.

Theoretical orientation. Theory may also affect the therapist's thinking about where to focus reflections. Many nondirective play therapists maintain that current feelings should be the sole focal point for reflection of feelings (Axline, 1969; Cochran et al., 2022; Green, 2014; Landreth, 2024; Punnett, 2016; Ray, 2011). Even when therapists observe affective themes in a session or across sessions, they might not share those observations with the child because they believe that doing so would detract from the child's remaining in the present. By contrast, more directive play therapists maintain that it is helpful to notice patterns in affective expression and to reflect those to children as well as reflect feelings from the present moment (Knell, 2016; Kottman & Meany-Walen, 2016; O'Connor, 2016).

Therapist's personal style. Your personal style of observation and communication may also influence your decision about the focus of feeling reflections. For instance, if you tend to look for connections between disparate thoughts, feelings, behaviors, attitudes, perceptions, and so forth, you might be more comfortable pointing out patterns to children. By contrast, if you tend to live primarily in the present moment, you might be most comfortable focusing only on the here-and-now with children. While this may seem simple and obvious, it is important to consider your personal style as it can impact your choice of interventions and predispose you to overuse certain interventions or neglect the appropriate use of others.

Multiple Feelings

Children often communicate several different feelings at the same time. You will need to decide whether to reflect all feelings or focus on only one or two feelings, depending in part on the child's developmental age. With verbally and intellectually advanced children, it can be productive to reflect several feelings simultaneously, especially if the feelings are mixed or have different intensity levels. With children who are developmentally or chronologically young, it may be better to focus on only one feeling at a time so they can process your feedback in a productive manner.

If you want to narrow the focus with a child who expresses several feelings at the same time, you will have to choose which feelings to reflect. Although this decision may depend somewhat on your theoretical orientation, it will most likely be determined by your intuitive judgment about which feeling is most important at that moment. This may be related to the pattern or the relative intensity of the various feelings. It may also stem from your sense of which feeling the child is ready to accept at that point in the therapeutic process.

If you want to acknowledge more than one feeling, you can provide some psychoeducation to the child that it is normal to have multiple feelings, even contradictory feelings, at the same time. By giving children permission to allow and express multiple feelings simultaneously, you can help them learn to accept and manage their feelings, which will support them in developing the means to self-regulate. One method of age-appropriate psychoeducation is using bibliotherapy with children's books such as *I'm Happy-Sad Today: Making sense of mixed-together feelings* (Britain, 2019), *Marcy's Having All the Feels* (Edwards, 2020), *Feelings Ninja: A social, emotional children's book about emotions and feelings* (Nhin, 2021), and *I Feel: A book of emotions* (Medina, 2022).

Monitoring Children's Responses

When you reflect a child's feeling, you should not expect the child to verbally acknowledge the reflection. Many times, the child will react in a nonverbal mode—either through body language or through play. The child may frown, smile, shrug, shudder, turn away from you, or use any number of other nonverbal responses.

The child may also react to your comments by doing something overt or covert in the play. *Overt reactions* may include behaviors such as turning and shooting you with a dart gun, having the father doll hit the mother doll, throwing the puppet down and stomping on it, having an animal figure comment on the reflection, and so forth. *Covert reactions* may involve a *play disruption*, whereby the child abruptly drops the current play and switches to a different type of play, different toys, or a different locale in the playroom (Kottman & Meany-Walen, 2018).

The child may react to a reflection with both verbal and nonverbal responses. You will want to monitor the intensity of these reactions for an idea of how the child is truly feeling about it. For instance, if Marybeth says mildly, "No, I am really not feeling angry right now," your guess about her feeling was probably wrong, and it may be appropriate for you to apologize or acknowledge that by saying something like, "Oh, I missed that one." If Marybeth has a rather violent reaction like screaming loudly, "No!!!! You are so stupid. Of course I am not angry," your guess about the feeling was probably correct. In such cases, you may consider various options for responding to the child's reaction. These options might include (a) responding with metacommunication about the child's reaction (e.g., "You seem really upset that I said you might be mad about that."; see Chapter 13), (b) ignoring the child's reaction, or (c) making a comment that invites the child to consider your hypothesis at a later time (e.g., "Well, it is something to think about."). By inviting the child to think your reflection over, you are planting a seed for further growth—something we like to do with all our clients.

Even when you believe your guess about the child's feeling is correct, it is essential not to argue with the child about this. Respect the child's right to decide which feelings to acknowledge at that particular moment. Sometimes the child is not ready to acknowledge a specific feeling, and it is important that they have control over this.

To a certain extent, the method of dealing with the child's reaction stems from the therapist's theoretical orientation. Some nondirective play therapists may notice the reaction but not verbally acknowledge it, preferring to integrate the response into their mental image of the interaction process rather than risk leading the child in a direction they do not choose to go. By contrast, more directive (and direct) therapists tend to make interpretations of the reaction to the child (e.g., "It looked like I reminded you about your father when I said that about you being angry.") or to acknowledge the reaction by commenting on the nonverbal communication (e.g., "You frowned when I said you were mad. I am thinking that maybe you don't like it when I think you are angry."). It is necessary to be cautious when verbally acknowledging the child's reaction. By presenting your thoughts in a tentative form, you can usually avoid evoking a defensive reaction or imposing your own interpretation of the child's reaction onto the child.

Expanding Concepts and Vocabulary

Many play therapists believe that it is part of their job to expand the child's feeling concepts and vocabulary (Goodyear-Brown, 2019, 2022; Kottman & Meany-Walen, 2016, 2018). By making guesses about feelings using words that express feelings more subtly than sad, mad, glad, and scared, you can help children learn about their own feelings. Although this process will not change children's abstract verbal reasoning skills, it may help them to verbally express their feelings to others.

Here are some feeling words that might be useful in play therapy sessions:

mad	irritated	frustrated	annoyed
enraged	outraged	angry	calm
glad	happy	joyful	excited
sad	overwhelmed	sorrowful	teary
scared	afraid	nervous	worried
anxious	terrified	horrified	concerned
disappointed	ashamed	embarrassed	antsy
proud	jealous	confused	lonely
powerful	shy	timid	bored
tired	gleeful	relieved	guilty
depressed	discouraged	distressed	peaceful
satisfied	dissatisfied	encouraged	distracted

Using your professional judgment and knowledge about child development, you can choose those feeling words that are appropriate for each individual child.

Applications in Different Theoretical Orientations

Most play therapists use the skill of reflecting feelings regardless of their theoretical orientation. There are no clear theoretical guidelines about how much emphasis should be on emotions in play therapy. Rather, it appears to be a matter of personal preference and style. However, there are theoretical guidelines about what feelings to reflect (here-and-now vs. patterns) and how to react to children's responses to reflections. Although we have provided some guidance in this chapter, we advise you to read texts on specific theories to further explore these issues (see Appendix A for selected references).

Examples of Reflecting Feelings

The following scenarios provide examples of reflecting feelings:

Example 1

Gloria (age 6) comes into the playroom with shoulders drooping and a sorrowful expression. She says, "My mom said I have to go to my dad's house this weekend instead of going to the swimming pool with my friends."

> "You seem disappointed that your mom says you can't go to the swimming pool with your friends."
>
> "You look sad and discouraged that you have to go to your dad's house instead of going to the swimming pool."
>
> "You wish you could go swimming with your friends instead of going to your dad's house. I am thinking you are feeling kind of sad that your mother made that decision."

Example 2

Oliver (age 8) bounces into the playroom, smiles, and exclaims, "I broke one of my brother's toys, and my mom thought it was his fault, so he got into trouble and I didn't."

> "You are kind of excited about getting away with breaking your brother's toy and not getting punished for it."
>
> "It sounds like you feel happy that your mother blamed your brother and not you."
>
> "You seem delighted that you got away with breaking your brother's toy without getting in trouble."

Example 3

Aurora (age 4) is looking for a particular toy that she likes and cannot find it in the playroom. She stomps her foot and says, "I hate you. I hate this room. I want my sword."

> "You are really mad because you can't find the sword. You are very unhappy because you wish you could find the sword and you haven't found it."
>
> "You want me to know you are very disappointed that the sword isn't where you expected it to be."
>
> "You seem very disappointed and angry that the sword isn't where it usually is."

"You want me to know that you feel angry because you aren't getting what you want."

Example 4

Hee (age 7) enters the playroom, looks down at the ground, and says, "I wish I could always stay here in this room with you."

> "You seem sad that you can't stay in the playroom with me all the time."
>
> "It sounds like you really feel happy and safe while you are here with me."
>
> "I am thinking that you're disappointed that you don't get to spend more time in the playroom with me."

Example 5

Luna (age 7) takes the smallest tiger figure and puts it under a book. In a high-pitched voice, Luna (pretending to be the voice of the smallest tiger) starts crying and whining, "Help!" She has the mother tiger tip the book off the smallest tiger. Then the daddy tiger comes over and growls at the smallest tiger and says, "Stop crying or I will bite you!"

> "Small Tiger, you seemed sad and scared when the book was on top of you and you couldn't get yourself free."
>
> "I am guessing that the smallest tiger was worried that no one was going to help get the book off."
>
> "Daddy Tiger, you sound very angry at Small Tiger for crying and asking for help."
>
> "I bet the mommy tiger was worried about the smallest tiger and she felt relieved when she got her out from under that book."
>
> "Small Tiger, I am guessing you were even more scared when Daddy Tiger said he was going to bite you if you didn't stop crying."

Example 6

Diego (age 9) has a dragon puppet that he uses to communicate many of his thoughts and feelings. He comes in, picks up the dragon, and has him roar at the therapist, then hide under a pile of other puppets. Then he has the dragon peek out from underneath the pillow at the therapist and growl, "I always get in trouble even though it's not my fault."

"Dragon, I can't tell if you are feeling mad at me or mad at someone else today."

"Dragon, you seem upset and feeling like something unfair happened today."

"I am thinking that the dragon is trying to tell me something—maybe that he is feeling worried or mad right now. Whatever he is feeling, he wants me to know he is unhappy."

"Diego, can you help me out? I can't tell if the dragon is annoyed about something that happened before you came to the playroom or if he is mad at me or someone else."

Example 7

Zuri (age 7) was recently told by her father and mother that they are getting a divorce. While she talks about this in her sessions, she never acknowledges any feelings about the impending divorce. In a session in which she is playing with puppets in the puppet theater, she has the little girl puppet yell at the father puppet for "ruining everything."

"Sounds like that little girl is mad at her father for something she didn't like that he did."

"Seems like she is angry because the father broke the rules and messed things up."

"I am guessing she is both disappointed in the father's behavior and sad because she feels like he has ruined something. It might be that she is mad at him too."

To the little girl puppet, "You sound really angry at your dad for something he did, and you feel disappointed in his for ruining something."

To the father puppet, "I am thinking the little girl is super mad at you for something you did that she thought you shouldn't do."

Practice Exercises

For each of the following scenarios, generate three possible ways to reflect feelings:

1. In his second session, Royal (age 7) comes into the playroom, picks up a stuffed animal, throws it on the floor, and stomps on it. He looks very angry and shouts, "I hate you, you slimy jerk."

2. Royal picks up a stuffed animal and starts pounding on the punching bag with it. He smiles and giggles every time the punching bag falls to the ground.

3. In his third session, Royal comes into the playroom and says, "I have had a really bad day at school—I got sent to the principal three times for yelling at my teacher. I am scared the principal is going to call my parents."

4. In the fifth session, Royal enters the playroom and lays on the pillows. In a flat voice and without any facial expression, he says, "I just won my spelling bee."

5. Tami Beth (age 8) has the mother doll say to the baby doll, "I wish you had never been born." The baby doll starts crying.

6. After using the wolf puppet to bite all the animal figures he labels as "prey" for six sessions in a row, Booker (age 5) comes to his next session, throws the puppet on the floor, smiles, and says, "I don't need that wolf anymore."

7. After her parents bribe her to come into the playroom by promising her candy at the end of her session, Pansy (age 4) throws herself on the floor and wails, "I wanted to play outside today, not come here and be with you. I hate you, and I hate all the toys in here."

8. Danny (age 6) buries ten marbles under the sand and says, "You won't be able to find those. I hid them very deep and you were closing your eyes when I did it, so you don't know where they are!"

9. Next, Danny turns to you, smiles, and says, "I will win again. I always beat you at everything."

10. Ah Lam (age 8) has recently found out that she has to go back to the hospital for more chemotherapy because her leukemia has returned. She starts burying the little girl figures in the sand without saying anything to you.

11. Ezra (age 9) came to therapy because he was expressing suicidal thoughts. In his eight sessions, he has played out various themes related to feeling as though he cannot live up to his parents' high standards. His parents and school report that he is doing better, and he tells you that he has no more thoughts about hurting himself. His insurance coverage has run out, and this is his last session. He refuses to look at you or talk for the first 15 minutes of the session.

12. Darcy (age 5) looks around the playroom and asks, "Why don't you have any dolls with leg braces like mine?"

13. Farheem (age 5) cradles the baby doll, feeding it. When he notices you watching him, he puts it down, walks away, and says, "I know boys are not supposed to play with dolls."

14. Santiago (age 4) walks into the playroom, looks at all the toys, smiles, and says, "I know I am going to have fun here."

15. Rebekah (age 4) picks up the gun and frowns. From having talked to her mother, you know that the family does not let their children use weapons of any kind and disapproves of you having guns in your playroom.

16. Declan (age 7) takes the baby doll, puts it under the pillows, turns to you, and says with a huge grin on his face, "I got rid of him. I never liked him anyway. We already have too many kids."

17. Amiko (age 5) draws a picture of a house, turns to you, smiles, and says, "My mother will like this. She will think this is a good picture. I am going to give it to her."

18. Felix (age 3), in his last session, with tears in his eyes, hugs you and heads to the door without saying anything.

For each of the following scenarios, be sure to include at least two different feelings to reflect:

1. Hyacinth (age 8) says, "My dad is in jail for abusing me. I hate him for hurting me. I wish he could come back and live with us at our house."

2. Hyacinth continues, "My grandmother is super mad at my mom for not protecting me. I can't decide if my grandmother is being fair or not. I am not sure how my mom could have protected me."

3. Leon (age 7) says to a little puppy puppet, "Too bad you ran into the street and got run over by the car. You should have listened to me when I told you to stay out of the street."

4. Leon makes a grave out of sand and, looking sad, buries a small dog figure. Then he brushes the sand off his hands and walks away from the sand tray, smiling.

5. Ishtar (age 6) has a father doll lock a mother doll and children figures out of the dollhouse. The mother doll cusses at him, the children hide behind their mother, and the father doll taunts them through the window.

6. Ishtar has one of the smaller child figures sneak in through the window of the house and tell the mother and other children to sneak into the house, too. Ishtar then uses the smaller child to

push the father doll out the front door of the house. The mother doll and other children dance around the house.

7. Billy Jack (age 9) says, "I got the 22 rifle I wanted for my birthday. But other people might think I am one of the guys who shoot people at the mall now."

8. Billy Jack continues, "I would only ever shoot targets or maybe a squirrel for food. But sometimes I wish I could shoot the school bully. That would make the world a better place if he wasn't around. I'd still probably get in trouble though."

9. Playing electronic Battleship in a session with you, Charlotte (age 10) sinks your ship, smiles, and yells, "Yes!" Then she makes eye contact with you and says, "I'm sorry I sunk your ship. I hope you're not too sad about it."

10. Rory (age 6) uses the dragon puppet to chase a bunny puppet. The bunny puppet squeals and runs away. The dragon puppet looks around, still trying to find the bunny puppet. When the bunny puppet gets clear, he does a dance.

Questions to Ponder

1. What is your reaction to the suggestion that you should refrain from asking children how they feel?

2. How do you feel/what do you think about the suggestion to avoid asking children *why* they feel a certain way?

3. Explain your thoughts on the phrase "makes you feel."

4. Discuss your perspective on the issue of focusing solely on feelings in the here-and-now as opposed to focusing on both present feelings and affective patterns.

5. Do you believe there is a time when you would choose to ignore feelings expressed in the here-and-now? Explain your answer.

6. Do you think it is appropriate to use play therapy skills to increase children's affective vocabulary and concept development? Explain. If you think this is important, how will you expand your feeling vocabulary as your first step?

7. Consider your own issues and the rules in your family of origin about feelings and expression of emotion. What were a few of your family members' rules about which feelings were allowed in your family?

8. What were a few of your family members' rules about expressing specific feelings? How might this affect your ability to reflect feelings in your play therapy sessions?

9. Are there specific feelings that you would be uncomfortable with children expressing in your sessions? What are they, and why would they be problematic for you? How will you prevent the expression of these feelings from being a problem in your play therapy sessions?

10. Are there specific ways people express feelings that might be problematic for you in your play therapy? What do you think causes your discomfort about those ways of expressing feelings?

11. How will you handle your reactions in the playroom when you have play therapy clients who express specific feelings in ways that are problematic for you?

8

Setting Limits

Historically, some experts working with children viewed setting limits as a technique that would undermine the therapeutic relationship. Instead, Ginott (1959) and other prominent play therapists (Schiffer, 1952; Slavson, 1943) advocated complete and unconditional permissiveness in therapy sessions so that children could act out whatever behavior they wanted or needed to and thereby optimize the effectiveness of therapy. These play therapists maintained that imposing predetermined limits would seriously hamper therapeutic progress because they would not be specifically tailored to individual children and their needs and problems.

Beginning with Axline (1947, 1969), Bixler (1949), and Moustakas (1953), this trend shifted. Axline (1947) stated that limits "are set up as a prerequisite to satisfactory therapy" (p. 131). Moustakas (1953) said, "Without limits there would be no therapy" (p. 15). Bixler (1949) stated this proposition even more emphatically in his article titled "Limits Are Therapy."

In most contemporary approaches to play therapy, therapists limit specific behaviors that are not acceptable in the playroom without limiting children's verbalizations or *symbolic* expressions of aggression or hostility. Limit setting usually involves some structured method of letting children know that these behaviors are not permitted (Cochran et al., 2022; Dion, 2018; Gonsher, 2016; Jayne et al., 2019; Kottman & Meany-Walen, 2018; Landreth, 2024).

Ginott (1961) listed 54 behaviors that should be limited in play therapy. This list included behaviors such as taking a playroom toy home, deciding whether to enter or leave the playroom at will, deliberately spilling sand on the floor in the playroom, painting toys or furniture, bringing a friend to a session, bringing food or drinks to the playroom, doing homework or reading books the child has brought to the session, lighting matches, starting fires, smoking, throwing sand or other things at the therapist, tying the therapist up, shooting darts on the therapist, kissing the therapist or sitting on their lap, hugging the therapist for long periods, eating mud or chalk, and urinating or defecating on the floor. Regardless of their theoretical orientation, most play therapists would agree with this truncated list of limits.

Norton and Norton (2008) suggested that play therapy limits fall into three distinct categories:

- *Absolute limits* are primarily designed to keep the child and the therapist safe. They are nonnegotiable and uniformly applied.
- *Clinical limits* are primarily related to clinical issues, such as leaving the toys in the playroom, staying in the playroom for the entire session, and leaving the session when it is over.
- *Reactionary limits* must be set when the child reacts to the therapist setting an absolute or clinical limit.

Kottman and Meany-Walen (2016) added a fourth category of limit setting: *relative* or *negotiable limits.* These are limits that the therapist and the child generate together (e.g., how many cups of water can be poured into the sandbox, where the child can play with the finger paints), working as a team to find compromise solutions when the child wants to do something that the therapist seeks to limit.

Although most therapists seem to agree on the types of behaviors that should be limited in play therapy, they may differ on the purpose of limiting, when to limit, and how to limit. There are myriad explanations of the rationale for limit setting in play therapy. For instance, Bixler (1949) suggested that limits (a) allow the therapist to be more accepting of children because they are not allowed to destroy property or hurt the therapist and (b) teach children the skills of conforming to the specific rules of different environments and relationships.

By contrast, Ginott (1959) described six different reasons for the use of limits in child-centered play therapy: (a) helping children use symbolic means for catharsis; (b) allowing the therapist to be accepting, caring, and empathic toward clients; (c) protecting children and the therapist from physical harm; (d) helping children increase ego controls by giving them practice in curbing socially inappropriate impulses; (e) keeping playroom behavior from violating legal, ethical, and social rules; and (f) preventing excessive outlay of money for repair of the physical plant and replacement of broken toys and play materials.

Landreth (2024), who also practices child-centered therapy, described the following seven reasons for setting limits:

1. Limits help children feel physically and emotionally secure in the playroom, which maximizes their potential for growth.
2. Limits help protect the physical safety of the therapist, which increases their ability to fully accept children.
3. Limits help children develop skills in decision-making, self-control, and self-responsibility.
4. Limits can anchor play therapy sessions to reality and help children focus on situations in the here and now.
5. Limits establish a sense of predictability and consistency in the play therapy relationship and environment.
6. Limits help maintain the parameters of the play therapy relationship within professional, ethical, and socially responsible guidelines.
7. Limits can reduce potential damage to toys, play therapy materials, and the playroom.

In Adlerian play therapy, the purpose of setting limits is to (a) build an egalitarian relationship with children in which power and responsibility are shared between the therapist and the client, (b) enhance children's self-control, (c) help children learn that they have the capacity for generating alternative appropriate behaviors and for redirecting their own socially unacceptable behaviors, (d) encourage children to develop a sense of responsibility for complying with limits and consequences, and (e) minimize power struggles in the play therapy process (Kottman & Meany-Walen, 2016).

Within each theoretical approach, the reasons for setting limits reflect the basic goals of that approach. Generally, however, most play therapists agree that limits can help to (a) keep both the child and the therapist safe in the playroom; (b) increase the child's awareness of and capacity for self-regulation and self-responsibility; (c) keep the relationship within legal, ethical, and socially acceptable boundaries; and (d) limit damage to property and play materials.

What to Limit

There is a consensus among most play therapists about the main goals of limit setting. Children are not supposed to do anything that might result in them hurting themselves, other children, their parents, or the therapist in the play therapy session. They are not supposed to be allowed to damage (on purpose) the toys or other play materials in the playroom, nor are they to harm the walls, floors, windows, furniture, or other physical property within the playroom. Other relatively universal rules are that children will stay in the session until the therapist has indicated the time for therapy has ended and will leave when the therapist has indicated the time has ended. Many therapists also have a rule that children should not leave the therapy room without permission to go to the bathroom, get a drink, and so forth. Most therapists also limit children from taking toys from the playroom, and some therapists limit children from bringing toys from other settings into the playroom.

These limits are usually considered to be nonnegotiable—especially the rules that prohibit harm to people and property—and practically all play therapists enforce them. Whether you implement other limits can depend on (a) your theoretical perspective, (b) the setting of your play therapy practice, (c) your personality, and (d) the individual situation and personality of specific child clients.

Influence of Theoretical Perspective

Most nondirective therapists (e.g., child-centered, experiential, Jungian, narrative, psychodynamic) attempt to keep limits to a minimum to create an atmosphere of optimal permissiveness. These therapists seldom use limits that would be classified as negotiable, sticking to the absolute and clinical limits, with an occasional reactionary limit. Ginott (1959) suggested avoiding conditional limits because they tend to be disruptive:

> Limits should be delineated in a manner that leaves no doubt in the child's mind as to what constitutes unacceptable conduct in the playroom. . . . A limit that states "you may splash me as long as you don't wet me too much" is inviting a deluge of trouble. (p. 162)

Play therapists who integrate both nondirective and directive elements (e.g., Adlerian, cognitive-behavioral, prescriptive, Gestalt, object relations) use all four categories of limits. They set limits that are absolute, clinical, and reactionary, often evoking some rules that are negotiable in nature. These rules usually revolve around behavior that could potentially be a minor nuisance or messy without being dangerous (e.g., whether the child can take paper and put it on the floor to paint there instead of the easel or whether the child is allowed to turn off the light in the playroom). The therapist and the child work together to establish negotiable limits by engaging in a discussion about what would be reasonable in the situation (Kottman & Meany-Walen, 2016, 2018). For instance, if the child wanted to pour six cups of water into the sandbox and you felt that only one cup was needed, you and the child could enter into a dialogue designed to find a compromise position—perhaps three cups.

It is important to note that the negotiated limit should be defined in a clear and measurable way, thereby avoiding Ginott's (1959) description of the drawbacks of conditional limits. Rather than using a vaguely stated limit (e.g., "It's against the rules to kick the ball hard."), you should work with the child until you arrive at a concretely stated limit (e.g., "It's against the rules to kick the ball so that it hits the lights, the window, or me.").

Play therapists on the more directive end of the continuum (e.g., ecosystemic, Theraplay) tend to use structuring to limit. They tell children which toys to use and what they will do in the session. Because they present the plan for playing as nonnegotiable, not as a choice, they act as if (of course) children will do what the therapist says they will do together. Thus, they avoid having to limit in a formal process. When children do not comply with the structure the therapists provide, these therapists may decide to switch paths, present a "new plan for playing," and introduce a different activity.

Some play therapists believe that acceptance of the child depends on permissiveness in the playroom (S. Bratton, personal communication, September 22, 2022). In service of communicating acceptance, these play therapists have few rules in the playroom. For Jungian play therapists, the playroom is an area where children can openly engage their destructive impulses, so few activities are limited (Green, 2014). In Gestalt play therapy, when a child expresses aggressive energy, the play therapist might be more permissive than when other issues are being played out (Fried & McKenna, 2020). In Adlerian play therapy, we are more likely to limit than many of these other approaches. While we strive to be accepting in the playroom, accepting does not require us to be permissive. We have had many clients deliberately test limits so that we will set rules and consequences for violating the rules. Sometimes too much permissiveness can communicate to a child that they are not safe in the playroom.

Personal application. As you are thinking about which approach to play therapy might be the most comfortable for you, it is important to consider how you feel about the different types of limit setting. You should think about whether you would be more comfortable with (a) a few limits that are nonnegotiable and clearly defined or (b) a moderate number of limits, some of which you would have to work out in conjunction with your clients. It would be helpful to consider whether you would be comfortable with structuring as a limit-setting device in your sessions—being directive and in charge of what play materials children use and what they do with them. It is also essential for you to think about your stance on permissiveness and how permissiveness is related to creating acceptance and safety in the playroom.

Influence of the Therapist's Setting

Practically speaking, the setting of your practice will also influence the types of behaviors for which you will want to set limits and how strictly you enforce various rules. The following examples illustrate the physical setting's influence on setting behavior limits:

- *George is a school counselor* who uses play therapy as an intervention modality. He is more likely than play therapists who work in mental health settings to limit wild behavior and inappropriate language because these behaviors are contrary to school rules. His view is that allowing children to flaunt school rules in the counselor's office can encourage them to flaunt rules in other areas of the school, which could result in negative consequences for them. Last year, George's office was near the principal's office, so he limited loud noises in his session. This year, his office is by the gym and the cafeteria, so he allows children to be very noisy in their sessions with him. No matter where his office is located, George provides time and activities to help children transition from the free and relaxed atmosphere in his office back to the classroom. George assumes that most children need help getting their behavior back into classroom-acceptable mode.

- *Huang is in private practice* and has an office in an expensive building with fine furniture and fancy toys. She sees both adults and children in her office. She is strict about enforcing rules with regard to damage to the property. Because she is personally responsible for expenses incurred if children inflict property damage, she does not allow them to violate the rules.

- *Youssef is an in-home family counselor* who works with parents and children in their own homes. He brings his own toys into the space designated by the family as the therapy space, sets down a blanket, and arranges his toys and art materials on the blanket. He must adjust his limit setting to fit with the rules and values of the families. For instance, the Taylor family is noisy and exuberant, with few rules and much physical conflict. Although Youssef tends to let the children in this family get loud in a session, he is consistent about enforcing the limits against hurting others, keeping toys in the play area, and structuring the session. In the Zander family, on the other hand, the parents are rigid and strict and allow little latitude for their children to act like children. In the Zander home, Youssef sets more limits on loud behavior so that the children will not be punished by their parents for violating family rules.

When Terry was an intern at a university clinic, she was rather lax about enforcing the rule against getting paint on the walls. However, after she graduated and became the clinic director, she became more vigilant about ensuring that clients did not get paint on the walls after realizing how much it would cost to repaint them and how inconvenient it would be.

These examples are meant to illustrate how the kinds and number of limits you set with clients may depend on the physical setting of your practice. You may think this is only common sense, but you will need to consider how your work setting and the nature of your job can influence how you set limits. We hope you will be proactive and intentional in making decisions about limits while also acknowledging the practical realities of your situation.

Influence of the Therapist's Personality

Your personality will influence what you limit in your play therapy sessions. You must feel comfortable with the behaviors you allow children to exhibit in the playroom. It is also important for you to feel secure about your own safety and the safety of clients. The following instances illustrate the influence of the therapist's level of comfort with particular situations:

- *Hilda has a strong need to maintain control* over herself and life situations. She equates being out of control with being in danger. This limits her ability to feel comfortable when she perceives children as being wild or out of control. She feels a need to impose limits on children's behaviors whenever she believes their behavior is getting out of control.

- *Jean-Françoise has a high tolerance level* for activities some might consider to be dangerous or out of control. He is comfortable when children are loud, acting out, or aggressive and never feels personally challenged or endangered. Jean-Françoise imposes very few limits on children.

- *Henrietta is personally timid* and does not like to take risks nor understands why anyone would want to do so. She believes that most things children do can constitute a threat to themselves or others. Henrietta imposes more limits on behavior than therapists who personally enjoy taking physical or emotional risks.

These examples may seem obvious, but determining your own preference for limits may not be so clear-cut. It is essential to consider how your personality may influence these preferences.

Your personality can also influence your ability to be accepting of children based on their behaviors. Some behaviors are simply intolerable or uncomfortable to certain people. If you do not limit behaviors that feel intolerable or uncomfortable, you might have a reduced capacity to accept or be empathic to a child demonstrating those behaviors. The following instances illustrate the influence of the therapist's ability to tolerate specific behaviors:

- *Tyrell hates snakes.* He becomes very agitated and breaks out into a sweat whenever a child gets near him with a rubber snake. With this in mind, Tyrell should limit having rubber snakes placed on or near his body because it might make him unable to focus on the child and their issues. He might even choose not to include rubber snakes in his playroom.

- *Aaliyah's religious beliefs preclude using profanity.* She is extremely uncomfortable with a child swearing in her playroom. If her discomfort would inhibit her from maintaining an acceptable level of positive regard for the child, she should limit this behavior.

- *Dirk is a very laid-back person.* He was a hospital nurse for ten years and is comfortable with every aspect of the human body. His theoretical orientation is psychodynamic, which allows for client regression. If a child wanted to "make poop" with some sand and water and smear it on the floor of the playroom, Dirk would be quite comfortable with this behavior and would choose not to limit it. However, many therapists, including the authors, would not be comfortable with this behavior.

- *Natalie needs structure and order.* She works in a psychiatric hospital and frequently conducts play therapy sessions with children who are chaotic and messy. When children come into the playroom, they often empty all of the contents of the shelves onto the floor. Although Natalie is uncomfortable with this behavior, she chooses not to limit it. Instead, she reminds them that they will have to start picking up the room earlier than usual when they do this.

As a play therapist, you must thoroughly examine your beliefs, personality, and issues to learn about the behaviors you will find acceptable or not in your play therapy sessions. If you remain unaware of those behaviors that might create difficulties in your ability to accept a child, you could inadvertently hurt the relationship with them and potentially cause them psychological harm. You need to explore your own history and current situation—examining your thoughts, attitudes, feelings, and prejudices—to determine whether there are behaviors you find intolerable or uncomfortable. Then, you can decide whether to work through these issues to maintain acceptance of children when they act out those behaviors. If you cannot do this, you may need to limit those behaviors to be accepting. With a child who continually exhibits behaviors that are intolerable to you, you may choose to refer that child to another counselor who does not share these issues.

Influence of the Individual Child

Developmental age, personality factors, and the life situation of individual children can be factors in deciding what to limit. Younger children usually need more rules and structure than older children. It is frequently helpful with young children (developmentally 2–5 years of age) to provide quite a few limits, especially those related to physical safety and property damage. Children in this age range often do not have the experience necessary to guide them in deciding what behaviors can be damaging to themselves, others, or the playroom. By setting limits and explaining the rationale behind each limit, you can teach younger children how to judge whether an activity is harmful.

Regarding personality factors, some children seem to need more structure than others. One method of conceptualizing children that can provide insight into the influence of their personalities related to limit-setting in the play therapy process was developed by Kissel (1990), who suggested that children having problems tend to fit into two distinct categories: *too loose* or *too tight*.

Children who are too loose need more structure and limits because they have difficulty with self-regulation and rule-governed behavior. Because they struggle with self-control, they may need you, at least in the initial stages of the play therapy relationship, to assist them in staying in control of themselves. Often, these children escalate their behavior in the playroom, almost as if they are trying to force you to set limits. Typically, this type of child needs more limits. It will usually be appropriate for you to limit more behaviors with children who are too loose than those who are too tight. You will probably avoid using too many negotiable limits because the negotiation procedure might be hampered by the thought processes and behaviors of children who are too loose.

By contrast, children who are too tight are rigidly self-controlled and will probably benefit from being encouraged to be freer and more spontaneous. With children who are too tight, you could contribute significantly to their growth by imposing few limits. You might allow them to experiment with behavior that is not entirely under control, such as shooting a dart gun at lights or throwing sand on the floor, as long as the results of these activities do not result in any permanent damage to you, the child, or the property.

Life situations that can impact what you limit are usually related to children's lives feeling out of control. For instance, children who are terminally ill, who have recently experienced a serious loss, or who have been sexually or physically abused may feel that they have no power in their own lives—that they are powerless to stop harmful things. Depending on how this sense of futility manifests in the playroom, you may decide to make shifts in what gets limited. Some children in these circumstances act recklessly in the playroom, necessitating many limits on their behavior. Other children may withdraw and refuse to try new behaviors in the playroom. With these children, you will probably decide to set fewer limits so as to encourage them to take more risks.

When to Limit

Rather than recite a list of limits in the initial session, most play therapists find it more helpful to set limits when the child is about to break a rule (Kottman & Meany-Walen, 2018). This approach helps to avoid power struggles with children who tend to be aggressive, for whom a set of limits would simply be a laundry list for future transgression. It also helps encourage timid children to try activities they might avoid if given a formidable list of things they are not allowed to do in the playroom.

The best time to limit is immediately before a child violates a rule. To anticipate potential problems, you must be alert to the child's nonverbal behaviors. Most children physically telegraph their intentions before they actually do something that would be deemed inappropriate in the playroom. For example, if Loretta is about to shoot you with the dart gun, she would pick up the gun, load it with darts, and aim it at you. If you are paying attention, you would have plenty of time to set the limit—after she aims the gun at you and before she pulls the trigger.

It is important to avoid setting a limit too early or too late. If you set a limit too early, children may argue about their intentions—taking offense because you have "accused" them of making plans for carrying out inappropriate behaviors. If you set a limit too late, you will miss the opportunity to prevent the targeted behavior. This can result in children feeling guilty for doing something unacceptable or triumphant for getting away with something inappropriate. And, despite your training, you may also experience some anger or irritation at the child for not following your playroom rules.

Some children become anxious if there is not a list of rules to govern their behavior (either by compliance or by defiance). These children would prefer a list of limits rather than having the playroom rules be nebulous or undefined. To help these children, L. Guerney (personal communication, October 2012) tells them, "If you are about to do something that is against the playroom rules, I will let you know." By stating this, she is avoiding the pitfalls of providing a list of limits while letting children who need structure know that there are rules and that she will not let them blunder into transgressions.

Practical Considerations in Limiting

Before we discuss specific steps of several approaches to limit setting, it might be helpful to discuss some practical considerations in delivering limits. You should monitor your personal reactions, attitudes, and feelings regarding interactions with the child, moderate your tone of voice and body language, and avoid lecturing the child and unnecessarily repeating their name.

One of the key components in successful limiting is conveying acceptance and respect for the child even when they are doing something inappropriate or unacceptable in the playroom. To do so, you must clearly understand your own issues, reactions, attitudes, and emotions so that you do not inadvertently convey disapproval to the child. By understanding your own trigger points and monitoring your own physical and emotional responses to the child, you will be more likely to be in control of the feedback you are sending via verbal and nonverbal channels. If there are behaviors that you cannot accept, you can refer children who repeatedly manifest them to another therapist, or you can work out your own issues outside the play therapy relationship, either with a personal therapist or a supervisor.

When you limit, the nonverbal aspect of the communication is usually even more important than the content of the message—both in voice (e.g., tone, pitch, volume, speed) and in physical reactions (e.g., body posture, body movement, facial expressions). It is essential to use your usual tone of voice without changing the tonal pattern from how you usually speak to the child. If, for example, you normally talk in a calm and level tone, without many tonal variations, this is the way you should limit. In contrast, if you speak in a lively, animated way, you should limit using that same varied tonality.

Do not use a sarcastic or singsong tonal pattern in how you talk with children, because both tones will sabotage the limiting process. If you limit in a snarky, facetious, or condescending tone of voice, children will tend to take this as a challenge, an insult, or a put-down. When limits are delivered in this way, children may decide to ignore them to show you that you cannot tell them what to do. If you set a limit in a baby or singsong tone of voice, children will tend to ignore the limit, as they will if you end your limits with a rising inflection, which turns a statement into a question. Children do not take these limits seriously because they infer from the tone of voice that limits are not being seriously set or that you are unsure of your ability to follow through with the limit.

It is important to have the same pitch you usually use. If your voice is relatively high, in most cases, you would want to limit in that pitch. Otherwise, you might communicate to the child that you are panicking or trying to control the child's behavior by overpowering them. If your voice is relatively low, in most cases, you would want to limit in that pitch; otherwise, you might communicate your own anxiety about the limiting process to the child. There are exceptions to this injunction, however. For some children, lowering your pitch makes the limit more effective because they may be more likely to comply with a limit delivered in a deeper voice. With other children, raising the pitch of your voice may convey urgency, which might influence compliance. As you would with any play therapy intervention, you need to pay close attention to how children react to various stimuli in the playroom.

Your body posture, body movement, and facial expressions convey your thoughts and feelings to the child. Again, the best strategy for delivering limits is to avoid changing these nonverbals from the usual. If you change any of the various physical means of communication, do so intentionally, having thought out what you wish your body language to convey. For example, if a child sits on your lap and you tell the child your lap is not for sitting on, if the child does not get off your lap, you must stand up in order to have your verbal and nonverbal communication be congruent. If you remain seated while setting this limit, you send a double message, which can be confusing to the child.

Whatever procedure you opt to use for setting limits, remember to keep it brief and concise. You will be more successful in limiting if you can avoid lecturing or otherwise drawing out the procedure. The most effective limit does not involve a lot of explaining or pontificating on your part. Keep it simple and quick.

Play therapists often use the child's name an inordinate number of times when limiting. This repetition seems to be related to the therapist's level of anxiety and their need to get the child's attention. The therapist may believe that saying the child's name multiple times will increase the likelihood of compliance. In our experience, this doesn't work. In limiting, you should use the child's name a minimal number of times to avoid telegraphing your trepidation about compliance.

Cultural Considerations in Limit-Setting

When setting limits, it is imperative to consider a child's culture and the methods used for discipline in that culture. However, it is impossible to know everything about every culture, and it is inappropriate to generalize information about specific cultures to every member of that population. Acknowledging this fact, it is often helpful to gather information about different cultures to inform your decisions about setting limits in a culturally sensitive and responsive way (Gil & Drewes, 2021; Ray et al., 2022b). For example, many Native American families place a high value on individual freedom and noninterference, so parents set few limits and expect children to discipline themselves (Glover, 2005, 2022). With African American children, as a way of "dismantling dehumanization commonly experienced in oppressive environments outside of the playroom" (Taylor & Turner, 2022, p. 150), play therapists must always ensure their verbal and nonverbal communication (especially in setting limits) send a message of safety, acceptance, warmth, and care. Some Asian children may find it daunting to engage in generating alternative behaviors during limit-setting if they have been socialized to demonstrate obedience and respect by always following the lead of adults (Cheng et al., 2022). For many Latinx families, an important component in building connections with children and their families is *personalismo*, which refers to relationships based on mutual respect and trust (Delgado & Aguilar, 2022). Personalismo may involve making small talk about a client's day, close physical contact (such as hugging or sitting very close to another person), gift-giving, and sharing personal information. Several of these cultural considerations may create situations in which play therapists would usually set a limit. With the Latinx population, that might be seen as a rejection of cultural values. Perez et al. (2007) suggested that some limits usually applied in the playroom are inappropriate for first-generation Mexican American children and should be adjusted because of cultural considerations. For instance, it may not be appropriate to limit taking toys or materials from the playroom because sharing toys is a natural part of play in this culture. Another limit that might be contraindicated would be staying in the playroom rather than being allowed to have a portion of sessions outdoors, where many Mexican American children are accustomed to play. Prohibiting friends or family members from accompanying the child to a session may violate the cultural value of *familismo*, which refers to the family assisting its members through good and bad times—the therapist might give serious consideration to eliminating this limit with this population (Perez et al., 2007). Although play therapists do not have to adhere strictly to the disciplinary pattern of each child's culture, they must learn what some of these patterns are and convey a sense of respect for the child's culture. When working to ensure that the playroom rules do not violate clients' cultural traditions, play therapists must also recognize that no uniform guidelines can apply to every member of a culture.

Styles of Limiting

There are many different strategies for setting limits in play therapy. Some are related to theoretical orientation, and some to the preferences of individual therapists. In this section, we will discuss the techniques outlined by Landreth (2024) and Kottman and Meany-Walen (2016).

Landreth's Method

Landreth (2024) used a three-step limiting procedure of acknowledging, communicating, and targeting (ACT):

1. *Acknowledge* the feelings, wishes, and wants of the child (e.g., "You seem really angry at me, and you want to shoot the gun at me.").
2. *Communicate* the limit to the child, using passive voice formulation (e.g., "I am not for shooting.") rather than active voice (e.g., "You may not shoot me.")
3. *Target* appropriate alternative behaviors and redirect (e.g., "Elizabeth, you can choose to shoot the doll or the bop bag instead of shooting at me.").

Landreth (2024) emphasized that the therapist must clearly define what is or is not acceptable. For the third step, he also suggested using the child's name to get their attention and using nonverbal cues to divert the child's focus from the original target of the behavior. He acknowledged that there are times when the therapist cannot follow these procedures in order—in certain situations, it might be more important to limit quickly and then acknowledge the child's behavior.

For those children who persist in a lack of cooperation in responding to the ACT procedure, Landreth (2024) outlined a fourth step, which is to state a final choice or "ultimate" limit. This involves a consequence for continued noncompliance (e.g., "If you choose to shoot me one more time, you choose not to play with the gun anymore today."). An important feature of this style of setting consequences is the inclusion of the child in making choices about how the interaction will proceed. Having to leave the playroom is one potential consequence, but if possible, the therapist should state a consequence that allows the child to continue the session with appropriate behavior.

Landreth (2024) emphasized that the therapist must exercise patience in this process and avoid using the fourth step whenever possible. He also stressed that the therapist's tone of voice and nonverbal behavior must continue to convey warmth, empathy, respect, and acceptance to the child even when they do not comply with limits.

Kottman and Meany-Walen's Method

Kottman and Meany-Walen (2016) described four steps for setting limits in Adlerian play therapy, which involves a collaborative process between you and the child, as follows:

1. State the limit nonjudgmentally, emphasizing that the limit is a rule specific to the setting (e.g., "It is against the playroom rules to shoot darts at people.").

2. Reflect the child's feelings or make a guess about the purpose of the child's behavior (e.g., "I can tell you are really angry right now." or "You want to show me that I can't control your behavior.").

3. Engage the child in generating alternative appropriate behaviors (e.g., "I bet you can think of something in the playroom you could shoot that would not be against the rules."). This statement opens the door for a negotiation process between you and the child in which you collaboratively devise a concrete, measurable *contract* for acceptable behavior (e.g., "OK, remember our agreement is that you can shoot anything but me, you, and the mirror.").

With most children, the third step is the end of the procedure. Kottman and Meany-Walen (2016) speculated that involving children in generating behaviors acceptable in the playroom gives them a sense of ownership and power that precludes further pursuit of the limited behavior. However, with children who persist in noncompliance, there is a fourth step, which involves first a renewed reflection of feelings or guesses about the purpose of the behavior and then a setting up of logical consequences for further transgressions (e.g., "We will need to decide what the consequences will be if you choose to shoot me again."). The consequences should be related to the proscribed behavior and should be respectful to the child—not harsh or punitive. It is usually helpful if the consequence does not last the remainder of the session. This provides the child with a chance to behave appropriately within the same time interval in which the transgression occurred. A timer set for 5 to 10 minutes can assist you in giving the child a chance to recover and play with that toy or handle that situation more appropriately. This technique is designed to provide the child with a reparative experience so that they leave the playroom with a better understanding of the playroom rules and know they are capable of following those rules.

You can decide about the timing of the fourth step. You can (a) wait to see if the child adheres to the agreement made in the third step without outlining consequences of noncompliance or (b) combine the third and fourth steps and define the consequences at the same time the contract is set. Kottman and Meany-Walen (2016) suggested that deferring the generation of consequences communicates a belief that the child will comply. However, this is a matter of personal preference—you will need to consider this on a case-by-case basis.

There are some behaviors that you will probably not be willing to let happen more than once, such as hitting someone or breaking a toy deliberately. With these situations, you could link the third and fourth steps or present the consequence as a choice before the child actually breaks the limit (e.g., "If you choose to try to hit me with the sword, you choose to lose the sword for 20 minutes. We have 40 minutes left in the session."). One difficulty with using this "preemptive strike" type of consequence setting is that it does not involve the child in generating the consequence. However, in some situations and with some children, it may be necessary to do this to prevent mayhem.

Examples of Limit Setting

Using the following three scenarios, we provide examples of each of the limit-setting methods described in this chapter:

Scenario 1

James (age 9) is described by his parents as "very angry all the time" and by his school principal as defiant and responding to requests and limits by being aggressive. He has been sent home from school several times for damaging school property and hurting other children. In his third session, James enters the playroom, picks up a plastic gun, and uses it to pound the plastic dolls in the dollhouse. Several of them break before the therapist can intervene.

- *Landreth method.* "I can tell you want to pound on those dolls with the gun. The dolls are not for smashing, though. James, you can decide to hit the pillows or the stuffed animals with the gun." James continues to pound. "If you choose to continue to pound the dolls with the gun, you choose not to play with the guns for the rest of this session."

- *Kottman method.* "It is against the rules in the playroom to smash the toys. I can tell you are really angry about something, and it is not OK to destroy the dolls. Let's think of something you can hit that would not violate the playroom rules." The therapist seeks to negotiate an agreement that James can smash egg cartons or rip paper to express his rage rather than hitting dolls. James refuses to negotiate or does not abide by the agreement and returns to hitting dolls. "I see that you have decided to keep breaking the rule about smashing toys to show me you don't have to listen to the rules. We will need to think of a consequence just in case you continue breaking toys." The therapist negotiates logical consequences that James will put the gun away for 15 minutes and then he can try to use the toy appropriately for the rest of the session.

Scenario 2

Lauren (age 4) starts tearing sheets of paper and putting them in the sink. Once they are sopping wet, she puts them in the sand tray.

- *Landreth method.* Seeking to create a permissive atmosphere in the playroom, a play therapist using the Landreth method might not limit Lauren's behavior. In this example, however, the therapist decides that this behavior has the potential to make a mess that would prevent other children from having access to the sand. "I can tell that you would like to put the wet pieces of paper in the sand, but the sand is not for putting sopping pieces of paper in. Lauren, you can choose to put the wet pieces of paper on the floor by the side of the sand tray instead." Lauren ignores the limit. "If you choose to continue to put the wet pieces of sand in the sand tray, you choose not to play with either the pieces of paper, the water, or the sand for the rest of today's play time."

- *Kottman method.* "It is against the playroom rules to put wet pieces of paper in the sand tray. It looks like you think it would be fun to put the wet paper in the sand, and you like to do fun things in here. If you keep putting the wet paper in the sand, it will make a very big mess and get too much water in the tray. What else could you put in the sand that won't make such a big mess?" "Where else could you put the sopping wet pieces of paper that would be fun for you?" "Where else could you combine some of the sand and the sopping pieces of paper that would be interesting or entertaining?" Note that you have a lot of different choices for engaging the child in figuring out acceptable alternative behaviors—you are limited only by your own imagination. The therapist would negotiate with Lauren to come to an agreement about what to do with the wet pieces of paper. Lauren refuses to negotiate or does not abide by the agreement. "You would like to show me that I can't tell you what to do. But if you choose to continue to put the wet paper into the sand, you choose not to play with the water, the wet paper, and the sand for 10 minutes."

Scenario 3

Leonard (age 5) is angry because the therapist has set a limit. He throws himself out of his wheelchair onto the floor and starts banging his head against the floor, screaming, "You mean bitch! You can't tell me what to do!" Regardless of the method of limiting, the therapist must intervene to prevent this child from hurting himself. This intervention may involve a therapeutic restraint, calling for a parent to restrain the child, or putting a pillow between the child's head and the floor. The Association for Play Therapy (APT; 2022a) has stated that restraint should only be used after the play therapist has exhausted all other preventive measures. When working with children who have a history of aggressive or violent behaviors or self-harm, play therapists should address with caregivers or legal guardians at the beginning of the therapeutic relationship the potential for needing to use physical restraint on a child. As APT (2022a) stated,

> Play therapists working in a setting in which restraint is commonplace should receive the necessary training and become thoroughly familiar with any laws in their state/country and legal and ethical code in their parent licensing body regarding the use of physical restraint. All play therapists should have a plan (even if it does not involve touch or restraint) for how they will manage extreme violent or self-endangering acting out on the part of a child in session, and this plan should be consistent with their training in restraint and the policies on restraint in the facility in which they are working. (p. 9).

If restraint is deemed necessary for the safety of the child or the therapist, it is essential to thoroughly document the incident and to process what happened with both the child and the caretaker immediately after restraining the child. The notification of the incident to the caregiver or legal guardian must include (a) a description of the child's behavior immediately before the restraint, (b) the behavior that triggered the restraint, (c) the efforts made by the therapist to de-escalate the situation, and (d) alternatives to the restraint that the therapist attempted prior to the restraint intervention. It is often helpful for the play therapist to discuss the situation with their supervisor as well.

Landreth method. The therapist moves to stop the child from hitting his head on the floor by putting a pillow between the child's head and the floor. "Your head is not for hitting. You are very angry because I told you the mirror is not for shooting. Leonard, you can choose to stop hitting your head, or you can choose for your mother to come into the playroom to put you back in your wheelchair and take you out of the playroom."

Kottman method. The therapist moves to stop the child from hitting his head by putting a pillow between the floor and his head. "It's against the rules to hit your head, Leonard. You are angry, and you want to show me that I cannot tell you what to do. I bet you can choose something soft to hit for 2 minutes to show me how mad you are at me." The therapist negotiates with the child, and they agree that he can hit a pillow for 2 minutes.

Practice Exercises

For each of the following 15 scenarios, decide whether you would limit the behavior and explain your rationale. Write out the steps you would take to limit using each of the two methods of limiting explained in this chapter, and explain what you would do if the child does not abide by the limit.

1. Jael (age 8) is a child who is struggling with math and reading at school. She is playing school, with the teacher doll yelling at the small girl doll. She goes toward the bathroom holding the little girl doll, saying, "I am going to flush her down the toilet. She will drown, which is just what she deserves at school for not doing her best."

2. Lennon (age 6) wants you to sword fight with him. You decline to engage in sword fighting, so he grabs a sword and approaches you, trying to climb into your lap and yelling, "If you won't fight, I will just cut off your head. Then you will be sorry you didn't want to have a sword fight with me."

3. Adia (age 4) starts chewing on the heads of the baby dolls, saying, "I am a giant who eats children. These babies have tasty heads."

4. Finnian's (age 4) parents are in the middle of a messy divorce and acrimonious custody battle. Finnian's presenting problems include night terrors, separation anxiety (from both his mother and father), excessive crying, and clinging to adults. In his fourth session, he takes all of the figures from the dollhouse and tries to stick them into the furnace duct in the playroom.

5. Lina (age 6) was referred to play therapy because she is disobedient and defiant at home and school. She is rude and disrespectful to both of her parents and bullies her two younger sisters. In her first session, staring straight at you, she starts to put crayons in

her mouth, apparently getting ready to chew and swallow them. She says, "I bet you can't stop me from eating these."

6. Niko (age 10) has been diagnosed as being on the autism spectrum. His parents report that he has no friends and frequently ignores his teacher. He seldom makes eye contact and seems to avoid touching other people. His parents and teacher asked you to work with him on social skills and self-esteem issues. In his sixth session, he is making mudpies in the sand tray when he accidentally splatters mud outside the sand tray onto the floor. He smiles and does it again. He begins to make a game of seeing how far out of the sandbox he can jettison the muddy sand.

7. Juana's (age 4) parents have brought her to play therapy because they think that her behavior is "out of control." She tends to ignore directions from her parents and regularly hits her younger brother and sister. In her second session, Juana takes the finger paints out of the cabinet and begins smearing them on her face and dress while humming and smiling. When you ask her to stop, she ignores you.

8. Continuing with the finger paints, Juana is now putting the finger paint on you.

9. According to reports from his father, Achinoam (age 5) has always tended to be timid. He dislikes trying new things and is anxious when he is not with one of his parents. When he started therapy, he cried in new situations, and his entire body shook, even when he was with one of his parents. Since the beginning of therapy, he has made significant progress in managing his anxiety about new situations and experiences. In the middle of his 14th session, he smiles at you, goes to the playroom door, and says, "I am going to go outside and play on that playground next door. See you later!"

10. Saffron's (age 8) behavior has changed recently after witnessing a car wreck in which several people were killed. Her parents report that her formerly compliant behavior has shifted, and she now seems both angry and fearful "all the time." In the fifth session, she comes stomping into the playroom and yells, "You can't stop me from doing whatever I want." She takes several toy cars and trucks and then deliberately starts breaking them.

11. Parinda (age 6) is the most "grown-up" child you have ever counseled. Every week, he comes into the playroom, sits down, and describes his week to you. He does not like to play with messy

materials such as finger paint or sand. He does not seem to be making much progress on his issues of being rigid and lacking spontaneity. You have only three more sessions with him, so in your seventh session, you decide to be a little more directive than you have been. You ask Parinda to squirt shaving cream onto a table and spread it with his hands. He tells you that he "absolutely won't do that." You ask him to try it "just one time," and he proceeds to aim the shaving cream nozzle at you.

12. Hope (age 8) was sexually abused by a neighbor boy when she was five years old. She did not show any ill effects at the time, but lately, she has started sexually acting out with several of her cousins. In her six sessions with you, she has been relatively seductive but has done nothing overtly sexual. In the seventh session, she approaches you and starts rubbing her crotch against your knee.

13. Hawk (age 7) is a self-described "brave boy" who has been diagnosed with attention-deficit/hyperactivity disorder. He loves to climb and jump from high places. He often talks about situations in which he emerges unscathed from "doing dangerous things." Hawk begins to climb up the shelves in your playroom, saying, "I am going to climb up to the very top and jump off, and I won't even get hurt."

14. Leanna (age 7) has been labeled by her teacher and her family as being "too perfectionistic." She tends to have extreme reactions to making mistakes—tearing up school assignments that are not 100% accurate or crying when she gets answers wrong in class. Her parents report she will not try anything if she thinks she won't be able to do it perfectly. In her first session, she tries to draw a tree and is dissatisfied with her efforts, so she tears up the drawing and then gets some paints to try a different approach. She accidentally spills some paint on the floor. She starts to sob loudly and takes the paint container to the sink, ready to dump out the entire container because "it's just too drippy."

Questions to Ponder

1. From your previous experience of being around children, describe your comfort level with managing children's misbehavior.
2. Based on your previous experience with children, your interactions with other adults, the practice exercises, and your sample

sessions with children, what kind of misbehavior do you think will evoke the most anxiety for you? Explain why.

3. What might be some triggers that could interfere with your ability to limit certain behaviors?

4. In what situations might your own personal values support setting a limit that might not be therapeutically appropriate?

5. What will be the hardest part of limiting for you? Explain.

6. What purpose do you think limiting serves in the playroom? Explain.

7. What kind of impact will your possible work settings have on how you limit? Explain.

8. What kind of impact will your own personality and/or issues have on the way you limit? Explain.

9. What is your position on conditional limits? Would you be comfortable negotiating certain limits with children, or would you be more comfortable with a binary (e.g., "Yes, you can do this." or "No, you cannot do this.") position?

10. For each style of limiting, what appeals to you?

11. For each style of limiting, what do you think would be difficult for you?

12. If you were to create your own strategy for limiting in the playroom, what steps would you include? Explain how each step would be helpful and how each fits into your beliefs about people.

13. How do you feel about physically restraining children? How would you decide whether to use physical interventions with a child?

14. What impact do you think setting limits on children's behavior will have on your relationship with them?

15. How do you plan to explore different populations with which you might work to learn more about cultural norms or traditions that might impact how and what you limit?

16. How will you adapt your strategies for limiting depending on the child's cultural background?

17. What is your stance on permissiveness in the playroom? What is your comfort level with being totally permissive, with very few limits? Do you think that you must be permissive to be accepting of children? Can you be accepting when allowing children to do things that might bother or offend you?

9

Returning Responsibility to the Child

When working with children, you may find yourself slipping into a habit of caring for them or making decisions for them that they could do or make for themselves. Whenever possible, it is essential to refrain from this practice, as it can be harmful to children's sense of self-confidence and self-efficacy. One method of avoiding doing things for children that they can (and should) do for themselves is the skill of *returning responsibility* to the child (Kottman & Meany-Walen, 2016; Landreth, 2024; Ray, 2011). This skill involves letting children know, either directly or indirectly, that you believe they have the capacity to successfully execute the behavior or make the decision in question.

When using this skill, your goals are to empower children, convey that you believe they can be successful, promote problem-solving skills, and give them an experience of trying something they might not otherwise attempt. By returning the responsibility to children, you can help to imbue them with a sense of self-efficacy and convey that the task or choice is within their reach. The experience of *trying* to do something is frequently empowering to children even when they are not totally successful at doing it. As children realize that they are in control of their own behavior and decisions, the very act of doing or choosing lets them experience a feeling of power. It does not matter whether they are successful in the attempted behavior or make the "correct" decision. By allowing them to handle the consequences of their own choices, you can encourage independence, self-responsibility, and creativity (Kottman & Meany-Walen, 2016, 2018; Landreth, 2024).

When to Return Responsibility

The skill of returning responsibility to children is often appropriate in situations in which they *explicitly* or *implicitly* ask for help, or you feel a need to help them even though they have not indicated a desire for assistance. Sometimes the responsibility relates to *behavior,* and other times it relates to *decisions*. Some examples of each of these instances:

Example 1

Child explicitly asks for help with behavior

> "Can you zipper my jacket?"
> "Will you turn the water off for me?"
> "Please help me put this on the shelf."

Example 2

Child explicitly asks for help with decisions

> "Will you tell me what color I should paint this flower?"
> "What do you think I should do after we finish this?"
> "What kind of animal is this little figure?"
> "What is that thing underneath the pillow?"

Example 3

Child implies that they need help with behavior

> "I can't figure out how to put these Legos together."
> "How do you get the stickers off this paper?"
> "I don't know what time it is."

Example 4

Child implies that they need help with decisions

> "I can't decide what color to use to draw this bear."

> "I am not sure what to build with these blocks." (looks at you in askance)
>
> "I wonder what kind of puppet to use to be the narrator of the story."

Example 5

You feel a need to help the child with behavior without being asked

> The child drags a chair over to the shelf.
>
> The child struggles to button their coat at the end of your session.
>
> The child is looking for a specific toy on the shelf and cannot find it (and you know where it is).

Example 6

You feel a need to help the child with decisions without being asked

> The child looks around the playroom, obviously having difficulty deciding what to do.
>
> The child touches several toys, picking them up and putting them down again.
>
> The child sits poised with the scissors and the paper but doesn't cut anything.

How to Return Responsibility

There are two main styles of returning responsibility to children: direct and indirect. The indirect approach has at least four variations: (a) using the child's metaphor, (b) using minimal encouragers, (c) restating content, reflecting feelings, or tracking, and (d) applying the whisper technique. At times, you might decide to combine elements of both approaches.

When you return responsibility to the child, it is often tempting to start with an acknowledgment of what the child wants and then use the word "but" as a segue to the part of the sentence returning responsibility (e.g., "I know you want me to pick the color you are going to paint the house, but in here, you get to decide what color you want to paint it."). In these instances, however, it is better to use the word "and" (e.g., "I know you want me to pick the color you are going to paint the house, and in here, you get to decide what color you want to paint it."). In this context, the word "and" conveys a positive message to the child without implying that the child has made a mistake or done something that should be corrected, which the word "but" often communicates.

Direct Approach

In the direct approach, you expressly tell children that it is up to them to execute the behavior or make the choice without assistance. If the child explicitly asks for help, you can simply tell them that it is up to them to carry out the behavior or make the choice (e.g., "In here, you can do whatever you want to do with the blocks.") or you can make an encouraging comment ("I bet you can decide what you want to do with the blocks.").

If a child seems to implicitly ask for help, you might initially make a guess about them wanting you to do something or make a decision for them (e.g., "You seem like you want me to tell you what color to paint the flower."). After this, you would tell them that they can take care of the situation or make the choice by themselves (e.g., "In the playroom, you can decide that for yourself.") or make an encouraging remark (e.g., "I believe in your ability to figure what you want to do."). When you feel a need to help children with behaviors and decisions even though they have not asked, you might decide to reflect a feeling before making an encouraging comment that suggests you have confidence that they can handle the situation themselves (e.g., "You seem a bit frustrated that you can't reach that game on the top shelf, and I bet you can figure out how to get it down.").

Indirect Approach

The other strategies for returning responsibility to the child are more indirect. As mentioned, there are four different variations of this approach.

Using the child's metaphor. You can be indirectly direct by using a metaphor to return responsibility to the child. For example, if the child asks you where the Steve character from the Minecraft game should hide from the zombie, you might respond, "Steve gets to choose a place to hide from the zombie for himself" or "Steve, I bet you can figure out a place to hide to make sure you are safe from the zombie." By talking to the child about the characters in the play or talking directly to the characters, you can empower the child to make decisions or take action without ever coming out of the child's metaphor. Obviously, this method works only if the child has been communicating through a metaphor.

Using minimal encouragers. Another method of indirectly returning responsibility is to either use minimal encouragers (e.g., "Mmmm . . ." "Hmmm . . ." "Well . . .") or not answer when the child asks for help (Landreth, 2024). By providing little to no feedback to the child, you allow the child time to decide or act without interference or input from you. This method seems to work best when the child obliquely asks for assistance. It also works when the child directly asks for help, but in those instances, it may be frustrating to the child.

Restating content, reflecting feelings, or tracking. You can also indirectly return responsibility to a child by restating the content of the child's request (e.g., "You asked me what that is."), reflecting the child's feelings (e.g., "You seem a little frustrated because you are sure that toy has a name and you don't know what it is."), or tracking (e.g., "You are touching all the sand tray figures on that shelf."). This approach works best if the child asks for or acts as if they want help.

Applying the whisper technique. The *whisper technique* is usually used in role playing (see Chapter 13), but it can also work in returning responsibility to the child. For example, if Harrison asks you to tell him where to hide the snake figure, you can use a whisper to ask him for direction (e.g., "Where should I tell you to hide the snake?" in a whisper voice). This technique puts the child in charge of generating an answer to their own question. The whisper technique seems to work best when the child asks for assistance or advice.

Combined Approach

There may be times when you will use a combination of indirect and direct approaches to return responsibility to the child. One example is when you do not know if the child can accomplish the task, so you will need to gather more information. In this case, you could start with an indirect approach by restating the content of the child's request or reflecting a feeling and watching the child's response. For example, if TingTing asks you to show her how to solve a puzzle ball, you could reflect a feeling and then restate the content of her request by saying, "You seem frustrated because you are having trouble solving the puzzle ball, so you are asking me to do it for you." After the child responds to this hypothesis, you can decide on your next intervention. If TingTing clarifies that she knows how to solve the puzzle ball but is anxious about her ability to do it quickly, you can use a direct response, acknowledging her feeling and returning responsibility to her with a comment like "You are feeling nervous about whether you can solve it as quickly as you want. I have confidence you can solve it if you work at it. There is no time limit. Remember last week? You solved it then."

If the child's response indicates they likely will not be successful at the task at hand, you might want to suggest a collaborative effort, with the two of you working as a team to successfully complete the task together. It is important to note that combining direct and indirect approaches with a suggestion of collaboration is appropriate only when the child is asking for help with behaviors. It is not appropriate with decision-making because, although there may be behaviors a child cannot successfully accomplish, they are always capable of making decisions in the playroom because there is no judgment about whether a decision is "right" or "wrong" there. Therefore, collaboration about decision-making is inappropriate because it would involve you in doing something for the child that the child can do alone.

When Not to Return Responsibility

It is not always appropriate to return the responsibility to the child. Although you will have to decide whether to use this skill with individual children in particular situations, there are several circumstances in which returning the responsibility to a child might be contraindicated (Goodyear-Brown, 2010; Kottman & Meany-Walen, 2016, 2018). These extenuating circumstances could include situations in which (a) you believe that the child is not capable of taking responsibility for the behavior, (b) the child is engaging in regressive behavior, and you believe that this behavior is appropriate for that particular child, (c) the child's history indicates that the child may need someone to take care of them in certain situations, and (d) the child is struggling emotionally or behaviorally and may benefit from special nurturing for a limited time.

Child Cannot Take Responsibility

It can be discouraging to a child who truly cannot do something to be told by an adult that they really can do it. In cases where you do not know whether the child can do something, it is usually more helpful and encouraging to suggest that you and the child work together on the project. You can suggest collaborating on the activity (e.g., "Let's do it as a team. You roll your wheelchair over close to the sink, and I will help you turn the faucet on.") or ask the child to give directions on how the task could be accomplished (e.g., "Tell me where you want it put on the high shelf."). This strategy avoids any implicit suggestion that the inability to complete the task constitutes incompetence on the part of the child, which can be very discouraging to the child.

Regressive Behavior

If your theoretical orientation (e.g., Jungian, prescriptive, psychodynamic) supports the concept that regression is therapeutically useful to children, you might choose not to return responsibility to the child if they are engaging in regressive behavior. For example, when nine-year-old Sophia uses a baby voice to say, "I am the baby. Will you wrap this blanket around me? I can't do it," you might simply choose to do this for her.

Child's History

Sometimes a child's history will suggest that the child is not psychologically capable or ready to take care of themselves in certain situations. This may be a result of a traumatic experience or some element in the child's caretaking that has contributed to their inability to take responsibility at the current time (Goodyear-Brown, 2010, 2019). One example of a traumatic experience that might affect the decision to return responsibility is the experience of Frank (age 8), who was stuck in an elevator for hours when he was five. If Frank feels tremendous anxiety connected to elevators and asks to hold your hand riding the elevator from your waiting room to the playroom, you might choose not to return this responsibility to him.

An example of a child whose upbringing might affect the decision to return responsibility would be Cathie (age 7). When Cathie was four, her mother was diagnosed with bipolar disorder with psychotic features and subsequently abandoned her family. Cathie and her two younger siblings were raised by their father with the help of her elderly grandmother, and they had to work very hard to make ends meet. Cathie is extremely needy and frequently asks you to do things for her that she could do herself. You might decide that she needs more nurturing than many other children, resulting in your decision not to always return the responsibility to Cathie, even when you believe she can take care of herself. Eventually, as Cathie began feeling better about herself and her ability to take care of herself, you could begin to return responsibility to her.

Child's Current Situation

There may be times when you decide that not returning the responsibility to the child is appropriate for them at that point (Goodyear-Brown, 2010, 2019; Kottman & Meany-Walen, 2016). This might involve the child having a particularly bad week or month at school, an anniversary of some traumatic experience, unusual family turmoil, a difficult foster placement, and so forth. In such cases, a child who is usually very self-reliant might ask for help. When this happens, you might decide to forgo returning the responsibility to the child. For example, since Ajayi (age 6) started in therapy, he has been comfortable with choosing the next activity for the playroom. The day after he is diagnosed with asthma, he tells you he "has no idea what to do next." Given your understanding of his uncertainty and anxiety about what this diagnosis might mean for him, you might decide to just do this for him rather than return the responsibility to him.

Applications in Different Theoretical Orientations

The skill of returning responsibility to the child is widely used in play therapy. Adlerian, child-centered, cognitive-behavioral, Jungian, Gestalt, prescriptive, and psychodynamic play therapists tend to return responsibility (a) when a child asks them to do something that the child can do without assistance or (b) when a child asks them to make a decision that the child has not attempted to make alone.

Nondirective play therapists generally use a simple approach to returning responsibility to the child, seldom combining direct and indirect responses. With children who want help with decisions, most nondirective play therapists use some variation of the direct format of saying to the child, "In here, you can decide." With children who want help with actions, most nondirective play therapists use an indirect approach, usually reflecting the child's feelings, restating the content of the request for help, tracking the child's behavior, or using a minimal encourager.

Directive play therapists may use more complex procedures to return responsibility to the child. They may (a) make a guess about the underlying meaning of the communication from the child or (b) make an interpretation to the child of why they have asked the therapist for help, directions, or permission before returning the responsibility to the child.

Examples of Returning Responsibility

The following examples represent numerous situations where a therapist would return responsibility to the child. After each scenario, we have listed several ways of returning responsibility and the style of returning responsibility (i.e., direct or indirect with variations) demonstrated.

Child Explicitly Asks for Help With Behaviors

Example 1

Bob (age 4) takes his leg braces off, sits on the ground, and says, "Will you help me up?"

> "I have confidence you can get up all by yourself, especially if you put your leg braces back on." (*direct and encouraging*)

> "You want some help with getting up off the ground." (*indirect, restating content*)

> "You seem a little nervous about whether you can get up. Want to work together to get you up?" (*combination of indirect and direct, combining a reflection of feelings with a suggestion of collaboration*)

Example 2

Sophia (age 9) looks at the paints and says, "You don't have any green paint. Will you make some for me?"

> "I am guessing you know how to make green for yourself." (*direct and encouraging*)

> "You'd like me to do that for you." (*indirect, restating content*)

> "You want me to make some green paint for you. I am pretty sure you know which colors to mix to make green. How about you tell me what to do, and we can help one another make the paint?" (*combination of indirect and direct, with a suggestion of collaboration*)

Example 3

Tungar (age 6), who fastened his belt by himself last week, says, "Please fasten my belt for me."

> "I noticed that you did that all by yourself last week, and I am guessing that you can do it by yourself again this time." (*direct and encouraging*)

> Therapist smiles and nods encouragingly but does not move to help. (*indirect, minimal encourager*)

> "Even though you did it last week, you're not feeling very confident that you can do it again. Why don't you show me how it gets started, and we can work together from there?" (*combination of indirect and direct, combining a reflection of feelings with a suggestion of collaboration*)

Child Explicitly Asks for Help With Decisions

Example 1

Scarlett (age 7) looks up from cutting into shapes and asks, "What shape should I cut next?"

> "You get to cut whatever shape you want." (*direct*)

> "You want me to tell you what shape to cut next." (*indirect, restating content*)

> Therapist whispers to the child, "What shape should I say?" (*indirect, using the whisper technique*)

Example 2

Anakin (age 5) puts the dolls away and asks, "What do you think I should do next?"

> "You can make that choice for yourself." (*direct and encouraging*)

> "Hmmm . . ." (*indirect, minimal encourager*)

> "You want me to tell you what to do." (*indirect, restating content*)

Example 3

Ceyrah (age 9) picks up a costume cape and asks, "What kind of superhero will I be if I wear this?"

> "In here, you can be whatever superhero you want to be." (*direct*)

> "Let's ask the cape and see if it knows." Therapist asks the cape, "What kind of superhero will Ceyrah be if she puts you on?" (*indirect, using metaphor*)

> "You want me to tell you what kind of superhero you would be if you put that cape on. You get to decide that for yourself." (*combination of indirect and direct*)

Example 4

Isaiah (age 10) picks up a toy and asks, "What does this do?"

"That is up to you." (*direct and encouraging*)

"You want to know what that does." (*indirect, restatement of content*)

Therapist whispers to the child, "What does that do?" (*indirect, using the whisper technique*)

Child Implicitly Asks for Help With Behaviors

Example 1

Davika (age 8) sits on the floor pouting and says, "I can't get my crutches to work."

"You sound like you want some help with getting your crutches to work, and I bet you can figure out a way to do that yourself." (*makes a guess about the underlying communication, then direct and encouraging*)

"You are feeling a bit frustrated and thinking that you can't get your crutches to work the way you want them to work." (*indirect, reflecting feeling*)

"You sound a bit discouraged. Let's figure out how we can work together to get your crutches to work the way you want them to work." (*combination of indirect and direct, combining a reflection of feelings with a suggestion of collaboration*)

Example 2

Niall (age 5) walks over to the sink and asks, "How do you make the drain close?"

"Try it, and I believe you can figure it out." (*direct and encouraging*)

"It sounds like you want me to show you how that works. Hmmm . . ." (*makes a guess about the underlying message and then indirect, minimal encourager*)

"I'm thinking that you would like to figure that out, and you're not sure you can do it yourself. Why don't you put your hand on top of mine, and let's see if we can close it together?" (*makes a guess about the underlying message and then combination of direct and indirect, with a suggestion of collaboration*)

Example 3

Lessie (age 6) points to her drawing and asks, "What color does this bunny want to be?"

> "In here, the bunny can choose any color to be." (*indirect, using the child's metaphor*)

> "In here, you get to pick whatever color you want for the bunny." (*direct*)

> "I'm guessing that maybe you think there is a certain color that bunny is supposed to be, and in here, you can decide on things like that because there is no 'right' color for bunnies to be." (*makes a guess about the underlying message and then direct and encouraging*)

Example 4

Agapito (age 6) glances up at the analog clock on the wall, looks sad, and says, "I don't know how to tell time when the clock doesn't show the numbers."

> "You can just make up a time, and that's what it will be in the playroom." (*direct and encouraging*)

> "You sound kind of sad that you don't know how to tell time with that kind of clock." (*indirect, reflecting feeling*)

> "I'm guessing you would like me to tell you what time it is. Hmmm . . ." (*makes a guess about the underlying communication and then indirect, minimal encourager*)

> "Well, sounds like you're not sure if you can figure out what the time is with that kind of clock, and you want some help with that. Any ideas about how we can figure out the time?" (*makes a guess about the underlying communication and then suggests collaboration*)

Child Implicitly Asks for Help With Decisions

Example 1

Koko (age 10) looks at the cabinet with games and says, "I can't decide which game to play."

> "You sound like you wish I would decide that for you, and in here, that is your decision to make." (*makes a guess about the underlying communication, then direct and encouraging*)

"You feel uncertain about what you want to play now." (*indirect*)

Therapist whispers to the child, "Which one looks like the most fun?'" (*indirect, whisper technique*)

Example 2

Kenisha (age 8) looks askance at the therapist and whines, "I don't like to play anything if it's not a video game."

"I have confidence that you can figure out something in here that you might want to play with." (*direct and encouraging*)

"You seem a bit confused about what you want to do since I don't have any video games in the playroom." (*indirect, reflecting feeling*)

"I am thinking that you wish I had video games in the playroom. I know that you can make your own plan for what you do next even though there aren't any video games in here." (*makes a guess about underlying communication, then direct and encouraging*)

Example 3

Oliver (age 4) says, "I wonder what this little thing is."

"In here, it can be whatever you would like for it to be." (*direct*)

"I wonder . . ." (*indirect, minimal encourager*)

"It sounds like you are thinking that I should tell you what that is, and in the playroom, you are in charge of making those decisions." (*makes a guess about underlying message, then direct and encouraging*)

Therapist whispers to the toy, "What are you?" (*indirect, whisper technique, using the child's metaphor*)

Therapist Wants to Help Child With Behaviors Without Being Asked

Example 1

Shannon (age 7) is jumping up to reach something on a high shelf.

"I know it is hard to reach that, and I bet you can think of a way you can get what you want." (*direct and encouraging*)

"That looks a bit frustrating, and you are continuing to try to get it." (*indirect, reflection of feeling*)

> Therapist says nothing but looks supportive. Therapist ponders where this pattern of wanting to do things for children that they can do for themselves originated. (*indirect, minimal encourager*)

Example 2

Demetrius (age 5) keeps on trying to fasten his shoes but is not experiencing success with this task.

> "You are determined to do that even though it is so hard. Shall we figure out a way we could work on it together?" (*indirect, reflection of feeling, then suggestion for collaboration*)

> "That seems really hard to do. I am thinking that we might work as a team to fasten those shoes. What should I do first?" (*suggestion for collaboration*)

> "I have confidence if you press really hard on the fastener you will get it to stick just the way you want it to stick." (*direct and encouraging*)

Example 3

Kamala (age 3) is trying to get the inflatable punching bag to stay down, but it keeps popping back up. She looks disgruntled about this.

> Therapist nods, looks empathic, and does not say anything. (*indirect, minimal encourager*)

> "Many of the kids who come here have trouble figuring out how to make it stay down. What if we work on it together and get it to work?" (*suggestion for collaboration*)

> "You look like you are feeling grumpy that the punching bag keeps popping up." (*indirect, reflection of feeling*)

Therapist Wants to Help Child With Decisions Without Being Asked

Example 1

Israel (age 6) looks around the playroom, obviously having difficulty deciding what to do, and says, "There's so much stuff."

> "There are a lot of things in here." (*indirect, restating content*)

> "Wow, it's pretty easy to feel overwhelmed with all the toys in here." (*indirect, reflecting feeling*)

"Hmmm . . ." (*indirect, minimal encourager*)

Example 2

Zyanya (age 8) is hard of hearing. He tells you he wants to figure out which instruments in the playroom are the quietest. Some of them are very quiet, so you wonder if he can actually hear each of them.

> "You look a little confused because you want to know which of the instruments is quietest, and some of them are so quiet you might not be able to hear them." (*indirect, reflection of feeling*)

> "You are trying each of the instruments, hoping you can figure out which one makes the quietest sound." (*indirect, tracking*)

> "Well . . . the quietest instrument . . ." (*indirect, minimal encourager*)

Practice Exercises

For each of the following 10 scenarios, (a) label the type of situation (e.g., child explicitly asking for help with decisions, therapist wants to help with decisions); (b) generate two ways of returning responsibility to the child; (c) identify the style of returning responsibility to the child (e.g., direct; direct and encouraging; indirect, reflecting feeling) for each response, and explain why you chose that particular style in this situation; and (d) describe some set of extenuating circumstances in which you would decide not to return responsibility to that child for that particular behavior.

1. Owen (age 6) is legally blind. He looks at the directions on a Shrinky Dinks arts and crafts package and says, "I can't read this."

2. Allena (age 6) asks, "Should I use red or green for this girl's dress?"

3. Colm (age 7) picks up a pair of scissors and says, "I don't think I am supposed to use this kind of grownup scissors."

4. Amadeus (age 5) says, "It is really hard to open this jar. Can you help me open it?"

5. Aabroo (age 9) tries to open the lid of a box, can't get it open, and sits down and begins to cry.

6. Patrick (age 8) looks at the therapist and says, "Am I allowed to cuss in here?"

7. Taiwo (age 3) picks up a tambourine and asks, "What does this thing do?"

8. Hunter (age 6) tries to get the lid off the sand tray and says, "This is just too hard for me to do by myself."

9. Charlotte (age 8) picks up a puppet and asks, "What do the other kids who come here use this for?"

10. Liron (age 9) says, "I'm bored. What is there to do in here?"

11. Thomasina (age 6) picks up a Bionicle toy and asks, "What do you do with this?"

12. Santiago (age 5) climbs up and stands on a stool, starts falling off, and yells, "Help me! I can't save myself!"

13. Fionuala (age 7) says, "I can't get the blocks to fit back in the box."

14. Saul (age 8) wants to know, "What do you do with this?" while holding out the dart gun.

15. Saul tries to shoot the dart gun, is not successful, and hands it to you, saying, "Why won't this work?"

16. Saul takes the dart gun back from you, saying, "Show me how to make it work."

17. Madelyn (age 9) brings a doll to you and asks, "What is the father supposed to do?"

18. Giovanni (age 6) picks up a dragon puppet and says, "This dragon can't decide whether to eat all the people who live in the castle."

19. Germaine (age 7) points to a horse with wings and asks, "What is this thing called? Can you make it fly for me?"

20. Rujita (age 6) is trying to comb her hair but becomes angry because there are so many snarls. She brings you a pair of scissors and says, "Will you cut out the snarls? That's what my real mom did when I lived with her."

21. Teague (age 8) asks, "How do you spell 'supercalifragilisticexpialidocious'?"

22. Belvedere (age 10) takes his hearing aid out of his ear and asks, "Can you fix this? It seems to be broken."

Questions to Ponder

1. Explain your understanding of the rationale for using the skill of returning responsibility to the child rather than doing things for children. Do you believe this can be helpful to children? Why or why not?

2. Based on your past experiences with children, your responses to the practice exercises, and your sample sessions with a child, which of the various ways of returning responsibility to the child will be most comfortable for you to use? Explain your reasoning.

3. Based on your past experiences with children, your responses to the practice exercises, and your sample sessions with a child, which of the various ways of returning responsibility to the child might be the most uncomfortable for you? Explain the factors that would contribute to your discomfort.

4. What are some situations in which you would not use the skill of returning the responsibility to the child? Why would this be the case in these situations?

5. Explain your thoughts on the optimal way to respond if a child asks you for help with behaviors or decisions in the playroom.

6. What are some situations in which you would feel a need to help a child with a behavior or a decision even though the child has not asked for help? What are your own personal issues connected to these situations?

7. How do you feel/what do you think about using encouraging statements such as "I bet you can figure that out for yourself" or "You really know a lot about fixing things. I believe that you can fix that without my help" as a part of the procedure of returning responsibility to the child?

8. How do you feel/what do you think about using minimal encouragers or silence to return responsibility to the child?

9. How do you feel/what do you think about using the whisper technique to return responsibility to the child?

10

Dealing with Questions

In play therapy, children will ask you questions. Having a strategy for dealing with these questions will help you be consistent in your relationship with the child. There are multiple options to respond to questions. The method depends partly on (a) the nature of the question, (b) your personal inclination, and (c) your theoretical orientation. Ultimately, your response to questions depends on a combination of these factors in the context of the play therapy session.

Nature of Children's Questions

Most questions that children ask in play therapy fit into one of four distinct categories: practical, personal, relationship, or the ongoing process of play therapy (Landreth, 2024; O'Connor, 2000). In deciding which strategy to use in answering a particular question, one important factor to consider is the type of question the child asks.

Practical Questions

Practical questions are those that ask for commonsense information. Although these questions can have an underlying hidden meaning, they are usually requests for simple data or feedback. Some examples of practical questions:

"What time is it?"

"What is this?" or "What do you do with this?"

"Can I go to the bathroom?"

"Where is my mother?"

"Where are the scissors?"

"Is today the day we get out of school early?"

"Can we play a game today?"

"Is this a snake or a dragon?"

"Can I hit the mirror with the hammer?"

"What do you do with this?"

Personal Questions

Children will sometimes ask personal questions about your situation or life. In our experience, when children ask personal questions, they usually need to increase their knowledge of our lives. They may do this because they feel exposed because we often know more about them than they know about us. They may ask personal questions because they want to enhance their feeling of connection with us or because they wish to explore our "credentials." Sometimes, their personal questions aim to check out a hunch about who we "really" are. Some examples of personal questions:

"Do you have any children?" or "Are you married?"

"Did you have to go to school to learn to play with kids?"

"How old are you?" or "Where do you live?"

"Why do you work with children?"

"What is your favorite color (or food)?"

"Why is your skin a different color than mine?"

"Why do you walk with a limp?"

Older children, or more "streetwise" younger ones, might ask questions too personal to shock you or gain a sense of power over you (Kottman & Meany-Walen, 2016; O'Connor, 2000). Other children who have poor boundaries or have experienced sexual abuse may believe that this type of question is acceptable social interaction. Some examples of inappropriate personal questions:

"Do you like sex?" or "Do you and your spouse 'do it'?"

"What do you wear to bed?"

"What kind of person do you think is cute?"

"Would you like to touch my privates?" or "Would you like it if I touched your privates?"

"Do you think I am growing pubic hair yet?"

Relationship Questions

With relationship questions, children ask about the therapeutic relationship and their personal relationship with you. By asking relationship questions, children are probing to find out how you feel about them. They may distinguish between your personal feelings and your professional perspective. Children want you to "really" care about them rather than care about them because it's your job. The purpose of this type of query may be to determine the strength of the relationship. Getting this information could help children avoid making an emotional commitment disproportionate to your emotional commitment (Kottman & Meany-Walen, 2016). Relationship questions usually have two different messages: an obvious, literal question and an underlying hidden, or "underneath," question. For instance, in the question "Who else comes here?" the obvious, literal question is a request for the names of other clients (which you cannot ethically share), and the underlying hidden question is "Are there other children that you care for as much as you care for me?" Examples of relationship questions include:

"Do you like me?" or "Am I your favorite kid?"

"How many other children come here?"

"Did you notice that I don't have arms like other kids?"

"Do you like Asian people?"

"If you could, would you want to adopt me?"

"Do you miss me when I'm not here?"

"Have you noticed that both of us wear glasses?"

Ongoing-Process Questions

Landreth (2024) listed questions children frequently ask in play therapy. Many of these questions seem to focus on the therapy's ongoing process. In these questions, children seem to be expressing curiosity about how play therapy works and the boundaries of the relationship between you, the play therapist, and them (Kottman & Meany-Walen, 2016). The goal of these questions is often soliciting your help or exploring the rules in the playroom. Sometimes, ongoing process questions are attempts by children to get you to read their minds or make decisions for them. Again, in many cases, there is an obvious, factual question (e.g., "Can I shoot the dart gun at you?") and a more subtle subtext (e.g., "What are the rules in here?" or "Will you let me do something to hurt you?"). Other examples of ongoing process questions include:

"Would you like it better if I draw a house instead of a person?"

"Can I throw this ball in your face?"

"How long do we have to stay in here?"

"How come you always talk about my feelings?"

"Why don't you ever answer my questions?"

"Don't you know how to play pitch and catch?"

"Will you tie my shoes?"

"When is my mom going to come and get me?"

"What do you tell my dad about what we do in here?"

Dual-Category Questions

The categories of questions presented here are not exclusive of each other. A question that seems to be a superficial practical question may also have a more subtle subtext that is really a relationship question or one about the ongoing play therapy process. For example, when Maryam asks, "Do any other kids who come here go to my school?" she may be asking a straightforward question about whether there is anyone in her school with whom she could get a ride to the clinic. She could also be asking a relationship question because she feels threatened by the possibility that you have warm feelings about other children she might know.

If a particular question fits into more than one category, it could be that the child is aware of both aspects of the question and intentionally asks a dual-purpose question. However, this would be too sophisticated for most young children. Usually, when a question is double-edged, the child is focused on the literal meaning of the question, and the more hidden meaning is out of their awareness. When you make a guess about the underlying meaning, the child often has a *recognition reflex*, an involuntary response acknowledging the accuracy of the guess and registering a new awareness on the child's part. As a play therapist, you should watch for those responses (Kottman & Meany-Walen, 2016).

Types of Responses

Although there are innumerable ways to respond to children's questions in play therapy, most possibilities will fit into one of eight categories. You can (a) answer the question, (b) ignore the question, (c) give a minimal encourager for an answer, (d) restate the question, (e) make a guess about the purpose of the question, (f) return the responsibility to the child, (g) reply to the question with another question, or (h) politely decline to answer the question. For each of these choices, we will explain the mechanics of the method, describe the kinds of questions for which such a reply would be appropriate, explore which theoretical approaches would use such a response, and (when possible) provide several examples.

Answering the Question

Sometimes the most sensible strategy for dealing with children's questions in therapy is to simply answer them, especially those you interpret as straightforward requests for information. This is particularly the case with practical questions with no underlying meaning and personal questions designed to gain reassurance by obtaining more information about who you are. For many play therapists, this is the usual method of dealing with questions seeking factual information, although some child-centered play therapists might initially reflect the content of the question and only answer if the child persists in asking (R. VanFleet, personal communication, September 10, 2021). In psychodynamic play therapy, therapists are unlikely to answer personal questions because they believe doing so would interfere with clients' transference experience (T. Tisdell, personal communication, June 15, 2023).

If you decide to answer questions, you should keep your replies as brief and straightforward as the queries, conveying simple information such as time, dates, directions, etc. Often, the most factual answer is "I don't know." Getting comfortable responding this way is helpful when you don't know the answer.

Some relationship questions warrant answers, but you may want to get more creative than with simple informational queries. With questions such as "Do you like me?" or "Can I be your kid someday?" or "Am I your favorite kid?", your answers should convey a sense of caring without necessarily giving a factual answer to the child. General responses that provide reassurance and caring tend to be more appropriate with questions for which the "real" answer could be either hurtful to the child or therapeutically contraindicated. The following responses are examples of general answers that provide reassurance and caring:

> "I care about all of the children who come to play with me here."
> "I think kids are the greatest people in the world."
> "I care about you a great deal."
> "You are a very special person."
> "You are a really important person to me."

With these questions, sometimes the best answer combines a guess about the purpose or an interpretation of the meaning of the query with a general caring response that conveys acceptance and understanding. Most nondirective play therapists would feel uncomfortable making a guess about the purpose of the question because it could be construed as leading the child. More directive play therapists (especially Adlerians) might find that making a guess about the purpose of the question is a valuable strategy for responding to difficult questions.

Some several examples of combining a guess about the purpose, meaning, or motivation of the child's question with a general reassuring answer:

Example 1

Brooklyn (age 6) asks, "Am I your favorite kid who comes here to play?"

> "You sound like you want to know if I like you. I care about you a lot."
> "I'm thinking perhaps you are worried about whether I like the other kids I see in here better than I like you. To me, you are a very special person."
> "It seems as if you may be a little jealous of the other children I work with. I really like playing with you."

Example 2

Mason (age 5) asks, "Would you like me to be your son?"

> "It seems like you really want me to feel close to you. You are important to me."
> "It sounds like maybe you would like to be my son. Even though you can't really be my little boy, I feel very close to you."

Example 3

Jiao (age 7) asks, "Will you remember me when I don't come here anymore?"

> "You seem worried that I might forget what a wonderful and special person you are. I will never forget that."

> "Might it be that you are afraid that you won't always have a place in my heart? You will always have a place there even after you stop coming to play therapy."

Ignoring the Question

In some cases, you might choose to ignore a child's question to encourage them to discover or determine an answer on their own. This response can work with any of the question categories, although it is probably more appropriate with practical and ongoing process questions because those are most likely intended to engage you in solving a child's problems for them. This response style is appropriate no matter what your theoretical orientation is. Although some children cannot tolerate you not answering their questions, they might keep asking to try and force you to answer.

When choosing to ignore a question, it is important not to ignore the child. You should make eye contact and smile in a caring way, nonverbally conveying confidence that the child can answer the question for themselves without your assistance.

Using Minimal Encouragers

Minimal encouragers are counseling responses designed to convey interest and understanding to the client in as few words as possible. This can be challenging if you tend to be a talkative person. Minimal encouragers include simple responses such as "Uh-huh," "I see," "Yes," "Well," and "Hmmm . . ." Another method of minimally encouraging the client is to repeat one or two words of the client's sentence or question (e.g., The child asks, "What color should I paint this picture?" and you reply, "What color?"). You can also smile and nod at the child. In instances when you choose not to reply to the child's question, eye contact and a listening posture are essential to convey to the child that you are attending to what is happening in the playroom.

It is usually appropriate in play therapy for you to avoid answering questions the child could answer without assistance. Using minimal encouragers is one method for communicating to the child that you are paying attention to what they are asking without answering the question. This technique is essentially a stalling tactic, whereby you hope the child will answer the question in the interval the minimal encourager provides. It works with all four types of questions but is probably most appropriate with practical questions and questions about the ongoing process—two categories that often involve the child asking questions they can answer without your input. Although nondirective play therapists are more likely than directive play therapists to use this strategy, all play therapists can comfortably use minimal encouragers and remain theoretically consistent.

Restating the Question

Restating the question is a response style that uses a reply as a verbal mirror for the child's question. The purpose is to return the initiative to the client, so they must then consider whether to ask the question again, find their own answer, or decide that the answer is not worth pursuing. Sometimes, repeating the gist of the question to the child also helps clarify the purpose or intent of their question. This strategy is appropriate for all four types of questions and is used most often in a nondirective approach.

When you restate the question, it can be presented as a statement or question, depending on the intonation of your delivery and the words you choose. When you want to make the restatement into a question, you would usually use the same words as if it were a statement but add a rising inflection at the end of the sentence to make it a question rather than a statement. Conversely, if you want to make it into a statement, use a lowering inflection at the end.

If you decide to restate a question as a statement, simply tell the child what the child was asking. You might paraphrase the question or use the child's exact words to best convey the meaning of the question. Examples of restating the question as a statement include the following:

> *Avery* (age 8): "What time is it?"
> *Therapist*: "You want to know what time it is."
>
> *Hercules* (age 6): "Do you have any children?"
> *Therapist*: "You are curious about whether I have any children."
>
> *Shannon* (age 5): "Do you like me?"
> *Therapist*: "You want to know how I feel about you."
>
> *Reginald* (age 7): "Do you like Black people like me?"

Therapist: "You want me to tell you how I feel about Black people, like you and your family."

If you decide to restate a question using a question, you can repeat the original question, changing only those words necessary to have the sentence make sense or to paraphrase the original question. Because many nondirective play therapists prefer to avoid asking questions, they may choose not to use this formulation to restate the question. The following are some examples of restating a question as a question:

Violet (age 8): "When is our time up?"
Therapist: "When is our time over?" or "What time will our time together be over today?"

Julian (age 6): "Do you have a little boy?"
Therapist: "Do I have a son?"

Olive (age 5): "Do you think I am special?"
Therapist: "Do I think you are a special kid?" or "Do I care about you?"

Wil (age 7): "Should I paint this wooden car?"
Therapist: "Should you paint the wooden vehicle?"

There are some questions, especially those about race, culture, or ethnicity, that should not be answered using this strategy. If a child asks, "Do you like trans people?" or "Do you think Black people matter?" it would be culturally insensitive to restate with a question. The child could easily interpret such an answer as conveying a lack of acceptance of their cultural background.

Guessing About Purpose/Interpreting

In some of the more directive approaches to play therapy, including Adlerian and ecosystemic, the therapist will make a guess about the purpose of the question, interpret the meaning of the question, or interpret the reason the child asked the question (Kottman & Meany-Walen, 2016, 2018; O'Connor, 2000). This process helps clarify the child's intention and assists the child in gaining an awareness of any underlying message communicated by the question. To avoid imposing your meaning onto the child's question, you might choose to deliver such responses as tentative hypotheses. This technique allows the child to give feedback about the accuracy and relevancy of your guess. Because the child may not provide that feedback in verbal form, you must closely observe their behavior and play during and after you share the hypothesis. It is also important not to get so attached to your hypothesis that you miss the child's reaction to it.

Although this strategy can be effective with practical questions with multiple interpretations, it can be even more helpful with questions about your personal life, the relationship between you and the child, and the ongoing therapeutic process. This is because of the dual nature of these three types of questions, with their frequent double messages. Making guesses helps children examine possible underlying meanings. The guess should reflect your best understanding of the message conveyed by the child's nonverbal communication and by the verbal component. It should also reflect any other information or behavior patterns you have observed in the child throughout the therapy process. Rather than coming "out of the clear blue sky," guesses should grow naturally out of what you have learned about the child in the ongoing relationship and from interactions with parents, teachers, siblings, and other sources of information about the child and their life.

Because interpreting goals and meaning depends on your theoretical perspective, the hypotheses generated by you will reflect your views about people and their motivations. The depth of interpretations will also depend on the stage of therapy, the particular child and their developmental level, and whether the interpretations are concrete or abstract, direct or indirect.

The following are examples of making guesses about the purpose of a question, interpreting the meaning of a question, or interpreting why the child asked a question:

Example 1

Chwen-Lan (age 8) asks, "What is this?"

> "You seem to think there is just one answer to what that is."
>
> "I am thinking that sometimes you are kind of nervous about making decisions for yourself."
>
> "It seems like sometimes you would like me to take care of you and tell you what things are."

Example 2

Mario (age 6) asks, "Can we play Cobra Paw today?"

> "You sound like you might have already figured out what you want to do today."

"I'm guessing you would like to decide what we are going to do in here today."

"It seems like you're wondering if I would be willing to play with you this morning."

"I know you like Cobra Paw because you are so fast at it, and I am not. I am guessing you're in the mood to win at a game today."

Example 3

Dolly (age 7) asks, "Where do you live?"

"You seem to be very curious about me and what happens in my life."

"I'm thinking you would like to know more about me."

"It seems as if you are feeling a little uncomfortable with me knowing more about you than you know about me."

Example 4

Dawud (age 5) asks, "What do you think I am going to do now?"

"You seem as though you wish I would make a guess about your plans."

"I am wondering whether you feel powerful knowing something that I don't know."

"It's almost as if you want me to tell you what to do next so you can tell me that you don't have to do what I want you to do."

Returning Responsibility to the Child

One method of handling questions is to return the responsibility back to the child (see Chapter 9). You would usually do this with practical questions asking for specific information about toys, game procedures, or playroom rules. You would also do this with questions about the ongoing process that ask you to take care of or make decisions for the child. This response style would be appropriate for both nondirective and directive play therapists, although there are some formats for stating the return (e.g., encouraging comments) that might better suit more directive therapists, such as Adlerians, who tend to make encouraging comments than it would nondirective therapists, who try to avoid leading the child. The following are examples of returning the responsibility to the child:

"You can decide that for yourself."

"I bet you can figure that out."

"In here, it can be whatever you want it to be."

"You are the only one who can know what you are going to do next."

Answering With a Question

You might sometimes choose to answer a question with another question. This could be done directly if you wanted to (a) gather more information about the topic addressed in the original question (e.g., "What did you want to use to hit the mirror?"), (b) clarify what the child is asking (e.g., "So you're asking if you can jump from the top of the pillows onto what?"), or (c) explore the purpose or underlying message of the question (e.g., "Do you really want to know if I like girls better than boys, or do you want to know if I like you or your brother better?").

This response style could work with any of the different types of questions, depending on the content and context of the query and your theoretical orientation. Nondirective play therapists do not usually ask questions in their interactions with children because they believe that asking questions increases the potential for leading the child. Therefore, those who adhere to these theoretical orientations would be less likely to use this response style than those who are more directive and willing to lead the client.

Another strategy for answering a question with a question would be to use the whisper technique (see Chapter 9). In this instance, when the child asks a question, you use a whisper voice to ask, "What should I say?" to get the child to dictate the contents and direction of the response. The whisper technique works best with practical questions and ongoing process questions. Using this strategy with personal or relationship questions would be awkward because they require actual input from you. Both nondirective and more directive play therapists can feel comfortable using the whisper technique originated by Landreth (2024). This technique gives control to the child. If you were a more directive therapist who wanted to share the control of the session, you could alternate using the whisper technique with other response styles.

Declining to Answer

You should decline to answer some questions, such as personal questions, that violate socially appropriate boundaries or are inappropriate in some other way. Examples of this type of question would be, "Why did you have to adopt your son? Can't you have kids?" "Do you like thong underwear?"

"How often do you have sex with your husband?" This refusal would usually be stated with a response such as, "I choose not to answer that question," "I don't answer private questions like that," or "That is private and isn't for discussing with other people." When you set a limit by declining to answer, you should avoid sounding judgmental about the question. Because this type of question can evoke a strong emotional reaction, you must remember to state your choosing not to answer the question without any disapproving nonverbal communication.

How and when you use this type of reply probably depends more on your personal preference and your desire to set appropriate boundaries than on your theoretical orientation. This response style would be appropriate across all of the approaches to play therapy.

Asking Questions

Some play therapists feel comfortable asking children questions during play therapy sessions, and others do not. This comfort level depends on your theoretical orientation and your personal style. For more directive play therapists (e.g., Adlerian, cognitive-behavioral, ecosystemic), asking questions is often used as a part of building relationships and exploring children's interpersonal and intrapersonal dynamics (Knell, 2016; Kottman & Meaning Walen, 2016, 2018; O'Connor, 2016). If you choose to ask questions, they should flow naturally from the conversation with the child or from the child's play and should be developmentally appropriate. You can ask the questions directly (e.g., "How does your family handle conflict?") or indirectly through a metaphor with children who prefer to communicate symbolically (e.g., "What happens in the alligator family when they get mad at one another?"). Remember, if you use the child's metaphor, you can also ask the toys questions (e.g., "Mr. Rabbit, what is scaring you right now?"). Most more nondirective play therapists (e.g., child-centered, Jungian, psychodynamic) choose not to ask questions because they can be a form of leading the client, which violates the basic principles of most nondirective approaches to play therapy.

In terms of personal style, are you a very curious person or a not-so-curious person? We are both super nosy, so we have a natural inclination to ask a lot of questions. This style can be intrusive to children, so it is helpful to recognize that asking a few well-considered questions is much more effective than asking a plethora of questions.

If you decide to ask questions in your sessions, you might want to be intentional with the kinds of questions you ask and focus on asking questions that will help with (a) your conceptualization of the child and (b) moving the child forward in the relationship or in understanding self and/or others. You will likely get more information from open-ended questions than closed-ended ones, which tend to yield "yes" or "no" answers. Questions that begin with how, what, when, and where work better than questions that ask the child "why" because often children have no idea why they did things, and these questions might sound accusatory.

The other important thing to remember is that the child should have control over whether they choose to answer your questions. Unlike many of the child's other relationships with adults, like teachers and parents/caregivers, in play therapy, the child gets to decide whether to give a verbal answer to questions. You will want to be careful not to show any kind of emotional reaction to the child simply ignoring the question. For many play therapists, this is difficult because they often have a countertransference reaction to being ignored. It is important to manage any emotional reaction you have when a child chooses not to answer your question. Even when a child does not give you a verbal answer, they will often convey information related to the question through nonverbal communication or the play. You can use three common types of responses when a child doesn't verbally answer your question. You can just let it go, you can make a here-and-now comment about the child deciding not to answer you (e.g., "You decided not to answer that question."), or you can make an interpretive comment about the child's purpose in not answering the question verbally. Among the multitude of purposes the child may have in ignoring your questions are (a) the question may address a sensitive area that the child is not yet ready to explore with you, (b) the child wants to demonstrate that you do not have the power to force an answer, or (c) the child has learned that ignoring adults is a reliable way of getting them to continue to engage.

Practice Exercises

For each of the following questions, decide which type of question it is. If there is an underlying hidden message, explain your interpretation of that message and describe how you arrived at this interpretation. Then, decide on several possible appropriate responses and explain how those responses would be helpful to the child.

1. Jolene (age 7), in her first session, timidly asks, "What should we do first?"

2. Abell (age 9), who is usually very shy, comes into the playroom and asks, "Do you think I am a good friend?"

3. Faith (age 4) likes to control the sessions in various ways. In the sixth session, she introduces the idea that you should play a guessing game with her. She asks, "Do you know what I am thinking?"

4. Ming (age 5) picks up a cell phone and says, "Why doesn't this really work?"

5. Sharee (age 8) likes to play with the dolls and uses them to talk for her. She picks up the little girl doll and the mother doll. She turns the mother doll toward you and asks, "Do you think my daughter, little Sherelle, has been bad again today? Should I give little Sherelle a spanking?"

6. In his tenth session, Cash (age 9), who plays exclusively with the inflatable punching bag, looks around the playroom and says, "What did you do with the punching bag? Don't you know it is my favorite thing to do in here?" Would you answer differently if you had removed the inflatable punching bag to encourage Cash to use some of the other toys than if the inflatable punching bag was broken?

7. Freya (age 6) is sitting in the corner looking sad, bored, and miserable. Although she is usually quite excited about coming to play therapy, she says, "Why do I have to keep coming here week after week?"

8. Riley (age 10), in his first session, says, "What are your credentials? Do you actually play with kids for a living?"

9. Aria (age 7) is stacking blocks and knocking them down. She does this for at least 30 minutes of every session. Her presenting problem is that she tends to be maladaptively perfectionistic. She asks, "What will happen if I accidentally knock down the stack?"

10. Elijah (age 5) makes very strong eye contact and asks, "How are you going to stop me from dumping this sand on the floor?"

11. Nora (age 7) brings into the playroom a list of 29 things she wants to do today. She immediately asks, "How many more minutes do we have left for today?"

12. Yasha (age 6) knows his mother is having a new baby in a month, her tenth child. He asks, "Are you going to have a baby soon?"

13. Isla (age 9) likes the doctor kit more than anything in the playroom. At the end of her third session, after repeatedly telling you

how much she likes playing with the doctor kit, she asks, "Do you like sharing your toys?"

14. Raul (age 7) has a father who is Latino and a mother who is Asian. When he comes to your office, he asks, "How do I know whether I am Mexican or Chinese? How am I supposed to fit in at school?"

15. Darcy (age 6), in her second session, asks, "Why do you always tell me what I am saying and tell me what I am doing? Don't you have any of your own thoughts?"

For each of the following situations, decide whether it might be appropriate to ask a question and explain your rationale for making that decision. If you think it would be helpful to ask a question, write two questions you might want to ask to help build the relationship with a child, help them better understand themselves, or get a clearer picture of a situation or relationship.

1. Harley (age 9) enters the playroom for his fourth session, looks around, and seems at a loss for what to do first.

2. Gentry (age 4) says, "This dolly is like my mama."

3. Saleem (age 6) says, "My dad likes my sister better than me."

4. Gretta (age 7) picks up the dog puppet, puts it very close to your face, and growls.

5. August (age 10) takes his prosthetic arm off, puts it on the table, and looks expectantly at you.

6. Glenna (age 4) comes into her session crying and wanting to sit on your lap.

7. Graham (age 10) walks into the playroom and says, "Nobody will play with me. They say I am too hyper."

8. Cong (age 8) says, "None of the toys in here are any fun at all. Why don't you have any fun toys?"

9. Kwamin (age 5) has his back to you and seems to be burying a tiger figure in the sand.

10. Aracely (age 6) wants to put the puppet theatre up, and she seems to be having trouble getting it to stay up without falling on its side.

For each of the following situations, label the therapist's question as either appropriate or inappropriate. If you don't think it was an appropriate intervention, what could you have done instead of asking that question? If you do think it was appropriate, what would you do if you asked the child this question and they chose not to answer you?

1. Pip (age 9) puts the board game away with 20 minutes left in the session. He stands in the middle of the playroom, looking around for something else to do. You ask, "What would you like to do next?"

2. Yeiri (age 6) is playing with the fairy figure, putting it on the top of the shelf, knocking it off, and screaming as it plummets to the ground. You ask, "Little Fairy, what could you do to keep yourself safe?"

3. Arlo (age 4) is playing in the dollhouse with the family figures. The mother figure keeps yelling at the father figure. You ask, "What do you think the mother is so mad about?"

4. Cora (age 8) says, "I don't like being an only child." You ask, "What don't you like about being an only child?"

5. Deion (age 5) is getting ready to climb onto a chair. He has already arranged several big pillows at the foot of the chair and seems to intend to jump from the chair to the pillows. You ask, "What is your plan to keep yourself safe?"

6. Bionca (age 7) arranges the tiger family from biggest to smallest, looks at you, and has the smallest tiger jump on the biggest one and knock it over. She smiles. You ask, "Little one, how did you feel when you jumped on the biggest one?"

7. Jack (age 10) is dancing to some music in his head. You ask, "What are you listening to?"

8. Meaghan (age 6) says, "My mom is going to have a baby." She takes the baby doll and gives it a hug, opens the door of the playroom, and throws it into the hallway. You ask, "What happened to the baby doll?"

Questions to Ponder

1. Will knowing what kind of question the child asks (personal, relationship, ongoing process, or informational) help you formulate your response? Explain.

2. Which category of question will personally give you the most trouble? Explain why that type of question might be difficult for you.

3. How will you handle inappropriate personal questions?

4. What kind of personal questions do you anticipate will evoke a strong emotional reaction from you? Explain where that reaction might originate for you.

5. Which method of dealing with questions will be the most comfortable for you? Explain your reasoning.

6. Which method of dealing with questions will be the least comfortable for you? Explain your reasoning.

7. What will your strategy be for dealing with relationship questions in which the underlying message seems to reveal the child's need for your attention and approval? Explain your reasoning.

8. How do you feel about asking children questions in therapy? What kinds of questions do you think are permissible to ask the child in play therapy? Explain.

9. How will you decide whether to ask a child a question?

10. What will your reaction be if a child ignores your question? How will you handle it if the child chooses to ignore your question?

11. How do you feel about the idea of avoiding "why" questions in the playroom?

12. What is your stance on the therapist taking the lead in play therapy? Explain your reasoning.

Integration of Basic Skills
The Art of Play Therapy

So far, we have presented each of the basic play therapy skills in isolation. This is the simplest way to teach the how-tos or "science" of play therapy. The primary drawback of this method is that it misses the "art" of play therapy. The art of play therapy consists of (a) the process of deciding when to use a skill with a particular child, (b) the integration of several skills to create a mélange that works more efficaciously and smoothly than would an isolated skill, and (c) the melding of the therapist's personality and interactional style with the play therapy skills. In this chapter, we will explore these issues.

Deciding When to Use a Skill

Choosing the appropriate skills to optimize the chances for a successful outcome in play therapy is essential, but it is not a simple task. The process of selecting which skill to use in a particular situation is multifaceted. It depends on the therapist's theoretical orientation, their intuition and experience, their personal preferences and personality, the individual child, the child's life context, the course of the play, the phase of the therapy, and any number of other factors.

Unfortunately, there is no way to order or assign weight to these factors—remember, this is the art aspect of play therapy, and art is not quantifiable. The key to selecting the "correct" skill is recognizing there is no correct skill. Almost any of the play therapy skills will work in most situations in the playroom. There is no magical formula for deciding which one to use in any particular moment, so you should not strain to generate the perfect skill for each and every situation.

What you must do is trust in the process of play therapy, in yourself, and in the children—they will be your best teachers. You need to believe that the play therapy process will flow in a way that is helpful to children. You need to believe that there is little you can do in the playroom that will do permanent damage to a child. You need to believe that children will show you what you need to know to help them and that they will let you know when you make a mistake. Children will almost always give you grace, even if you mess something up. Having made that disclaimer, we want to explain how each of these facets can affect the selection of skills.

Theoretical Orientation

Each theoretical orientation provides a certain degree of guidance about when and how to use specific skills. As you study play therapy, you should begin to narrow the field of possible approaches to play therapy and focus your investigations on the theoretical orientations that most interest you. To learn the specifics, you will need to read books, book chapters, and journal articles devoted to those particular theories (see Appendix A for recommendations). For most nondirective play therapists (e.g., child-centered, experiential play therapy, Jungian analytical, object relations/attachment-based, psychoanalytic), the primary skills you will use are tracking, restating content, reflecting feelings, returning responsibility to the client, and limiting. For practitioners of these approaches, the primary focus in using these skills is fostering the therapeutic relationship with the client. Most more directive play therapists (e.g., Adlerian, cognitive-behavioral, ecosystemic, family, Gestalt) use the same skills nondirective play therapists use. In addition, they often ask questions, answer questions, design therapeutic metaphors, role play, model, metacommunicate, and interpret. In Theraplay, many of these skills are not used because it has its own protocols for interacting with clients. If you are considering doing prescriptive or integrative play therapy, you will need to know a great deal about many different theories to have a broad range of possible interventions from which to choose (Gil et al., 2015; Kaduson et al., 2020; Schaefer & Drewes, 2016).

Intuition and Experience

Many times, the decision to use a particular skill stems from the therapist's intuition about what will work best at that moment with a particular child. The therapist's intuition may be due to their ability to recognize almost undetectable nonverbal cues from the child; it may be related to the therapist's ability to put together clues about the child's attitudes, feelings, thoughts, and perceptions to form patterns of insight; or it may be linked to myriad other factors.

Making this decision requires you to hone your intuition and learn to listen to it—intuition can be an excellent guide in deciding when and how to apply the available skills in play therapy. It can help you choose (a) when to track, restate content, or reflect a feeling; (b) whether to track the child or the play object; (c) which feeling to reflect; (d) whether to help a child or to return the responsibility to the child; (e) when to use a skill in isolation and when to combine several skills for an integrated intervention; and (f) when to modify a skill or technique based on whatever you expect to work best with a specific child.

Experience can also be helpful in this process. By observing and remembering how various children react to a specific intervention, you will begin to form general guidelines for when particular skills will and will not work. From experience, you will learn that some skills work wonderfully with certain types of children while others do not. You will learn how to time your various interventions for optimal effect and what feels best for you in terms of the proportion of skills used in each phase of play therapy.

Experience can also guide you in deciding how each skill will work best for you. From past interactions with children, you will discover that some applications of the various skills do not seem to work for you. Although you may have observed other play therapists successfully using these skills, you might still not feel comfortable or confident using them. For instance, we have trouble setting limits with *passive voice,* the use of limiting phrases like, "I am not for shooting..." or "Sand is not for throwing on the floor..." (Landreth, 2002). Although children almost always abide by the limits we set when we use other styles, we have noticed they tend to ignore us when we use Landreth's passive voice to limit. We have seen it work very well for many other therapists, and we realize that it is a valuable skill—for other play therapists.

Personal Preference and Personality

Therapists' personalities and ways of being in the world will also significantly impact their application of the various play therapy skills. These factors tend to influence the interventions they use and how they use them. For instance, therapists who are uncomfortable with feelings seldom reflect feelings—they may instead concentrate on tracking and restating content and ignore opportunities for reflecting emotions. Therapists who are given to caretaking others often have difficulty returning responsibility to children—they usually prefer to do things for them rather than watch them struggle with decisions and behaviors. Therapists who are disposed to be loquacious tend to choose the most long-winded method of presenting a particular intervention, and those who favor complexity over simplicity frequently choose the most complicated method of applying a skill.

It is appropriate and acceptable for your personal preferences, personality, beliefs, attitudes, culture, and experiences to influence your therapeutic process as long as this does not cloud your clinical judgment or prevent you from offering the best care for your clients. Because the interaction between how you counsel and who you are is inevitable, it is imperative for you to know yourself well enough that you can monitor your use of skills, strategies, and techniques—do not let your own issues determine what you do and how you do it to the detriment of your clients.

Attitudes and Beliefs About Cultural Differences

You will need to examine your own conscious and unconscious attitudes and beliefs about cultural differences as they may impact how you work with clients (Gil & Drewes, 2021; Ray et al., 2022b). By reflecting on your own prejudices and beliefs, you can cultivate cultural humility and grow your ability to be culturally sensitive and responsive to a diverse population of children and families. Hook et al. (2017) posited that there are two different aspects of cultural humility: intrapersonal and interpersonal. *Intrapersonal dynamics* involve your awareness of your own personal cultural identities and background and their influence on your ability to be honest when evaluating your reactions to your clients. Your *interpersonal dynamics* include curiosity and openness to others and a willingness to adapt your application of skills, strategies, and techniques in the playroom to the beliefs and values of clients who might be different than you. Ray et al. (2022a) suggested that "Through cultural humility, the play therapist honors the reality that there are a multiplicity of truths and experiences based on a person's identities, background, and experiences" (p. 15). Play therapists should consider those different truths and experiences when making decisions about actions and interactions in the playroom.

To fully step into a *multicultural orientation,* in addition to embracing cultural humility, you will need to explore cultural opportunities and cultural comfort (Ogawa et al., 2022; Owen et al., 2016). "Cultural opportunities are the moments during a counseling session where there is an opening to directly attend to clients' cultural identities" (Ogawa et al., 2022, p. 29). In play therapy, cultural opportunities present themselves through (a) symbolic or pretend play, (b) children's stories about their lives, (c) children's reactions to the therapist's race, ethnicity, or other cultural identity, and (d) repetitive themes in children's play. Ogawa et al. (2022) proposed that it is essential for play therapists to "be aware of and capture cultural opportunities in play therapy by responding to them therapeutically, even in those instances when they are presented briefly or subtly" (p. 30). Your ability to respond to cultural opportunities in a thoughtful, culturally sensitive, and culturally responsive way will depend on your willingness to engage in ongoing self-exploration and your desire to capitalize on cultural opportunities. It will also depend on your *cultural comfort,* defined as "the feelings that arise before, during, and after culturally relevant conversations in session between the therapist and the client" (Hook et al., 2017, p. 28). By cultivating ease, openness, calm, and relaxation about your ability to "engage with clients' various cultural identities in an open, fluid, relaxed, and connected way" (Ogawa et al., 2022, p. 37), play therapists can capitalize on cultural opportunities.

The Individual Child

The personal preferences and personalities of the children with whom you work will also affect the process of play therapy. Children may react better to some skills than others. This is also true for the various methods of applying each of the skills. For instance, some children simply hate it when you reflect feelings, and they reject any attempt to discuss emotions in a session. You will have several options with these children: You can avoid feeling reflections with them, decide that reflections are exactly what they need and increase the number of reflections you make in each session, or gradually phase in more reflections of feelings over a period of time so they can learn to cope with having feelings bandied about the room. Innumerable factors will influence your decisions to adopt play therapy with individual children. These include your knowledge of child development and child psychopathology, your understanding of theory, your intuition and experience with children who have acted in similar fashions, your knowledge of different cultures and your ability to provide culturally sensitive and responsive responses, your ability to capitalize on cultural opportunities, and the interaction of your personality with the child's personality.

It is essential to focus on the individual child in your play therapy sessions and to remember that play *is* communication. The child will let you know which skills are effective and helpful and which are not—partly through verbal feedback and nonverbal reactions to the various interventions but mostly through the play. Your main job is to truly listen, observe patterns, and be willing to adjust your interaction with the child and your choices of specific strategies to accommodate what works with them.

Context of the Child's Life

The context of the child's life is another factor in deciding which skills and techniques to use in a session. When choosing intervention strategies, you will need to consider the child's cultural and ethnic background, along with current and recent events in the child's life. This is important because the child's reactions, feelings, attitudes, thoughts, and behaviors will vary depending on their situation and cultural background. You will also need to consider the interactional patterns that occur in the child's family to avoid duplicating any dysfunctional patterns in your relationship with the child. The presenting problem may also impact the child's attitudes and interactional patterns in sessions, and you may need to adjust your interventions accordingly. The culture of the child and their family should be one of the factors you consider when making decisions about your interactions with your clients in play therapy sessions.

You will need to keep informed of the circumstances of each child's life. This will allow you to adjust intervention styles as needed for situations that might result in the child behaving in a new or unusual manner in the playroom. This might include a death in the family, a birthday, a failing report card, a special holiday, a lost pet, or a similar event. For example, a child whose grandparent recently died may need more reflections of feelings than other children (Coenen, 2020; Steele, 2015). A child who has had a traumatic experience, like witnessing parental violence or being in a car wreck, may need to be more in control of the interactions in the playroom than a child who has never experienced trauma (Goodyear-Brown, 2022; Myers, 2016). A child whose parent has recently been deployed by the military may need more nurturing, which might preclude returning responsibility to them (Herzog et al., 2015; Umhoefer et al., 2015).

Some presenting problems influence the therapist's choice of or application of skills in sessions. The therapist's knowledge of the various aspects of specific diagnoses, developmental crises, relationship difficulties, and other reasons for coming to play therapy will help to individualize intervention strategies (Gil et al., 2015; Kaduson et al., 2020; Kottman & Meany-Walen, 2018; Schaefer & Drewes, 2016).

An example of this type of adaptation would be play therapy with children with attention-deficit/hyperactivity disorder (ADHD) who need more structure (Grant, 2017b; Kaduson, 2015). In a playroom, this involves setting limits early and often. Because children with ADHD tend not to generalize cause-and-effect relationships, you might decide to explain the consequences for violations of limits at the same time you set the limits, even if you would not normally do so. Most children with ADHD do not read nonverbal cues well, and they tend not to notice or heed indirect or subtle feedback, so you would probably use direct rather than indirect formulations for your interventions. To avoid overwhelming them with input, you would probably not want to link several different skills.

Children's cultural identities will also have an essential role in helping you decide how and when to use specific skills in your play therapy (Gil & Drewes, 2021; Gil & Pfeifer, 2016; Post & Tillman, 2015; Ray et al., 2022b). However, one example might be when working with gender-expansive children. In such cases, it will convey respect for them if you inquire about their pronouns and share yours with them. It will also help you to be aware of tendencies you might have based on the gender assigned at birth to your clients. You will want to reflect feelings equally with children assigned female at birth and children assigned male at birth rather than reflecting more feelings with those assigned female than male (Jayne & Wehmeier, 2022). As another example, when working with children who have physical disabilities, you may be tempted to do things for them they can do for themselves. With such children, it may be even more important than it is with nondisabled children to return responsibility to them when they are capable of doing things. It is also useful to engage with children who are neurodiverse in ways that echo their sensory preferences by mirroring their movement, behavior, or communication style (Swan & Schottelkorb, 2022). Many clients who are Black, Indigenous, and people of color (BIPOC) have experienced prejudice, racism, and microaggressions and may have developed low self-esteem. You may be able to capitalize on cultural opportunities in your sessions with children in these populations by reflecting their feelings, returning responsibility to them, and encouraging them as a way to build the therapeutic relationship and foster positive self-esteem (L. Taylor & Turner, 2022).

The Course of the Play

In play therapy, "the play is the thing," and you will need to adapt your application of the various skills to what is going on in the play. For example, if the parents of Daisy (age 8) are getting a divorce and she is working through her emotional reaction to this life circumstance, it will probably be advantageous to increase the number of feeling reflections you are using in the session. If Julian (age 6) is very detail-oriented and likes to describe specific situations and relationships in his life, he will feel heard and understood when you spend part of every session restating content to ensure he realizes that you are listening to him and honoring his efforts at communication. If Olive (age 5), who is slow to warm up and tends to always follow the rules, is challenging some of the playroom rules, you may want to give her some slack and let her attempt some behaviors she would not normally be brave enough to try. The gist of what we are saying with these examples is that each session, each moment in a particular session, is a world in and of itself. You must be alert to what is happening in the play in the here-and-now and be willing to adjust your choice of interventions based on what is happening in the play at that particular moment.

The Phase of the Therapy

It makes intuitive sense that the therapist would choose interventions that carry limited psychological risk for the child early in the therapy process and interventions that could feel psychologically risky to the child later in the therapy process. Of course, you must decide whether to adapt your practice to accommodate this. If you do, you must choose which skills might potentially have psychological risks for specific child clients. The play therapy process unfolds differently according to the various theoretical approaches, so it will be necessary for you to explore the particular approach you want to follow to know what happens in each phase and what the therapist's role is in each. For instance, if you were doing Adlerian play therapy (Kottman & Meany-Walen, 2016), in the first phase, building an egalitarian relationship with the child, you would use more nondirective skills such as tracking, restating content, and reflecting feelings. In the second phase, where you concentrate on exploring the child's interpersonal and intrapersonal dynamics (the child's "lifestyle," in Adlerian terms), you would use more directive techniques, such as inviting the child to make sand trays or art, as a tool for gathering information about how the child sees self, others, and the world. During the third phase, the focus is on helping the child gain insight, so you would be more likely to work through the child's metaphor and do more metacommunication or interpretation, as discussed in later chapters. When you get to the fourth phase, your primary job would be to use direct and indirect teaching—such as delivering therapeutic metaphors, bibliotherapy, modeling, and role playing—to support the child in making changes in their thinking, behaving, and feeling.

Integrating and Infusing Skills

As you gain mastery of each of the basic and advanced play therapy skills, you may notice that your application of the skills still feels rather stilted and artificial. Two methods of skill integration could help to change this. One of these—the integration of various skills with one another—is rather narrow and concrete. The other—the infusion of skills into your own natural way of communicating and interacting—is more global and abstract.

Although you can concentrate on both of these transformations at the same time, the integration of skills will be an easier and quicker process, whereas the infusion of skills into your interactional style will be a slower and potentially more painful evolution. We suggest that you begin by practicing blending skills with one another. Later, you can move to the gradual process of working toward congruence and confluence between how you communicate as a person and as a play therapist.

Integrating Skills

To start the transformation from isolated skills to integrated skills, you must first learn the mechanics of how to blend the basic skills into intervention techniques. You must also discover which skills meld smoothly and which skills clash. Several obvious natural combinations work well together, but what works for one play therapist might not suit another, so you will need to experiment. It will also be helpful for you to practice using skills in isolation and in combination and experiment with making decisions about when to integrate and how to time your interventions. There is no scientific formula for doing this either. It will depend on the child's developmental level, the child's situation, the child's standard way of processing information, the phase of therapy, and various factors related to your own comfort, personal style, and expertise.

Mechanics of blending skills. The procedure for blending one skill with one or more other skills is relatively simple: Take whatever you would have said or done for the first skill and decide how you can fit it into what you would have said or done for the second. The following are some suggestions for doing this blending:

1. Make the blended intervention into a compound sentence that just combines the two different skills.

2. Blend the two skills into a simple sentence, using a feeling word as a descriptor for how the child is doing something or reacting to something.

3. Use several different sentences for your intervention, each containing a different skill.

4. Talk about or to the play object, sometimes using a metaphor and/or acting as if the play object is alive, has feelings, can talk, and so forth.

5. If you have enough information about the child and their situation, make a cause-and-effect attribution linking two different elements—most of the time, these statements have the words "because" or "since" to emphasize the cause-and-effect connection between the different components.

These are some basic mechanics of combination, but this list is not exhaustive. Different ways of integrating skills are limited only by your imagination and willingness to experiment. While most play therapists would probably be willing to follow the first three examples above, nondirective play therapists might be uncomfortable about the directive/interpretive nature of the last two. These two methods would perhaps be more comfortable for therapists willing to lead the client rather than letting the client always take the lead.

The following examples illustrate several different mechanics of integrating various basic skills:

Example 1

You want to blend a reflection of feeling with a tracking intervention. Your reflection of feeling is "You seem angry today," and your tracking intervention is "You are hitting that punching bag." Possible combined interventions are as follows:

> "You are hitting that punching bag, and you seem angry today." (*compound sentence*)

> "You seem to be thumping that punching bag in an angry way today." (*using reflection of feelings as a descriptor*)

> "You are hitting that punching bag. You sure seem angry today." (*combining two sentences*)

> "I bet that guy (the punching bag) thinks you are pretty angry today, you are whacking him so hard." (*referring to a play object, assuming it can think or has feelings*)

> "You're hitting that punching bag because you are feeling angry today." (*cause-and-effect attribution*)

Example 2

You want to blend a restatement of content with a tracking intervention. Your reflection of feeling is "It seems like you are kind of sad right now," and your restatement of content is "You are missing your grandmother." Possible integrated interventions include:

> "You're missing your grandmother, and it just seems like you are kind of sad about that right now." (*compound sentence*)

> "You're feeling sad about missing your grandmother." (*using reflection of feelings as a descriptor*)

> "You are missing your grandmother. You seem sad right now." (*two sentences*)

> "You're feeling sad because you miss your grandmother." (*cause-and-effect attribution*)

Example 3

You want to blend a reflection of feeling with returning responsibility to the child. Your reflection of feeling is "You act like you're a little nervous about deciding that for yourself," and your returning responsibility to the child is "In here, you can choose for yourself." Possible integrated interventions include:

> "You act like you're a little nervous about deciding for yourself, and in here, you can choose." (*compound sentence*)
>
> "In here, you can decide things for yourself, even though you might feel a little nervous about making a choice." (*using reflection of feelings as a descriptor*)
>
> "You act like you're a little nervous about deciding that for yourself. In here, you can choose for yourself." (*two sentences*)
>
> "You seem a bit nervous because in here you can make the decision for yourself." (*cause-and-effect attribution*)

Additional tips for the generation and delivery of effective integrated interventions are to limit the length of your comments, monitor the nonverbal elements of the communication to make sure you are not sending confusing messages in which the verbal and nonverbal components contradict one another, avoid hidden messages or underlying subtexts, and consider the developmental level of the child. Combining two different skills will frequently expand the verbiage and complicate the message, which can result in an intervention that children do not understand. The best solution to this possibility may be to keep all interventions as simple and short as possible. The longer you talk, the more likely it is that children—especially younger children who are less developmentally sophisticated than older children and teens—will not listen to or comprehend the message.

Your tone of voice and emphasis on different words will affect the meaning conveyed by the intervention. Because integrated interventions are often longer and more complex than isolated skills, they are more likely to be distorted by nonverbal communication. For example, depending on your tone and emphasis, the integrated intervention "You act like you're a little nervous about deciding that for yourself. In here, you can choose for yourself" can convey an extremely encouraging or discouraging message. By emphasizing the word "you" in the second sentence in an upbeat, positive tone, you can communicate confidence and a sense of empowerment to the child. In contrast, by stressing the words "in here" in a sarcastic or doubting voice, you can convey doubt that the child could make decisions anywhere other than the playroom. Pay close attention to your patterns of nonverbal communication to avoid inadvertently delivering a message that could be potentially discouraging to the child.

Certain words can convey a message you might not intend, such as the conjunctions used in forming compound sentences. An example of this difficulty would be when you combine a reflection of feelings with returning the responsibility to the child using the word "but." This might result in an integrated intervention like "You seem unsure about whether you will make the right decision, but in here, you can decide." To an insecure child, this might convey the message that "We are going to let you decide even though you will probably get it wrong." Using "and" instead of "but" can prevent this from happening.

Because you may not have time to analyze possible subtexts before delivering your interventions, you may be unable to avoid every occurrence of this potential pitfall. However, it is important to closely monitor children's reactions and responses to these therapeutic responses, especially when they are first introduced. This will allow you to take corrective measures with the child and avoid this problem in similar integrated interventions in the future.

Deciding which skills meld and which clash. Although there are a few general guidelines for choosing which skills to blend, for the most part, this decision depends on personal inclination and experience.

Both tracking and restatement of content are simple, concrete skills. In combination, these two skills can complement one another and prevent an overabundance of isolated interventions that sound so obvious that they become insulting to the child. Integration of tracking and restatement of content can make your statements more interesting than they are in isolation.

Reflections of feelings blend well with all the other basic skills—tracking, restatement of content, limiting, returning responsibility to the child, and responding to questions. Most procedures for setting limits include a step for reflecting feelings, so these skills tend to be integrated. Reflection of feelings can also add power and depth to tracking and restatement of content. By adding reflection of feelings to returning responsibility to the child, you can probe the underlying issues related to the child's wanting or needing help in deciding or acting.

Tracking and restating content do not combine well with limiting because they do not usually add anything to the limiting process. Depending on the limiting procedure, however, some therapists will feel comfortable adding returning responsibility to the child. For example, the direct, encouraging approach to returning responsibility to the child (e.g., "I bet you can figure out a way to do that.") works very well in Adlerian limit setting (see "Kottman and Meany-Walen's Method" in Chapter 8). This strategy can fit into the third step of Adlerian limiting by inviting the child to help generate appropriate behaviors and in the fourth step of deciding on logical consequences.

You will need to experiment with your application of skills to further explore which skills work well together for you and which skills clash when you use them in combination. Again, you will need to monitor children's reactions to your combinations and your feelings as you deliver the combinations to gather information about this process.

Infusing Skills

As you gain confidence in the mechanics of combining the basic skills, you should shift your attention to situations in which you still feel uncomfortable in the playroom—those times when you continue to feel as though your interventions are weak and your delivery does not flow in a smooth, natural way. As you recognize patterns in these feelings of discomfort, it will be helpful to work on meshing your personal interactional style with your mastery of the basic play therapy skills.

Your awareness of being uncomfortable in the playroom is the first step in this process because, in many cases, this discomfort results from you not being yourself there. As your ability to recognize awkwardness in yourself while doing play therapy increases, you can consider the cause of your uneasiness. You will need to decide whether the uncomfortable feelings are related to (a) your efforts to do things "correctly," which may undermine your natural way of interacting; (b) your own anxiety about particular topics or skills; (c) the normal awkwardness involved in learning a new skill; (d) some other factor, such as your own uncertainty about how to respond if a child makes a racist, sexist, homophobic, or other comment that violates your values; or (e) a mismatch between your natural way of communicating and your current theoretical orientation. As you notice situations where you feel you are not being yourself in the playroom, you must ask yourself how you could be more natural and comfortable. It might help to visualize yourself in the playroom using the skills in your own words or visualizing yourself using the skills in more comfortable situations, such as with your friends and family. Sometimes, you can practice the basic play therapy skills (and the more advanced play therapy skills discussed in later chapters) with members of your family, other children you know, or your friends to smooth out your delivery and develop a method of saying things that will feel more natural to you. It is also helpful to practice more familiar ways of phrasing the various interventions in the playroom to help you develop your own personal style for play therapy. You may also need to reexamine your choice of theoretical orientation to see if you can find one that is better suited to your natural way of interacting with others or to your philosophical beliefs about people and how they change.

The most important factor in becoming an artful play therapist is acquiring experience being in a playroom with children, experimenting with the various play therapy skills, and learning to listen to and trust your own judgment and knowledge about children. Another essential factor is your willingness to continually work on your own growth and to notice and honor your own intuition about yourself and your own process—as a professional and as a person, both in and out of the playroom.

Practice Exercises

In each of the following scenarios, (a) write your intervention, (b) label which skills you used and explain why you chose those skills, and (c) if you used an integrated intervention, describe the method you used to combine the isolated skills. You do not have to confine yourself to the methods described in this chapter. Please use your imagination and your personal way of communicating to adapt the skills creatively. Because we believe that it is easier to use combined interventions with children you know relatively well, we use continuing sagas of two children for these exercises so you have an ongoing therapeutic process with which to work. It would be helpful to generate two or three different interventions for each scenario to explore different ways of handling a situation.

Scenario 1

Ellen (age 7) presents with a problem of low self-esteem. She is African American and was adopted at age 2 by a White family. She had been removed from her birth mother's home because her mother's mental illness precluded her taking care of Ellen.

1. In your first session, Ellen looks around and says, "I don't know what to do. There's so much stuff in here."

2. She picks up a dart gun and aims it at you. She says, "Am I allowed to shoot you with the dart?"

3. After your response, she puts the dart gun away and says, "You know I don't want to be here. My parents are making me come. They think you will help me feel better about my life."

4. During your third session, Ellen asks you what color she should paint a person she is making. She looks at you and says, "Should I paint this person the same color as I am?"

5. After you respond, she says, "I think I will paint this person blue—that's a good color for people. Much better than the color I am or the color you are."

6. In the fourth session, Ellen comes in and says, "Nobody at school likes me. Nobody wants to be friends with me." She takes a brown doll figure from the doll families, buries it in the sand tray, and says, "There. Got rid of her."

7. After you respond, she says, "Should we unbury her or leave her there under the sand? Nobody really wants her around."

8. In your sixth session, Ellen comes in and seems very sad. She takes some construction paper and starts tearing it into tiny pieces. As she tears the paper, a tear rolls down her face.

9. She blows her nose, wipes her face with a tissue, and says, "Do you like me as much as you like the other kids who come here? You probably don't."

10. In your 10th session, Ellen enters and suggests the two of you have a dance party. She has brought a tablet and wants to play music. As she starts some music, she dances around the room, saying, "Why aren't you dancing with me?"

Scenario 2

J. R. (age 8) lives with his mother and four older sisters. His parents are in the middle of an acrimonious divorce, and J. R. has recently developed some symptoms of depression and anxiety. He alternates between clinging to his mother, acting helpless, and being defiant and uncooperative at home.

1. In your second session, J. R. takes the largest male figure from the dollhouse and throws it in the trash can.

2. As he continues to play in the doll house, he has the smallest doll figure get bossed around by everyone else in the doll house. The smallest figure finally says to the rest of the doll family, "You are not the boss of me!"

3. He takes the largest female figure and says, "This is the mother." Then he has the mother doll say to the smallest child doll, "Your dad leaving is all your fault, you know. You will have to be punished."

4. After he says this and you respond, he puts all the doll figures back in the doll house, announcing, "Boys should not be playing in the doll house. That is only for girls."

5. At the beginning of your next session, J. R. looks at the doll house several times, then takes some cars and crashes them into one another.

6. He looks at the doll house again, goes over and moves the small doll over to the bed, and puts it in the bed. He picks up the mother doll and puts her right by the bed. In the mother doll's voice, she says, "What are you doing? Trying to get out of doing your chores?"

7. J. R. turns to you and, in a soft, sad voice, says, "Where can he hide? She always wants him to do chores. She thinks he is going to be the man of the house."

8. J. R. hands you the dolls, says, "It's your turn now," and walks over and starts to cook you a meal in the kitchen area.

9. He says, "I am going to make some food for you. What do you want to eat? What is your favorite food?"

10. He waits a moment, takes the plastic food, frowns, and throws it on the floor, saying, "Nobody would want to eat anything I know how to fix."

Questions to Ponder

1. What role does intuition play in your life?

2. On a scale of 1–10 (with 1 being none and 10 being more than anyone else you know), how would you rate the strength of your intuitive sense of what is going on with other people? Explain your rating.

3. On a scale of 1–10 (with 1 being none and 10 being more than anyone else you know), how would you rate your ability to trust in your own intuition? Explain your rating.

4. How well do you understand yourself and your own issues? What are the main issues you think might interfere with your ability to work with children and their families?

5. As compared with the science of play therapy, how important is the art of play therapy? Explain.

6. Which of the different elements in the art of play therapy are important to you? Explain your reasoning.

7. What will be your biggest obstacles in moving toward being more congruent in your interactions in the playroom and in other relationships in your life? Explain.

8. What do you think will be the most important strategies for integrating your own personal style of communicating and interacting with the skills of play therapy?

9. How will you continue to cultivate cultural humility in your play therapy practice?

10. What can you do to increase your cultural sensitivity and cultural responsiveness in your play therapy practice?

11. What can you do to become more aware of cultural opportunities in your playroom?

12. What is your plan to continue growing your cultural competence?

13. What are some attitudes, values, beliefs, and biases that might get in the way of your ability to be with certain clients?

14. How do you plan on practicing using your play therapy skills so that you can get more adept at integrating your own personal style of communication with play therapy skills?

15. Are there certain populations of clients with which you anticipate struggling to be culturally sensitive and culturally responsive? Which populations? How might you increase your cultural comfort in doing play therapy with those clients?

What are your thoughts about using "but" or "and" in your interactions with children? Paying attention to your own communication patterns, how often do you use "but" instead of "and"? If you want to increase your use of "and," how would you go about doing so?

Advanced Skills and Concepts

Recognizing and Communicating Through Metaphors

A metaphor is a form of language which describes something in terms which aren't factually accurate, to bring about an accurate sense of the thing being described.

—Debbie Waller, *The Metaphor Toolbox*

Client-generated metaphors "have the potential to be 'gold dust,' a precious gift from the client, emanating from their language, culture, and worldview, an unconscious attempt by the client to say: 'This is how it is for me right now'" (Lloyd, 2018, p. 11). Metaphors can clarify, inspire, and deepen understanding. They can keep us safe by allowing us to communicate about situations and relationships that might be difficult to talk about directly so we can maintain "plausible deniability" while still communicating our feelings, attitudes, and beliefs about important topics. Sometimes, the decision to use metaphors to communicate these messages is conscious, and sometimes it is beyond our awareness.

Why Metaphors Are Important

Children naturally communicate the stories of their lives through metaphors.

> Every story a child tells, acts out through play, or writes contributes to a self-portrait—a portrait that he can look at, refer to, think about, and change, a portrait others can use to develop an understanding of the storyteller. Each time a child describes an experience he or someone else has had, he constructs part of his past, adding to his sense of who he is and conveying that sense to others. Each time a child makes up a story about something that might have happened to himself or to another, he expands his world. (Engel, 1995, p. 1)

In play therapy, metaphors are found in the scenes that children act out alone or ask you to role play; they are in the stories that children tell about events that have happened to them or to others; they are in the fantasy stories that children make up; they are in the artwork or sand trays that children create; they are in the behaviors children manifest in the playroom; and they are in plot summaries from video games, movies, television shows, and books that children act out or discuss in your playroom. In play therapy, many children use stories and metaphors to explore and reveal the self, consider the world and how it works, investigate relationships with others, explore how to solve problems, and communicate with you. Your job as a play therapist will be to recognize when a child is communicating through a metaphor, notice the various metaphors as they occur, listen to metaphors and try to understand what they mean for that particular child in that specific context, and use the child's metaphors as a vehicle for communicating with the child. If your theoretical orientation is one of the more directive approaches to play therapy, you may even decide to design and deliver therapeutic metaphors to help a child gain insight and/or learn new skills. Here are four examples of the myriad metaphors that pervade the play therapy process:

> Alonzo (age 6) has a Black mother and an Asian father. The family lives in a small Midwest city where his father attends graduate school. Alonzo has had a difficult time making friends in his predominantly White school and has had multiple experiences of bullying and racism in the neighborhood and at school. Alonzo arranges all of the dolls in two "camps" on the edges of the sand tray, sorted by skin color. He puts a brown doll in an ambulance, moving it from camp to camp, but no one will let the doll get out of the ambulance, and no one will help him.

Lois (age 8) comes to play therapy with a presenting problem of generalized anxiety. In your first session, she chooses a small bunny and has it hide beneath the pillows in the playroom. When you reflect the bunny's feelings, Lois says in a high voice, "I'm not coming out. There are too many dangerous things here. I need to keep myself safe."

Roger (age 7) has been diagnosed with attention-deficit/hyperactivity disorder. His presenting problem is impulsivity and refusal to complete work in school. He comes into the playroom, scoots around the room, crashes into your chair, and says, "I am a runaway truck, and I cannot stop. Even if a car gets in my way, I just run right over it. Nobody can even slow me down, no matter how hard they try."

Savannah (age 10) has been struggling with interpersonal relational aggression at school, where the "queen bee" girl has decided she isn't going to be friends with Savannah, and none of the other girls in the fourth grade are "allowed" to be friends with her either. She draws a picture of herself, looks at it sadly, tears it up, and puts it in the trash.

Recognizing Metaphors

One of your primary tasks in play therapy is to recognize clients' metaphors—noticing the various images and stories present in the play and acknowledging their metaphoric potential. By listening to stories in the playroom for their symbolic content, you can begin to see the child's world through their eyes, connecting the images and stories in the play to the situations and relationships in the child's life.

Once you begin listening and looking for metaphors, you will find them everywhere in the play, including in children's stories, puppet shows, drawings and paintings, descriptions of their friends and family members, and playroom scenarios. Metaphors will be everywhere and in everything that happens. Your first mission is to begin to notice them and acknowledge to yourself that there may be some kind of symbolic message in the play. After you have gotten into the rhythm of recognizing that there may be a hidden story in the play, you can consider what these metaphors mean in the context of your clients' lives.

Understanding the Meaning

"Metaphors, in their essence, are bridges of understanding, vehicles that transport us beyond the confines of literal language. They are keys that unlock hidden chambers of meaning and connect us to the depth of our emotions and experiences" (Neurospicy Creative, 2023, p. 1).

Metaphors are symbolic, not direct, so the meaning of the metaphor may be hidden inside the story or the play. As the play therapist, you must try to understand the meaning of the metaphor to better comprehend the child's feelings, attitudes, relationships, and views about self, others, and the world.

Some play therapy approaches, such as experiential play therapy (Norton & Norton, 2006, 2008) and Jungian analytical play therapy (Allan, 1988; Green, 2014), support the idea that certain symbols have common meanings shared across different children and cultures. In other words, when a child tells a story using a specific symbol, that symbol would have a particular universal interpretation. For instance, in a story about a bird, the bird would signify transformation. In a description of a house, the house would symbolize the child's family. Allan (1988) suggested that therapists must be cautious in interpreting the meaning of all symbols according to a universal standard. However, play therapists who adhere to these perspectives tend to view the meaning of certain symbols as being the same across children and cultures.

Other play therapists view metaphors as idiosyncratic and phenomenological (Fried & McKenna, 2020; Kottman & Meany-Walen, 2016, 2018; Landreth, 2024; Oaklander, 1978/1992, 2015). For those play therapists, especially those who practice from an Adlerian, child-centered, or Gestalt orientation, symbols in metaphors are unique to a particular child at a specific moment in time. From this perspective, the only way the metaphor can be completely understood is to consider the child's history and culture, the developmental level of the child, the time context of the storytelling, and a multitude of other factors.

J. P. Lilly (personal communication, September 11, 2020) combines these two ways of thinking about symbols and metaphors. He has maintained that there are archetypal meanings of certain symbols that are true across all peoples, no matter their culture or individual experiences. In addition to this archetypal meaning, Lilly suggested that there can be a culturally influenced layer of meaning for any given symbol and a personal interpretation layer for the meaning of that symbol. Even if you are unsure about archetypal meanings, we encourage you to consider how culture and personal experiences can influence the meaning people make of symbols and how cultural and personal experiences can impact the meanings of stories they make up.

You will have to consider your own views about the interpretation of the meaning of symbols and metaphors. Regardless of your stance, it will be important to try to understand the message of the metaphor and convey your desire to understand it to the child. You will need to do so in an accepting, patient way without pressuring the child to communicate more directly. With many children, your willingness to listen and try to understand the message of the metaphor is enough to produce a shift in how they look at themselves, others, and the world.

Even when the meaning of the metaphor eludes you, it can be helpful to consider possible meanings. By thinking about the different messages that could be conveyed by a particular story or play sequence, you can better understand the child's interpersonal and intrapersonal dynamics. In many cases, there is no single "correct" message to be derived from the play. By considering all the possible messages in that metaphor, you can learn much about the child and their way of viewing the world.

Sometimes, the specific content of the story is not that important. What the child is trying to convey may be a feeling or an attitude rather than concrete information about a certain situation—the affective tone of the story may be the message of the metaphor. For instance, if Sam tells you the story of his football team winning the Super Bowl, he may not really care who won the game—he may just be happy and optimistic that his life is going how he wants it to go.

Not every story or play scene has hidden dimensions. There are often no underlying layers of meaning in a child's narrative. A story about a bird and a bee may just be a story about a bird and a bee. A "nonmetaphor kid" (see Chapter 14) usually has no hidden meaning in their story because the child's communication is concrete rather than symbolic.

Examples of Metaphors and Possible Meanings

After each of the following examples are several possible interpretations of the meaning of the metaphor. All, some, or none of these interpretations might be correct for that particular child under the specific circumstances.

Example 1

Camille (age 7) is playing in the castle. She has a dragon "flame" all the members of the castle guard, kidnap the queen, and take her to a "safe place where no one will bother her."

- Camille wants to be rescued from a difficult situation and doesn't want to deal with the problems in her family at home.
- Camille wants to be special and have someone treat her like she is important to them.
- Camille feels that someone in her life is dangerous to others but protective of her.
- Camille is an introvert and wishes the other people in her life didn't bother her all the time.
- Camille feels that she is not safe in her current environment and wishes she had someone to protect her.

Example 2

Jin (age 6) tells you this story: "There once was a tiger living in a tiny cage where there wasn't enough room to run and play. He hated living in the cage and wanted to run away. One day, the tiger escaped, but a pack of wolves saw him and attacked him. The wolves hurt the tiger badly and he died."

- The tiger symbolizes Jin, and he wants to run away.
- Jin believes that being trapped is still safer than dealing with the world. He is afraid that if he escapes from his current situation, his life will be even worse.
- Jin is being bullied somewhere by a group of aggressive people, either at school or in the neighborhood.
- Jin believes that trying to get his needs met is dangerous.
- Jin wishes he had more fun in his life but is afraid of taking risks.
- Jin recently went to the zoo and saw a tiger in a small cage and felt sorry for him.

Example 3

In her 10th session, Flower (age 9) plays with several of the figures of people, one of whom is a different color than the other figures. As she tells her story, the figures who are all the same color start throwing things at the figure who is a different color. That figure runs away crying.

- Flower is experiencing racist attacks, perhaps through physical or microaggressions.
- Flower feels different than other children.
- Flower wants to find a place of belonging and significance but does not feel that she is welcomed in the communities with which she interacts.
- Flower is being bullied by others in her neighborhood or at school.
- Flower doesn't feel like she fits in her family and feels that she is being rejected by the other members of her family.

Example 4

When Ocean (age 5) was four years old, his mother died. His father seems to have difficulty taking care of himself and his three children. Ocean tells you the story of a garden where the gardener took care of the flowers, which were all happy and bright. However, the gardener was taken away by a scary monster, and now the flowers are all droopy, and the weeds are taking over the garden.

- Ocean's mother was the "gardener," and now that she is gone, all the flowers (symbolizing her children) are struggling.
- Ocean believes that the cancer that killed his mother is a scary monster.
- Ocean recognizes that his father is having difficulty taking care of the family.
- Ocean's mother had a garden in their yard, and through neglect, the garden is now dying.
- In Ocean's culture, gardens symbolize growth and a sense of well-being.

Example 5

Eva (age 9) describes the plot of a movie she watched recently. The way she tells the story, the hero had no chance against the overwhelming number of villains attacking him, and he dies at the end of the movie. You, having seen an action thriller or two yourself, including the actual superhero movie Eva described, know that the plot resolution of that movie involved the hero defeating the overwhelming number of adversaries.

- Eva believes that there are so many obstacles in her life that she cannot overcome them all.
- Eva has a pessimistic view of the world and believes that heroes do not win, no matter how hard they try.
- Eva feels as though everyone in her life is out to get her and that she has no friends or allies.
- Eva believes her situation is hopeless and no one can help her.
- omeone Eva looks up to is struggling, and she is feeling helpless to help that person.

Using the Metaphor to Communicate

It is essential to avoid "breaking" the metaphor, such as by asking the child to explain the meaning of the metaphor or interpreting the meaning of the metaphor to the child (Kottman & Meany-Walen, 2016, 2018). Breaking the metaphor conveys a lack of respect for the child's decision to communicate indirectly and implies that the child should be direct and concrete. Instead of breaking the metaphor, a play therapist can enter the metaphor and use it to communicate indirectly with the child, using the child's symbolic language.

Whether or not you completely understand the underlying meaning of the child's metaphor, it is possible for you to use the metaphor to communicate with the child. When a child uses indirect modes of expression, especially stories and metaphors, you will likely obtain a more positive response if you show you are willing to use the same indirect mode of expression.

You can use the child's metaphor as a vehicle for basic intervention skills, such as reflecting feelings or returning responsibility to the child, or for more complex interventions, such as teaching problem-solving techniques, conveying new information, suggesting alternative solutions to problems, or making interpretations. If you are working with a child experiencing prejudice or bullying of some kind, you can also use the child's metaphor for broaching the possibility of racism, ablism, sexism, or homophobia. The metaphor can also serve as a vehicle for asking questions about the child's life or relationships, using an indirect forum for asking.

In all of these situations, you simply use whatever is happening with the characters in the child's story as an opportunity to apply that particular skill. For example, Leo (age 7) is telling a story about a bunny that a fox is chasing. You could use basic skills to track the behaviors of the bunny, restate the content of the fox's comments, and reflect the feelings of both the bunny and the fox. You could ask the bunny about the different ways they tried to get away from the fox or suggest asking the bear or the wizard to help the bunny hide from the fox.

When using the child's metaphor, consider which character in the story represents the child's point of view. This will guide you in making choices about which character to use as a focal point for the interventions. If you wish to convey empathic understanding to the child, it is better to concentrate on the character representing the child in the metaphor. If you wish to facilitate the development of empathy in the client, focusing on other characters in the story may be helpful.

Monitoring the Child's Reaction

If you use a child's metaphor to communicate with the child, it is important to monitor their reaction to your adaptation. Most of the time, the child will go along with your use of the metaphor and continue to use it to communicate more information. In cases where both of you feel comfortable with a particular metaphor, you and the child can use the same metaphor in subsequent sessions as a recurring mode of communication.

Alternatively, some children might have an adverse reaction to you co-opting the metaphor. This negative reaction could be a subtle nonverbal response, such as a head shake or a frown, or a blatant rejection, such as a repudiation of any changes you might have made in the story or a refusal to use that particular metaphor in future interactions. However, this doesn't happen often. Most children love it when the therapist uses their metaphor to communicate with them.

When an adverse reaction occurs, you should examine whether it was (a) to the direction you were taking the metaphor or (b) to the co-opting of the metaphor. If the former, the child may reject the specific part of the metaphor that they do not like (e.g., "The rabbit wouldn't ask for help. What are you talking about?") or convey more generalized disapproval (e.g., "I don't want to tell this story anymore. You don't know what you are talking about."). If this happens, you may need to adjust your direction or use of the metaphor. For example, Leo may not like it if you suggest ways the bunny can elude the fox. Leo may identify with the fox and see nothing wrong with it picking on smaller creatures. For future uses of Leo's metaphors, you might need to be more careful in assuming which character represents Leo.

Sometimes, you might just "get it wrong" in the metaphor, just as you might make a mistake in a more direct form of communication.

You may have inaccurately reflected a feeling or missed the gist of a restatement of content. When this happens, the child's reaction is usually a relatively mild correction, such as "No, the bunny isn't scared. He likes being chased."

Some children might not wish to "share" their metaphors with you. With these children, their adverse reaction to you using their metaphor can be a violent rejection of anything you do with the metaphor. It is usually better with these children to avoid adapting their metaphors and instead generate other ways of making suggestions with them, both directly and indirectly.

Examples of Using Metaphors to Communicate

The following examples show how a therapist might use metaphors to communicate with the four children whose cases are described at the beginning of this chapter:

Example 1

Alonzo has put a small brown doll in an ambulance, moving it from camp to camp, but no one helped or let the doll out of the ambulance.

> "Nobody seems to be willing to help the small brown person. Might there be some racism happening to the person in the ambulance?" (*tracking, interpretation, question, broaching possibility of racism*)

> "He does not seem to be able to get the help he needs." (*interpretation*)

> It looks like he can't find a place where he could belong and feel safe." (*interpretation*)

Example 2

Lois, after moving the bunny to hide under a pillow, has said, "I'm not coming out. There are too many dangerous things in here. I need to keep myself safe."

> "So, you've figured out one way to keep yourself safe, Bunny. What else could you do to keep yourself safe?" (*restatement of content, returning responsibility to the child, invitation for alternative problem-solving*)

> "What is the bunny scared of here in the playroom?" (*question*)

> "You sound pretty proud of your ability to keep yourself safe." (*reflection of feeling*)

Example 3

Roger has come into the playroom, scooted around the room, crashed into your chair, and said, "I am a runaway truck, and I cannot stop. Even if a car gets in my way, I just run right over it. Nobody can even slow me down, no matter how hard they try."

> "You believe that you cannot stop yourself." (*interpretation and cognitive reframe*)
>
> "Mr. Truck, how are you feeling right now, not being able to stop?" (*question*)
>
> "What would happen if someone helped the truck put on his brakes?" (*invitation to problem solve or generate alternative behaviors*)

Example 4

Savannah has drawn a picture of herself as a clown and put it in the trash.

> "You are seeming pretty discouraged." (*reflection of feelings*)
>
> "I am guessing you feel like others don't take you seriously." (*interpretation*)
>
> "Lots of people don't like clowns and don't want to be around them." (*interpretation*)

Helping Clients Shift Their Metaphors

Sometimes clients' metaphors are self-defeating or discouraging. If you are a directive play therapist, it can be useful (after you understand the meaning of the metaphor and have acknowledged the feelings, attitudes, and thoughts expressed through it) to help clients shift their metaphors by adding different elements, shifting the direction of the story or changing the resolution of the client's story (Lloyd, 2018).

You can do this by asking a question or making a suggestion. For instance, with Alonzo, you could ask whether the two of you could work to find someone (a figure or puppet) to help Alonzo, or you could bring in a character that looks like the little brown figure and have it join Alonzo. You could also suggest that the ambulance take the little brown figure to a hospital you set up in another part of the room, populated with figures with several different skin colors. With Roger, you could suggest he control his runaway truck using an escape lane, emergency escape ramp, or truck arrester bed, a traffic device that enables vehicles with braking problems to stop safely. You could ask him how he might slow the truck when it is out of control. With Savannah, you could ask her to do another drawing of herself as a princess instead of a clown. Or you could offer to help her tape the torn picture of the clown back together and help the clown work on feeling important or special because they can make children laugh and have fun. These are just a few examples of how it is possible to shift the client's metaphor.

Before you ask a client to shift one of their metaphors, you first reflect their feelings or validate how they feel about what is happening in the metaphor. This conveys respect and understanding rather than dismissal. Whether to try to shift a metaphor is one of those art versus science of play therapy dilemmas—it works best when your analysis of the situation is that the client is feeling stuck, and that feeling is reflected through the metaphor. If the metaphor is simply a reflection of what is happening with the client in the moment, it is often better to simply use restatement of contents, reflection of feelings, interpretation, or a question to help the client explore the relationship, situation, attitude, or emotion represented by the metaphor.

Therapeutic Metaphors

As described by Lankton and Lankton (1989), "Stories are gentle methods that don't demand a response, but that stimulate 'thinking, experiencing, and ideas for problem resolution'" (pp. 1–2). "Storytelling is an alternative communication strategy. For counselors, it should be used as a technique within the context of an overall treatment plan rather than as a treatment approach in and of itself" (Flanagan, 2019, para. 7). A therapeutic metaphor is "an intervention by the clinician that is presented to the client in story form: as anecdotes, parables, fairytales, etc. Its nonthreatening presentation can create new insights and different, or original, perspectives on a client's approach to problem resolution" (Cohen, 2018, p. xi). A therapeutic metaphor is usually offered to a client to help the client reach their goals on the most effective and efficient path. Metaphors can be used to fill the experiential gap between what is or has been and what can be (Burns, 2017).

In designing a metaphor, you may include characters in the story who represent the various people or situations in the child's life (e.g., allies, obstacles) and put a hero and allies into situations in which they have to cope with problem situations similar to the child's difficulties. The characters express feelings parallel to those experienced by the child and the other people in the child's life. You can explain each character's perspective in the story to shed light on different ways to view the problem. After struggling with the problem and trying different possible solutions, the main character comes to some kind of a resolution of the difficulties. The purpose of including characters and circumstances similar to the child, their situation, and the people in their life is to help the child identify with the characters, explore the various perspectives presented in the story, and consider applying the potential solutions to problems in the story to their own situation. Rather than pointing out the parallels between the child's life and the story, let the child decide whether to acknowledge the similarities or to act as if the story is "just a story."

Designing and Delivering Therapeutic Metaphors

Some therapists have suggested ways to design therapeutic metaphors for work with children (Burns, 2017; Deverage, 2022; Flanagan, 2019; Gordon, 2017; Hammel, 2019; Mills & Crowley, 2014; Pernicano, 2022; Webber & Webber, 2023). Flanagan (2019) suggested the following steps for structuring a story:

1. *Set the stage for the story.* To set the stage, you would create a scenario that features a child (represented by a human, an animal, or an animated object) living in a particular situation. This character should be depicted in a way that's positive and appealing.

2. *Tell about the problem.* In the next step, describe a problem the central character struggles with. It should have some similarity to your client's struggle. End this part of the story with a declaration that no one really knows what to do about this problem.

3. *Organize a search for helpful resources.* During this part of the story, explain how the central character and their allies try to find resources to solve the problem. The search usually culminates in identifying several resources, such as a wise, kind, gentle, and mysterious old person or an animal or alien creature who can serve as a special helper for the central character.

4. *Refine the therapeutic intervention.* The initial therapeutic strategy was not supposed to be effective in solving the problem, so for this step of the model, you should include a process for changing or perfecting potential solutions. During this step in the story, the central character learns an important lesson and begins the behavior change process.

5. *Integrate the lesson.* In the final step in the story's progression, the central character articulates the lesson(s) they have learned.

Another process for designing metaphors for children in play therapy has been described by Kottman and Meany-Walen (2016, 2018). This seven-step process begins with deciding on the therapeutic goal for telling a story and ends with a celebration of the eventual resolution. These steps are as follows:

1. Decide what your therapeutic goal is for telling the story. Be specific about what you want to use the story to teach or communicate. It is helpful to write down your goal for the story so you can use it as a guidepost for where you want it to go.

2. Describe the setting and initial situation with enough detail so the child can visualize it. The beginning scene should not be exactly the same as the child's circumstances, but it should have several similarities. The story can be set in a natural environment (e.g., "in the forest"), in a mythical environment (e.g., "once upon a time in the dragon's palace"), or in a realistic environment (e.g., "in a school where I used to work").

3. Describe the characters in enough detail that the child gets a sense of what they are like. The cast of characters should include (a) the protagonist of the story, representing the child; (b) the antagonist of the story, representing someone or some situation that is giving the protagonist problems; (c) a resource person, representing someone wise or relatively uninvolved in the struggle who can provide advice, an alternative perspective, or possible solutions to difficulties encountered by the protagonist; and (d) one or two allies for the protagonist, representing someone willing to go through the difficulties with the protagonist and can provide support, encouragement, advice, an alternative perspective, or possible solutions. Depending on the setting and the interests and developmental level of the child, these characters can be realistic, fictional, or fantastic. We have found that it frequently helps the child's acceptance of the story if the protagonist and most of the other characters are the same sex as the child.

4. Describe the primary problem, dilemma, or struggle encountered by the protagonist and their allies concretely and in enough detail so that the child can visualize and understand the difficulty. The problem situation can have some parallels to the child's difficulty, but the correlation should not be so obvious that it precludes the child from continuing to believe that the metaphor is only a story.

5. As the story progresses, the protagonist must also progress in their method of coping with the problem. This may involve

trying some solutions that work, gaining new coping skills that aid in handling the problem, or adopting a new perspective on the situation so that it does not seem insurmountable. The resolution should not come too easily, however. The protagonist may experience setbacks or try several ways of dealing with the problem before the situation moves toward resolution. This ensures that the child does not see the progress as just a glib reassurance that "everything will be all right." Rather, the child should understand that the protagonist has earned the solution. The protagonist must also be responsible for making final decisions and putting most of the effort toward the resolution. The resource person and the allies can help along the way, but they should not be responsible for overcoming obstacles or providing the solution to the problem.

6. Describe the resolution in a concrete manner that makes it clear what has changed in the protagonist's feelings, attitudes, perception, or behavior related to the problem. It may be helpful to leave some aspects of the problem unsolved to avoid implying that all problems can be resolved. However, at the end of the story, the protagonist must have made progress in learning how to cope with the situation. The resolution should include the protagonist (a) gaining insight into themselves and the situation, (b) gaining insight into others and the ways that they see themselves, (c) gaining insight into relationships and interactions with others, (d) developing improved attitudes toward themselves, others, and life; or (e) acquiring skills that can aid in coping with problem situations in the future. These gains should be related to changes the child needs to make in their life.

7. After the resolution, the protagonist and other characters (sometimes including the antagonist) should have a celebration that affirms the changes that have taken place in the protagonist. This celebration can be a party, a ceremony, or simply a conversation in which the protagonist explains to the other characters what they have learned through the struggles, and the other characters congratulate the protagonist on progress or changes made. You might choose to add a moral or message to the end of the story, but children may not always respond positively to this method of consolidation, possibly because it can tend to be heavy-handed or sound judgmental.

In our experience, therapeutic metaphors work better in play therapy if the storytelling method is appropriate to the child's developmental age. Younger children (3–8 years developmentally) seem to be more interested in animal characters than in people. It also helps with these children to (a) act out the story with animal puppets or figures, (b) make a drawing or painting as you are telling the story to illustrate the metaphor, or (c) show them a "book" illustrating the story that you have constructed before the session. A visual component is essential for most children in this age range because it facilitates their understanding and acceptance of the story. With children in this age range, we usually tell them that "the animals can talk in this story." Then, we use a different voice for each animal when telling the story.

You will also need to keep the story relatively short with these younger children. We try to make stories for very young children (3–4 years) just 2 to 3 minutes long. For children 5 or 6 years old, we might have a 3 to 4 minute story. For children 7 or 8 years old, the story should not last more than 5 or 6 minutes, or you may start to lose their attention.

With older children (7 years or older developmentally), you can decide whether to use animal characters, "real" people characters, cartoon characters, or fictional characters from books, video games, television shows, or movies. The identity of the characters should be determined based on the child and their preferences and interests. With some children, you can use characters they have already generated in stories the child has told. Other children may have a clear interest or hobby that could guide you in character definition. Many children like to hear stories about real people—other children, their families, and friends. We usually make up these real people or use acquaintances that have been heavily disguised to ensure that the child could not possibly recognize them.

Many older children do not need to have the visual input that is necessary with younger children. It is frequently helpful to experiment with this visual input—using visual aids with some metaphors but not others and watching how each child responds to the type of delivery used. Some older children like to help act out the metaphor, especially if you frame the story as a movie or radio show that you will record so they can watch or listen to it at home. You can also do this with puppet shows or plays using the other toys in the playroom.

Developmentally older children can tolerate longer stories. You may also want to try this with different variations for individual children, but most children 8 years or older can sustain interest in a metaphor that lasts as long as 8 to 10 minutes.

If you do not wish to generate metaphors for individual children, there are sources of therapeutic metaphors designed for those with specific presenting problems or situations. You can use these stories in precisely the form they were written or adapt them for individual children. Following is a list of sources for therapeutic metaphors:

- *How to Tell Stories to Children* (West & Sarosy, 2021)
- *101 Stories for Enhancing Happiness and Well-Being* (Burns, 2017)
- *Inspiring Short Stories for Kids: Motivational Book about Self-Confidence, Perseverance, Gratitude, Courage, and Other Values* (AMghs Publishing, 2023)
- *Therapeutic Storytelling: 101 Healing Stories for Children* (Perrow, 2012)
- *An A-Z Collection of Behaviour Tales: From Angry Ant to Zestless Zebra* (Perrow, 2017)
- *Tales for the Hidden Mind* (Taub, 2021)
- *Using Art, Play, Metaphor, and Symbol with Hard-to-Reach Young Clients* (Webber & Webber, 2023)
- *The Magic in Metaphor: Empowering Children Through Healing Stories* (Sears, 2023)
- *Using Trauma-Focused Therapy Stories: Interventions for Therapists, Children, and Their Caregivers* (Pernicano, 2022)
- *The New Social Story Book* (Gray, 2015)

Bibliotherapy is another way of delivering metaphors without having to invent them. In bibliotherapy, you can use therapeutic books specifically written for certain kinds of problems or books that just happen to cover topics related to an individual child's issues (Elswick, 2018; McNicol & Brewster, 2019; Pardeck, 2013; Ward & Allred, 2023). You would choose a book to help children understand their experiences, learn coping strategies, and/or consider different perspectives. Clients often identify with characters and sometimes with the stories themselves. Books used in bibliotherapy should relate to specific issues in children's lives and suggest ways for them to confront and solve their problems (Ginns-Gruenberg & Bridgman, 2021; Kottman, 2020; Murray, 2021). You should always preview books to ensure they are suitable for the particular child, relevant to their current situation, developmentally appropriate, well-written, and illustrated (for picture books). The books should engage the imagination and senses. You will need to choose whether you want to engage in reactive or interactive bibliotherapy

(Gladding, 2020). In *reactive bibliotherapy*, children read (or have read to them) specific books or stories in which there is a potential for them to identify with the characters or the story as a means of increasing their understanding and insight without you engaging them in conversation about what they have learned from the book. *Interactive bibliotherapy* involves children reading (or having read to them) stories or books and then having a discussion with you to facilitate, reinforce, and integrate specific concepts. When doing interactive bibliotherapy, you can even ask children to create the story in a sand tray or act it out (Kottman, 2020; Van Hollander, 2022). Rubin (2020) has suggested a myriad of practical ways to integrate stories and bibliotherapy (even using comic books and manga) featuring superheroes and villains in play therapy.

We have a bias that children's literature books are much better for bibliotherapy than "therapeutic" books, which can often be rather pedantic in trying to make a "point" about children's issues and the solutions to the targeted problem, which can inadvertently suggest that there is something wrong with them. "Therapeutic" books are often not as well written as children's literature.

Although generic metaphors can be extremely helpful, we encourage you to design metaphors for specific children. The prospect of this process can be a little intimidating. However, once you have delivered several metaphors you have created, especially for individual children, and you see how excited and honored they are to have a story made just for them, you may be willing to risk trying this intervention even if you do not feel that creativity is your strength.

Examples of Therapeutic Metaphors

The following examples present one possible metaphor for each of the children described:

Example 1

Samantha (age 8) was a slow-to-warm-up little girl who did not enjoy school, where she felt pressured by the expectation for her to try new things. When her school district switched to online schooling during the COVID-19 pandemic, she was happy to be learning remotely. As the school district returned to in-person education, Samantha started exhibiting symptoms of school phobia, refusing to go to school and begging to be home-schooled or to continue with online education. Neither one of these options was possible because both of her parents had to work, and their district had phased out the online learning program. Samantha's parents brought her to play therapy to help ease her transition back to attending school in person. The therapeutic goal for the following metaphor was to suggest that, while it was scary to have to go back to school in person, some good things could happen there—like making friends and getting to go to art and music classes, both of which Samantha loved.

A metaphor designed for Samantha:

> Once upon a time, there was a little turtle named Terapina. She had a beautiful shell, and she preferred staying in her shell instead of going out into the swamp where she lived. She felt safer in her shell under the log where her family lived and was just not sure she wanted to explore the swamp. Her parents were a bit worried because they knew that Terapina needed to learn many things that she couldn't if she just stayed in her shell under their log. They wanted her to be able to go out and make new friends and experience the sights, smells, tastes, and sounds available in the swamp. Her parents asked her many times to come out of her shell and go out into the swamp, but she stayed tight and refused to leave the warm, squishy mud under the log.
>
> One day, when her parents were out and about, gathering watercress and arugula for the family to eat, Terapina heard a bird singing a lovely song out in the swamp. She peeped out from her shell to hear the song better, but she still wanted to hear more of the song, so she crept out from under the log and into the water on the edge of the swamp. She saw a little brown bird singing its heart out. She edged closer to the bird, who looked at her and seemed to smile. She whispered, "What is your name, little bird?" The bird replied, "My name is Sally Swamp Sparrow. What's your name?" Terapina told Sally her name, and Sally hopped over and sat on top of Terapina's shell. Terapina loved having Sally on her shell and listening to Sally's song. Sally suggested they use the mud along the edge of the swamp to make pretty patterns with their feet. It was such fun, and the patterns they made together were perfectly wonderful. Terapina wanted to continue making patterns but was getting a bit hungry. She asked Sally where there might be some food they would both like, and Sally guided her to a rock that had some delicious worms under it. Sally used her nose to move the rock, and they shared the snack of worms they found there.
>
> After the snack, Terapina was tired, so she decided it was time to go back under the log to take a nap. She said goodbye to her new friend and asked if they could play the next day. Sally agreed to meet the very next day, and Terapina trundled back to the family's log. Her parents were so excited to hear about her adventures, and they

celebrated her courage and newly formed connection with a friend who also loved music and making art. Terapina promised to continue exploring the other exciting experiences available in the swamp.

Example 2

Rodrigo (age 9) was embarrassed because he still wet the bed. His parents had tried all sorts of remedies, including waking him up several times during the night to go to the bathroom. His father had recently tried to shame him into going all night without wetting the bed, telling him he could never be a man until he stopped his "unmanly behavior." Rodrigo was convinced that he couldn't stop wetting the bed, so nothing anyone did seemed to help. The therapist's goal for Rodrigo's story was to help him explore ways that he could shift his self-talk around the bed-wetting.

A metaphor designed for Rodrigo:

> When I was a teacher, I had a kid named Antonio in my class who had a problem with spilling. No matter what happened, whenever he had a glass of water, milk, or juice, he spilled it all over himself and everything else. He was embarrassed about this behavior. Many of the kids in his class started making fun of him, which was even more embarrassing. His mother and father tried to help him think of a way to stop spilling, but nothing they suggested seemed to work. All three of them were very frustrated.
>
> One day, Antonio came to school early to talk to me about his problem. I really wasn't sure what to suggest to him, so I asked two of his friends, Calvin and Darius, to help us come up with some ideas for how he could get over this problem. Calvin pointed out that when Antonio even picked up a glass, he got so worried that his hands shook, making it hard to hold. Calvin mentioned that he had heard Antonio mumbling to himself, "I just know I am going to spill this water," even before he had spilled anything. It seemed to me that maybe what was happening was that Antonio had already decided that he was going to spill, so it came true every time. I asked Antonio if he could come up with a way to change the way he thought about himself and spilling. Antonio told me that he did kind of always think he was going to spill, and then he got so nervous and worried that it was hard not to spill. Antonio decided that he would start telling himself, "I am going to drink this glass of water without spilling." Calvin and Darius suggested that he keep an empty glass nearby so that if he thought he might spill, he could pour whatever was in the glass into the empty glass and thereby prove to himself that he could pour instead of spilling. Antonio decided to try both of these ideas.
>
> On the first day, it was hard for him to remember to tell himself, "I am going to drink this without spilling," but Calvin and Darius

reminded him at lunch, and his mother reminded him at dinner. He spilled a little bit one time during the day, but he managed to get most of it into the empty glass. The second day, it was easier for him to remember to tell himself that he was not going to spill and he didn't even need the empty glass. He decided that always having an empty glass was kind of stupid anyway and that he wanted to try just telling himself that he was going to drink without spilling. On the third and fourth days, the plan went perfectly. On the fifth day, Antonio spilled his drink twice. He was so upset that he was ready to give up the plan, but Calvin and Darius reminded him that not everything works out perfectly and that everybody has to practice when they learn something new. They also told him they would be disappointed and a little mad if he didn't keep trying to make the plan that they had helped to think up work. So, for the rest of that week and the next, Antonio continued to tell himself that he could drink without spilling, and it worked—most of the time.

At the end of the second week, Antonio stayed after school to tell me how things were going. He said, "It isn't working perfectly, but things are a lot better than they used to be. I think I had just convinced myself that I could not drink without spilling, and now I know that I can. I just have to concentrate on telling myself that I can do it, and I have to give myself a break when I am not perfect." I was so impressed by Antonio's willingness to try a new way of thinking about himself and his not giving up that I invited Antonio, Calvin, and Darius to go out to McDonald's with me after school. Antonio drank an entire big drink without spilling a single drop.

Practice Exercises

Exercise 1

For each of the following scenarios, write three possible explanations of the meaning of the metaphor. List three ways you could use the metaphor to communicate with the child, labeling the type of intervention each represents (e.g., reflection of feeling, interpretation).

1. DeWayne (age 9) tells you the following story: "I have a friend who was a very good basketball player. He liked to challenge other people to a game of "H-O-R-S-E" because he always won. One day, he challenged a boy who had just moved into the neighborhood and the new kid beat him. He demanded a rematch and the new kid beat him again. He decided he just wouldn't play basketball anymore."

2. Shekinah (age 4) is playing with the dolls in the dollhouse. The mother doll starts yelling at the children, who run and hide under the bed. The mother doll goes into the bedroom in the dollhouse and yells at the kids for messing up the stuff under the bed.

3. Luke (age 7) wants to pretend to be a character from the video game Fortnite. He informs you that he will be the Grizzly because he is the most powerful character and that you will be the Crash because she is not powerful at all. Then he says, "You know girls aren't as strong as boys are."

4. In the play with Luke, he tells you that you must help him attack the other characters to win the game. He hands you a sword and says, "Help me get them." After about two minutes, he takes your sword away and says, "You aren't very good at this. I guess I don't need your help. You go back and guard the fort, and I will get the other characters by myself. That way I will be the last one standing and win the game."

5. Zehra (age 8) has been expressing frustration with you because you continue to reflect her feelings even though she told you repeatedly that she does not like it when you talk about feelings. She begins to complain about her mother, saying, "She never does anything I tell her to. I try and try to get her to listen, but sometimes I just feel like a bug that she squashes. She just doesn't care about what I think."

6. Ho (age 6) takes all the pillows and makes a wall around himself. He looks at the wall, frowns, and starts getting other toys, stacking them on top of the pillows to make the walls taller. He gets in the middle of the walls, sits down, and smiles.

7. Demi (age 4) has the mother doll rocking one of the baby dolls, singing to it. Suddenly, Demi begins making crying noises that seem to emanate from the baby. The mother doll tries to comfort the baby, but it continues to cry. The mother doll seems to be getting frustrated, frowning, and muttering to herself. Finally, after all her efforts to comfort the baby fail, the mother doll throws the baby doll on the floor.

8. Tom (age 9) relates a story of a television show he has watched in which the hero has a friend whom he really trusts, but the friend suddenly metamorphosizes into a monster who stabs the hero in the back, killing him.

9. Macy (age 5) paints a house and a five-person family. Then she takes the black paint and very carefully paints over the entire piece of paper until there is no picture or blank paper left.

10. Tyler (age 7) picks up the handcuffs and wants to put them on you with your hands behind your back, saying, "You will be powerless, and I will have all of the power." When you limit having your hands handcuffed behind your back, he takes them and throws them on the floor, saying, "You are no fun. You never do anything I want you to do."

11. Latifa (age 8) has just found out her father has a new job, and the family is moving to a different town. In the playroom, she carefully arranges a town in the sandbox, with every figure meticulously arranged. Then she picks up the magic wand and frantically stirs up the sand, saying, "This is a tornado. It is destroying the town."

12. Kellum (age 7) has just been introduced to his father's fiancée and her two children. He enters the playroom and begins to use the puppets to act out the story of Cinderella, emphasizing the evilness of the stepmother and her daughters.

13. Paulina (age 6) has a continuing story that she tells you about a busy beaver who is always telling everyone what to do and how to live their lives. The beaver has no friends, but it cannot stop itself from being bossy and trying to get everyone to live their lives as they are supposed to. No matter what feedback the other animals in the forest give the beaver, it continues to engage in this self-defeating behavior.

14. Every time Felipe (age 5) gets frustrated or angry with you, he brings the alligator puppet over and tries to bite your arm. When things are going smoothly in your relationship, he does not even seem to notice the alligator puppet, but the minute he gets irritated with you, out comes the alligator puppet—teeth at the ready.

Exercise 2

Following the guidelines outlined in this chapter, design a therapeutic metaphor for each of the following children. Write down your therapeutic goal for the story you develop.

1. Adam (age 8) has a history of getting into fights with other children on the playground and in the neighborhood. He is a very small child, and he tends to pick on children who are bigger than

he is. He usually gets beaten up but prides himself on not letting other people intimidate him. He has told you several times that the only way to get any respect is to "show them they can't push me around."

2. Sudinez (age 5) has been in three foster families in the past four years. None of the moves have been the result of her behavior, as she is a sweet and compliant child. However, she has incorporated these experiences into her self-image as proof that no one will ever like her and that she will never have a forever family.

3. Joselyn (age 9) hates his name. He gets teased a lot by the other children in school about "having a girl's name." He is getting increasingly sullen and angry both at home and at school. He told you last session that he thinks his parents gave him this name because they did not want him. He is their youngest child, and his sister recently told him that he was an "accident."

4. Karolina (age 10) and her family have moved several times because her mother is in the army and keeps getting transferred. Karolina has started having nightmares where all her friends are flushed down a giant toilet.

5. Chin-Hae (age 7) is encopretic at school. He was potty-trained at age 3, but when he began kindergarten, he started soiling his pants on a regular basis. His kindergarten teacher was extremely harsh and would not let children use the restroom except at recess and lunch, but his first- and second-grade teachers have been very nurturing and supportive, encouraging him to go to the bathroom whenever he needs to. Chin-Hae refuses to use the bathroom at school and may have a bowel movement in his pants twice or thrice daily.

6. Jerzy's (age 8) father died two years ago of cancer. Jerzy adjusted reasonably well to this loss but has recently been having nightmares. She has also been clinging to her mother and crying for "no apparent reason." Her mother recently started dating seriously and is talking about marriage. Although Jerzy initially seemed to like her mother's new boyfriend, in the past month, she has refused to have anything to do with him, telling her mother, "I don't want a new father. I want my old one back."

Questions to Ponder

1. What type of metaphor presentation discussed in this chapter (e.g., children's stories, play scenes, plots) might be the hardest for you to recognize? Explain.

2. What will be the most difficult aspect for you of recognizing and using children's metaphors in play therapy? Explain.

3. Will you be more comfortable communicating with children directly or communicating indirectly through metaphor? Explain.

4. Do you believe there are certain universal meanings to specific symbols, that each person formulates their own meaning for symbols, or some combination of the two? Explain your reasoning.

5. If you do not understand the meaning of a metaphor, how much discomfort will this cause you? How will you deal with your discomfort?

6. What is your reaction to the suggestion that breaking the child's metaphor is disrespectful?

7. How will you handle it if a child rejects your attempts to use their metaphor to communicate in a play therapy session?

8. How will you use your understanding of the child's ethnic or cultural background in your attempts to decipher their metaphors?

9. Do you think you might use therapeutic metaphors in your play therapy practice? Explain your reasoning.

10. If you think you might use therapeutic metaphors, explore the situations in which you think you will most likely use this technique in your play therapy sessions.

11. What do you think will be the most problematic factor for you in designing and delivering therapeutic metaphors?

13

Advanced Play Therapy Skills

In this chapter, we will discuss several play therapy skills that apply to a wide range of different approaches to play therapy. We have chosen to cover (a) metacommunication, (b) mutual storytelling, (c) co-telling a story with a child, and (d) role playing in this chapter because they can be used across several different theoretical orientations, and they lend themselves to relatively simple and concrete description. For each of these play therapy skills, we describe the skill, explain its purpose, provide several examples of how it can be used, and offer practice exercises so you can experiment with its application. We also briefly describe several important umbrella strategies across theoretical orientations, such as sand tray therapy, art techniques, dance, movement, and music. For more information on these and other play therapy strategies, see the resources listed in Appendix C.

Metacommunication

In metacommunication, the counselor metacommunicates; that is, the counselor steps outside the interaction and communicates about the communication taking place in the relationship. By metacommunicating, the counselor can help children begin to notice and understand their own patterns of communication (Kottman & Meany-Walen, 2016, p. 111).

The *metacommunication skill* is a hallmark of Adlerian play therapy. Some non-Adlerian play therapists call this skill "soft interpretation" (J. P. Lilly, personal communication, September 11, 2020). There are several types of situations in which metacommunication would be an appropriate response, including the following:

- Patterns in the interactions between the therapist and the child (e.g., "I notice that you seem to get mad when I tell you that dumping the sand on the floor is against the rules.").
- Patterns in how the child communicates (e.g., "It seems like whenever Little Brown Bear thinks one of the other puppets isn't listening, her voice gets louder.").
- Nonverbal communication on the part of the child (e.g., "You looked at me like you were checking out whether I was mad because you were winning the game.").
- The child's reactions to the therapist's statements and questions (e.g., "You looked kind of sad when I asked you how your weekend with your mom went.").
- Patterns in the child's behaviors, reactions, cognitions, emotions, or attitudes across several sessions (e.g., "Mr. Dragon seems very sad whenever he mentions his sister getting lost in the forest.").
- Patterns in the child's behaviors, reactions, cognitions, emotions, or attitudes in the playroom that extend into other situations and relationships outside the playroom (e.g., "I have noticed that you like to be the boss in here with me. I am guessing that you also like to be the boss on the playground with the other kids.").
- Patterns in the child's behaviors, reactions, cognitions, emotions, or attitudes that typify their personality, coping strategies, interpersonal interactional style, approach to problem-solving, approach to conflict resolution, or self-image (e.g., "It seems as though you use pouting and acting really mad to get other people to do what you want.").

These situations can sometimes overlap. For example, the child's reactions to your statements and questions could be expressed through the child's nonverbal communication, or patterns in the interaction between you and the child could manifest themselves in the patterns of the child's communication.

Depending on whether the patterns or reactions emerge as part of the child's metaphor or as a function of the child's behavior, communication, or interaction, you could metacommunicate directly or via the metaphor. As we said in Chapter 9, matching the child's communication is essential if they feel more comfortable communicating metaphorically than directly.

Purpose of Metacommunication

The purpose of metacommunicating is to help children begin to notice and understand their own patterns (Kottman & Meany-Walen, 2016). In many cases, children are unaware that they are acting or reacting in a certain way. Even when they are aware of their patterns, they often do not have the abstract verbal reasoning skills to conceptualize what these patterns mean about themselves and their interactions. By pointing out the patterns in children's behavior, reactions, attitudes, emotions, communication, and cognitions, the therapist can help children think about possible meanings in the patterns and help them gain insight into the issues related to underlying themes. Because the play therapy process frequently involves unspoken communication, the therapist needs to pay attention to children's nonverbals, especially when they seem to be asking a question without words. It can also be helpful to notice and comment on children's reactions to the therapist's interventions to give a voice to those reactions. Unlike adults in therapy, children do not always give clear verbal feedback about what the therapist has said. It becomes incumbent on the therapist to articulate those reactions so that children become aware of their own responses to therapeutic interventions and can use that information in the growth process.

Phrasing and Styles of Metacommunication

Because the patterns and reactions that metacommunication is concerned with are covert or implicit, it is speculative in nature. Therefore, it is better for you as a play therapist to phrase metacommunication in a tentative way to avoid imposing your reality on the child. When you make guesses (rather than assertions) about the child's patterns, the child has a chance to respond to the metacommunication without feeling a need to be defensive or to overpower you. Sometimes the child is not ready to acknowledge that particular pattern, other times you may have made an incorrect guess about underlying issues or communication patterns, and sometimes the child wishes to correct or clarify your interpretation. To maintain a tentative stance, you can include conditional words and phrases such as "might be," "maybe," "I would guess," "I am thinking," "kind of," "seems as though," and so forth. By keeping hypotheses tentative, your goal is to make clear to the child that they do not have to acknowledge the communication or agree with the contents of the message.

There are three basic styles of metacommunication. One is to simply describe the behavior or the pattern without adding any speculation or guess about what the behavior or pattern means (e.g., "You frowned right after I said that about your mom." or "Wombat Woman bounced up and down after she defeated the snake."). The second method is to focus on interpreting the meaning of the behavior or pattern, with little or no emphasis on the description of the behavior or pattern (e.g., "I am thinking when I say that your mom seems happy being married to your stepdad, you get kind of mad." or "Wombat Woman seemed very excited when she defeated the snake."). The third method is a combination of the first two—the therapist describes the behavior or pattern and speculates about what it might mean (e.g., "You frowned right after I said that your mom seems happy being married to your stepdad. I am thinking you got kind of mad when I said that." or "Wombat Woman seemed excited and proud when she defeated the snake. It seemed as though maybe she was nervous about whether she could beat him or not.").

Play therapists who tend to be nondirective will either avoid metacommunication or restrict themselves to describing the behavior or pattern without adding any speculation or guessing about what it means. Other, more directive play therapists are more likely to use all three methods.

Children's Reactions

It is important to pay attention to children's reactions to metacommunication. Some children do not seem to understand or respond to metacommunication. Sometimes, this is because the therapist's interpretation is incorrect or inaccurate, and for some reason, the child is not comfortable or willing to correct the therapist. It may also be due to the children's developmental level or cognitive ability. Understanding metacommunication requires relatively high levels of cognitive and receptive language skills, and some children have not yet developed the ability to comprehend such therapeutic comments. Other children are concrete thinkers and may be unable to recognize patterns or underlying issues even when the therapist highlights them. Metacommunication is not a skill that works well with these children and should probably be avoided with them.

Many children are reluctant to "own" certain feelings, reactions, or attitudes or to acknowledge certain underlying issues, and they may not respond in predictable ways to metacommunication about those patterns. Sometimes, these children simply ignore the metacommunication, or they overreact, vehemently denying the accuracy of the metacommunication or impugning the intelligence or insight of the play therapist. With these children, the play therapist can consider whether it would be helpful to continue to metacommunicate about the patterns and themes in the hope of eventually helping them to gain insight into and become comfortable acknowledging whatever is going on with them. This may be the most appropriate course of action, or it may be more therapeutic to wait until a child is more open to acknowledging their underlying issues and themes.

With children who we believe can understand the content of the metacommunication but have some other reason for not responding constructively, we often metacommunicate about their reactions to our original metacommunication. Other times, especially with children who have extremely negative reactions to a metacommunication, we might simply say, "Well, it's something to think about," rather than getting into a power struggle with them about whether they accept our interpretation of a particular behavior.

Examples of Metacommunication

Here are a few scenarios that have several examples of possible metacommunications.

Example 1

Barry (age 7) becomes aggressive with his play therapist whenever he does not get his way in a play session. He sometimes shouts at the therapist, gets very close physically, and does other things that seem intended to intimidate the therapist into doing what he wants. The therapist might metacommunicate by making comments such as the following:

> "You seem to get mad when I don't do what you want me to do."
>
> "I have noticed that sometimes you yell at me and stand close to me when I don't do what you want."
>
> "I am guessing that you think I will do what you want if you yell at me and stand really close to me."

Example 2

Elena (age 5) is a warm, open child. She has always been affectionate to her therapist, greeting her with hugs and kissing her on the cheek before she leaves a session. After the therapist announces that she is having a baby and they are going to take a break in their time together, Elena stops physically showing her affection and seems generally aloof in her sessions. The therapist might metacommunicate by making comments such as the following:

> "It seems like you are feeling kind of sad because we are going to take a break from seeing one another."

> "I have noticed that since I mentioned that we were going to take a break, it seems like you have stopped giving me hugs, and you are not smiling very much when we are together."

> "Since I mentioned that I am going to have a baby, it seems like you have stopped giving me hugs, and you don't smile very much in here. I am thinking that you might be kind of sad and mad at me because we are going to take a break for a while."

Example 3

Aditya (age 6) has been diagnosed as being on the autism spectrum. He is always quiet in his play therapy sessions, but he is even more quiet whenever he has had a rough day at school or gotten into a conflict with one of his siblings on the way to his session. This is especially true whenever his mother reports such problems to the therapist in the waiting room before his session. The therapist might metacommunicate by making comments such as the following:

> Aditya, sometimes it seems like you are especially quiet when you have had a hard day at school."

> "I have noticed that you don't seem to talk much on the days when your mom tells me that you have had a rough day."

> "I am guessing that you feel kind of bad about how your day went today, and you're just not feeling like talking very much. That happens sometimes when kids have had a hard day."

> "I am thinking that you feel kind of embarrassed when your mom tells me that you haven't been getting along with your brother, and you just don't want to talk about that when it happens, so you get really quiet in here, letting me know that the squabble with your brother is not something you want to discuss."

Example 4

Justine (age 4) is afraid of many things, including snakes, bugs, fire trucks, and ambulances. Whenever she sees any of the things she fears or discusses them in a session, her voice gets higher and louder, and her speech speeds up. The therapist might metacommunicate by making comments such as the following:

> "I noticed that whenever you see a toy fire truck or ambulance in the room, you get a little louder."
>
> "You seem to be a little nervous whenever you look over there at the shelf with the fire truck and the ambulance."
>
> "It sounds like your voice got louder when you saw the toy fire truck. I am thinking you feel a little nervous about having it in the playroom."

Example 5

Alexander (age 7) was physically abused by his birth mother. When he was four, he was placed in kinship foster care with his aunt. When the play therapist moves their chair closer to Alexander to be able to see his painting, Alexander flinches and moves away. The therapist might metacommunicate by making comments such as the following:

> "I noticed that when I moved my chair closer so I could see your painting, you kind of got all scrunched up."
>
> "It looked to me like when I moved my chair closer to you, you felt a little scared about me being that close to you. I can move away if that would be more comfortable to you."
>
> "It seemed like you got kind of scrunched up when I moved my chair so I could see what you were painting, like maybe you thought that I might hurt you if I was that close. I am guessing you wish I would move my chair further away from you."

Example 6

Solidad (age 6) tends to try to please the adults in her life and is highly anxious in this area. She is using Model Magic to create an animal figure. When she asked the therapist what she should make, her therapist returned the responsibility for making that decision to her. Whenever she adds a piece of Model Magic to the figure, she glances over, visually checking the therapist's reaction. The therapist might metacommunicate by making comments such as the following:

> "I noticed that you were looking over here, kind of checking out what I was thinking about what you are making."

> "It seems like you are worried about whether I am going to like what you are making."

> "You seem to be looking over here like you are worried that I might not like what you are making."

> "I am thinking that you want to make sure that I like what you are doing with the Model Magic."

Example 7

Basajaun (age 9) does not like it when the therapist metacommunicates about his nonverbal reactions, especially those centered around the leg braces he wears. Whenever the therapist mentions his reactions to the leg braces, Basajaun says things like "Don't talk about that" or "You don't know anything." The therapist might metacommunicate by making comments such as the following:

> "Whenever I mention something about how you feel about your leg braces, you tell me not to talk about it."

> "It seems to me that you would like me to stop noticing it when you have a reaction to how your leg braces are working today."

> "I am thinking that you would like to get me to stop pointing it out when you are unhappy with your leg braces and how they are working."

Mutual Storytelling

Mutual storytelling is a counseling strategy developed by Ricardo Gardner (1971, 1993) in which the therapist asks the child to tell a story with a beginning, a middle, and an end. The therapist then tells a story using the same beginning—characters, setting, and dilemma—as the child's story. The new story should incorporate more constructive problem-solving skills and a more functional resolution than the child's original story. The idea behind mutual storytelling is that children's stories represent their worldview in some way. The stories might represent their ideas about relationships, perception of problem situations in their lives, ideas about appropriate ways to solve problems, or views of themselves and others. The purpose of mutual storytelling is to use the children's stories as a springboard for offering (a) different views about relationships, self, and others; (b) different ways to perceive the problem situations in their lives; and (c) more socially acceptable ways to solve problems. The therapist's story is usually intended to teach behaviors—new ways of coping with problem situations and different strategies for interacting with others.

How to Use Mutual Storytelling

The first step in this process of mutual storytelling is to ask children to tell a story. Children like to tell stories to adults who are willing to listen, so this invitation to tell a story is usually sufficient to get this process started. To make the story more concrete, the play therapist may suggest ways for the children to incorporate toys and other play media into the storytelling process (Kottman & Meany-Walen, 2016). With younger children (7 years or younger), it is helpful to set the stage by asking the children to choose a group of puppets, animals, or other toys to be the characters in the story, to pretend these characters can talk, and to use them to tell a story.

Older elementary school children (8 years or older) may balk at using puppets and animals, but they are often willing to use miniature figures, such as sand tray figures, to tell stories. The therapist can also encourage a child in this age range to tell stories if the therapist sets the scene by saying that the child is the guest on a television or radio show invited to tell the audience a story. The therapist will then play the television or radio show host and retell the story from that role. The therapist can add a certain amount of authenticity by recording the story. An additional advantage to this approach is that the child can listen to the recording as many times as they wish. There are also many different computer programs (some free and some commercial) designed to guide children in creating stories and storyboards.

Because it is important that the child be invested in the story, we suggest that it be original—not the plot of a movie, book, video game, or television show. However, some children struggle to make up a story from scratch by themselves. We just go with what children say about this process—it's not worth getting into a power struggle with them if they are convinced they can't make up original stories. With these children, we let them use a borrowed plot because they almost always impose their worldview onto the way they recount the story. They filter the plot of the borrowed story through their own way of looking at relationships and situations. In this way, the story reveals more about them than the movie, book, video game, or television show in its original form (Kottman & Meany-Walen, 2016, 2018).

Many times, children will tell very short stories without much detail or plot. These stories often end abruptly when the children run out of ideas and stop the narrative. Depending on how you expect a child to react, you may choose to probe a bit to elicit more details of the story. Some children tolerate this probing well and might even enjoy your interest in the story. These children will frequently reengage themselves in the story after a couple of questions from you and will tell more of the story without further prompting. Other children will resent your probing and react as if you were criticizing their ability to tell a story. You must watch for their nonverbal responses to probes and adjust your own behavior accordingly.

The second step in the mutual storytelling process is to listen to the story metaphorically. As you listen to the child's story, think about how it represents the child's worldview and the situations and relationships in the child's life. It is helpful to consider the following questions as a way to structure your understanding of the story (Gardner, 1993; Kottman & Meany-Walen, 2026, 2018):

- How does what the characters do in the story fit with what you already know about the child?
- How does the situation in the story resemble situations the child normally encounters?
- Which one of the characters in the story represents the child?
- How does the character who represents the child feel in the story?
- Which of the characters in the story represent the important people in the child's life or the people involved in a particular situation with which the child is currently struggling?
- How does the affective tone of the story represent the child's perceptions of the world? Does the affective tone convey the idea that the child is optimistic or pessimistic?
- How does the story represent the child's perceptions of self?
- What does the story tell you about the way the child thinks about their ability to cope with problem situations?
- How does the story represent the child's attitudes toward other people?
- What does the story reveal about the child's perceptions of patterns and themes in relationships and interactions?
- How are the patterns and themes in relationships and interactions in the story similar to what you have observed in the child's patterns and themes in relationships and interactions?

- What is the usual method of coping with conflicts or problem situations in the story?
- How is the usual method of coping with conflicts or problem situations in the story similar to the child's usual mode of handling conflict or resolving problems?
- What is your affective response to the story?

Based on thoughts generated by these questions and others you may have, formulate some ideas about what the story reveals about the child, the child's life, relationships with others, self-image, and their methods of dealing with difficulties. There may be theory-specific questions you would ask about the story. For instance, if you were a cognitive-behavioral play therapist, you might ask yourself how the story reveals the child's self-talk. If you were an Adlerian play therapist, you might consider what the story reveals about the goals of misbehavior, the Crucial Cs, and the child's personality priorities.

The third step in this process is retelling the story, with a more adaptive, socially appropriate middle and end. In preparation for the retelling, you would consider the following questions:

- Which character(s) would you leave in the story for retelling? Why?
- Would you add any character(s)? If yes, what traits would you incorporate in any added character(s)?
- Why would that (those) character(s) be important with this child?
- What positive characteristics or traits would you want to encourage in the child through this story?
- Do you want to incorporate some kind of consequences for negative behaviors in the story? If so, what consequences would be appropriate without sounding moralistic or judgmental?
- If the affective tone of the original story was negative or pessimistic, how can you incorporate a more positive, optimistic affective tone?
- How can you incorporate more constructive patterns of interacting with others?
- How can you include more socially appropriate methods of resolving conflicts or resolving any difficulties in the story?
- How can you encourage the child to focus on their strengths?
- How can you use the elements of the story to teach new ways of viewing other people?

- How can you use the story to give the child feedback about how others see them?
- How can you use the story to improve the child's faith in their ability to solve problems?
- How can you incorporate more descriptions of the characters' feelings and reactions?

This seems like many factors to consider as you listen to a child tell you a story that may last only 30 seconds to a minute or two. As you begin using mutual storytelling, you may want to give yourself extra time to go through these two lists before you retell the story. This extra time can involve making an audio recording of the original story, listening to it outside of the session, and returning to the next session with your modified version. It can involve you simply thinking about the original story for several minutes and then retelling it later in the session.

As with therapeutic metaphors (see Chapter 12), there are several ways to deliver the retelling. You can use the same modality the child did (e.g., puppet show, video recording, miniatures, animal figures) or a different one (e.g., painting or drawing a picture or mural, making a book, making a personalized video recording). It is essential to present the retelling without emphasizing that you are retelling the story—you don't want to imply that anything was wrong with the original version. As you introduce your version of the story, it is helpful to tell the child that you were so interested in the story and the characters in their story that it inspired you to think of a story you wanted to tell about those same characters.

It is likely that every play therapist will have a unique interpretation of the meaning and underlying messages of a child's original story and will design a completely different retelling than any other play therapist. There is no one perfect retelling of the story, so there is no reason to agonize over every nuance of the retelling in an attempt to get it "right." You may retell a story one way or another in the session when the child tells the original story and in other ways in subsequent sessions.

Examples of Mutual Storytelling

The following examples present a possible retelling for each of the children described:

Example 1

Skylar (age 7) has a learning disability that affects his ability to read, understand, and complete written assignments. He is referred to play therapy by his school counselor, who reports that he tends to be shy and withdrawn in his special education classroom but aggressive on the playground. The school counselor speculates that this pattern is related to his struggles with academic subjects and that the other students make fun of him for this. Skylar is strong and physically powerful, so he may be getting his revenge while out on the playground. Skylar uses the animal puppets to tell the following story:

> There once was a bear cub, and he wasn't very good at climbing trees and getting honey from the bees. When he played with the other bear cubs, they made fun of him. They said, "You are so dumb—the bees are smarter than you. You can't even climb the tree. What is wrong with you?" He would swat them with his paw and say, "I am not dumb. You are the dumb ones!" Nobody wanted to be friends with him. They said, "Go away and leave us alone. Go play with the bees."

A possible retelling of this story:

> There once was a bear cub named Snarl, and he had some trouble climbing trees and getting honey from bee hives. He was frustrated by this and tried many different ways to learn to climb better. Snarl was still having trouble despite all his efforts to climb. He also struggled with getting honey from the beehives up in the tree. When he wanted to play with the other bear cubs, they said, "Why do you have so much trouble climbing? What can't you get honey from the beehives? What is wrong with you?" Snarl said, "I don't know, but I really want to learn how." Two other bear cubs, Fuzz and Buzz, said, "We will help you learn." The other bear cubs were still mean to him, saying, "You are not even a bear. You should know how to climb and get honey." Fuzz and Buzz help him practice climbing every day, and Snarl slowly began to get better at climbing. He even managed to get a little bit of honey from the beehive. He felt proud of himself and said to Fuzz and Buzz, "Thank you so much for helping me. I don't think I could have learned to climb without your help." Snarl climbed the tree to get some honey to give them in thanks. He ignored the other young bear cubs and decided to work on being better friends with Fuzz and Buzz because they had helped him with his problem.

Example 2

Lindey (age 9) lives with her mother and stepfather. Although she once got along with her stepfather, the more he tried to impose rules and discipline on the children, the angrier Lindey became. Lindey's mother and stepfather were willing to work things out, but they were at a loss for how to cope with Lindey's alternately defiant and clinging behavior. Lindey sat on a chair and told this story:

> There once was a kitten that nobody wanted. She tried to find a place to live, but her mother didn't want her to live with her, and her father didn't want her to live with him. She went to her grandmother's house, and she didn't want her either. She was kind of sad, but then she got mad. She went back to each house and knocked them all down. The kitten thought that she would feel better when she did this, but she didn't. She felt worse than ever.

A possible retelling of this story:

> There once was a kitten named Lilly who thought nobody wanted her. Lilly's father said she couldn't live with him because he worked at night and was afraid he couldn't take good care of her. Her mother said Lilly could live with her, but Lilly did not get along with her mother's new husband, so Lilly went to her grandmother's house. Gram was very old, and she had trouble taking care of herself. Even though Gram wanted Lilly to stay and live with her, she knew that would not be best for the kitten. Gram was also very wise, though, and she knew how much Lilly's father, mother, and stepfather all loved her. Gram asked Lilly if she could help Lilly figure out some new ways that Lilly could try to get along with her stepfather. They talked it over and had some good ideas, but the kitten was still not sure it would work out for her to live with her mother and stepfather. Gram asked Lilly if she would be willing to come to a meeting with her mother, her stepfather, and her grandmother so they all could talk about the problems they had been having. Gram reminded Lilly that her stepfather had never been a parent before, so he might need some help from Lilly learning how to be a dad. The kitten knew her grandmother would be on her side, so Lilly agreed to try to work it out. They had the meeting and decided to give it another chance. Lilly returned to her mother's and stepfather's house and started training him how to be a good dad. Her stepfather really wanted to be a good dad, so he listened to what Lilly had to say. But at the same time, he stuck to some of the rules that were important to him. He explained to Lilly why those rules were important to him. Things were still not perfect, but they got better every day.

Example 3

Li Quang (age 5) rules over his family by using temper tantrums to get what he wants. Whenever his mother and father try to get him to comply with their requests, or they say "no" to him, he throws himself on the floor, yells, screams, bites, cries, and throws things at them. He acts out the following story with the animal figures:

> This is the big lion. He says, "I am the king, and everybody has to do what I say." These are all the other animals who live in the woods. They say, "What will you do if we don't do what you say?" The big lion says, "I will roar at you and scratch you and make you do what I want." The other animals say, "OK, we will do what you tell us to do."

A possible retelling of this story:

> Leo, the big lion, was mighty and always wanted the other animals who lived in the jungle to do what he told him to do. He got mad when they didn't do what he wanted because he thought the other animals should follow his rules. Leo decided the best way to get the other animals to do what he wanted would be to roar and swipe them with his claws. He hurt several animals, so they all hid when he came to their part of the woods. Leo was disappointed that no one wanted to be friends or play with him anymore, so he told the animals he had hurt that he was sorry. He asked them how he could be friends with them again. They said, "You cannot always be the boss. You will have to take a turn. Sometimes you can be the boss, but sometimes we want to be the boss, too. And you cannot roar or scratch just because you don't get your way." Leo decided to try their way and see how it worked. He didn't like letting the other animals get their way, but he did it anyway, and he was pretty happy because he had a lot of new friends.

Co-Telling a Story With the Child

Co-telling a story is when the play therapist takes turns with a child telling a story. There are many ways to do this. The play therapist can introduce a topic (e.g., ways to cope with being scared, making friends, dealing with rejection) by describing the characters, the setting, and the initial problem faced by the characters in the story. The therapist would then pass the telling to the child, who would pass it back to the therapist, and so on, taking turns until either or both the therapist and the child come to a conclusion, ending the story. The play therapist can also ask the child to choose the topic and start the story, with the therapist taking over the second part and then passing the telling back to the child. It can also be fun to have a conversation whereby the therapist and child collaboratively decide what the story is about, choose the characters and the problem, and then decide who will start the story. There are many ways to organize the telling. For example, (a) the therapist and the child can each tell a sentence at a time, alternating sentences; (b) they could tell a paragraph at a time, switching off at the end of each paragraph; or (c) the storytelling can be *free form*, without a set formula for how the story is told. We often use a collection of sand tray figures or a page of clipart pictures gathered from the internet as the springboard for the story. With children who can read, we sometimes write nouns or verbs on 3 × 5 cards, then take turns drawing a card and incorporating the word into the next part of the story. We also do *stretching stories* (Ashby et al., 2002; Kottman & Meany-Walen, 2018), taking turns telling segments of the story while acting out the movement in the story together. As you can see, there are a million ways to co-tell stories with children—don't feel constrained to follow our lead on this—give yourself permission to "make stuff up."

Role Playing and Engaging in Play

Regardless of their theoretical approach, many play therapists use role playing or engaging in play with the child in their sessions. There are several methods used to role-play or engage in play with the child, with the choice depending on the therapist's personal preference and theoretical orientation. These methods include the whisper technique (Kottman & Meany-Walen, 2016; G. Landreth, personal communication, September 24, 2010) and other methods such as role reversal, behavior rehearsal, and creative dramatics.

Whisper Technique

The *whisper technique* consists of an interaction between the therapist and the child in which the therapist gives the child control of the direction and content of the play (or the role playing). This method of playing ensures that the child has input into what happens in the interaction; it can also be a strategy for returning responsibility to the child.

How to use the whisper technique. When using the whisper technique for role playing, you will use at least three different voices: (a) your own "regular" voice, (b) a character voice, and (c) a whisper voice. You would use your voice to make therapeutic comments such as tracking, restating content, reflecting feelings, metacommunicating, and so forth. You would use the character voice (or voices) to represent the character(s) you are playing. The whisper voice would be used to ask the child for directions. By whispering, "What should I say?" or "What should I do?" you can involve the child in the decision-making process to encourage them to be engaged and take responsibility.

In our interactions with children, we have noticed that most are more likely to respond with directions when we ask in a whisper. We are not sure why this strategy works so well. When you initially use the whisper, some children are unsure what to do. However, they will usually begin to respond if you persist in asking them for directions with a whisper, occasionally giving them a prompt by whispering things like "Now you are supposed to tell me what to say" or "I am going to wait to do something until you tell me what to do." If they do not respond to the prompts, you may want to metacommunicate what could be happening with them. For example, they could be afraid to take a risk by telling an adult what to do; they could suspect that you are trying to trick them in some way; or they may not be in the practice of controlling anything, and so they have no ideas for what should happen next in the role play.

Beginning therapists tend to struggle with remembering to use their own voice to continue to interact in a therapeutic way with the child. They get so caught up in the playing that they let that particular aspect of the whisper technique lapse. It will be important to remember that you are still the therapist even when you are a partner in the child's play.

When the child is stuck. There will be situations in which the child seems "stuck," such as when the child plays the same role repeatedly with the same behaviors, talk, and so forth, and without seeming to gain insight or learn new behaviors. This repetition may stem from the child using the play for abreaction—to gain a sense of mastery over a certain experience or relationship or as catharsis—or to express painful feelings. When this happens, the child will tend to be relaxed and calm after the play scene has ended. At other times, though, the child will seem agitated and confused after the play has ended. In these cases, the child may be exhibiting *posttraumatic play* (Gil, 2017; Goodyear-Brown, 2019), which is play in which the child feels retraumatized rather than helped toward a sense of mastery.

If it seems as though the child is stuck, you will need to consider how the play is affecting the child. If the play seems to be soothing the child somehow, it is probably appropriate to let the child continue to be stuck until they feel the need to move somewhere else with the play. You should avoid interfering with the child's quest for mastery simply because you are bored with the play.

However, if you believe that the child is engaging in repetitive posttraumatic play, you can decide to take the role playing in a different direction and not use the whisper technique to ask the child for the next set of instructions. When this happens, you can simply do or say something to move the play past the stuck part. This may involve suggesting alternative endings to the story, teaching different coping strategies for dealing with problem situations, introducing new characters that provide help or advice to the other characters, and so forth. Most nondirective play therapists would probably choose not to be this directive. They would most likely deal with this issue in another way—perhaps by choosing not to participate in a role-playing or playing situation that seems to be evoking a posttraumatic response. If you are in this situation and are struggling with whether the child is stuck in a productive, useful way or in a nonproductive, self-destructive way, you might want to consider getting supervision about the case or consulting with an experienced play therapy colleague. It is quite possible that being stuck with the child's stuckness is related to one of your own issues rather than the child's.

Other Methods

Several other methods are used to play or role-play with the child, including instant replay, role reversal, or release therapy (Gil & Dias, 2021; Harvey, 2016; Irwin, 2014; Kottman & Meany-Walen, 2018). Some therapists role play using puppets or costumes to present metaphors or mutual storytelling, assigning parts to themselves and the child. Other therapists structure role playing to help the child practice new behaviors, or they use instant replay within the role play to experiment with a variety of ways to handle problem situations. *Instant replay* is a technique in which the therapist asks the child to repeat a recent interaction but with a different attitude or style of approaching the situation. The therapist would use this technique to give a child feedback that their usual way of interacting with others is not appropriate and to invite the child to practice more appropriate interactional patterns.

To increase a child's empathy, understanding of others' feelings, and ability to comprehend other perspectives, the play therapist may set up *role reversal* situations. In role reversal, the therapist pretends to be the child, and the child pretends to be some important person in the child's life, usually one with whom the child has a pattern of conflict or misunderstanding. Because the purpose is to teach the child new perspectives or skills, the therapist would not usually use the whisper technique to ask for directions. Instead, they would decide what to do or say without letting the child control the interaction.

In some cases, the therapist may be working with a variation of *release therapy*, in which the child acts out a traumatic event over and over until the event's impact on the child is lost. By participating in this play, the therapist can have some control over how the child plays out and processes the event.

Examples of Playing or Role Playing

In the following examples, we demonstrate several methods of engaging in play and role-playing with Ricardo (age 7), including the whisper technique, instant replay, teaching and practicing new behaviors, and role reversal.

Whisper Technique

Ricardo: "Let's play heist."

Therapist: "OK." In a whisper, "Who do you want me to be?"

Ricardo: "You be the cops, and I will be the robber."

Therapist: "So you decided that you want to be the robber, and you want me to be the cops." In a whisper, "What happens next?"

Ricardo: "I am going to drive the truck up to the bank, go in, threaten the guards with a gun, and grab the money. I will then drive away in my getaway truck. You just drive the cop car into this barricade. You get mad because you are not going to be able to catch me."

Therapist: "You want me to crash the car into the barricade. It sounds like I might be a little frustrated with not being able to catch you." In a deep "cop" voice, "I am so mad. That barricade is blocking my way, and I can't catch up to the robber."

Ricardo: "I am getting away with all the money!"

Therapist: "You have a lot of confidence in yourself, Mr. Robber. You are sure you will be able to get away with all that money." In a whisper, "What should I be doing?"

Ricardo: "You try to go around the barricade, but it doesn't work, so you get even madder."

Therapist: In the cop voice, "I am so mad. I tried so hard to go around that barrier, but I can't find a way around it. I am scared the robber is going to get away with the money, and that is very frustrating."

Ricardo moves the truck into the play school building.

Ricardo: "Haha! You thought you would be able to catch me. Now I am in my hideout, and you will never find me."

Therapist: "You sound very proud of yourself for getting away from the cops and being safe in your hideout." In a whisper, "What should I do?"

Ricardo: "Try to find me. But you won't get past the barricade into my hideout. I am safe."

Therapist: "You sound satisfied with getting away and being safe." In the cop voice, "I will find a way around this barricade."

Therapist tries going around the barrier, but Ricardo adds more objects to the barricade, preventing circumnavigation.

Therapist: "I am worried that the robber will not be caught and will get away from me and the other police officers."

Ricardo: "Yup. Home free and safe. You lose!"

Therapist: "You knew just how to keep the cops from catching you, and you are in a safe space." In a whisper, "What should I do?"

Ricardo: "Just give up, drive your cop car away and say, 'The end.'"

Therapist: "So the story is finished now. The end!"

Instant Replay

Ricardo: In a very bossy voice, "I want to play with that game up there on the shelf. Get it for me right now."

Therapist: "I would be glad to help you get that game, but when you talk to me like that it hurts my feelings, and I don't feel like doing favors for you. Let's try that again. Try asking me to get the game in a different way."

Ricardo: In his regular voice, "I want to play with that game up there on the shelf. Could you get it for me?"

Therapist: "I would be delighted to get it for you. Thank you for asking in such a polite way."

Teaching/Practicing New Behaviors

Therapist: "OK, Ricardo, the next time your brother Jesus tries to get you into trouble, what are you going to do?"

Ricardo: "Ignore him and go tell my mom, without using a whiny voice, that Jesus hit me or whatever he did."

Therapist: "Let's practice that. I will be Jesus and your mother, and you be yourself. I am Jesus, and I come up and push you. What do you say?"

Ricardo: "Nothing. I turn and walk away. Then I go to my mom and say, 'Mom, I just wanted you to know that Jesus pushed me. I walked away and didn't do anything back.'"

> *Therapist: In a high-pitched "mom" voice, "Wow, Ricardo. You did it—you didn't let Jesus push you into getting in trouble. I am proud of you." In a regular voice, "How did that feel? Let's try it again using a different strategy."*

Role Reversal

> *Therapist: "Ricardo, from what you have told me, you seem to get yourself into trouble with your teacher when you use a crabby voice, or you try to tell her what to do. To give you an idea how she feels when you speak that way, let's pretend that you are the teacher and I am you." In a crabby voice, "I can't believe you gave me a 'C' on this work. I want you to change this grade right now." In a regular voice, "Now, what would the teacher say?"*
>
> *Ricardo: "I can't change the grade. You missed all these problems."*
>
> *Therapist: In a crabby voice, "You are so mean. You never do what I want. I hate you." In a regular voice, "What would the teacher say if you said that?"*
>
> *Ricardo: "Ricardo, I am sorry that you feel that way, but we don't talk that way to people in our room. You need to go to the office."*
>
> *Therapist: "How did that feel when you were being the teacher and I talked to you that way?"*
>
> *Ricardo: "Bad. I didn't like it. I got mad, but I didn't think the teacher would yell at me. She never has before."*
>
> *Therapist: "Let's try it now, and I will talk in a more polite way about the same situation. Let's see how you feel."*

The number of counseling skills and techniques that can be adapted for use in the playroom is limited only by your imagination. If you are willing to be creative and take some risks by experimenting with various intervention strategies, you can generate a plethora of interventions that might be helpful in play therapy. It would be impossible to list and describe every play therapy technique in an overview such as this. You can learn more about play therapy techniques in the suggested resources in Appendix C.

Play Therapy Strategies

There are six main play therapy strategies representing broad "umbrella" categories of tools play therapists can use, depending on their theoretical orientation, personal inclination, and specialized training, supervision, and experience (Kottman & Meany-Walen, 2018). These six strategies are adventure therapy; storytelling and therapeutic metaphors; movement, dance, and music experiences; sand tray activities; art activities; and structured play experiences. Rather than providing a detailed description of these strategies, we will provide the basic gist of each.

Adventure therapy is "the use of games, activities, initiatives, and peak experiences to facilitate the development of group process, interpersonal relationships, personal growth, and therapeutic gain" (Ashby et al., 2008, p. 1). Adventure therapy activities can be used as stand-alone methods for accomplishing a specific therapeutic objective or as part of a sequential process designed to move clients forward by cycling through icebreakers, deinhibitizers, trust- and empathy-building exercises, and challenge/initiative and problem-solving exercises (Ashby et al., 2008; Kottman & Meany-Walen, 2018).

Described in this chapter and Chapter 12, *storytelling and therapeutic metaphors*

> can be used in many ways and provide a vast amount of information about the child to the play therapist. The therapist can gain knowledge of the child's developmental stage, their language ability, their play skills, their attachment style, and their understanding of their life experiences. (Murray, 2021, p. 95)

> By telling a story, reading a book, or helping a client shift a metaphor from a negative one to a positive one, you can allow a client to keep a safe distance from difficult material and still communicate significant concepts or skills. (Kottman & Meany-Walen, 2018, p. 99)

Movement, dance, and music experiences especially appeal to children who need to keep moving or love music. The play therapist can use these for assessment as well as an intervention. They can help assess clients' capacity for relationships, body image, self-confidence, creativity, self-regulation, comfort with their bodies, and problem-solving. As interventions, dance, movement, and music techniques can help clients explore feelings, attitudes, and patterns of behavior; access their body's wisdom; practice new ways of interacting with others; build trust; share control; increase cooperation; handle problem situations; and enhance their relationships with others (Devereaux, 2014; Kottman & Meany-Walen, 2018; LeFeber, 2014). According to S. Taylor (2021), music, dance, and movement work with all four of the major therapeutic powers of play designated by Schaefer and Drewes (2014): facilitating communication, fostering emotional wellness, enhancing social relationships, and increasing personal strengths. These experiences can be customized to the needs and preferences of individual children.

Sand tray therapy uses small toys and a sand tray as a vehicle for exploration and expression, whereby clients choose figures from a collection of miniatures and put them into a tray of sand (Kottman & Meany-Walen, 2018). Sand tray therapy is

> an expressive and projective mode of psychotherapy involving the unfolding and processing of intra- and inter-personal issues through the use of specific sand tray materials as a nonverbal medium of communication, led by the client or therapist and facilitated by a trained therapist. (Homeyer & Sweeney, 2023, p. 6)

D. Sweeney (2021) suggested that sand tray therapy provides clients unable or unwilling to verbalize with a language of miniatures as a way to express themselves. In addition, it has a unique sensory and kinesthetic quality that appeals to many clients, supplies a safe place for abreaction, is effective in helping overcome client resistance, and is a vehicle for accessing deep interpersonal and intrapersonal issues.

Many play therapists use *art activities* in their interactions with clients. Some clients spontaneously draw, paint, use modeling clay, or build structures with paper and other materials, whereas others need to be invited to engage in artistic creation. Art in the playroom can help clients explore feelings, relationships, and cognitions; understand interpersonal or intrapersonal dynamics; gain insight into their patterns; practice new behaviors or attitudes; and so forth (Kottman & Meany-Walen, 2018). There are innumerable possibilities for clients to express themselves artistically, such as by drawing or painting, creating images with stickers, constructing, sculpting, collaging, and making puppets or masks—to name just a few. Again, the application of this strategy is limited only by play therapists' imagination and willingness to try new methods of working with clients.

Structured play experiences can range from simple children's games (e.g., "Mother, May I?", red light/green light, blowing bubbles, pitch and catch) to more elaborate activities, such as puppet shows, role plays, tabletop games, and scenarios done in the dollhouse or kitchen area (Kottman & Meany-Walen, 2018). Play therapists can use structured play activities as an assessment process designed to help them understand clients' intrapersonal or interpersonal dynamics, as a vehicle for helping clients gain insight, or as a way to help clients make changes. They can be used as interventions to help clients explore new patterns of interacting with others and communicating, to help them learn and practice new ways of solving problems, or to help them gain insight into their patterns of thinking, feeling, and behaving. Structured play experiences can be a part of everything you might want to do in a playroom if you are willing to be directive or go along with a child who initiates structured play activities.

Practice Exercises

Exercise 1

For each of the following scenarios, write two responses involving metacommunication.

1. Luke (age 7) has been diagnosed with attention-deficit/hyperactivity disorder and struggles in school academically and socially. He was referred to play therapy because he has low self-confidence, especially about school and friendships. Every time you return responsibility to him, he shakes his head, looks sad, and says, "I can't do that. You know I don't know how."

2. Yvonne (age 5) is in foster care because her mother is in a drug rehabilitation program. She comes into the session smiling, chattering, and bouncing. She is excited because she visited with her mother before her session.

3. Royal (age 9) does not like talking about his incarcerated father. Whenever you comment or ask a question about his father, he moves to the other side of the room and sits with his arms crossed.

4. Raisa (age 6) tells you that her grandmother yelled at her this afternoon. She seems sad, so you reflect that feeling by saying, "You seem very sad about that." She says, "No, she can't do anything to make me sad. I hate her because she is always mean to me."

5. Whenever you ask Grady (age 8) a question, he shrugs and frowns.

6. Raylene (age 4) has always had an excellent relationship with you. After you tell her that you are moving to another town and you will help her father find a new play therapist for her, Raylene seems to withdraw from the relationship, no longer making eye contact or chatting informally with you. You notice Raylene turning the dollhouse upside down.

7. Silus (age 8) is a pleaser but often has trouble following the playroom rules. Whenever you set a limit with him, he becomes compliant and quiet for the next 5 to 10 minutes. Then he gradually escalates, becoming louder and more defiant, until you set another limit. After this limit setting has happened several times in a session, he asks if you still like him.

8. Whitney (age 7) tells you that the other African American kids on the playground are picking on her because her skin is "very dark." She says, "I can't help how dark my skin is. Why are they blaming me?"

Exercise 2

Following the steps described earlier in this chapter (see "How to Use Mutual Storytelling"), formulate an understanding of the child and their issues and design a retelling of their original story. If you wish, you can develop several retellings for each story.

1. Bethesda (age 7) has had a series of losses in her life over the past year: Her dog died, her best friend moved away, two other friends dumped her, and her grandmother moved into a retirement community. Once optimistic, she has lately developed a pessimistic attitude, which has affected her relationships with her classmates, teacher, younger brother, and parents. She paints a picture and tells the following story:

    > This is an apple tree. It is sick. First, its apples all fall off, except for one. Then its leaves all fall off, except for one. It starts to get droopy, and the gardener thinks it is going to die. The day even gets cloudy, and you can't see the sun anymore. There's no rainbow either.

2. Garrin (age 9) was sexually and physically abused by his aunt when he was six years old. He tried to tell his parents about it, but they initially did not believe him. He is angry with his mother and father for not believing him and for not stopping his aunt. Garrin has nightmares and frequent crying outbursts. He also has a short temper and often hurts his two younger brothers. Recently, his parents caught him fondling one of his brothers. He tells you that he cannot think of a story but will tell you the plot of a movie he saw instead. His story:

    > There was this guy, and he saw some guys robbing someone's house. He tried to tell the police, but no one listened to him. Then the police decided that it was really him that robbed the house. It turned out that someone got killed in the robbery, and the police blamed him. They started chasing him to try to catch him, but he got away. I don't think the police ever believed him though, that he didn't do anything wrong.

3. Joo (age 5) has selective mutism. She talks to her parents and her younger sister but not to anyone else. She never speaks at school. Her kindergarten teacher has tried various interventions, but none have worked. She has never talked to you in her seven sessions with you. You ask her to tell her mother a story using the puppets while you leave the room and record it. She consents to do this. Here is her story:

> An, the rabbit, liked to hop around in his yard, but he didn't like to go outside the yard. He said, "I am afraid that someone outside the yard will hurt me if I go out there." So, he just stopped going out of the yard. His mother tried to get him to go out of the yard. She said, "Don't be afraid. No one will hurt you." But he just would not do it. He told his mother, "You can't make me go out there."

4. Harvey's (age 9) mother has bipolar disorder. She frequently stops taking her medication, leaves Harvey with his grandmother, and disappears for days. She has been hospitalized twice in the past three years. Harvey's grandmother is seeking legal custody of him, but she is afraid that his mother will take him and disappear with him. Harvey is struggling in school and has mood swings that seem erratic. Harvey's grandmother fears he may be "working on being nuts like his mom." Harvey uses miniatures to tell the following story through dialogue.

> *Female figure:* "Hi. My name is Nelly. I am a crazy nut."
>
> *Another female figure:* "My name is Jane. Nelly, you just have to shape up. I can't believe all the things you do. You just have to stop."
>
> *Smaller male figure:* "I don't have a name, and I hate you both. Why don't you just leave me alone?"
>
> *Nelly:* "OK. I will leave you alone, but I am never coming back. You just don't know what I will do."
>
> *Jane:* "We don't care. Just get out of our lives."
>
> *Smaller male figure:* "I do care. No, I don't care. I just don't know. I hate you both. I wish you were dead, and I wish I was too."

5. Jan (age 7) has asthma. Her parents tend to let her have her way rather than risk provoking an asthma attack. She is exceptionally bright but is not performing up to her potential in school. She makes an elaborate tableau with animal figures and puppets and tells the following story:

> This is the princess. She was asleep for a long time, and she was so beautiful that all the other people and animals in the kingdom came to look at her. Now that she is awake, she is in charge of the kingdom, and everybody has to do what she wants. Sometimes they don't like it, but that doesn't matter. When they don't do what she says, like this horse didn't, she puts them into a cage and doesn't give them any water or food. Pretty soon, they promise to do what she wants.

6. Vijay's (age 6) little brother recently died of sudden infant death syndrome. Since then, his parents have been extremely protective of him, to the point that they do not let him out of their sight. He has begun to develop nightmares and seems unusually anxious for a child his age. He uses three animals to tell the following story:

    > This is the father sheep, this is the mother sheep, and this is the baby sheep. The baby sheep says to the mother and father sheep, "I am going out of the fence to see what else is on the farm." The father sheep says, "No, you cannot do that because you might get hurt." The mother sheep says, "We have to make sure you are safe." The baby sheep says, "But I am tired of being in the fence. I want to go and look around the farm." The mother and the father sheep still say, "No. You have to stay here with us so we will know you are safe."

Exercise 3

For the following scenarios, make up two ways you could use role playing with the child. Label the technique (e.g., whisper, instant replay, role reversal) you used.

1. In his first session, Finn (age 8) gazes around the room for a while and then says, "Let's play with the army men."

2. Ginger (age 5) was sexually abused by her mother's boyfriend, who is now in jail. She loves to play with puppets. She asks if you will play with her. You know that she has some issues about being able to say "no" to others and about whether her mother will continue to love her since she "caused" the boyfriend to be incarcerated.

3. Guillermo's (age 9) father died when he was a baby. He has always assumed the role of the "man" in the house. His mother recently started dating again, and Guillermo treats all of his mother's

dates with aggression and contempt. This behavior has caused a rift between him and his mother. In this session, they both come into the playroom.

4. Iseult (age 7) is the youngest of seven children. All of her older brothers and sisters have alternately spoiled and bossed her. She tends to think she must be in charge of every situation, and she uses her charm and her temper to get what she wants. She comes into the session and says, "I don't care what you want to do. Today, we are going to play house. I am in charge!"

5. Martin (age 4) had a temper tantrum in the waiting room because his mother took a toy away after he hit her with it. He comes into the playroom mad at her and prepared to be mad at you. He says, "Let's do a puppet show about mean moms."

Questions to Ponder

1. Based on the descriptions, examples, and practice exercises provided in this chapter, what is your reaction to the skill of metacommunication?

2. Which do you think would be the most comfortable for you of the three basic styles of metacommunication (describing the behavior, focusing on the meaning of the behavior, and both describing and speculating about the meaning of the behavior)? Explain your reasoning.

3. Would you use mutual storytelling in your play therapy practice? Explain your reasoning.

4. Based on the examples and your own experience, is there a particular type of child with whom you would be more likely to use mutual storytelling? Explain your reasoning.

5. What kinds of pressures would you put on yourself to be able to retell a child's story immediately after they tell the original story? How can you give yourself permission to retell the story either later in the same session or even in another session?

6. Do you think you would use role play or playing with a child in your play therapy practice? Explain your reasoning.

7. Which method of role playing or playing with the child (e.g., whisper technique, instant replay, role reversal) appeals to you the most? Explain.

8. Which of the advanced skills described in this chapter would you be most comfortable using? Which would you be the least comfortable using? Explain.

9. What would you fear most about using these advanced skills in your work with children? What is your plan for making sure these fears do not prevent you from using any techniques that would be appropriate in your work?

10. Which of the six play therapy strategies (adventure therapy; storytelling and therapeutic metaphors; movement, dance, and music experiences; sand tray activities; art activities; and structured play experiences) discussed in this chapter do you want to explore more deeply?

11. Which of the play therapy strategies do you think might be fun to try in the playroom?

12. Some of the play therapy strategies are not used in nondirective approaches to play therapy. How do you feel about that restriction?

13. Which of the play therapy strategies do you find intimidating? What might you do to manage your anxiety if you decide you would like to use that strategy in your play therapy practice?

14. How will you adapt your interventions depending on the ethnicity or cultural background of the child?

14

Assessing Themes and Patterns in the Child's Play

Play therapy themes can be useful in improving clinical practice by helping the play therapist become more attuned to clients, develop more in-depth case conceptualization, identify clients' therapeutic issues, and communicate their needs and progress to their parents and caregivers (Holliman, 2021). As a play therapist, you will want to pay attention to patterns and themes in a child's play behavior, attitudes, and verbalizations to help you understand their personality and assess difficulties related to the presenting problem and any other factors involved in their coming to play therapy. Interpretation of the meaning of the child's behavior, attitudes, and verbalizations will depend, to an extent, on your theoretical orientation. In your work with children, you may monitor and assess factors or elements such as patterns of play suggesting themes in the play; developmental issues; how the child plays out the presenting problem and other significant concerns; repetitive play that seems to upset, rather than soothe, the child; level of aggression or challenge to the authority of the play therapist; the child's desire for secrecy or privacy; overtly sexual play, artwork, or verbalizations; the child's level of anxiety; the child's willingness to take risks; the child's desire for order and structure; the child's desire for power and control; and whether the child naturally communicates directly or in metaphor.

Play Themes

There are many ways of thinking about themes in play therapy and how you can understand and use them. Hollimon (2021) even acknowledged "it is neither necessary nor even possible to establish a definitive canon of play therapy themes" (p. 155). While we have not included an exhaustive review, we have tried to provide an overview of the important approaches to identifying and understanding themes in play therapy.

Ray (2011) posited that recognizing themes in children's play can deepen the therapist's understanding of children's subjective experiences. Sharing these themes with parents in parent consultation can help parents understand and empathize with their children. Ray distinguished between play behavior and play themes. She suggested that *play behaviors* are what children actually do in the playroom, whereas *play themes* are coherent metaphors children use to communicate the meaning they make of their life experiences as expressed through their play behaviors. As she explained, "The theme informs the therapist of the internal meaning-making system within the child" (Ray, 2011, p. 106).

Ray (2011) also described three characteristics that can help identify and understand the meaning of play themes: repetition, intensity, and context. *Repetition* involves play behavior that occurs multiple times in a single session or over several different sessions—the repetition usually indicates that this play is important and has meaning to children and their process. *Intensity* is "marked by the energy and focus applied to play behaviors within the session" (Ray, 2011, p. 107), which can be communicated through silence, an increase in emotion during the play, volume of voice, or vehemence in expression or movement. *Context* (which might include an understanding or knowledge of children's early development, personality traits, family circumstances, the presenting problem, and significant life experiences) can give you a framework through which to understand the meaning of themes.

Ray (2011) listed the following as examples of play themes: relationship, power/control, dependency, revenge, safety/security, mastery, nurturing, grief/loss, abandonment, protection, separation, reparation, chaos/instability, perfectionism, integration, hopelessness, helplessness, anxiety, self-sufficiency, and resiliency. For each of these themes, she described internal statements she maintained are the metaphoric communication represented by the play behaviors, including the following examples:

> Relationship—"It's important to me that we are connected." "I want to connect with you or others."

> Power/Control—"I must be in control of my environment to feel safe."
> "I must have power over you or others to be worthy."
> Hopelessness—"I have given up. Nothing will get better for me or
> others." "There is no one who can help me."
> Protection—"I must protect myself from someone or something." "I
> must protect others from someone or something." (Ray, 2011, p. 115)

VanFleet et al. (2010) focused on understanding play themes in child-centered play therapy. They advocated looking for behavioral patterns in which play is repeated, situations in which children do similar activities with different toys, sessions in which children are playing with unusual intensity and focus, specific play sequences that happen in several different play sessions, occasions when the play scenarios continue across sessions, and times when there is a shift in the affective tone of the play. VanFleet et al. enumerated common play themes that are evident in play therapy sessions: power and control, aggression, emotions, good against bad or evil, winning and losing, mastery of developmental tasks, mastery of anxiety or fears, reenactment of trauma, identity exploration and formation, boundaries and limits, grief and loss, nurturance and love, regression, attachment and connection, safety or protection paired with threat and danger, resilience, persistence, problem identification and solutions, wishes, and cultural symbolism.

Based on Erik Erickson's (1995) model of psychosocial development, Ryan and Edge (2012) and Sarah et al. (2021) suggested that seven themes occur in child-centered play therapy: trust, mistrust, autonomy, shame/doubt, initiative, guilt, and industry. Each theme has multiple subthemes (e.g., for the theme of trust, subthemes include nurturing, protection, comfort, rescued, attunement, having enough; for the theme of shame/doubt, subthemes are helplessness, self-doubt, and external approval). They used the *Child Initiated Pretend Play Assessment* (Stagnitti, 2007), a standardized, norm-referenced assessment tool, to measure play themes.

According to Kottman and Meany-Walen (2016, 2018), themes are recurring patterns in the children's early recollections; in their play behavior in the playroom; in their choices of toys and how they use them; in their interactions with other family members; in their descriptions of different situations and relationships in their lives; and in their views of self, others, and the world as expressed directly and through metaphors. These might include patterns in how the characters in the child's play, art, and stories interact with others, react to stressful situations, work to solve problems, deal with circumstances that are out of their control, talk about themselves and their capabilities, and so forth.

Adlerian play therapists use a commonsense method of understanding themes rather than a "standard" list of themes because they believe each person has their own way of understanding the symbols present in their communication.

Other approaches to play therapy also offer unique ways of classifying and understanding play themes. Studying thematic play therapy, L. Hillman (2014) did a factor analysis of Helen Benedict's (2001) coding system of play therapy themes that originally included 41 play theme content codes, 19 interpersonal-relationship process codes, and two process codes to find whether there was an underlying structure to the play themes. Hillman found nine factors: empowerment/loss of self-control, safety, violent violations, parentified internalizing, hyper-arousal/dissociation, maltreatment communication, people pleasing, attack/protect from self, and uncertainty/loss. Thematic play therapists look for unique characteristics and scenarios with idiosyncratic meanings for individual children related to common themes across children (Patton & Benedict, 2015). These themes include family (e.g., separation, reunion, nurturance), safety (e.g., danger, rescue), and aggression (e.g., good guys vs. bad guys, death, aggressor/victim). Green et al. (2009), writing from the perspective of Jungian play therapy and psychodynamic play therapy, suggested several patterns/themes that warrant special attention when working with children: death, failed nurturance, separation, safety, aggressive play, boundary violations in play, and sexualized play.

Notice that some themes recur across the writings of this plethora of experts in different approaches to play therapy. Each theoretical orientation will posit different themes as important in understanding children, depending on the philosophical beliefs about people, how their personalities form, and how therapists can help them make changes posited by that orientation. You will need to decide whether you want to incorporate any of these lists of the various play themes in your work with children and how you want to use them as tools in therapy and communicate about them with parents and/or teachers to deepen their understanding of the child.

How the Child Plays Out the Presenting Problem and Other Significant Concerns

By the time the child enters the playroom, you will have heard at least one version of the presenting problem—usually from the adult who has decided that the child needs counseling. The child will often have a different stance on the presenting problem and other significant concerns than the important adults in their life. You can obtain insight into the child's perspective by observing the play and the child's interaction with you. For example, you could learn how Arturo (age 5) views his parents' impending divorce by watching how he plays with the dollhouse and the doll family. He might set up two separate houses and have the doll children running back and forth between the two, crying. He might set up two houses and have the doll children refuse to enter one of them. He might have the doll children freely move between the houses, expressing relief that their parents are not fighting anymore. All three of these possible scenarios indicate different ways Arturo might react to the divorce.

Many times, the child does not view the presenting problem described by parents or teachers as an impediment or difficulty. The child may be struggling more with some other issue that the adults do not view as significant. When this is the case, these themes frequently get played out in the play. For example, Bashira's (age 6) father brings her to counseling because he thinks that she is depressed and feeling displaced because of the birth of her baby brother. However, if Bashira plays happily with the baby doll in a very nurturing way, feeding him with a bottle and cuddling him, you might speculate that her problems lie elsewhere. When Bashira makes a sand tray with a unicorn with only three legs and the other figures pick on him and call him names, you might recognize that Bashira's concern is related to possible bullying at school or in her neighborhood because of her physical differences.

Repetitive Play That Upsets

Children frequently repeat play sequences in therapy, which is not usually a problem. By repeating a scenario, a child can often resolve negative feelings connected to a traumatic experience through abreaction or catharsis. Repetitive play can also be useful in generating and practicing different responses to troublesome situations or relationships and in helping a child gain a sense of mastery over specific experiences. When repetitive play serves a therapeutic function for the child, they will seem comforted or satisfied at the end of the play.

There are times, however, when a child seems agitated or retraumatized by repetitive play. This type of repetitive play is called *posttraumatic play* (Gil, 2017; Terr, 1990) and is not therapeutic for the child. When this happens, it is often important to take note of specific scenarios that are distressing to the child. The therapist should interrupt the play to help the child break out of the posttraumatic play and replace it with play that is self-nurturing. Gil (2017), Goodyear-Brown (2019), and Kottman and Meany-Walen (2016, 2018) have suggested ways to help children with this process.

Aggression and Challenging Authority

Behaviors that represent aggression and challenges to the play therapist's authority include (a) repeated defiant responses to limiting, (b) attempts at physical or verbal aggression toward the therapist, (c) violent use of toys (e.g., punching, kicking, slamming), and (d) violent themes in the play (e.g., murder, mayhem, torture). To determine if the level of aggression or challenge to authority is within the "normal" range, you may find it helpful to compare each child's pattern of aggression or challenge with that of other children who come to play therapy. It is also helpful to consider the purpose of the behavior for this particular child (Kottman & Meany-Walen, 2016). Some children have witnessed or experienced a great deal of violence and may not have learned other ways to interact with the environment. Other children may be angry because of life circumstances that involve such things as racism, bullying, or abuse. Many children are simply testing limits to see how you will respond. There are also children who feel that this is a setting where they can safely express their true feelings, including rage, which might not be accepted in other settings.

If you believe that this behavior is therapeutic in some way for the child, even if it is outside the normal range, it is probably appropriate to let the behavior continue as long as there is no danger to the child, you, or the playroom. However, there are many times when ignoring the behavior (or refraining from limiting it) seems to exacerbate the child's problems by sanctioning behavior deemed unacceptable in most settings. This frequently seems to be the case with children diagnosed as having conduct disorder or oppositional defiant disorder. Their "venting" may only increase their hostility and aggression rather than serving an abreactive or cathartic function. If you consistently find that you, the child, or the playroom are at risk or that the behavior is not therapeutic and cannot be redirected, it may be appropriate to terminate play therapy sessions and try some other form of intervention.

Desire for Secrecy or Privacy

Some children manifest behavior in the playroom that suggests a strong need for secrecy or privacy. This behavior may involve a pattern of hiding themselves or building barriers between you and them. It may also include hiding or burying toys. Some children tell you they have a secret or that there are things they cannot discuss. There are several common interpretations of this behavior. Some children manifest this behavior because they believe they have something to hide or something they think is too shameful to share with others (e.g., children who have experienced abuse or are encopretic). For other children, this behavior suggests that they live in an environment where they do not feel they have access to privacy (e.g., children who live in crowded quarters or whose parents are enmeshed or intrusive). Some children use these behaviors as a way of asserting control over the course of the play therapy session (e.g., children who want to hide and have you find them).

Overtly Sexual Play, Artwork, or Verbalizations

These behaviors would include sexually explicit (a) acts by the child (e.g., "humping" the therapist's leg); (b) acts by the toys (e.g., the child places a boy doll on top of a girl doll and moves their pelvic regions together in a rhythmic manner); (c) drawings, paintings, or clay sculptures (e.g., drawings with exaggerated genitals); or (d) suggestions or comments by the child (e.g., asking whether you want to "get sexed"). Blatantly sexual behavior may indicate that the child has experienced sexual abuse or witnessed sexually explicit material or activities. However, this is not always the case. Some children are simply exploring sexuality or newly acquired information about sex through their play. While it is imperative to further investigate the origins of this behavior and the possibility that the child has been abused, it is critical to consider the child's developmental level and watch for patterns or repeated occurrences of this kind of behavior to accurately interpret the meaning of this play.

Level of Anxiety

A child's anxiety should be assessed over time to determine if it is chronic and part of the overall problem or just a temporary reaction. Most children manifest at least some nervousness during the first session or two of play therapy. Anxiety is frequently demonstrated in opposite extremes of behavior. Anxious children might not make eye contact with you or constantly stare at you; they may stand very close to you and not venture into other parts of the room; they may wander aimlessly; they may chatter incessantly or not utter a word. These are all normal reactions to being in a new situation in which the rules and requirements are not immediately apparent. By the third or fourth session, most children seem to relax and enter into the play with enthusiasm. With children who continue to express high levels of nervousness and inhibition after the initial adjustment, you will probably want to assess the level of anxiety they manifest in other situations to determine whether chronic anxiety is contributing to their difficulties.

Willingness to Take Risks

It is often helpful to evaluate a child's willingness to take risks. We find it easiest to think about this factor on a continuum ranging from children who take too few risks to those who take too many risks. Children who take too few risks are afraid of making a mistake or of being a failure. Their unwillingness to take risks inhibits their acquisition of new skills and the development of self-confidence. In the playroom, these children are reluctant to try new behaviors and may refuse to engage in any kind of play that could result in them experiencing less-than-perfect performance (which they would classify as failure). They typically play with blocks, sand, or other easy, "safe" play materials, refusing to explore more psychologically "risky" materials. These children ask (overtly and covertly) for direction and reassurance to an unusual degree—they are unwilling to make any decision for themselves. Behavior that fits into this extreme of the continuum may be an indicator of high levels of anxiety or tendencies toward maladaptive perfectionism (Ashby et al., 2004; Williams, 2018).

Some children take too many risks because they are not afraid of anything. These children can be a danger to themselves and others because they do not consider the consequences of their actions. In the playroom, they might climb on top of shelves or precariously stack a pile of toys. They tend not to anticipate potential negative consequences and may be highly impulsive. Behavior that fits into this extreme of the continuum can be an indicator of attention-deficit/hyperactivity disorder, poor impulse control, abuse, sensory integration problems, or some other difficulty. If it continues after being limited or redirected, you may want to refer the child for psychological testing or occupational therapy assessment to rule out a problem that might be better treated through medication or occupational therapy.

Desire for Order and Structure

Children with a strong desire for order and structure usually do a lot of sorting and tidying up in the playroom. They may also ask you for more guidance than other children typically do. With nondirective therapists, these children may even purposely violate rules to get the therapist to provide more structure for them. There are two somewhat contradictory basic interpretations of this behavior. One interpretation is that many of these children live chaotic lives where they frequently feel out of control. Sorting toys into categories and putting play materials into the "correct" location on the shelves in the playroom provides them with a sense of orderliness and consistency that is otherwise missing from their lives. The other interpretation is that children who manifest this kind of behavior live in families in which age-inappropriate order and structure are demanded of them. These children's sorting and tidying behavior is usually accompanied by a certain level of worry about the consequences of disorder—they are afraid they will get into trouble if they do not impose order on the relative chaos of the playroom.

Desire for Power and Control

A large percentage of children referred for play therapy have a strong desire for power and control over themselves or other people. You can assess their desire for power and control by watching them interact with other family members, observing the scenes they act out with puppets and dolls, and watching their reactions to limits. Children with an elevated need for control strive to avoid compliance with anyone else's rules. They like to boss other family members, classmates, teachers, and you. When they play out scenes in the playroom, there is always one puppet or doll who is clearly "in charge" of everything and everyone. Adlerian play therapists maintain that this behavior manifests in children who have (a) too much power within their family and in interactions with others, (b) too little power in their interactions within their family and in interactions with others, or (c) chaotic, out-of-control families and environments (Kottman & Meany-Walen, 2016).

To help alleviate a child's need for power and control, it can be helpful to consult with parents and give them suggestions for adjusting the power and control the child has outside of the playroom. When adjusting their interactions with children who crave power and control in the playroom, Adlerian play therapists consider the circumstances that might have led to that craving. With children who have too much power, it can be helpful to start sharing power with them from the beginning of the play therapy process. With children who have too little power and children from chaotic, out-of-control families and environments, Adlerian play therapists tend to initially inundate them with power, continuously returning responsibility to them and allowing them to control the unfolding of the play, with the ultimate goal of gradually shifting so that they are sharing power with the children.

Metaphoric Communication or Direct Communication

It is helpful to assess whether a child is a metaphor kid, a nonmetaphor kid, or comfortable coming in and out of the metaphor. As you watch the child in the playroom and listen to how their stories unfold, you will begin to recognize each type of child's typical behaviors and communication. This distinction is important because it will serve as a guide for discerning the best way to communicate with them.

A metaphor kid is usually a child who thinks, speaks, or tells stories in the form of metaphor or fictionalized story. Sometimes this child is an abstract thinker. Sometimes there is sensitive material that the child needs to distance themselves from for protection by telling you things that happen via a story about an animal, a fictional character, or a "good friend." The healing power of play that works best with these children is metaphoric teaching. With these children, you don't want to "break" the metaphor, so you are not going to say things like "Which of those puppets is your mother?" in the middle of a puppet show about a family or "I am guessing that you chose a gorilla for your brother because sometimes he seems to get away with bullying other people" when the child is telling you a story about a gorilla who picks on other animals and never gets in trouble for this behavior. When you break a child's metaphor, the child may react with a *play disruption* (Gil, 2017; Kottman & Meany-Walen, 2018) by abruptly dropping the story and switching to some other activity. Children may also have some other way of indicating that they feel angry, disappointed, or betrayed by your unwillingness to go along with the metaphor they have set up as their way to communicate about a particular topic.

A nonmetaphor kid is a child who doesn't usually naturally communicate metaphorically. These children often prefer to tell you the story of what happened directly. They often prefer that you tell them what you want them to know directly, too, and without the distance of the metaphor. Direct teaching works well with them.

Then, some kids come in and out of the metaphor. These children might start to tell you a fictional story, then switch to direct communication to tell you the connection between the fictional story and events or people in their lives, then switch back to a fictional story. These children are comfortable with you telling a fictional story as a teaching tool (metaphoric teaching), with you explaining something to them directly (direct teaching) or with some combination of the two.

Developmental Issues

When working with children, it is imperative for you to consider each child's developmental level (International Centre for Children and Family Law, 2023; Kottman & Meany-Walen, 2018; Ray, 2011, 2015). Many behaviors that would be perfectly acceptable at one age are inappropriate at another age. You will need to consider whether there is a gap between the child's chronological and developmental ages. Some possible explanations for an overall developmental delay include (a) child neglect, which can prevent the child from getting the stimulation necessary for proper development; (b) trauma, resulting in the child being stuck at a certain age; or (c) neurological problems that prevent age-appropriate levels of maturity. For instance, it would not be unusual for Hillary at 3 or 4 years old to speak in "baby talk." However, if Hillary is 10 years old, this could present social problems and might be an indicator of other difficulties, such as developmental delay, regression, or trauma. Sometimes, the child's overall development is within the normal range, but certain areas seem to be delayed. An example of this would be Howard (age 10), age-appropriate in every way in the playroom, except that he will grab a baby bottle and start sucking on it every time the therapist mentions his grandfather. In such a case, the therapist needs to explore the child's history and current circumstances to determine the cause of the issue in that particular area.

In this chapter, we have listed many of the elements that we assess as we work with a child. We try to communicate to parents our understanding of these factors and what they mean in that particular child's life, along with a formal diagnosis in situations in which it is necessary. We base our therapeutic goals on our assessment of the child's personality, strengths, presenting problem, and other situations or relationships that might be troubling to the child. We also use our assessment of these facets of the child to plan our interventions. These are not the only factors to consider when assessing children and their behavior. Other play therapists may consider these and a wide variety of diverse factors in their assessment of children and their issues. You will want to consider what is important to you in observing what happens in your playroom. As you gain experience, you will continue to refine your ideas about what is important to look for in the patterns of children in your play therapy sessions.

Using Your Understanding of Play Therapy Patterns and Themes

How a play therapist responds to play therapy patterns and themes depends at least partially on their theoretical orientation and personal preferences. Some play therapists choose to enter into the child's metaphoric play and use the patterns and themes to help the child gain a deeper awareness of their own intrapersonal and interpersonal dynamics or help the child learn new, more adaptive ways of coping with their life circumstances. Other play therapists will simply observe the patterns and themes without sharing them with the child client. This will be contingent on their beliefs about whether it is important to help children increase their level of conscious understanding of their underlying issues inherent in their play (Yasenik & Gardner, 2012, 2018).

You will have a plethora of options for what you choose to do with the patterns and themes you notice in your work in the playroom. As we do in Adlerian play therapy, you could metacommunicate about the themes and patterns to the child as a vehicle for helping the child gain insight (Kottman & Meany-Walen, 2016). You could use the themes and patterns to deepen your understanding of the child's subjective experiences and as a tool for helping parents and teachers to better understand the child, as many child-centered play therapists do (Ray, 2011). Reflecting feelings that lie underneath the themes and patterns evident in the child's behavior can help the child feel heard and understood (Van Fleet et al., 2010). It will be helpful to use themes and patterns in assessing psychosocial developmental levels (Ryan & Edge, 2012; Sarah et al., 2021) or to deepen your understanding of a child's issues and track therapeutic progress across sessions (Patton & Benedict, 2015).

Practice Exercises

In the following scenarios, describe the theme or pattern you notice and explain two possible interpretations of what the theme in the play could mean. For each theme you notice, how do you think you might "do" with the theme?

1. John (age 9), in several different sessions, takes a small telephone figure and buries it in the sand. A mother figure keeps crying and trying to find the telephone in the sand.
2. For four sessions in a row, Bethan (age 4) throws the baby doll on the floor and stomps on it, then takes a blanket and puts it over the baby doll.

3. At the end of every session, Hector (age 7) wants you to wrap him in a blanket and feed him from a bottle.

4. In the playroom, when you give Jess (age 6) a choice of activities, she always rejects every possible activity you suggest, even when you incorporate her interests and usual way of expressing herself in the choices.

5. Toto (age 8) always wants to sword fight with you. When you engage in this activity, his "team" always loses, even when he is more adept at swordfighting than you are.

6. Momal (age 9) likes to arrange all of the LEGO blocks by color and shape. She asks you to bring in Ziplock bags to put them in but then gets very upset if she comes to the playroom and they are in the "wrong" place.

7. Nasrin (age 5) likes to arrange the dominoes in a row and then knock them down. When he accidentally knocks them down before he is ready, he gets angry and threatens to throw them across the room. When you limit this behavior, he returns to arranging the dominoes in a row.

8. Sloane (age 10) usually wants to play a board game or a card game. When you play with her, she changes the rules if she thinks she will lose.

9. Jorge (age 8) usually wants to play a board game or card game. When you play with him, he changes the rules if he thinks you will lose the game.

10. In every session for six consecutive weeks, Greta (age 4) takes a male doll, puts it on top of a female doll, and moves the male doll up and down on the female doll.

Questions to Ponder

1. What do you think about the distinction that Ray (2011) makes between play behaviors (what children actually do in the playroom) and play themes (coherent metaphors children use to communicate the meaning they make of their life experiences as expressed through their play behaviors)?

2. How do you think you might measure the three characteristics Ray (2011) describe that can be helpful in identifying and understanding the meaning of play themes (repetition, intensity, and context) as you work with children in the playroom?

3. What is your reaction to the possible "underneath" internal statements made by children for each of the themes posited by Ray (2011)? Explain your reasoning.

4. Might you ever consider using something like the *Child Initiated Pretend Play Assessment* (Stagnitti, 2007), a standardized, norm-referenced assessment tool to measure play themes? Under what circumstances might you decide to use this assessment instrument?

5. What are your thoughts about Adlerian play therapists using a commonsense method of understanding themes rather than a "standard" list of themes because they believe each person has their own way of understanding the symbols present in their communication? Explain your thoughts on this subject.

6. How do you predict you might respond to a child who seems stuck in posttraumatic play? What might the factors that determine how you will respond to this?

7. Are there certain themes or patterns that might evoke a countertransference reaction in you? How will you be able to discern whether your reaction is related to your own countertransference?

8. How do you think you will handle it if you have a client who is consistently challenging your authority in the playroom?

9. What do you anticipate your reactions will be to a child client who manifests overtly sexual play, artwork, or verbalizations? If you have an adverse reaction to these behaviors, how will you keep yourself consistently expressing unconditional positive regard and empathy for the child?

10. How comfortable will you be interacting with a child who never communicates directly and relies exclusively on metaphor to communicate what is happening in their world? Explain your reasoning.

15

Working With Parents, Caregivers, and Teachers

Parents, caregivers, and teachers can be invaluable partners in the play therapy process. They are usually the primary sources of knowledge about children's personalities, developmental history, relationship patterns, problem-solving skills, and learning styles. They can also provide information concerning family dynamics, children's classroom behavior and school performance, presenting problems, and previous attempts at intervention. As part of a collaborative team, parents, caregivers, and teachers provide support for the changes children make through play therapy. Post (2014) stated that there is consensus among play therapists that effective consultation with parents maximizes beneficial outcomes for children.

> "Effective parent consultation can help parents better understand why play therapy is beneficial for their children, how play therapy interventions are purposeful and that the effectiveness of the interventions can be assessed. In addition, these consultations can provide parents support and hope, both of which help prevent early termination by the parents." (p. 1).

She suggested that parent consultation can help maintain and foster a strong therapist-parent alliance, assess parental assessment of therapeutic progress, and provide parents with education on parenting skills and community resources. Consulting with parents helps to decrease defensive reactions on the caregivers' part and increases the likelihood of them following suggestions for changes (Cates et al., 2006). The consultation process may also reduce the possibility of premature termination and missed appointments. In a survey of 423 members of the Association for Play Therapy, Lolan (2021) found that 94% of the play therapists surveyed believed that engaging parents and caregivers as part of the play therapy process is related to the positive impact of play therapy. The play therapists surveyed suggested that to be effective, parent and caregiver consultation includes (a) employing good communication skills with parents and caregivers, (b) using basic counseling skills when communicating with them, and (c) providing education for them and linking them to resources.

Wherever the specificity of the terms is not indicated, the term "parents" will refer to both "parents and caregivers," and "adults" will refer to both. The American Psychiatric Association (APA) defines a *caregiver* as "a person who attends to the needs of and provides assistance to someone else who is not fully independent," and Merriam-Webster as "a person who provides direct care, as for children, elderly people, or the chronically ill." While we recognize that these terms are not necessarily interchangeable, we believe there needs to be an acknowledgment of the crucial role caregivers provide in a child's life, whose role is often no different than that of parents.

Working With Parents and Caregivers

Through their work with a play therapist, parents and caregivers can make changes in their relationship with their children, in their parenting strategies, and in family dynamics, which can result in significant systemic shifts that can bring about or support changes in the child (Goodyear-Brown, 2021; Homeyer & Bennett, 2023; Kottman & Meany-Walen, 2016, 2018). When you work with parents and caregivers, some of the issues you may want to address include (a) teaching parenting skills and discipline strategies, (b) helping them explore personal issues that might interfere with optimal application of parenting skills, (c) helping them understand and change family dynamics to create a more positive environment for the children, (d) working with them to explore marital issues that might affect the children, (e) helping them better understand the children, (f) helping them learn more about child development, (g) helping them better understand themselves and their relationship with the children, (h) providing information about child development, and (i) discussing school issues that might have an impact on the children.

Of course, you will not want to overwhelm parents and caregivers by working on all of these topics at the same time. As you talk to the adults, observe them with their child, and watch how the child plays house and does family puppet shows, drawings, or sand trays, you will get a feeling for how you want to prioritize your work with the parents, caregivers, and other family members. It is important to remember that the adults are often very nervous about what you might discover about their parenting or that you will be critical of how they do things. Even really good parents are frequently convinced that if their child has a problem, it must be because they are doing something wrong. This may make them defensive, tearful, timid, or untruthful. Initially, you need to be mindful that parents and caregivers may be rather skittish, and you will want to approach giving them feedback or suggestions with caution and gentleness.

You should build a relationship with the adults before introducing the expectation that they and other family members may need to change how they think about their child and/or how they interact with one another (Homeyer & Bennett, 2023). Helping them be heard, understood, supported, and cared for will lay the groundwork for collaboration and teamwork between you and these adults. You will want to convey to them how important they are in their child's life. Parents and caregivers need to know that we value their knowledge of the best way to build a relationship with their child. They also have information about the child's developmental history, temperament, traumatic experiences, and strengths and struggles. The adults also know the history of the presenting problem, what they have tried to make things better, the impact of their culture on their child, and other information that will help you as you explore the child's interpersonal and intrapersonal dynamics. Because of the closeness of the relationship and the time spent with their child, parents and caregivers are in a unique position to support their child by gaining insight into their patterns and making changes in their behavior, thinking, feeling, and interaction. From the first time you communicate with the adults, it will behoove you to stress that you and the child will need their help and play a crucial role in ensuring therapeutic progress. It is also important to convey some information about what play therapy is and what it is not before you start seeing the child. By explaining that play therapy isn't "just playing" but a gradual process that takes time for changes to manifest, you can prevent some of the potential complaints or dissatisfaction with the process.

As the consultation proceeds, you will need to constantly remind yourself to maintain boundaries so that the consultation does not become therapy for the adults. If you believe that the adults' issues are so severe or complex that the consultation is crossing over into personal or marital counseling, you must refer them to those services rather than continuing to spend the bulk of consultation sessions on their issues. When working with parents and caregivers, we should always monitor our own reactions to them. If we are spending more time outside the session thinking about what to do with an adult than we are thinking about what to do with the child, or if the adults' portion of the sessions seems to be expanding into more time than we spend with the child, there is a good chance that the adults are superseding the child as the client. When this happens, we usually refer the adults to someone else for personal counseling or seek out supervision for ourselves to ensure that we can remain objective and supportive without turning the consultation into counseling.

Homeyer and Bennett (2023) outlined six primary components of parent and caregiver consultation: (a) establishing a therapeutic relationship with the adults, (b) asking about progress at home and school, (c) sharing information about treatment progress, (d) monitoring and updating treatment plans, (e) teaching therapeutic parenting skills, and (f) connecting parents and caregivers to resources. They also discussed the skills needed for consulting with parents and caregivers, including gathering information, reflecting feelings and meaning, clarifying nonverbal expressions, and asking follow-up questions.

Cates et al. (2006) examined the structure of parent/caregiver consultation in play therapy and provided a general outline of the components of effective consultation. They suggested that the play therapist use the initial meeting with parents to establish rapport; gather information about the child, the presenting problem, family dynamics, and cultural considerations; explain the process of play therapy; give them some ideas about how to introduce the idea of coming to play therapy to the child; discuss the child's right to privacy and the limits of confidentiality; give a tour of the playroom; and have a conversation about the logistical aspects of the parent consultation (i.e., how often it will occur, potential topics). During the subsequent consultation sessions, the play therapist uses active listening and encouragement skills to provide empathic support to parents and caregivers, give them updates about the child's progress, get input from the adults about the child's functioning at home and in other settings, modify treatment goals when necessary, provide education about child development and other factors related to helping parents and caregivers better understand the child, make suggestions about how the family can improve their management of the child's behaviors, teach the adults advocacy skills, and discuss readiness for termination of therapy.

Even though there is support in the literature for working with parents, caregivers and teachers, many play therapists choose to minimally interact with these particular adults. In some cases, the play therapist's theoretical approach does not emphasize including the adults in the process; in other cases, it is because the play therapist is uncomfortable working with adults. There are probably as many reasons for not working with parents, caregivers, and teachers as there are play therapists who choose not to do so. You will need to decide what you think and feel about working with the adults involved in the lives of your child clients. If you are uncomfortable working with adults, you may need to examine the issues underlying your reluctance. If you feel unprepared because of a lack of training or skill, you should seek education and supervision in this area. There are many ways to work with children's parents, caregivers, and teachers. If you decide it is necessary to work with the adults in your clients' lives, you will need to consider the many possibilities and choose which will work best for you and your client.

Most play therapists acknowledge doing some form of consultation or education with parents of the children they see in play therapy. Several approaches to play therapy discussed in this book incorporate specific strategies for working with parents and caregivers (Autplay Therapy, FirstPlay, Theraplay, TraumaPlay) and teachers (Adlerian play therapy and child-centered play therapy). There are various strategies for working with parents, some using consultation models and others psychoeducational training. It is beyond the scope of this book to provide in-depth coverage of all the different approaches to including parents, caregivers, and teachers in the process of play therapy. To give you a "taste" of several of these approaches, we will provide an overview of psychoeducational programs that involve teaching parents nondirective play therapy skills: filial therapy, Child-Parent Relationship Therapy (CPRT), Parent-Child Interaction Therapy (PCIT), and Familial Encouraging Connection Therapy (FECT). We will also discuss parent consultation procedures from Adlerian play therapy, child-centered play therapy, and TraumaPlay.

Psychoeducational Programs for Teaching Parents Nondirective Play Therapy Skills

Filial Therapy

Filial therapy is a "theoretically integrative form of therapy in which practitioners train and supervise parents (or other caregivers) as they conduct special nondirective play sessions with their own children" (VanFleet, 2014, p. 2). In filial therapy, as parents and caregivers practice the nondirective play therapy skills and gain skill and confidence, they begin to hold "special play sessions" with their children at home (B. Guerney, 1964; L. Guerney, 1997, 2015; VanFleet, 2014; VanFleet & Topham, 2016). The play therapist monitors the adults' play therapy skills, the child's play behavior, and improvements in the adult–child relationship during regular meetings with the adults. Although filial therapy was initially conceptualized as an intervention for children ages 3 to 12 years, this range has been broadened to include toddlers and adolescents (VanFleet & Topham, 2016). Filial therapy synthesizes theoretical concepts from psychodynamic, humanistic, interpersonal, behavioral, cognitive, developmental/attachment, and family systems theories (VanFleet & Topham, 2016). "The instruction to parents in play therapy skills is based on learning and reinforcement principles, but the instruction is affectively oriented with an emphasis on the client-centered principles of empathy and acceptance" (L. Guerney, 1997, p. 131).

There are four primary skills taught in filial therapy: structuring, empathic listening, child-centered imaginary play, and limit setting (VanFleet & Topham, 2016). Structuring is the skill of beginning and ending play sessions so that children recognize that the special play time is different from their usual interactions with parents. Empathic listening is the skill of recognizing the child's feelings and conveying understanding and acceptance to them. In child-centered imaginary play, parents and caregivers engage in roles suggested by children and follow their lead in the play. Setting limits in filial therapy involves a three-step process: (a) stating the rule and redirecting the play (e.g., "You may not shoot the dart gun at me, but you can do almost anything else you would like to do."), (b) giving a warning if the child breaks the same rule more than once (e.g., "Remember that you may not shoot the dart gun at me. If you try to shoot it at me again, we will end our special play time for today. You can do just about anything else during our time together."), and (c) enforcing the consequences by stopping the session if the child breaks the same rule a third time.

There are five phases in the filial therapy process: (a) training in play therapy skills, including mock play sessions; (b) observed practice of parents' beginning play sessions with their children; (c) independently conducted sessions by parents; (d) generalization; and (e) discharge planning (VanFleet & Topham, 2016). In the training phase, the counselor presents the rationale, theoretical concepts, and empirical evidence for child-centered play therapy and filial therapy. Training continues with demonstrations of filial therapy, instruction in child-centered play therapy skills, and mock sessions in which the counselor plays the child as the parents practice conducting play sessions. In the observed practice phase, parents use empathic responding, tracking, limit setting, and structuring to practice with their child as the counselor observes. In ideal situations, the counselor may even record the practice sessions and use the recordings to give feedback to the parents. When the counselor is satisfied that parents have mastered these skills, the "home sessions" begin, with parents conducting special playtime sessions at home at least once a week with the target child. Parents record these sessions when possible, bringing the recordings to review with the counselor. When this is not possible, they report what is happening in their home sessions with the counselor, discussing what happened and any concerns they might have. In the generalization phase, the counselor and the parents discuss ways to generalize the skills they use during the filial therapy sessions into the rest of their relationships and other situations with their children. During the discharge planning phase, parents and the counselor discuss the child's progress and decide whether to fade the special playtime sessions or continue them. This is determined on the basis of whether treatment goals have been met and whether the parents are satisfied with the child's progress.

Child-Parent Relationship Therapy (CPRT)

Building on the Guerneys' work in filial therapy, Landreth and Bratton (2020) have developed their own 10-session version of filial therapy they call Child-Parent Relationship Therapy (CPRT). According to Landreth and Bratton (2020), CPRT is "based on the belief that a parent acting as an agent for change in the place of a play therapist has potential for significant and lasting gains" (p. iii). A unique aspect of CPRT is that it is designed to foster improvement in the child, the parents, and the parent-child relationship. CPRT aims to help parents (a) increase their acceptance and empathy for their child, (b) better understand their child's emotional needs and respond to those needs sensitively, (c) improve their ability to set more realistic developmental expectations and limits for their child, and (d) become more confident in their parenting abilities (Bratton et al., 2015). This program combines didactic instruction with parent-child play sessions and supervision through the ten sessions, with each session dedicated to a specific content:

1. Training objectives and reflective responding
2. Basic principles for play sessions
3. Parent-child session skills and procedures
4. Supervision format and limit setting
5. Play therapy skills review
6. Supervision and choice giving
7. Supervision and self-esteem building responses
8. Supervision and encouragement versus praise
9. Generalizing skills
10. Evaluation and summing up (Landreth & Bratton, 2020).

Parent-Child Interaction Therapy (PCIT)

Parent-Child Interaction Therapy (PCIT) is an evidence-based parent training program combining play therapy concepts and strategies with behavioral parent training (McNeil & Hembree-Kigin, 2010; Niec, 2018; Quetsch et al., 2016). PCIT is based on principles from behavioral, developmental, and social learning theories that suggest that when parents use controlling or coercive methods of dealing with a child's behavior, they often unintentionally reinforce inappropriate, noncompliant behavior. PCIT is designed to help parents learn to establish and maintain a secure, nurturing relationship with their child, along with appropriate and consistent discipline. As parents improve on these skills, the anticipated end results for their child are increased prosocial behaviors (e.g., sharing, taking turns, using polite language) and decreased inappropriate behavior (e.g., noncompliance and defiance). PCIT was originally targeted at helping parents of children between 2 and 8 years old exhibiting externalizing behavior problems, but it has since been expanded to several other populations (Niec, 2018).

PCIT is conducted in two phases: child-directed interaction and parent-directed interaction, with three different assessment periods, one at the beginning of treatment, one in the middle, and one at the end (McNeil & Hembree-Kigin, 2010). Assessments examine child, parent, and family functioning through structured clinical interviews, parent and teacher rating scales, behavior observation, and specific measures of parent functioning and stress. The same assessments are administered in each of the periods. The therapist gives parents feedback about the results of the assessments, which are used to guide the training (Herschell & McNeil, 2005). At the beginning of each training phase, specific skills are taught to parents in a didactic session. These sessions include descriptions of each of the skills taught in that phase, examples of each of the skills, and role playing. In subsequent sessions, parents are coached in applying the skills either using a radio earpiece and a one-way mirror or an in-room coaching format. During the coaching portion of the sessions, the therapist uses praise and descriptions of their observations of the parents' impact on the child, coupled with redirection and constructive correction of the parents' application of the skills.

In the first phase (child-directed interaction), which usually lasts between 7 to 10 sessions, parents learn and practice basic play therapy skills, plus strategic attention and selective ignoring (McNeil & Hembree-Kigin, 2010). The skills they acquire during this phase are also referred to as the "PRIDE" skills: praise, reflection, imitation, description (behavioral), and enthusiasm. The Praise skill consists of expressing favorable judgment about the child's activities, products, or attributes. Reflection is a restatement of content. Using the Imitation skill, the parent mimics or accompanies the child's behaviors or activities. Description (behavioral) is the play therapy skill of tracking. Enthusiasm means to show excitement or interest in what the child is doing and saying. Parents are taught to avoid asking questions, giving orders or commands, and making critical comments. They also learn to attend to any appropriate behaviors exhibited by their child and to ignore attention-seeking minor inappropriate behaviors.

The second phase (parent-directed interaction), which also lasts between 7 to 10 sessions, teaches strategies for parents to learn how to be authoritative and gain compliance from the child with their directives (McNeil & Hembree-Kigin, 2010). The skills taught in this phase conform to the acronym "BE DIRECT":

- Be specific and clear with commands so that children understand what is required of them.
- Every command should be stated positively because when parents tell the child what they want the child to do (rather than what they don't), the child is more likely to comply.

- Developmentally appropriate commands guarantee that the child can actually do what the parent is asking.
- Individual commands work better than multiple commands, which can confuse the child.
- Respectful and polite commands encourage the child to also be respectful and polite.
- Essential commands help parents remember that they should evaluate whether a command is necessary or trivial.
- Choices, when given, can help the child learn independence and problem-solving skills.
- Tone of voice that is neutral and calm demonstrates that the parents are relaxed and in control.

After parents master the skills in this phase, they get additional information on developing house rules, managing problematic behavior in public, handling potential problem behaviors, and recognizing the need for a "booster" training session. This part of the training is designed to help parents generalize and transfer the skills they have learned.

Familial Encouraging Connection Therapy (FECT)

Familial Encouraging Connection Therapy (FECT) (Kottman, 2023a, 2023b) is a program based on Adlerian psychological theory designed to teach parents and caregivers an active method of playing with their children as a way to build connection, communication, and understanding. During a series of 10 to 12 instructional sessions and structured homework assignments, parents and caregivers (a) explore their own attitudes and experiences with play, (b) delve into the rules in their culture about play and interacting with children, (c) learn and practice basic non-directive play therapy skills that they can use when building a strong connection with their children, (d) explore their own rules about children, play, and parenting/caregiving, and (e) learn new tools for deepening their understanding of children's behaviors and personalities as a way for them to better understand their child and enhance their ability to provide emotional support to their children. Through regularly scheduled supervised play sessions, parents and caregivers master non-directive play therapy skills, such as tracking behavior, restating the content of children's verbalizations, reflecting their feelings, returning responsibility to them, giving them choices in the play, providing encouragement, and setting appropriate limits with children as part of the process of building a stronger connection with their child. They explore ways to recognize the goals of their child's misbehavior and learn powerful strategies for dealing with misbehavior. They will also learn ways to foster their child's ability to (a) connect with others, (b) feel courageous enough to try new things, (c) have confidence in their abilities, and (d) believe that they are important and special. A major part of this program is discovering play activities that are both fun and structured to share with their child to enhance positive adult-child interactions.

Parent/Caregiver Consultation Models

Adlerian Parent/Caregiver Consultation

Adlerian therapists have historically advocated working with the parents and caregivers of children receiving counseling, whether through consultation or psychoeducational programs (Kottman & Meany-Walen, 2016; T. Sweeney, 2019). Adlerians believe that parents and caregivers are the most influential people in a child's life, so parent/caregiver consultation is an integral component of Adlerian play therapy (Kottman & Meany-Walen, 2016). Parents and caregivers are invaluable sources of information about children and their patterns of solving problems and interacting with others, developmental history, patterns of problematic behavior, and attempted solutions. These influential adults can also help support any changes in thinking, feeling, and behaving that a child might make as a result of the play therapy process. In many situations, a child's maladaptive behavior actually works for them—the child achieves the goals toward which they are striving. When this is the case, a child's problematic behavior will not change until the systems in which they live change, so parents and caregivers will need to shift their patterns of relating to them.

Adlerian consultation with parents and caregivers usually begins with an entire session, with a conversation devoted to discovering the adults' perceptions of the presenting problem, the child's usual way of interacting with others and solving problems, ongoing family or school issues, and any other concerns. If you are an Adlerian play therapist, after this initial session, you would tailor the configuration of the consultation to the needs of the parents and caregivers and the requirements of your practice setting. If you are in a mental health setting, you would usually consult with parents and caregivers for at least a short time every session, if possible. Depending on the situation, you might meet with the adults for 20 minutes and the child for 30 minutes in a routine play therapy session or meet with the child for the entire session two or three times and then meet with the adults for an entire session. It is also possible to ask parents and caregivers to attend Adlerian parenting training classes like Active Parenting (Popkin, 2014) or Positive Discipline (Nelson et al., 2016; Nelson et al., 2019). If you are a school counselor, you may have limited access to parents and caregivers. Because of their schedules and settings, you may have to consult with the adults via telephone or e-mail or provide parenting classes rather than conducting regular meetings in person. During these conversations, you can obtain information about functioning in settings other than school, family dynamics that could be affecting the child, and the child's assets. You can also suggest different ways of handling problems and new ways of relating to the child at home.

The Adlerian parent/caregiver consultation process follows the same four phases as the counseling process with the child (Kottman & Meany-Walen, 2016). To build the relationship in the first phase, you would use paraphrasing, summarizing, reflecting feelings, metacommunicating, and encouraging. Even during these initial interactions, you would observe the adults' interactional patterns, descriptions of their perceptions about the child's difficulty, and the methods of discipline they have tried. These observations will provide clues about the adults' personality priorities and Crucial Cs (courage, capable, connect, and count), which can inform the subsequent consultation with them (Dickinson & Daly, 2020).

In the second phase, you would ask questions to learn about the adults' perceptions of and attitudes toward the child. You could use questioning strategies, art techniques, or sand trays to explore these significant adults' lifestyles and their impact on the child's interpersonal and intrapersonal development. With the parents and caregivers, you could use those same techniques to explore their families of origin, marital relationships, family values, parenting methods, and so forth. This gathering of information is used to formulate hypotheses about the interaction between the adults and the child and to develop a treatment plan that incorporates work with both.

In the third phase, you would use your understanding of the adults' personality priorities and Crucial Cs to tailor your feedback so they can truly hear them and follow through with suggestions. The purpose of the consultation during this phase is for the adults to better understand the child and themselves. You would work with parents and caregivers to enhance their ability to recognize the interaction between their lifestyle and that of the child so that they can be more aware of how their own lifestyle issues might interfere with their ability to optimally interact with the child. As the adults gain insight into their own lifestyles, they can start to make changes in their attitudes toward themselves, one another, other people, and the world in preparation for the reorientation/reeducation phase.

As a part of the reorientation/reeducation process, you would use teaching techniques such as discussion, modeling, and behavior rehearsal with parents, caregivers, and teachers. The adults will learn new skills connected to parenting, including setting logical consequences, providing encouragement, fostering Crucial Cs, tailoring discipline to the child's goals of misbehavior, improving communication skills, and determining problem ownership. Many parents and caregivers also need more information about developmental patterns to enhance their understanding of "typical" behaviors that occur at certain ages.

Many resources outline Adlerian ideas that can be used in parent/caregiver consultation. The following is a list of books that you could use to guide you in consulting with the significant adults from an Adlerian perspective or creating a psychoeducational program for them:

- *Active Parenting: A parent's guide to raising happy and successful children* (4th ed.) (Popkin, 2014)
- *Ain't misbehavin': Tactics for tantrums, meltdowns, bedtime blues, and other perfectly normal kid behaviors* (Schafer, 2011)
- *Honey, I Wrecked the Kids: When yelling, screaming, threats, bribes, time-outs, sticker charts and removing privileges all don't work* (Schafer, 2009)
- *A Parent's Guide to Understanding and Motivating Children* (Lew & Bettner, 2000)
- *Positive Discipline: The classic guide to helping children develop self-discipline, responsibility, cooperation, and problem-solving skills* (Nelson, 2006)
- *Positive Discipline for Preschoolers: For their early years—raising children who are responsible, respectful, and resourceful* (4th ed.) (Nelson, Erwin, & Duffy, 2019)

It is helpful to consider which system might be causing a child the most difficulty (Kottman & Meany-Walen, 2016). This will help determine the amount of time and effort devoted to parent and/or teacher consultation and education. If the presenting problem centers around home and family, the play therapist focuses solely on consulting with parents and caregivers. When the presenting problem is primarily related to school issues, it often makes more sense for the play therapist to concentrate on consultation with teachers.

Child-Centered Parent Consultation

Schottelkorb et al. (2015) proposed a model for child-centered parent consultations that includes five elements: (a) forming and maintaining a relationship with parents using the core relationship conditions of child-centered play therapy, (b) being fully present and listening and responding to parents, (c) conveying respect to parents as the experts on their child, (d) sharing relevant information with parents, and (e) teaching therapeutic skills with the CONNECT model (Helker et al., 2007). The seven components of the CONNECT model are (a) Convey acceptance through actions and words, (b) Offer understanding through acknowledgment of feelings and wishes, (c) Notice children's behaviors, (d) Negotiate acceptable choices, (e) Encourage improved self-esteem, (f) Communicate limits through the ACT process (Acknowledge the feelings, Communicate the limit, Target the alternative), (g) Trust yourself to be genuine. According to Stulmaker and Jayne (2018), if you are a child-centered play therapist, your goals in child-centered parent consultation would be to provide them with the core conditions of empathic understanding, unconditional positive regard, and congruence; encourage parents' understanding of their children's behavior and "internal frame of reference" (p. 7); help the parents develop stronger empathy and acceptance for their children; and foster systemic change in children's lives. In this model, the initial parent consultation would typically last for 50 minutes and would be the forum for you to establish an empathic relationship with parents. During the second and subsequent consultations (following every third or fourth session with the child lasting from 30 to 50 minutes), you would address parents' current concerns and progress outside the playroom. You would also want to update parents on your observations about changes in the child, themes that have emerged in the play therapy, and your treatment plan. You might also teach specific parenting skills. In the final consultation, you would explain the termination process, summarize the child's progress, give recommendations for further growth, and describe factors that might support a return to play therapy or some other intervention in the future. Stulmaker and Jayne (2017) provide guidelines for CCPT parent consultation.

TraumaPlay Parent Consultation

In describing her work in TraumaPlay with parents, Paris Goodyear-Brown said, "So much of our work with parents is parallel process work, providing corrective emotional experiences, powerful paradigm shifts, and *in vivo* moments of having parents and children delight in one another" (2021, p. 2). The program in TraumaPlay invites parents to shift the language they use to describe their child, explore their parenting roles, ignite their compassion for their child and themselves, and examine their own feelings about their parenting. If you were working with the TraumaPlay model, by educating parents about what is developmentally appropriate for their child, especially in families that have experienced traumatic events, you would work with them on resetting their expectations for their children, moving the bar they set to something achievable by their children. You would also use the "Circle of Security" model (Hoffman et al., 2017) to work with parents to become "Safe Bosses," who provide both a secure base and a safe haven for their children. You would invite parents to (a) explore their own early attachment relationships and their attachment with their child, (b) learn self-regulation and how to co-regulate with their child, (c) set boundaries with their child, (d) learn to stay present with their child, (e) explore how to have more fun with their child, and (f) practice listening empathically to their child (Goodyear-Brown, 2021).

Research Support for Working With Parents and Caregivers as an Adjunct to Play Therapy

A large body of research supports including parents in the play therapy process. LeBlanc and Ritchie (2001), Bratton et al. (2005), Lin and Bratton (2015), in their meta-analyses of the play therapy research, concluded that parental involvement is an essential element in the efficacy of play therapy. Filial therapy studies have consistently shown improvement in child behavior, parental empathy and acceptance of children, parenting skills, parental stress, and parent satisfaction (Cornett & Bratton, 2015; Gilmartin & McElvaney, 2020; Mirzaie et al., 2019). Child-Parent Relationship Therapy (CPRT) has over 40 empirical studies that have provided research support for improving parental empathy, child behavior, and parent-child relationship stress (Bratton et al., 2015; Swan et al., 2019); reducing adopted children's global behavior problems, reducing parent-child relationship stress, and increasing parents' empathic behaviors (Carnes-Holt & Bratton, 2014; Opiola & Bratton, 2018); decreasing parenting stress and parental secondary trauma symptoms

(Tal et al., 2018); and improving family functioning (Cornett & Bratton, 2014). Even delivered in a two-day model, CPRT proved to be helpful to parents (Perryman et al., 2017). Many empirical investigations have demonstrated the efficacy of parent-child interaction therapy (PCIT) in decreasing child behavior problems, increasing parenting skill, and decreasing parental stress (Lieneman, 2017; Thomas et al., 2017). Working with parents is an integral component in Theraplay (described in Chapter 3), which has been shown to effectively reduce externalizing and internalizing symptoms of toddler and preschool children and improve parents' mental health functioning (France et al., 2023; Money et al., 2020; Tucker & Smith-Adcock, 2017).

Working With Teachers

Teachers are also influential in children's lives, and they can provide in-depth information about a child's development, learning styles, self-concept, friendship skills, interpersonal strengths and limitations, communication skills, problem-solving strategies, learning struggles, changes in functioning, and academic ability and interest (Kottman & Meany-Walen, 2016, 2018). Some approaches to play therapy (Adlerian, child-centered, Jungian, prescriptive, and psychodynamic) also include consultation with teachers when the problem is related to school behavior or performance. Just as it is essential in consulting with parents and caregivers, regardless of your theoretical orientation, it is crucial to build a relationship with teachers before making any suggestions for change. As you build a trusting relationship with teachers, you can shift into making suggestions about developing new ways of relating to children, new methods of classroom management, and new strategies for understanding children and their issues. Addressing the following issues in consultation with teachers can be extremely valuable: (a) classroom dynamics that might interfere with a particular child's ability to function at the optimal level at school, (b) personal issues that might interfere with the teacher's ability to optimally apply classroom management skills, (c) personal issues that might get in the way of the teacher's ability to interact in appropriate ways with a particular child, (d) children's intrapersonal and interpersonal dynamics, (e) classroom discipline strategies, (f) improvement of the teacher's relationship with a particular child, and (g) the impact of family dynamics on children. Again, it is important to avoid overwhelming teachers by making suggestions for changes in all these areas. Stepping back and deciding where you can have the most positive impact on something that will make a big difference in a child's experience at school is an essential step in this process. Also, unless you are a school counselor, you may not have sufficient time to consult with teachers. When possible, it is valuable to invest time and energy to cultivate relationships with teachers so they can actually "hear" any suggestions you make about how things go for children at school.

If you do have the opportunity to consult with teachers, it is important to build rapport with them by listening to their concerns while providing empathy, support, and encouragement as you gather information about what happens in the classroom and on the playground. You could ask the teacher to talk about the presenting problem and any attempts that have been made to solve it, the child's educational history, and any family information that might be relevant. During subsequent consultation visits, it will be constructive to get feedback about the child's behavioral, emotional, and academic functioning in the school while simultaneously supporting the teachers using active listening and encouragement. As time passes, your ultimate goal would be to help the teacher begin to make changes in attitude about, understanding of, and interactional patterns with the child. You can do this through didactic teaching or metaphoric storytelling, whichever you believe will be the most effective with that teacher.

Several approaches to working with teachers involve adapting the filial therapy model to train preschool and elementary school teachers as therapeutic agents, including Child–Teacher Relationship Training (CTRT), Kinder Training, and Teacher-Child Connection Training (TCCT). In CTRT (Helker & Ray, 2009; Morrison, 2006), teachers are trained in child-centered play therapy skills so they can develop a better comprehension of children's feelings, experiences, and needs; increase their awareness of methods that can be used to build children's confidence and self-esteem; and develop more positive affective relationships with children. Multiple empirical studies support the efficacy of CTRT in improving children's behavior problems (e.g., Coggins & Carnes-Holt, 2021; Morrison & Bratton, 2011; Post et al., 2020a, 202b). Post et al. (2022b) found support for CTRT, which positively impacts teachers' attitudes and behaviors and children's classroom behaviors.

Kinder Training (formerly called Kinder Therapy) was designed as a way for school counselors (or other mental health counselors working in the schools) to train teachers in child-centered play therapy techniques and the theoretical concepts of Adlerian psychology for the purpose of improving teacher-child relationships (Chen & Lindo, 2018; Chen & Cheng, 2021; White & Wynne, 2009). In Kinder Training, teachers are encouraged to develop beliefs and learn interpersonal skills that will help them create classrooms that foster students' social interest and learning. Kinder Training is based on the Adlerian concept that people are holistic beings who view the world subjectively and are socially embedded, self-determining, and goal-directed (White & Wynne, 2009). Teachers are taught to consider each child's mistaken goals of behavior: attention, power, revenge, or display of inadequacy. The play therapy skills taught in the Kinder Training are tracking, reflecting feelings, encouraging, and setting limits, following the child-centered model of play therapy. Kinder Training involves didactic group training for teachers, practice with other teachers followed by supervision from a counselor, weekly individual play sessions with a specific child followed by supervision, and classroom coaching. Classroom coaching is designed to help the teacher generalize the therapeutic language of play therapy into the classroom and transfer the Adlerian principles into classroom management applications. Researchers have provided evidence that Kinder Training can be used to increase teacher skills in interacting with their students, improve students' school adjustment, and reduce externalizing classroom behaviors in preschool children (Chen & Lindo, 2018; Chen & Cheng, 2021).

Building on Kinder Training, Kottman (2023c) developed Teacher-Child Connection Training (TCCT), a ten-session model for training preschool and elementary school teachers in concepts and skills drawn from Adlerian play therapy using didactic teaching, group process, demonstrations, role playing, in-school practice sessions, and live supervision/consultation. The goals of this program are to (a) educate teachers on the value of building relationships with the students in their classes, (b) train teachers in non-directive play therapy skills they can use to enhance their connections to students in their classes, (c) help teachers master encouragement skills, (d) train teachers in how to assess and foster the Crucial Cs, and (e) coach teachers in recognize the goals of children's misbehaviors, assess the needs children are meeting through those misbehaviors, and give teachers playful tools for responding to children's misbehaviors (Wassenaar, 2023).

Practice Exercises

1. Consider the methods of working with parents, caregivers, and teachers described in this chapter and seek out more information about each of them. Imagine yourself working with a parent or caregiver using one of these formats. If there is a

teacher version of that method, imagine yourself working with a teacher. What issues come up for you as you visualize this?

2. Because of the nature of this book as an "intro" to play therapy, the descriptions of the selected methods of working with adults who have a significant role in children's lives are somewhat limited. If one or more of these methods for working with parents, caregivers, and/or teachers has a particular appeal, find books, chapters, and articles about that approach and learn more about it. What kinds of things would you want to know? What information will help you decide if you would like to use this particular method for working with adults as an adjunct to your work with parents, caregivers, and/or teachers?

3. There are many other methods of working with parents, caregivers, and/or teachers that would be appropriate for play therapists. Explore some of these approaches and decide which of them you believe would work for you. Consider whether they would be philosophically and theoretically consistent with the approach to play therapy you believe is best suited for you.

4. Filial therapy, CPRT, PCIT, and FECT are programs that teach parents basic play therapy skills. Compare and contrast two of these different approaches to parent and caregiver training.

5. How do you think teaching play therapy skills to parents and caregivers will help them with their parenting? With their relationship with their children?

6. Imagine a situation in which it feels like your parent/caregiver consultation has gone off the rails, and the adult is now acting as if they are the client and not the child. What are some ways you can handle this situation? How would it be different if you were consulting with a teacher rather than a parent/caregiver?

7. Draw a parent or caregiver you think might be difficult for you to develop and maintain an empathic connection with. Add something to the drawing that might help you work with that parent or caregiver.

8. Do the same activity as in #7, but with a teacher in mind.

9. Draw a picture or write a poem about any fears or concerns about working with parents, caregivers, and/or teachers in your play therapy work.

Questions to Ponder

1. What are your thoughts on the importance of working with the adults in a child client's life? Do you believe that it is essential, desirable, or unnecessary? Explain your reasoning.

2. How comfortable do you think you will be working with adults as an adjunct to working with children in play therapy? What part of the process would be comfortable for you? What part of the process would be uncomfortable for you?

3. Do you think you would be more comfortable working with parents/caregivers or teachers? Explain the factors that might be involved in your level of comfort.

4. You can include many things in consultation with the adults in a child's life. Consider the following factors that might be areas of focus in parent/caregiver consultation. Which would you consider to be important? Explain your reasoning.

5. Teaching parenting skills and discipline strategies.

6. Helping parents and caregivers explore personal issues that might get in the way of optimal application of parenting skills.

7. Helping parents and caregivers consider changing family dynamics so that the family is a more positive environment for the child.

8. Working with parents and caregivers to explore marital issues that might be affecting the child.

9. Helping parents and caregivers better understand the child.

10. Helping parents and caregivers better understand family dynamics.

11. Helping parents and caregivers better understand themselves and their relationship with the child.

12. Providing information about child development.

13. Discussing school issues that might have an impact on the child.

14. Consider the following factors that might be areas of focus in teacher consultation. Which would you consider to be important? Explain your reasoning.

15. Helping teachers explore classroom dynamics that might hinder a particular child's ability to function at the optimal level at school.

16. Helping teachers explore personal issues that might hinder optimal application of classroom management skills.

17. Helping teachers explore personal issues that might hinder their ability to interact in appropriate ways with a particular child.

18. Working with teachers to help them understand children better.

19. Working with teachers to help them understand a particular child better.

20. Working with teachers to help them gain a better understanding of classroom dynamics.

21. Teaching classroom discipline strategies.

22. Working with teachers to help them improve their relationship with a particular child.

23. Helping teachers to understand how family dynamics affect children.

24. If you are doing filial therapy, CPRT, or FECT without doing play therapy directly with the child, how do you think you would you feel about just working with the parents directly? What would be the advantages and disadvantages of working with the parents/caregivers without working with the child as your primary play therapy modality?

25. Many counselors, even those not child-centered, use filial therapy or CPRT as an adjunct to their work with children. What are your thoughts on whether you would consider this as a possibility?

26. Why do you think parents and caregivers are not taught to interpret the meaning of play to the child in filial therapy?

27. One of the basic PCIT skills is praise, which involves conveying a judgment about a child's behavior. What is your reaction to teaching parents and caregivers to praise their children?

28. In PCIT, the goal is to teach parents how to be authoritative. How do you define being an authoritative parent? What is your reaction to this goal?

29. In CTRT and Kinder Training, teachers learn basic play therapy skills. How do you think knowing these would help a teacher in their classroom?

30. What do you think would be teachers' reservations about using play therapy skills in their classrooms?

31. There are four phases in Adlerian parent and teacher consultation. Why do you think each of these phases would be necessary?

32. How would you feel about custom-designing consultation based on your understanding of the adults' Crucial Cs and personality

priorities as they do in Adlerian consultation? What do you think would be the advantages and disadvantages of doing this?

33. What are your thoughts and feelings about teaching a parenting class to the parents and caregivers of your child clients?

34. How will you tell when it is time to refer a parent, caregiver, or teacher for personal or marital counseling rather than continuing consultation? Are there some ways you could set professional boundaries so that you are not getting involved in counseling adults at the same time you continue your consultation?

16

Professional Issues in Play Therapy

A thorough reading of the current play therapy literature reveals several important issues facing mental health and school counseling professionals who use play therapy as a treatment modality. These include (a) legal and ethical issues, (b) cultural competence and cultural humility, (c) inclusion of aggressive toys in the playroom, (d) technology in the playroom, and (e) public awareness of play therapy and the professional identity of play therapists. In this chapter, we explore these issues and encourage you to consider how they could affect you and how you can respond to the professional challenges they present. We also include some advice for beginning play therapists gleaned from selected experts in play therapy.

Legal and Ethical Issues

Play therapy is generally understood as a secondary profession or identity. Play therapists come from a wide range of professional disciplines (e.g., mental health counselors, school counselors, social workers, marriage and family therapists, psychologists, and psychiatrists). Each of these professional disciplines has its own code of ethics (e.g., counselors follow the guidelines set up by the American Counseling Association, and psychologists follow the guidelines set up by the

American Psychological Association). While these codes provide general ethical guidelines for clinical practice, they are not specifically designed to guide professionals who work with children or utilize play therapy interventions (Ashby & McKinney-Clark, 2015; Seymour & Rubin, 2006).

To address the dilemma caused by the lack of a code of ethics tailored to play therapists, the Association for Play Therapy (APT) developed *Play Therapy Best Practices,* which outlines best practices for the instruction, supervision, and practice of play therapy (APT, 2022b). These best practices address many of the issues traditionally addressed in a professional code of ethics with a particular focus on play therapy. The sections on the therapeutic relationship cover traditional commitments and responsibilities to the client, respecting individual differences, rights of clients, clients served by multiple resources, therapist needs and values, dual relationships, sexual intimacies, multiple clients who have a relationship with one another, group work, payment, termination and referral, and computer/Internet technology. These best practices also highlight the nuanced application of ethical constructs to play therapy practice, including the obligation to the child client and their parents or guardians, the challenge of informed consent from children who may legally lack the capacity to give consent, and honoring child clients' freedom to choose whether and how to engage in play therapy. Additional sections also offer guidance for applying ethical constructs in the specific context of working with children. A section on parents and family addresses working with parents and other family members. A section on confidentiality includes best practice guidelines about the right to privacy, group work, documentation, research and training, and consultation. A section on professional responsibility covers knowledge of standards, professional competencies, advertising and soliciting clients, credentials, public responsibility, and responsibility to other professionals. There is also a section on relationships with other professionals that provides guidelines for appropriate interactions with employers and employees, consultation, fees for referral, and subcontracting. A section on evaluation, assessment, and interpretation explains that play therapists must only provide assessment services for which they are qualified, and they must take special care when making diagnoses of mental disorders. In the teaching, training, and supervision section are guidelines for educators and practitioners providing training, training programs, and supervisors. Finally, a section on research and publication covers research responsibilities, informed consent, and reporting results and publication responsibilities.

Similar to other areas of professional practice, play therapy ethics are guided by the meta-ethical principles of nonmaleficence—"Do no harm"—and beneficence—"Whenever possible, promote good" (Singh & Ivory, 2014). Numerous authors (e.g., Ashby et al., 2015; Ashby et al., 2017) have identified the core issues related to play therapy ethics as including (a) informed consent, (b) competence, (c) confidentiality, and (d) multiple relationships. While these issues are common to all the helping professions, there are numerous specific applications to play therapy and working with children.

Informed consent in play therapy raises the issue of client competency. Client competency refers to children's right to participate in giving informed consent and making decisions about their treatment independent of parental consent (Ashby et al., 2015). Each state sets its own guidelines concerning a minor's competency based on a variety of factors that may include age; ability; experience; education and/or training; degree of maturity demonstrated; conduct and demeanor; and capacity to understand the nature, risks, and consequences of an action or procedure. Although it may not be a legal requirement, ethically, the play therapist must explain any treatment or intervention to the child client in language they can understand and obtain their consent to treatment, even though they may not have the legal right to give consent. When parents are divorced, the custodial parent must grant informed consent and is usually able to make decisions about treatment plans, releases of information, and confidentiality related to a child client's treatment. Because various states have different statutes about the rights of noncustodial parents, the play therapist should request a copy of the divorce decree and custodial agreement to clearly understand what rights the court has granted to the noncustodial parent. It is also helpful to ask the custodial parent to sign a release so the play therapist can share information with the noncustodial parent if they request it.

Competence is also a significant issue in play therapy practice. Because play therapy is a secondary practice, specialized training and supervision in play therapy are considered the standard of care for practicing play therapy (Association for Play Therapy, 2022). While play therapy is not a protected practice that requires additional credentials, competence in play therapy is required. To provide professional guidelines for developing competence in play therapy, the International Association of Play Therapy established the Registered Play Therapist (RPT) credential. To be eligible for the credential, licensed or state-certified clinicians (e.g., school counselors, social workers, counselors, psychologists) must complete designated training and minimal levels of supervised experience (see the Association for Play Therapy's 2023 Credentialing Standards for Registered Play Therapists). While the RPT is not proof of competence in play therapy, holding this secondary credential (in addition to licensure or certification in a primary profession) offers support in establishing play therapy competence.

Confidentiality in play therapy is an additional challenge in practice as the primary client is almost always a child. In most states, children under age 12 do not have the legal right to confidentiality. However, the Association for Play Therapy's (2022b) *Play Therapy Best Practices* document states:

> The play therapist recognizes and respects that the child is the primary client, and thus, informs the child and their significant adults of the purposes, goals, techniques, procedural limitations, potential and foreseeable risks and benefits of the services to be performed in age-appropriate language for the understanding of the client. The play therapist takes steps to ensure that the child and their appropriate significant adults understand the implications of diagnosis, the intention of tests and reports, fees and billing arrangements. The client has the right to expect confidentiality and to be provided with an explanation of its limitations, including disclosure to appropriate significant adults, supervision and/or treatment teams and governmental authority and to obtain clear information about any documents or documentations in their case records; to participate in the ongoing treatment plan as is appropriate to their developmental level. (p. 3)

The duty to warn and mandatory reporting of the reasonable suspicion of child abuse is included in most states' statutes governing the counseling of minors. As a result, play therapists have a responsibility to warn or protect a third party when a clear threat is expressed against a specific person or physical property. It is mandatory for play therapists to report any reasonable suspicion of child abuse—thus, child abuse or neglect also constitutes an exception to confidentiality and must be reported to the appropriate authorities. Children need to have this exception to confidentiality explained in language they can understand, and the legal guardian must be informed about this exception to confidentiality in informed consent.

With child clients, the "Do no harm" injunction involves defining clear and definite boundaries with the child and the child's caregivers about the play therapist's participation in social and personal relationships that might constitute a dual relationship with the child or the child's family. If an issue that might potentially cause a problem within the relationship (e.g., a need to disclose, consultation with teachers or other school personnel), the play therapist would discuss this with the client and their caregivers. If a problem arises, the play therapist should consult with professional colleagues or a supervisor to get input on how to handle the situation. The play therapist would keep adequate clinical notes about the treatment plan, interventions, and outcomes. When necessary, the play therapist would refer to other therapists or professionals.

Another issue related to multiple relationships and boundary crossings is the use of touch in play therapy. Unlike most therapy systems with adults, some play therapy modalities utilize the therapeutic use of touch (e.g., Booth & Jernberg, 2010). Given the complicated ethical considerations in the use of touch in the mental health treatment of children (e.g., McNeil-Haber, 2004), the Association for Play Therapy published the *Paper on Touch* (2022a). This paper defines appropriate clinical uses of touch and outlines the clinical, professional, and ethical issues related to touch in play therapy. The authors of this position paper suggested that play therapists should be trained in the developmental, therapeutic, ethical, and pragmatic issues related to the use of touch in play therapy, as well as the interpretation of touch in the cultures of the children with whom they might work. It is essential for play therapists to make sure they have informed consent for the use of touch in their sessions from both the child and the child's caregiver(s), and any touch that occurs meets the child's needs and forwards progress toward treatment goals. The paper also addresses the issues related to touch with abused or traumatized children, touch in group work, and physical restraints with children.

1. Carmichael (2006) provided the following suggestions for play therapists who must deal with the legal and ethical issues related to working with children:
2. Play therapists should always practice within the limits of their training, education, and supervised expertise.
3. Play therapists should be familiar with all state statutes concerning privilege and confidentiality and understand their limits.
4. Play therapists should have written informed consent that explains confidentiality for the child client and the parents or legal guardian. This document should be signed and dated by the client and parents (or legal guardian) before treatment begins.
5. Play therapists must keep objective, accurate records of all sessions and other interactions with clients, parents or guardians, and other concerned individuals (e.g., teachers, physicians, etc.).

6. Play therapists should have malpractice insurance that covers their legal costs in case of a lawsuit.

7. Play therapists should always confer with colleagues, a supervisor, and/or legal counsel if they are unsure of appropriate legal or ethical procedures.

As part of ethical practice, it is important to know how to use and apply an ethical decision-making model (e.g., Pope et al., 2021). Such models provide formalized steps for handling ethical dilemmas, especially when ethical standards conflict with legal codes or contradict one another. While these models can be applied to decision-making in play therapy, several authors have called for an ethical decision-making model specific to play therapy. Seymour and Rubin (2006) proposed an ethical decision-making model for play therapists from various professional backgrounds (e.g., counseling, social work, psychology). The model by Seymour and Rubin is intended explicitly for play therapy practitioners. Seymour and Rubin's Principles, Principals, Process Model (or "the P3 Model") "combines the historical ethics codes (Principles) of the professional disciplines providing play therapy with the contemporary voices of all the persons (Principals) involved in the ethics circumstance through dialogue (Process)" (p. 106). The P3 Model is based on a conceptualization of play therapy that is fundamentally relational and acknowledges that consideration of social context is critical in ethical decision-making. As a result, the P3 Model emphasizes the consideration of the client's voice, highlighting the power differential between the child and the play therapist. The model also acknowledges the central place of culture as the perspective of the community is of particular importance in framing any ethical decision.

If you wish to be a play therapist, you will need to obtain copies of the Association for Play Therapy's *Play Therapy Best Practices* (2022b) and the *Paper on Touch* (2022a). You will need to become well-versed in these documents, as they are the play therapy profession's equivalent of a code of ethics. It will also be essential for you to know the code of ethics for your own profession (e.g., mental health counselors, school counselors, social workers, psychologists, psychiatrists, and nurses). It is also important to find a model for making ethical decisions related to working with children and become familiar with a set of procedures, such as the one provided by Seymour and Rubin (2006), designed to help solve ethical dilemmas. You must also keep abreast of your state's laws and guidelines related to therapeutic work with children, duty to warn, child abuse and neglect reporting, privilege and confidentiality, informed consent, rights of noncustodial parents, and any other matters related to working with clients in general and child clients specifically.

Cultural Competence and Cultural Humility

Socioeconomic, cultural, racial, ethnic, religious, and political factors together have a tremendous impact on children and how they view and interact with the world. Culture is widely recognized as being inextricably intertwined in all facets of our being and becoming (Spector, 2017). As a result, all mental health treatment, including play therapy, is considered multicultural (Watkins et al., 2019). With the rapidly changing demographics of the world, play therapists need to be able to work with children from a wide range of diverse backgrounds. The primary professional associations to which therapists belong (e.g., the National Association of Social Workers, American Counseling Association, American Psychological Association, American School Counselors Association, and American Association of Marriage and Family Therapists) all highlight the importance of cultural competence in treatment. For instance, the National Association of Social Workers (NASW) ethical code (2015) indicates that "Social workers should have a knowledge base of their clients' cultures and be able to demonstrate competence in the provision of services that are sensitive to clients' cultures and to differences among people and cultural groups" (National Association of Social Workers, 1.05-B). The American Counseling Association (ACA) Code of Ethics (2014) states, "Counselors recognize that culture affects the manner in which client's problems are defined and experienced" (American Counseling Association, E.5.b.). In addition, the *Play Therapy Best Practices* guidelines from the Association of Play Therapy (2022b) state that "play therapists must actively participate in the provision of interventions that illustrate an understanding of the diverse cultural backgrounds of their clients" and "play therapists should make every effort to gain knowledge about diverse populations by increasing their understanding of multicultural counseling from a social context" (A.2).

Traditional models of multicultural competence provide a contextual roadmap for working with clients and include (a) knowledge related to clients' cultural backgrounds, (b) reflection and increased personal awareness of therapist values and biases, and (c) applying culturally appropriate skills and interventions when working with diverse clients (Coleman 2004; Sue et al., 1992). Gil and Drewes (2021) noted that multiculturally competent play therapy should include the exploration of cultural values regarding family roles, physical discipline, interpersonal affection, play or work patterns, closed family systems, normalization of conflictual patterns of interaction and sensitivity to issues of inequality, injustice, racism and oppression, and privilege. Some examples relevant to play therapy that are important to explore are:

1. Country of origin and cultural identity
2. Generations of the family that have emigrated
3. Languages spoken and where those languages are spoken
4. Parent/caregiver knowledge of English—understanding of written word, receptive vocabulary, and expressive vocabulary
5. Eating and sleeping patterns and arrangements at home
6. Expectations of children in the culture
7. Level of acculturation
8. Important holidays, celebrations, and cultural responsibilities
9. Attitudes of the family toward play
10. Playmates of the child at home and in the neighborhood
11. Usual play materials and activities
12. Family members' attitudes toward discipline
13. Parent/caregiver patterns of discipline
14. Responsibilities and expectations of the child at home (A. Stewart, personal communication, October 2009).

Several authors have noted that the construct of cultural competence focuses on a priori knowledge of culture and may limit recognition of within-group diversity (Edwards, 2016) and limit recognition of power dynamics, prejudices, and implicit bias (Agner, 2020). Mosher et al. (2017) noted that cultural humility can add a counterbalance to the traditional construct of cultural competence by emphasizing the motivation to learn from others, self-examination of cultural awareness, showing interpersonal respect, working to develop mutual partnerships that address power imbalances, and an openness to new cultural information from others. Mosher et al. (2017) suggested the following questions to foster a posture of cultural humility in working with clients.

1. What is it like to be this client?
2. What is it about this client that makes them culturally unique?
3. What aspects of this client's cultural background are important to them?

4. How does this person's culture impact their reasons for attending counseling?
5. How might this client's cultural context strengthen or support them when working toward goals?
6. How might this client's (and my own) cultural background impact our interaction and our ability to meaningfully connect and work together?

Mosher et al. (2017) also identify several hallmarks of culturally humble therapists. These include intentionally self-reflecting and consistently reducing limitations and biases, learning from clients' cultural backgrounds and experiences, searching for opportunities to build respectful, mutual partnerships with clients, and staying motivated to learn more about various cultural beliefs.

Ray et al. (2022b) highlighted the importance of a multicultural orientation framework (e.g., Owen et al., 2011) in play therapy. These authors see this orientation as having three pillars: cultural humility, cultural comfort, and cultural opportunities. Cultural humility (Davis et al., 2018) is the primary pillar and entails the play therapist holding an attitude of humility and focusing on the client in therapeutic interactions. Cultural comfort involves awareness and attunement to personal values and beliefs, as well as levels of comfort in addressing cultural contexts in treatment (Perez-Rojas et al., 2019). Closely related to the construct of cultural comfort, cultural opportunities represent the markers in therapy where a client's cultural beliefs, values, or other aspects of their cultural identity could be explored (Davis et al., 2018). These cultural opportunities can include broaching and bridging in sessions and during parent consultation. *Broaching* refers to the therapist's "deliberate and intentional efforts to discuss issues across racial, ethnic, and cultural domains that may impact the client's presenting concerns" (Day-Vines et al., 2020, p. 107). Similarly, *bridging* includes the play therapist's efforts to "explore shared identities and/or similar experiences as well as to navigate differences that may exist through cultural and systemic biases and misunderstanding, in order to achieve a strengthened therapeutic alliance and better treatment outcomes" (Lee et al., 2022). Together, cultural humility, cultural comfort, and cultural opportunities offer avenues for play therapists to intervene with an effective multicultural orientation (Ray et al., 2022b).

Research has consistently shown that clients of color report microaggressions and implicit racial biases from mental health professionals (Hook et al., 2016; Owen et al., 2017). Yee and Cheng (2022) identified five potential clinical errors that can perpetuate racism in play therapy and provide examples where a multicultural orientation (Ray et al., 2022b) can offer pathways to avoid these errors. The first clinical error is adapting a color evasion approach. That is, instead of taking the opportunity to broach or bridge, cultural topics are avoided. This can manifest in the therapist over-emphasizing any cultural similarities they might share with the client and client's family, while avoiding any discussion of cultural differences. Yee and Cheng (2022) identified the second clinical error as the therapist having an inflexible agenda. An agenda in the playroom is not necessarily problematic, and play therapists are often well-meaning in their agenda-setting. Being inflexible with agendas can cause therapeutic ruptures, sometimes related to a form of "saviorism" where one (generally someone in a more powerful position) has to "save" another (usually an oppressed or marginalized person) in some manner (Wycoff, 2020). Adopting a stance of cultural humility and carefully examining biases and motives while taking an active listening stance toward the client and family can aid the play therapist in developing appropriate flexibility of agenda (Yee & Cheng, 2022).

A third clinical error identified is the therapist's failure to address issues of race, ethnicity, and culture with parents and caregivers. Yee and Cheng (2022) suggested that this error can be avoided by adopting a stance of cultural humility and intentionally broaching by noticing cultural similarities with parents and caregivers, highlighting cultural differences, and inviting discussion so that parents and caregivers feel seen and understood. They also noted that a lack of appropriate toys for processing racial trauma is another potential clinical error that can perpetuate racism in the playroom. O'Connor (2005) stated that "children should have access to toys that accurately reflect the diversity to which they are exposed in their day-to-day lives" (p. 570). He recommended that play therapists include dolls, figures, and puppets of various ages, ethnicities, genders, and abilities. Yee and Cheng (2022)recommended going beyond this form of representation in the playroom to include culturally meaningful toys (e.g., religious symbols, ethnic food, traditional attire) and aggressive release toys that might allow for the processing of racial trauma (e.g., guns, handcuffs, rope, blood). The fifth clinical error identified is the failure of the therapist to advocate for children's rights. Play therapists should actively work for structural changes to promote optimal health and social justice for children (Yee & Cheng, 2022).

Developing effective play therapy strategies that work with a wide variety of culturally and ethnically different clients is essential. In addition to the need for you, as a play therapist, to recognize your own assumptions, biases (overt and implicit), and worldview, an integration of suggestions from Ray et al. (2022b), O'Connor (2005), Gil and Drewes (2021), and Davis et al. (2018) suggests the following guidelines for conducting play therapy with multicultural populations:

1. As a play therapist, you must be open to and respect the historical, psychological, sociological, and political dimensions of the child's particular culture and/or ethnic group. While not obligating the client or family to act to educate you on their culture, you should work to understand the child's experience in the context of their culture and/or ethnic group. You will need to convey to the child and their family that you respect and value their belief systems. In the playroom, you would have both culture-neutral and culture-specific play materials. An example of a culture-neutral toy would be a set of play dishes in primary colors and without decoration. Examples of culture-specific toys would include dolls with ethnic features, pictures that show images of diversity, crayons with a variety of skin tones, and so forth.

2. You must investigate (through reading and interaction with knowledgeable individuals) the role of play in diverse populations to gain an understanding of the potential attitudes toward play of children from different ethnic groups and cultures. Children's play can be profoundly influenced by cultural factors such as gender role stereotyping and attitudes toward expressing emotion. Enhanced understanding can also prevent you from making comments or interpretations that might violate children's cultural identities.

3. You must work to be familiar with the values, beliefs, customs, and traditions of the child's culture. It is also essential that you understand and appreciate the "nuances" in the behavior and communication of play therapy clients who are culturally different from you (Coleman et al., 1993, p. 68). This is especially true with regard to language. You should take particular care to avoid any bias in communicating with children who do not speak English with a majority culture dialect.

4. The play therapist should cultivate and express an appreciation for the strengths and unique qualities of different cultures. As children talk about the various aspects of their culture, the play

therapist can highlight the assets of their culture. One way to do this would be to incorporate stories, games, songs, and poems from various cultures and languages in the play therapy process.

5. When working with clients from cultures or ethnic groups different from their own, play therapists should acknowledge their awareness of these differences to the client and their parents by bridging and broaching. This can create an open dialogue and allow for the discussion of any issues or concerns.

6. You must remember that becoming truly knowledgeable about other cultures is an ongoing process. You will need to continuously seek out more information and experience with a multicultural focus while maintaining a posture of cultural humility.

7. You must remember that it is inappropriate to generalize about all clients who belong to a specific cultural or ethnic group. While it is helpful to consider knowledge of cultural patterns to explore hypotheses about values, behaviors, and attitudes, it is critical to understand the particular individual within that culture and their intersecting identities.

8. Although parents, caregivers, and children can be sources of information about their culture, asking them to act as your primary informant for their culture is inappropriate.

9. You must examine the appropriateness of the philosophy underlying their approach and the efficacy of various intervention strategies for specific children. You must seek to find a match between children and their cultural backgrounds with the techniques used with them in play therapy. This would involve surveying the psychological and multicultural literature and interacting with other mental health professionals and the children's support systems. In this area, it would be helpful to seek out information on specific cultural groups and which counseling strategies and interactional patterns are traditionally effective with members of those groups.

10. You must avoid taking any distinctly "-centric" perspectives (e.g., Eurocentric, Afrocentric) on play therapy interventions. One method of evaluating various interventions and deciding which is optimal is *pluralcentrism,* a perspective that acknowledges the impact of mainstream culture but encourages acceptance of diverse cultural and ethnic perspectives.

11. You must continuously work to be aware of your own culturally based biases, values, beliefs, and attitudes. It can be very

beneficial for you to strive for increased cultural humility and learn to appreciate your own culture. This will help to eliminate cultural encapsulation and widen your worldview.

12. You must try to actively interact with multicultural populations. This can include attending religious ceremonies, visiting ethnic community centers, watching movies and theater productions focused on specific cultures, visiting children's homes and schools, and so forth.

13. You must remain aware of the possible impact that social, economic, and political discrimination has had—and continues to have—on children and their families.

14. When there are differences between cultural mores and the traditional standards that play therapists practice, you may need to develop compromise positions (e.g., accepting gifts from clients for whom gift-giving as gratitude is an important cultural tradition).

You will need to consider where you are in your own journey of cultural humility and cultural competence. We recommend ongoing consultation with other play therapists (or supervision where appropriate) to increase your personal awareness of values, biases, and cultural assumptions. You will need to continue developing an appropriate therapeutic posture of active listening to understand your clients' experiences and establish comfort in practicing broaching and bridging with clients and caregivers. Whenever possible, you must seek to identify any cultural opportunities in session and ways in which your theoretical approach to play therapy can best be adapted to meet clients' needs. We also urge you to continue to learn about your own and others' cultures and intersecting identities through personal experience in cultural settings, workshops, books, and discussion groups.

With each play therapy client, you will want to think about the following issues as you decide whether play therapy is the best approach with that particular child: (a) family and cultural attitudes toward receiving mental health care, (b) verbal expressiveness, (c) willingness to talk directly about problems, (d) availability of culture-specific intervention strategies, (f) family and cultural explanations of causes of "abnormal" behavior, (g) family and cultural attitudes toward individual versus group approach to problem-solving, (h) willingness of the family to wait for symptom alleviation, (i) level of acculturation, and (j) family and cultural attitudes toward and expectations of "expert" professionals (Ray et al., 2022b; Gil & Drewes, 2021). You will want to tailor your approach to the child and their family based on your understanding of the dynamics involved in these issues.

Inclusion of Aggressive Toys in the Playroom

An ongoing controversy in play therapy literature centers around including aggressive toys (e.g., bop bags, weapons, handcuffs, soldiers, play alligators, etc.) in the play therapy setting. In many playrooms, aggressive toys are part of the standard selection of play materials (Kottman & Meany-Walen, 2016; Landreth, 2024). Traditionally, many play therapy experts such as Jennifer Baggerly, Louise Guerney, Garry Landreth, and Daniel Sweeney (cited in Trotter et al., 2003) have argued that having aggressive toys in the playroom allows children to express anger and fear and to act out these feelings in symbolic ways. Trotter et al. (2003) made a case for weapons providing a means for children to safely test the limits in the playroom and to test the boundaries of the therapeutic relationship: "Children discover that regardless of the intensity of the feelings that they may communicate, they will not only be accepted, but be encouraged to be themselves" (p. 122). Green (2009) supported the inclusion of aggressive toys as a way to allow children to express their rage as a means of encouraging the psychic integration of the shadow aspects of their personalities: "By containing rage, therapists facilitate children's transformative process, sublimating aggression into assertiveness, which brings forth positive feelings" (p. 89). More recently, Yee and Cheng (2022) have argued that having aggressive release toys (e.g., guns, handcuffs) may be necessary for the processing of racial trauma. These experts believe that the play therapist should create a permissive atmosphere where any symbolic forms of aggression are allowed (and perhaps even encouraged).

On the other side of the controversy, several play therapy experts (Drewes, 2008; Schaefer & Mattei, 2005) have made the case that Bobo (a free-standing inflatable life-sized clown punching bag often included in many playrooms) and other aggressive toys are unnecessary and perhaps actually harmful as play therapy materials. These authors reviewed the historical research on the effects of encouraging aggressive play fantasy and the value of cathartic expression of aggression in play. Although the research they reviewed is mainly from the 1950s through the 1970s, it was consistent in its finding that "when adults permit and encourage children's release of aggression in play, the children are likely to maintain this behavior at its original level or actually increase it" (Schaefer & Mattei, 2005, p. 107). They found no controlled studies with children to support the belief that the expression of aggression in play leads to a decrease in subsequent aggressive behavior. Based on their conclusion that if children are encouraged to express aggression, they actually unlearn their previous socialization against acting aggressively, Schaefer and Mattei (2005) and Drewes (2008) suggested that having aggressive toys in the playroom is contraindicated for children referred to play therapy for aggressive behavior. They conceded that such toys may be appropriate for children who are timid and inhibited. Drewes (2008) pointed out that, even when aggressive toys are not stocked in a playroom, children will simply pretend their fingers are guns, toy keys are handcuffs, and so forth. She stated, "The lack of realistic, functional toys to express aggression does not stop children from telling their story, expressing their story, or enacting their fantasies" (Drewes, 2008, p. 60).

The arguments on either side of this issue suggest that it is an all-or-nothing situation. We perceive things a little differently. We tend to consider this decision on a case-by-case basis. We believe that aggressive toys can help some children symbolically express anger and aggressive feelings and explore limits in the playroom (Kottman & Meany-Walen, 2016). Children can sometimes use aggressive toys to protect themselves metaphorically from dangers and unsafe situations. As children act out keeping themselves safe through symbolic play with the weapons in the play therapy session, they often build a sense of self-efficacy. We do not believe that this works with all children, however. We often use aggressive toys to teach inhibited, anxious, too-tight children to loosen up a bit. With children who are referred for excessively aggressive behaviors and with children who seem "stuck" in ritualized aggressive acting out with such toys as the Bobo and the dart gun, we remove these objects from our playrooms. We also do not use these toys when we work with children in schools, in which the inclusion of aggressive toys may violate school policy. We tend to use interactions with aggressive toys to teach children more socially appropriate expressions of anger and aggression and to practice strategies for getting their needs met without trampling on the needs of others.

The use of aggressive toys is a controversy you will need to consider well. There are excellent arguments on both sides of the issue. Parker et al. (2021) found that personal beliefs, cultural influences, and theoretical orientation significantly impacted play therapists' decisions on including toy guns and aggressive toys in the playroom. As you address the issue, it would be helpful to read the available resources that explore the pros and cons of including aggressive toys in the play-room and the research cited by Schaefer and Mattie (2005) and Drewes

(2008). Although Drewes (2008) made an excellent argument that "a policy of best practices requires that the results of research findings be incorporated into [play therapists'] treatment approaches" (p. 63), you must determine whether you will let the lack of research supporting the cathartic benefits of aggressive play influence the materials you will include in your playroom. You could also consider following our lead by deciding on a case-by-case basis whether you want to have aggressive toys in your playroom, depending on your work setting, the child's presenting problem, and the unfolding of the play therapy process. Drewes included a plea for play therapists to conduct more research into this area. You might decide to follow her suggestions for potential hypotheses to test in this area.

Technology in the Playroom

Another controversy in play therapy is the use of technology in the playroom. Technology-based play therapy interventions are increasing (e.g., Snow et al., 2012; Stone, 2019, 2022), but the inclusion of technology in play therapy continues to be an issue of debate. Altvater et al. (2017) conducted a qualitative study of play therapists to investigate their impressions and experiences with technology in the playroom. They reported that the play therapists sampled had "a mixed reaction to their comfort and preferences for using technology in play therapy" (pp. 245-246). In a more recent study, Gavin et al. (2020) interviewed 40 credentialed play therapists, finding that "some play therapists support the use of technology-based interventions in play therapy, and others are cautious of the emergent practice" (p. 7). Stauffer (2018) summarized a collegial debate between seven veteran play therapists about several topics, including the use of technology in the playroom. She concluded:

> The use of technology in the playroom is a personal choice that play therapists will have to weigh and measure continually. On one hand, children are comfortable and agile with electronic devices and the advantages of the digital traces they leave. On the other hand, children nowadays may have fewer opportunities to engage with an attentive adult in an un-plugged setting who can communicate understanding and build a relationship with them. Although play therapists will have to ponder whether and to what extent to include technology in and between sessions, all of us can agree that the relationship provides the true impetus for change through play therapy (p. 23).

Proponents of the selective use of technology in the playroom (e.g., Hull, 2016; Stone, 2019, 2022) suggested that including technology in the playroom can make play therapy more inviting and the therapy process less threatening. Hull further noted that similar to traditional play materials, technological gameplay can offer a safe emotional distance from real issues; including technology in the playroom allows the client to be the expert and teach the play therapist something important to them. As early as 1991, Gardner noted that using video games with children in therapy has several therapeutic opportunities, including the practice of releasing or controlling aggression, dealing with success and failure, foreseeing consequences of actions, and acting on past consequences. Altvater (2021) argued that children live in a culture of technology and, as a result, "it is imperative to determine how it could be welcomed into treatment" (p. 172). Play therapists have suggested numerous applications of technology in the playroom, including, but not limited to, virtual reality, augmented reality, and mixed reality (García-Vergara et al., 2014; Lamb & Etopio, 2021; Smith et al., 2023; Stone, 2019, 2022) and video games (Colder Carras et al., 2018; Griffiths, 2003; Kottman et al., 2021).

In contrast to the positive perspective of including technology in the playroom, some play therapists argue for the importance of carefully selecting toys for the playroom and not including any that would interfere with the client's free expression, such as video games or other electronics (Landreth, 2024; Ray, 2011). Some play therapists have concerns about technology interfering with the therapeutic process (Pykhtina et al., 2012). Linn (2009) argued that technology can lead to engulfment in a virtual world and internalization of thoughts and feelings, while most play therapy seeks to help children externalize their anxieties, fears, or concerns. Landreth (2024) and Ray (2011) suggested that technology in the playroom interferes with the essential therapeutic conditions of client-centered play therapy.

Stone (2022) argued that the play therapist who uses technology in the playroom "is not endorsing an acceptance of all and everything digital, nor are they suggesting that there are no concerns about the use by the client of society as a whole" (p. 12). Stone pointed out that technology is a culturally appropriate tool (given the technology culture of most child clients) to accomplish traditional play therapy goals of relationship building, information gathering, and direct intervention.

McNary et al. (2018) made the following suggestions for play therapists interested in joining the conversation about opportunities for integrating technology in play therapy sessions:

- Engage in training on incorporating technology into play therapy.

- Learn about any technology clients are using at home and school.
- Consult with School-Based Registered Play Therapist (SB-RPT) counselors, psychologists, and social workers to see whether play or technology-based counseling interventions are being used in school settings.
- Consult with Registered Play Therapist-Supervisors (RPT-S) who have received training in technology and are incorporating it into their practice.
- Invite clients who use digital play outside the playroom to teach you about their favorite games or worlds (even if you choose not to allow digital media into the playroom).
- Add physical items to the playroom representing figures in digital worlds/games (e.g., sand tray figures from video games).
- Discuss the availability and potential benefits of technology that can be used in play sessions with clients' families.
- Closely monitor your clients' progress if you choose to employ technology as a tool in play therapy.
- Seek supervision from an RPT-S familiar with ways to incorporate technology into play therapy.

You will have to decide what you think about using technology in the playroom. As you can see, it's a topic that evokes strong reactions from practitioners—your personal attitudes toward technology will probably impact your decision about incorporating technology in your play therapy practice.

Public Awareness of Play Therapy and Professional Identity of Play Therapists

In an early article, Schaefer (1998) noted that it is essential for the play therapist profession to develop the ability to explain what play therapy is and how it can be helpful to children. Despite significant changes in the therapeutic landscape since that time, it is still often difficult for people who are not familiar with play therapy (even those in the mental health and school counseling professions) to understand how "just playing with kids" could possibly be helping children deal with their problems. Numerous authors have called for increased advocacy to help play therapy "gain the respect it deserves in the mental health field" (p. 208; Tarroja et al., 2013).

The mission of the Association for Play Therapy is "to promote the value of play, play therapy, and credentialed play therapists." To that end, the Association for Play Therapy has a section on its website (www.a4pt.org) entitled "Parents Corner" that includes videos, articles, and downloads addressing the questions, "What is play therapy?" "Does my child need play therapy?" "What does a play therapy session look like?" and "Where can I find a play therapist?" This section of the website also describes mental health conditions and behavioral disorders amenable to intervention through play therapy. Additional sections of the website aimed at parents, mental health professionals, and others provide answers and research citations to the questions, "Why play?" "Why play in therapy?" "What is play therapy?" "How does play therapy work?" "Who benefits from play therapy?" "How will play therapy benefit a child?" "How long does play therapy take?" "How may my family be involved in play therapy?" "Who practices play therapy?" (*https://www.a4pt.org/page/PTMakesADifference*). The website also includes research citations supporting the efficacy of play therapy. These efforts are significant because a growing body of research suggests that the more that parents are knowledgeable about mental health services, the more likely they are to take their children to therapy (Cunningham et al., 2008). In a study investigating public perceptions of the utility of play therapy, Hindman et al. (2022) found that the more adults knew about play therapy, the more they viewed it as beneficial and that exposure to additional information about play therapy increased positive perceptions.

For the field to flourish, it will be necessary to continue to enhance the professional identity of play therapists. One significant step has been the identification of play therapy competencies. Building on the earlier work of Nalavany et al. (2005) and the three broad play therapy competencies identified by APT (knowledge and understanding of play therapy, clinical play therapy skills, and professional engagement in play therapy) Association for Play Therapy, 2023), Turner et al. (2020) identified twenty-seven indicators of competence in play therapy. These specific competencies strengthen the profession's integrity by adding focus to play therapy, training, and supervision, and they also significantly contribute to the professional identity of the play therapist.

One additional method of promoting the professional identity of play therapists is for increased numbers to seek formal professional credentialing in play therapy. By creating standards for the credentialing of play therapists, professional organizations have added an avenue for the increased acceptance of play therapy as a legitimate professional specialty in the fields of mental health and school counseling.

Because play therapy is a secondary profession or identity (e.g., Ashby & McKinney-Clark, 2015), formal credentialing in play therapy is not necessary for competent and ethical practice. However, seeking something like the Registered Play Therapist credential from the Association for Play Therapy helps "consumers identify licensed clinical mental health professionals, with specialized training and experience in play therapy" (APT, 2023). Similarly, the Canadian Association for Play Therapy certifies play therapists "to ensure qualified clinicians in the practice of play therapy" (Canadian Association for Play Therapy, 2023). These registrations and certifications strengthen the professional identity of the play therapist by codifying the training and supervised experience required for this specialized training and formalizing the specialized credentialing of play therapists.

You should consider how comfortable you are with the idea that you can be a powerful advocate for the field of play therapy. Your efforts could be something as simple as disseminating information—to consumer groups, health care providers and policymakers, the media, governmental agencies, and elected officials—about what play therapy is and how it can help children and their families. You can write articles, give interviews, and talk to a wide range of audiences. Even if you decide that advocacy is not consistent with your personality or professional goals, it is essential that you learn how to explain what play therapy is and why it works to parents and colleagues. By becoming comfortable with your ability to explain play therapy, you can make a difference in its acceptance within your community.

You should consider whether to pursue a formal play therapy credential. Professional credentialing increases the profession's credibility, which makes it a professionally responsible action to take. Becoming registered or certified in play therapy can also recognize you as an expert in working with children in your community, which can lead to more referrals from the public and other professionals. Meeting the ongoing continuing education requirements of a professional credential encourages practitioners to stay current in their field, which otherwise might not be a priority, helping to legitimize play therapy as a professionally viable area of specialization.

Advice to Beginning Play Therapists

Over the three editions of *Play Therapy: Basics and Beyond*, we have asked a collection of play therapy experts (some of who are no longer with us, but their wisdom still rings true) to answer, "What advice would you give to beginning play therapists?" Arranged in alphabetical order according to the therapists' last names, here is their advice to you:

- "Be yourself. Don't try to act like a play therapist. Children spot an actor/phony, and your work goes nowhere." *Felicia Carroll, Gestalt play therapist*

- "When thinking about taking our play therapy skills to the infant populations, the problem emerges that the traditional types of play therapy approaches, where the therapist may see the child for individual play therapy sessions without the parent in the room, becomes an outrageous scenario. The practice wisdom is that all infant mental health interventions are relationally oriented and therefore must directly include the parents or caregivers within the therapy sessions." *Janet A. Courtney, PhD, FirstPlay founder*

- "There are so many wonderful play therapy approaches out there. Explore them and then find the one that feels most like you, so that you can embody its philosophy when you are in the playroom. Your own congruence and belief in your approach is not only essential to your well-being and love for what you do but is also a key ingredient for helping a child and their family heal." *Lisa Dion, synergetic play therapist*

- "Be well grounded in one theory that helps you be a 'detective' into the child's issues and becomes the initial lens to start thinking about issues. Then master child-centered/child-led treatment before going into an integrative-prescriptive approach. Remember that one size does not fit all . . . that over time you will need to learn to master other theories and ways of working to serve your clients. Trust your instincts, listen to yourself and what you are picking up on or feeling. Know that children are very forgiving of therapist mistakes and missed cues, if the therapist is authentic and sincere in their approach and demeanor. It is okay to admit mistakes to a child. It helps them grow to have a role model who can model that it is okay not to be perfect. Always have a supervisor, no matter how experienced you become, be it a direct supervisor, peer supervisor, or consultative supervisor, as needed. We all get impacted by our clients and need another perspective from time to time. Take good care of yourself; use regular self-care. If we do not care for ourselves, we cannot adequately and consistently care for others. And finally, realize that we cannot save everyone. Not every client can be helped or will stay until termination. However, always remember we do make a difference in the lives of those we help (children and parents). We become a model and proof that there are helping, caring people out there." *Athena Drewes, integrative-prescriptive play therapist*

- "In the world of play therapy, there's a fundamental truth that new practitioners should always keep in mind: the therapeutic relationship is the cornerstone of our work. Invest your energy in forging a deep and genuine connection with the children and families you'll be helping. Show them that you truly care and can be trusted.

    o When it comes to the sessions themselves, allow the child to take the lead in play. This is their language, their way of expressing themselves. Don't rush into structured activities or become overly reliant on workbooks and manuals. Instead, trust your instincts and adapt your approach to what feels right for that particular child in that moment.

    o But it doesn't stop with the children; extend that same caring and empathetic approach to the parents and families you'll encounter. They, too, need to feel safe and connected in this process.

    o Furthermore, don't underestimate the value of building relationships within the broader play therapy community. Be generous with your knowledge and resources, and you'll find that support and collaboration with your peers are invaluable.

    o Authenticity is key. While it's natural to be inspired by seasoned therapists, don't try to mimic them. Instead, let their wisdom inform your own unique style. Your authenticity and genuine care will form the strongest bonds with your clients.

    o Lastly, commit to being a lifelong learner. Seek supervision and continuous professional development, even when it's not mandatory. Play therapy work can be emotionally taxing, so prioritize self-care and personal growth. Trying to go it alone can lead to burnout faster than you might expect.

    o As you step into the world of play therapy, remember to keep these insights close to your heart. They've been a guiding light for me throughout my journey, and I hope they serve you just as well. Here's to the meaningful connections and positive transformations ahead in your play therapy work." *Jackie Flynn, Integrative play therapist specializing in EMDR*

- "Sit under the teaching of each of the creators of the models that you want to be able to implement (or their next-generation protégés). In the prescriptive paradigm, the hope is that clinicians will be well-versed in each of the models that they incorporate in treatment. Learn each model in its purest form (which I believe is most effectively done by absorbing the theory, the language, the technologies, and the heart of a particular way of working in play therapy). Then inform your practice decisions with the evidence base and literature about which populations/diagnoses/childhood problems benefit the most from each way of working. Get good and ongoing supervision. Have fun and learn from your mistakes! And remember that the relationship provides the scaffolding upon which other treatment choices can rest." *Paris Goodyear-Brown, prescriptive play therapist*

- "Becoming a play therapist is a process, a journey. Understand that this takes time and learning about different approaches and most certainly about diversity. Be diligent in exploring who you are as a play therapist, what resonates within you, and taking care to value and understand how approaches may shift regarding cultural, racial, neuro, and other forms of diversity that will exist in your child clients." *Robert Jason Grant, AutPlay therapist*

- "Learn it and learn it well. Be sure not to mix up treatment and diagnostic goals. Diagnostic protocols that have been validated should be chosen. Stick with methods that have empirical support and don't be pulled into methods that somebody made up one day that sound 'like they ought to work.' A theoretical base for the methods really is in order also. Without a good theoretical and empirical base, a therapist flips around techniques without a genuine rationale or understanding of effects." *Louise Guerney, child-centered play therapist and filial therapy trainer*

- "TRUST THE PROCESS!" *Dana Holtz, Adlerian play therapist*

- "Get good supervision; listen to parents and children; be aware of your own limitations and expectations; and learn how to 'be' with the child." *Susan Knell, cognitive–behavioral play therapist*

- "KNOW THYSELF!! Understand what works for you, what attracts you as a theoretical approach and follow what suits you." *J. P. Lilly, Jungian play therapist*

- "Learn one method of play therapy thoroughly, so you know what it can do and cannot do. Then learn other methods thoroughly.

Don't try to mix them all up in the same session so you are confusing the child and yourself." *Evangeline Munns, Theraplay therapist*

- "I'm a big proponent of people experiencing the power of the projective techniques I use; to remember what it is like to be a child; to work through some of their own childhood issues. Beginning therapists need to relax and trust themselves. And they need to continue to go to workshops, training, read, etc." *Violet Oaklander, Gestalt play therapist*

- "The most important thing for a play therapist is to know yourself very well, including your own personal challenges. Be in an authentic relationship with yourself so that you can be an authentic relationship with other human beings. The relationship is the key to any path." *Dee Ray, child-centered play therapist*

- "Keep learning and expanding your therapeutic repertoire!" *Charles Schaefer, prescriptive play therapist*

- "Observe children of all ages at play in their natural environments. Hear the voices and the scripts they use. These are invaluable to adding an authentic voice when playing with children in play therapy. Have fun. Happiness and laugher create resilience." *Aideen Taylor de Faoite, narrative play therapist*

- "Trust your intuition. Learn to tolerate your own aggression. Setting limits is essential. You need to be containing so that the child can feel safe showing you intolerable parts of self." *Timothy Tisdell, psychodynamic play therapist*

- "Get good solid training—not just single day workshops or conferences, but more in-depth training, and get play therapy supervision. It's probably good to master just a couple methods for starters and then branch out. I usually recommend CCPT [child-centered play therapy] to start as the empathic attitudes and basic skills can also be important with other play therapy methods.

    o Always involve the family one way or another, and develop skills for doing that if you don't have them already.

    o Learn WHY you are doing the things that you do. Don't become technique-oriented. Know the theory and basic research, but mostly, know the rationale for what you are doing and why you are applying it to a particular child or problem.

    o Play more yourself! Learn or relearn the power of play firsthand.

- o If you're working with a trainer or supervisor who points out your flaws but not your good points, find a new one who is encouraging and not too critical.
  - o Give yourself time to develop, and stretch yourself to learn things that are new. Find excitement in doing that." *Risë VanFleet, child-centered play therapist*
- "The best ways to learn are to watch someone who is competent and to practice yourself and get constant supervision. Other ideas are to:
  - o Observe seasoned play therapists in the playroom.
  - o Practice encouragement, tracking, and logical consequences on a daily basis—not just in the playroom.
  - o Develop a theory base that you believe in and live by.
  - o Attend Association for Play Therapy workshops and conferences in addition to taking classes.
  - o Spend time with children.
  - o Develop a strong foundation in child development." *JoAnna White, Adlerian play therapist*

Practice Exercises

1. Prepare a short speech/presentation (3-6 minutes) explaining what play therapy is and how it can help children. You could actually practice presenting it to fellow students or colleagues.

2. Design a plan for becoming more culturally humble and competent, including a rationale for why growth in this area is important to you.

3. Design a plan for enhancing your professional identity as a play therapist, including a rationale for why growth in this area is important to you.

4. For each of the following ethical dilemmas in play therapy, explain the ethical issues, how you would deal with the situation, and your rationale. Use the ethical suggestions in this chapter, the *Play Therapy Best Practices* document from the Association for Play Therapy, and the code of ethics of your professional organization.

5. You have been working with a mother for three years on some very intense issues from her childhood. She wants you to continue working with her and also see her daughter in play therapy.

6. You are a school counselor, and a fourth-grader wants to start seeing you for play therapy. She adamantly tells you that she will never speak to you again if you tell her parents that she is coming for play therapy.

7. You are working with a child diagnosed with schizophrenia whose parents do not want him to continue on his medication. They want you to treat the problem with play therapy and no other medical intervention.

8. You are a child-centered play therapist working with a child diagnosed with autism spectrum disorder, level 1. His insurance will no longer pay for your services because the company says that play therapy will not help him. His family cannot afford your services.

9. Your theoretical orientation is Gestalt, and a parent calls you, asking if you can do systematic desensitization on a child with a snake phobia.

10. You are a school counselor working with a very active kindergarten child. The teacher wants you to "get him to stay in his seat and be quiet." The child is perfectly content to continue on his current path, and his parents are not dissatisfied with his behavior. How will you determine your goals for working with this child?

11. You have a 9-year-old client who is so reluctant to come to therapy that her parents have had to carry her into your playroom every week for the past month.

12. You have a client who is dealing with some issues related to his parents' negative attitude toward him, and his parents want to observe his sessions.

13. You have an 8-year-old client who has specifically asked you not to tell her parents about some problems she is experiencing at school.

14. You do not have a release to talk to a client's school counselor, who calls wanting information about your sessions.

15. You believe a child is making significant progress, but her parents think nothing is happening. They want to see your notes on the case to prove that "you are just wasting our time and money."

16. You have no training in play therapy but really like children and have some toys in your office. You have the reputation in your community of being a play therapist and get many professional referrals.

17. You are a Registered Play Therapist but have no training in clinical supervision. Someone in your community calls and asks you to serve as his play therapy supervisor.

Questions to Ponder

1. Which ethical issues related to play therapy practice will be the most difficult for you? What about that issue will be difficult for you?

2. Which ethical issues related to play therapy practice will be the easiest for you, and why?

3. What is your stance on having aggressive toys in your playroom? What are the pros and cons as you see them?

4. What is your stance on having/utilizing technology in your playroom? What are the pros and cons as you see them?

5. What are the next steps for you to develop increased cultural humility and an enhanced multicultural orientation?

6. Where do you need to grow to increase knowledge of your own culture and your related worldview and assumptions?

7. What information, consultation, supervision, and/or practice do you need in broaching and bridging with clients and their families?

8. What is an area in which you are most comfortable and/or confident in the area of cultural competence and cultural humility? How can you capitalize on this area of strength in your play therapy practice?

9. What do you think about the need to increase public awareness of the value of play therapy?

10. How important do you think the development of a professional identity as a play therapist is? What are your plans in this area for developing your professional identity as a play therapist?

11. How important is it to become registered and/or certified as a play therapist? What are your plans for registration and/or certification as a play therapist?

12. Do you think you might eventually want to be a play therapy supervisor? If so, what would be appealing about this to you? If not, why not?

13. If you had access to play therapy experts, which ones would you want to interview? Why would you choose those particular experts to interview? What would you want to ask them?

References

Agner, J. (2020). Moving from cultural competence to cultural humility in occupational therapy: A paradigm shift. *The American Journal of Occupational Therapy, 74*(4), Article 7404347010p1-7404347010p7. https://doi.org/10.5014/ajot.2020.038067

Akay, S., & Bratton, S. (2017). The effects of Adlerian play therapy on maladaptive perfectionism and anxiety in children: A single case design. *International Journal of Play Therapy, 26*(2), 96–110. http://doi.org/10.1037/pla0000043

Alber, D. (2019). *A little spot of anger: A story about managing big emotions.* Diane Alber Art.

Allan, J. (1988). *Inscapes of the child's world.* Spring.

Allan, J. (1997). Jungian play psychotherapy. In K. O'Connor & L. M. Braverman (Eds.), *Play therapy theory and practice: A comparative presentation* (pp. 100–130). Wiley.

Allen, F. (1942). *Psychotherapy with children.* Norton.

Altvater, R. A. (2021). The culture of technology and play therapy. In E. Gil & A. A. Drewes (Eds.), *Cultural issues in play therapy* (pp. 172–190). Guilford.

Altvater, R. A., Singer, R. R., & Gil, E. (2017). Part 1: Modern trends in the playroom—preferences and interactions with tradition and innovation. *International Journal of Play Therapy, 26*(4), 239–249. https://doi.org/10.1037/pla0000058

American Counseling Association. (2014). *ACA code of ethics.* https://www.counseling.org/resources/aca-code-of-ethics.pdf

AMghs Publishing. (2023). *Inspiring short stories for kids: Motivational book about self-confidence, perseverance, gratitude, courage, and other values.*

Anderson, J., & Richards, N. (1995, October). *Play therapy in the real world: Coping with managed care, challenging children, skeptical colleagues, time, and space constraints* [Conference presentation]. First Annual Conference of the Iowa Association of Play Therapy, Iowa City, IA, United States.

Ansbacher, H. L., & Ansbacher, R. R. (Eds.). (1956). *The individual psychology of Alfred Adler: A systematic presentation in selections from his writings.* Basic Books.

Ashby, J. S., Blasko, L. S., Bruner, L. P., & Martin, J. (2002). The stretching story. In H. Kaduson & C. E. Schaefer (Eds.), *101 favorite play therapy techniques* (Vol. 3, pp. 181–183). Jason Aronson.

Ashby, J. S., Kiperman, S., & Rosenbaum Wood, L. (2017). Ethics in play therapy consultation and supervision. In L. Steen (Ed.), *Emerging research in play therapy, child counseling and consultation* (pp. 32–47). Guilford.

Ashby, J. S., Kottman, T., & DeGraaf, D. (2008). *Active interventions for kids and teens: Adding adventure.* American Counseling Association.

Ashby, J., Kottman, T., & Martin, J. (2004). Play therapy with young perfectionists. *International Journal of Play Therapy, 13*(1), 35–55. https://doi.org/10.1037/h0088884

Ashby, J. S., & McKinney-Clark, K. (2015). Ethics in play therapy. In D. Crenshaw & A. Stewart (Eds.), *Play therapy: A compressive guide to theory and practice* (pp. 32–47). Guilford.

Association for Play Therapy. (n.d.). *Why play therapy?* https://www.a4pt. org/page/WhyPlayTherapy

Association for Play Therapy. (2022a). *Paper on touch: Clinical, professional & ethical issues.* https://cdn.ymaws.com/www.a4pt.org/resource/ resmgr/resource_center/Paper_on_Touch_2022__-_Final.pdf

Association for Play Therapy. (2022b). *Play therapy best practices: Clinical, professional & ethical issues.* https://cdn.ymaws.com/www.a4pt.org/ resource/resmgr/publications/best_practices.pdf

Association for Play Therapy. (2023). *Credentialing standards for the registered play therapist.* https://cdn.ymaws.com/www.a4pt.org/ resource/resmgr/credentials/RPT_Standards.pdf

Astramovich, R. L., Lyons, C., & Hamilton, N. J. (2015). Play therapy for children with intellectual disabilities. *Journal of Child and Adolescent Counseling, 1*(1), 27–36. https://doi.org/10.1080/23727810.2015.1015904

Axline, V. (1947). *Play therapy: The inner dynamics of childhood.* Houghton Mifflin.

Axline, V. (1969). *Play therapy* (Rev. ed.). Ballantine Books.

Axline, V. (1971). *Dibs: In search of self.* Ballantine Books.

Ayling, P. (2019). Containing feelings and setting limits in play therapy: Working with aggression. In P. Ayling, H. Armstrong, & L. G. Clark (Eds.), *Becoming and being a play therapist: Play therapy in practice* (pp. 122–136). Routledge. https://doi.org/10.4324/9780203711224-10

Bailey, R., & Jones, S. M. (2019). An integrated model of regulation for applied settings. *Clinical Child and Family Psychology Review, 22,* 2–23. https://doi.org/10.1007/s10567-019-00288-y

Baldwin, K., Velasquez, M., & Courtney, J. A. (2020). FirstPlay therapy strengthens the attachment relationship between a mother with perinatal depression and her infant. In J. Courtney (Ed.), *Infant play therapy: Foundations, models, programs, and practice* (pp. 83–100). Routledge.

Beck, A. (1976). *Cognitive therapy and the emotional disorders.* International Universities Press.

Beck, J. (1995). *Cognitive therapy: Basics and beyond.* Guilford.

Beckley-Forest, A., & Monaco, A. (Eds.). (2021). *EMDR with children in the play therapy room: An integrated approach.* Springer.

Benedict, H. E. (2001). *Benedict's expanded themes in play therapy* [Unpublished working document]. Baylor University.

Benedict, H. (2006). Object relations play therapy. In C. Schaefer & H. Kaduson (Eds.), *Contemporary play therapy: Theory, research, and practice* (pp. 3–27). Guilford.

Benedict, H., & Hastings, L. (2002). Object relations play therapy. In J. Magnavita (Ed.), *Comprehensive handbook of psychotherapy* (Vol. 1, pp. 47–80). Wiley.

Benedict, H., & Mongoven, L. (1997). Thematic play therapy: An approach to treatment of attachment disorders in young children. In H. Kaduson, D. Cangelosi, & C. Schaefer (Eds.), *The playing cure: Individual play therapy for specific childhood problems* (pp. 277–315). Jason Aronson.

Bent, D., Schalk, R., Van Regenmortel, T., & Noordegraaf, M. (2022). Systematic review of common and specific factors in play therapy for young people with intellectual disability. *International Journal of Developmental Disabilities,* 1–14. https://doi.org/10.1080/20473869. 2022.2086433

Bixler, R. H. (1949). Limits are therapy. *Journal of Consulting Psychology,* *13*(1), 1–11. https://doi.org/10.1037/h0061770

Blalock, S. M., Lindo, N., & Ray, D. C. (2019), Individual and group child-centered play therapy: Impact on social-emotional competencies. *Journal of Counseling & Development, 97*(3), 238–249. https://doi. org/10.1002/jcad.12264

Blanco, P., Muro, J., Holliman, R., Stickley, V., & Carter, K. (2015). Effect of child-centered play therapy on performance anxiety and academic achievement. *Journal of Child and Adolescent Counseling, 1*(2), 66–80. https://doi.org/10.1080/23727810.2015.1079117

Blom, R. (2006). *The handbook of Gestalt play therapy: Practical guidelines for child therapists.* Jessica Kingsley.

Booth, P., & Jernberg, A. (2010). *Theraplay: Helping parents and children build better relationships through attachment-based play* (3rd ed.). Jossey-Bass.

Booth, P., & Winstead, M. (2015). Theraplay: Repairing relationships, helping families heal. In D. Crenshaw & A. Stewart (Eds.), *Play therapy: A comprehensive guide to theory and practice* (pp. 141–155). Guilford.

Booth, P. B., & Winstead, M. L. R. (2016). Theraplay: Creating secure and joyful attachment relationships. In K. J. O'Connor, C. Schaefer, & L. Braverman (Eds.), *Handbook of play therapy* (2nd ed., pp. 165–193). Wiley.

Borenstein, M., Hedges, L. V., Higgins, J. P., & Rothstein, H. R. (2021). *Introduction to meta-analysis.* Wiley.

Bradway, K. (1979). Sandplay in psychotherapy. *Art Psychotherapy, 6*(2), 85–93. https://doi.org/10.1016/0090-9092(79)90003-6

Bratton, S., Ceballos, P., Sheely-Moore, A., Meany-Walen, K., Pronchenko, V., & Jones, L. (2013). Head start early mental health intervention: Effects of child-centered play therapy on disruptive behaviors. *International Journal of Play Therapy, 22*(1), 28–42. https://doi. org/10.1037/a0030318

Bratton, S., Opiola, K., & Dafoe, E. (2015). Child-parent relationship therapy: A 10-session filial therapy model. In D. A. Crenshaw & A. L. Stewart (Eds.), *Play therapy: A comprehensive guide to theory and practice* (pp. 129–140). Guilford.

Bratton, S., Ray, D., Rhine, T., & Jones, L. (2005). The efficacy of play therapy with children: A meta-analytic review of the outcome research. *Professional Psychology: Research and Practice, 36,* 376–390. https://doi.org/10.1037/0735-7028.36.4.376

Britain, L. (2019). *I'm happy-sad today: Making sense of mixed-together feelings.* Free Spirit.

British Association of Play Therapists (2022). *Play therapy competences.*

Brody, V. (1978). Developmental play: A relationship-focused program for children. *Child Welfare, 57,* 591–599. http://www.jstor.org/stable/45393490

Brody, V. (1997). *The dialogue of touch: Developmental play therapy* (Rev. ed.). Jason Aronson.

Brooks, B., Fiedler, K., Waddington, J., & Zink, K. (2013). Minors' rights to confidentiality, when parents want to know: An ethical scenario. *VISTAS Online,* Article 26. https://www.counseling.org/docs/default-source/vistas/minors-rights-to-confidentiality-when-parents-want-to-know-an-ethical-scenario.pdf?sfvrsn=12

Bixler, R. (1949). Limits are therapy. *Journal of Consulting Psychology, 13,* 1–11. https://doi.org/10.1037/h0061770

Bundy-Myrow, S., & Booth, P. (2009). Theraplay: Supporting attachment relationships. In K. O'Connor & L. M. Braverman (Eds.), *Play therapy theory and practice: Comparing theories and techniques* (2nd ed., pp. 315–366). Wiley.

Burns, G. (2017). *101 stories for enhancing happiness and well-being: Using metaphors in positive psychology and therapy.* Routledge.

Canadian Association for Play Therapy. (2023). https://canadianplaytherapy.com/

Cangelosi, D. (1993). Internal and external wars: Psychodynamic play therapy. In T. Kottman & C. Schaefer (Eds.), *Play therapy in action: A casebook for practitioners* (pp. 347–370). Jason Aronson.

Canning, C. (2021). *Bellies to the sky: A bedtime breathwork book.* Beaver's Pond.

Carey, L. (1990). Sandplay therapy with a troubled child. *Arts in Psychotherapy, 17,* 197–209. https://doi.org/10.1016/0197-4556(90)90002-8

Carey, L. (1999). *Sandplay: Therapy with children and families.* Jason Aronson.

Carmichael, K. D. (2006). Legal and ethical issues in play therapy. *International Journal of Play Therapy, 15*(2), 83–99. https://doi. org/10.1037/h0088916

Carnes-Holt, K., & Bratton, S. C. (2014). The efficacy of child parent relationship therapy for adopted children with attachment disruptions. *Journal of Counseling & Development, 92*(3), 328–337. https://doi.org/10.1002/j.1556-6676.2014.00160.x

Carroll, F. (2009). Gestalt play therapy. In K. J. O'Connor & L. D. Braverman, *Play therapy theory and practice: Comparing theories and techniques* (2nd ed., pp. 283–314). Wiley.

Carroll, F., & Oaklander, V. (1997). Gestalt play therapy. In K. J. O'Connor & L. M. Braverman (Eds.), Play therapy theory and practice: A comparative presentation (pp. 184–203). Wiley.

Carroll, F., & Orozco, V. (2019). Gestalt play therapy. *Play Therapy, 14*(3), 36–38.

Cates, J., Paone, T., Packman, J., & Margolis, D. (2006). Effective parent consultation in play therapy. *International Journal of Play Therapy, 15*(1), 87–100. https://doi.org/10.1037/h0088909

Cattanach, A. (2006). Narrative play therapy. In C. Schaefer & H. Kaduson (Eds.), *Contemporary play therapy: Theory, research, and practice* (pp. 82–99). Guilford.

Cattanach, A. (2008a). *Narrative approaches in play with children.* Jessica Kingsley.

Cattanach, A. (2008b). *Play therapy with abused children* (2nd ed.). Jessica Kingsley.

Cavett, A. M. (2014). Stress inoculation. In C. Schaefer & A. Drewes (Eds.), *The therapeutic powers of play: 20 core agents of change* (pp. 131–141). Wiley.

Cavett, A. (2015). Cognitive-behavioral play therapy. In D. A. Crenshaw & A. L. Stewart (Eds.), *Play therapy: A comprehensive guide to theory and practice* (pp. 83–98). Guilford.

Chen, S.-Y., & Cheng, Y.-J. (2021). Effects of kinder training on preschool children's externalizing behavior: A single-case design. *Journal of Child and Adolescent Counseling, 7*(3), 176–192. https://doi.org/10. 1080/23727810.2021.1948270

Chen, S.-Y., & Lindo, N. A. (2018). The impact of kinder training on young children's on-task behavior: A single-case design. *International*

Journal of Play Therapy, 27(2), 78–91. https://doi.org/10.1037/pla0000066

Chen, S.-Y., Roller, K., & Kottman, T. (2021). Adlerian family play therapy: Healing the attachment trauma of divorce. *International Journal of Play Therapy, 30*(1), 28–39. https://doi.org/10.1037/pla0000146

Cheng, Y.-J., Chung, R. K., & Ogawa, Y. (2022). Cultural opportunities with Asian populations. In D. Ray, Y. Ogawa, & Y.-J. Cheng (Eds.), *Multicultural play therapy: Making the most of cultural opportunities with children* (pp. 182–205). Routledge.

Cochran, N. H., Nordling, W. J., & Cochran, J. L. (2022). *Child-centered play therapy: A practical guide to therapeutic relationships with children.* Taylor & Francis.

Coenen, C. (2020). *The Creative Toolkit for Working with Grief and Bereavement: A Practitioner's Guide with Activities and Worksheets.* Jessica Kingsley.

Coggins, K., & Carnes-Holt, K. (2021). The efficacy of child-teacher relationship training as an early childhood mental health intervention in Head Start programs. *International Journal of Play Therapy, 30*(2), 112–124. https://doi.org/10.1037/pla0000154

Cohen, M. (2018). *Metaphor: Its therapeutic use and construction.* Resource Publications.

Colder Carras, M., Van Rooij, A. J., Spruijt-Metz, D., Kvedar, J., Griffiths, M. D., Carabas, Y., & Labrique, A. (2018). Commercial video games as therapy: A new research agenda to unlock the potential of a global pastime. *Frontiers in Psychiatry, 8,* Article 300. https://doi.org/10.3389/fpsyt.2017.00300

Coleman, H. L. K. (2004). Multicultural counseling competencies in a pluralistic society. *Journal of Mental Health Counseling, 26,* 56–66. https://doi.org/10.17744/mehc.26.1.kwcptmjrar8bbfc6

Coleman, V., Parmer, T., & Barker, S. (1993). Play therapy for a multicultural population: Guidelines for mental health professionals. *International Journal of Play Therapy, 2*(1), 63–74.

Cornett, N., & Bratton, S. C. (2014). Examining the impact of child parent relationship therapy (CPRT) on family functioning. *Journal of Marital and Family Therapy, 40*(3), 302–318. https://doi.org/10.1111/jmft.12014

Cornett, N., & Bratton, S. C. (2015). A golden intervention: 50 years of research on filial therapy. *International Journal of Play Therapy, 24*(3), 119–133. https://doi.org/10.1037/a0039088

Courtney, J. A. (Ed.). (2020). *Infant play therapy: Foundations, models, programs, and practice*. Routledge.

Courtney, J., & Nolan, R. (Eds.). (2017). *Touch in child counseling and play therapy: An ethical and clinical guide*. Routledge.

Courtney, J., Velasquez, M., & Toth, V. B. (2017). FirstPlay infant massage storytelling: Facilitating corrective touch experiences with a teenage mother and her abused infant. In J. Courtney & R. Nolan (Eds.), *Touch in child counseling and play therapy* (pp. 48–62). Routledge.

Cunningham, C. E., Deal, K., Rimas, H., Buchanan, D. H., Gold, M., Sdao-Jarvie, K., & Boyle, M. (2008). Modeling the information preferences of parents of children with mental health problems: A discrete choice conjoint experiment. *Journal of Abnormal Child Psychology, 36*, 1123–1138. https://doi.org/110.1007/s10802-008-9238-4

Czyszczon, G., Riviere, S., Lowman, G., & Stewart, A. (2015). In D. A. Crenshaw & A. L. Stewart (Eds.), *Play therapy: A comprehensive guide to theory and practice* (pp. 186–200). Guilford.

Daley, L. P., Miller, R. B., Bean, R. A., & Oka, M. (2018). Family system play therapy: An integrative approach. *American Journal of Family Therapy, 46*(5), 421–436. https://doi.org/10.1080/01926187.2019.1570386

Dasari, M., & Knell, S. (2015). Cognitive behavioral play therapy for children with anxiety and phobias. In H. Kaduson & C. Schaefer (Eds.), *Short-term play therapy for children* (3rd ed., pp. 25–52). Guilford.

Davis, D. E., DeBlaere, C., Owen, J., Hook, J. N., Rivera, D. P., Choe, E., Van Tongeren, D. R., Worthington, E. L., Jr., & Placeres, V. (2018). The multicultural orientation framework: A narrative review. *Psychotherapy, 55*(1), 89–100. https://doi.org/10.1037/pst0000160

Day-Vines, N. L., Cluxton-Keller, F., Agorsor, C., Gubara, S., & Otabil, N. A. A. (2020). The multidimensional model of broaching behavior. *Journal of Counseling and Development, 98*(1), 107–118. https://doi.org/10.1002/jcad.12304

Delgado, M. R., & Aguilar, E. V. (2022). Cultural opportunities with Latinx populations. In D. C. Ray, Y. Ogawa, & Y.-J. Cheng (Eds.), *Multicultural play therapy: Making the most of cultural opportunities with children* (pp. 165–181). Routledge.

Denham, S. A., Bassett, H. H., Thayer, S. K., Mincic, M. S., Sirotkin, Y. S., & Zinsser, K. (2012). Observing preschoolers' social-emotional behavior: Structure, foundations, and prediction of early school success. *Journal of Genetic Psychology, 173*, 246–278. https://doi.org/10.1080/00221325.2011.597457

Denny, L., Coles, S., & Blitz, R. (2017). Fetal alcohol syndrome and fetal alcohol spectrum disorders. *American Family Physician, 96*(8), 515–522A.

Deverage, S. (2022). *The psychology of storytelling: Understanding and managing effective storytelling strategies for personal and professional growth*. NFT Publishing.

Devereaux, C. (2014). Moving with the space between us: The dance of attachment security. In C. Malchiodi & D. Crenshaw (Eds.), *Creative arts and play therapy for children with attachment problems* (pp. 84–99). Guilford.

Dickinson, R., & Daly, E. (2020). Using personality priorities in Adlerian play therapy parent consultation. *The Journal of Individual Psychology, 76*(4), 342–360. https://doi.org/10.1353/jip.2020.0034

Dillman Taylor, D., Thompson, K., & Kottman, T. (2022). Strengthening the efficacy of Adlerian play therapy through the measurement model. *International Journal of Play Therapy, 31*(3), 164–173. https://doi.org/10.1037/pla0000176

Dion, L. (2018). *Aggression in play therapy: A neurobiological approach for integrating intensity*. Norton.

Drewes, A. (2008). Bobo revisited: What the research says. *International Journal of Play Therapy, 17*(1), 52–65. https://doi.org/10.1037/1555-6824.17.1.52

Drewes, A., & Schaefer, C., (2018). *Puppet play therapy: A practical guidebook*. Routledge.

Dreikurs, R., & Soltz, V. (1964). *Children: The challenge*. Hawthorn/Dutton.

Drisko, J., Corvino, P., Kelly, L., & Nielson, J. (2020). Is individual child play therapy effective? *Research on Social Work Practice, 30*(7), 715–723. https://doi.org/10.1177/1049731519854157

Eadeh, H. M., Breaux, R., & Nikolas, M. A. (2021). A meta-analytic review of emotion regulation focused psychosocial interventions for adolescents. *Clinical Child and Family Psychology Review, 24*(4), 684–706. https://doi.org/10.1007/s10567-021-00362-4

Edwards, A. (2020). *Marcy's having all the feels*. National Center for Youth Issues.

Edwards, J. B. (2016). Cultural intelligence for clinical social work practice. *Clinical Social Work Journal, 44*, 211–220. https://doi.org/10.1007/s10615-0150543-4

Elswick, S. (2018). *Using picture books to enhance children's social and emotional literacy.* Jessica Kingsley.

Engel, S. (1995). *The stories children tell: Making sense of the narratives of childhood.* Freeman.

Erickson, E. (1950). *Childhood and society.* Norton.

Erickson, M., & Rossi, E. (1981). *Experiencing hypnosis: Indirect approaches to altered states.* Irvington.

Esmaili, S. K., Mehraban, A. H., Shafaroodi, N., Yazdani, F., Masoumi, T., & Zarei, M. (2019). Participation in peer-play activities among children with specific learning disability: A randomized controlled trial. *The American Journal of Occupational Therapy, 73*(2), https://doi.org/10.5014/ajot.2018.028613

Etemadzadeh, M., Hooman, F., & Makvandi, B. (2023). The effectiveness of play therapy in improving attention and working memory in students with specific learning disorders. *International Journal of School Health, 10*(1), 26–33. https://doi.org/10.30476/INTJSH.2023.97787.1280

Evans, C. (2021). Trauma-informed Adlerian play therapy: A case study. *The Journal of Individual Psychology, 77*(3), 362–373. https://doi.org/10.1353/jip.2021.0025

Fantozzi, P., Sesso, G., Muratori, P., Milone, A., & Masi, G. (2021). Biological bases of empathy and social cognition in patients with attention-deficit/hyperactivity disorder: A focus on treatment with psychostimulants. *Brain Sciences, 11*(11), Article 1399. https://doi.org/10.3390/brainsci11111399

Fernandez, K. T. G., & Sugay, C. O. (2016). Psychodynamic play therapy: A case of selective mutism. *International Journal of Play Therapy, 25*(4), 203- 209. https://doi.org/10.1037/pla0000034

Fink, G. (2017). Stress: Concepts, definition and history. In J. Stein (Ed.), *Reference module in neuroscience and biobehavioral psychology* (pp. 1–9). Elsevier. https://www.sciencedirect.com/science/article/abs/pii/B9780128093245022082

Flanagan, J. S. (2019, July 8). Using therapeutic storytelling with children: Five easy steps. *John Sommers-Flanagan.*

https://johnsommersflanagan.com/2019/07/08/
using-therapeutic-storytelling-with-children-five-easy-steps/

France, L. A., McIntosh, S., & Woods, K. (2023) Using Theraplay to support children and families: A scoping review. *Early Child Development and Care, 193*(9-10), 1097–1111. https://doi.org/10.1080/03004430.2023.2227775

Frey, D. (2015). Play therapy interventions with adults. In D. Crenshaw & A. Stewart (Eds.), *Play therapy: A comprehensive guide to theory and practice* (pp. 452–464). Guilford.

Freud, A. (1928). *Introduction to the technique of child analysis* (L. P. Clark, Trans.). Nervous and Mental Diseases Publishing.

Freud, A. (1946). *The psychoanalytic treatment of children.* Imago.

Freud, S. (1955). *Analysis of a phobia in a five-year-old boy* (J. Strachey, Trans.). Hogarth Press. (Original work published 1909)

Freud, A. (1968). Indications and counter-indications for child analysis. *Psychoanalytic Study of the Child, 23,* 37–46.

Freud, S. (1995). *The basic writings of Sigmund Freud.* Modern Library. (Original work published 1938)

Fried, K., & McKenna, C. (2020). *Healing through play: Using the Oaklander model.*

Gallo-Lopez, L., & Schaefer, C. E. (Eds.) (2010). *Play therapy with adolescents.* Jason Aronson.

Garcia, G. (2017). *Listening to my body.* Skinned Knee.

Garcia, G. (2021). *Amaya's anger: A mindful understanding of strong emotions.* Skinned Knee.

García-Vergara, S., Brown, L., Park, H. W., Howard, A. M. (2014). Engaging children in play therapy: The coupling of virtual reality games with social robotics. In A. Brooks, S., Brahnam, & L. Jain (Eds.), *Technologies of inclusive well-being: Serious games, alternative realities, and play therapy* (pp. 139–163). Springer. https://doi.org/10.1007/978-3-642-45432-5_8

Gardner, B. J. (2015). Play therapy with adolescents. In D. A. Crenshaw & A. L. Stewart (Eds.), *Play therapy: A comprehensive guide to theory and practice* (pp. 439–451). Guilford.

Gardner, J. E. (1991). Can the Mario Bros. help? Nintendo games as an adjunct in psychotherapy with children. *Psychotherapy:*

Theory, Research, Practice, Training, 28(4), 667–670. https://doi.org/10.1037/0033-3204.28.4.667

Gardner, K., & Yasenik, L. (2008). When approaches collide: A decision-making model for play therapists. In A. Drewes & J. A. Mullen (Eds.), *Supervision can be playful: Techniques for child and play therapist supervisor* (pp. 39–68). Jason Aronson.

Gardner, R. (1971). *Therapeutic communication with children: The mutual storytelling technique.* Jason Aronson.

Gardner, R. (1973). *The talking, feeling, and doing game.* Creative Therapeutics.

Gardner, R. A. (Ed.). (1993). *Storytelling in psychotherapy with children.* Jason Aronson.

Garofano-Brown, A. (2010). Child-centered play therapy and child development: A single case analysis. In J. Baggerly, D. Ray, & S. Bratton (Eds.), *Child-centered play therapy research: The evidence base for effective practice* (pp. 231–248). Wiley.

Gavin, S., Meany-Walen, K. K., Murray, M., Christians, A., Barrett, M., & Kottman, T. (2020). Play therapists' attitudes toward using technology in the playroom. *International Journal of Play Therapy, 29*(1), 1–8. https://doi.org/10.1037/pla0000104

Gil, E. (2013, October). Strengthening attachment through laughter and play: Using playful rewarding interactions to motivate shifts in perception [Conference presentation]. Association for Play Therapy International Conference, Palm Springs, California, United States.

Gil, E. (2015). *Play in family therapy* (2nd ed.). Guilford.

Gil, E. (2017). *Posttraumatic play in children: What clinicians need to know.* Guilford.

Gil, E., & Crenshaw, D. A. (2016). *Termination challenges in child psychotherapy.* Guilford.

Gil, E., & Dias, T. (2020). Dramatic play therapy. In H. Kaduson & C. Schaefer (Eds.), *Play therapy with children: Modalities for change* (pp. 141–156). American Psychological Association.

Gil, E., & Dias, T. (2021). Dramatic play therapy. In H. G. Kaduson & C. Schaefer (Eds.), *Play therapy with children: Modalities for change* (pp. 141–156). American Psychological Association. https://doi.org/10.1037/0000217-010

Gil, E., & Drewes, A. A. (2021). Redefining and broadening the definition of culture. In E. Gil & A. A. Drewes (Eds.), *Cultural issues in play therapy* (2nd ed., pp. 1–11). Guilford.

Gil, E., Konrath, E., Shaw, J., Goldin, M., & Bryan, H. (2015). Integrative approach to play therapy. In D. A. Crenshaw & A. L. Stewart (Eds.), *Play therapy: A comprehensive guide to theory and practice* (pp. 99–113). Guilford.

Gil, E., & Pfeifer, L. (2016). Issues of culture and diversity in play therapy. In K. J. O'Connor, C. E. Schaefer, & L. D. Braverman (Eds.), *Handbook of play therapy* (2nd ed., pp. 599–611). Wiley.

Gil, E., & Shaw, J. A. (2009). Prescriptive play therapy. In K. O'Connor & L. D. Braverman (Eds.), *Play therapy theory and practice: Comparing theories and techniques* (pp. 451–488). Wiley.

Gilmartin, D., & McElvaney, R. (2020). Filial therapy as a core intervention with children in foster care. *Child Abuse Review, 29*(2), 159–166. https://doi.org/10.1002/car.2602

Ginns-Gruenberg, D., & Bridgman, C. (2021). Using bibliotherapy as a catalyst for change. In H. Kaduson & C. Schaefer (Eds.), *Play therapy with children: Modalities for change* (pp. 75–92). American Psychological Association.

Ginott, H. (1959). The theory and practice of therapeutic intervention in child treatment. *Journal of Consulting Psychology, 23,* 160–166. https://doi.org/10.1037/h0046805

Ginott, H. (1961). *Group psychotherapy with children: The theory and practice of play-therapy.* McGraw-Hill.

Gladding, S. (2020). *The creative arts in counseling* (6th ed.). American Counseling Association.

Glasser, W. (1975). *Reality therapy: A new approach to psychiatry.* Harper & Row.

Glover, G. (2005). Musings on working with Native American children in play therapy. In E. Gil & A. Drewes (Eds.), *Cultural issues in play therapy* (pp. 168–179). Guilford.

Glover, G. (2022). Cultural opportunities with Indigenous populations. In D. C. Ray, Y. Ogawa, & Y.-J. Cheng (Eds.), *Multicultural play therapy: Making the most of cultural opportunities with children* (pp. 128–145). Routledge.

Glover, G., & Landreth, G. L. (2016). Child-centered play therapy. In K. J. O'Connor, C. E. Schaefer, & L. D. Braverman, *Handbook of play therapy* (2nd ed., pp. 93–118). Wiley.

Gonsher, A. M. (2016). Limit-setting in play therapy. In K. J. O'Connor, C. E. Schaefer, & L. D. Braverman (Eds.), *Handbook of play therapy* (2nd ed., pp. 539–548). Wiley.

Gonzalez, C. L., & Bell, H. (2016). Child-centered play therapy for Hispanic children with traumatic grief: Cultural implications for treatment outcomes. *International Journal of Play Therapy, 25*(3), 146–153. https://doi.org/10.1037/pla0000023

Goodyear-Brown, P. (2010). *Play therapy with traumatized children: A prescriptive approach*. Wiley.

Goodyear-Brown, P. (2019). *Trauma and play therapy*. Routledge.

Goodyear-Brown, P. (2021). *Parents as partners in child therapy: A clinician's guide*. Guilford.

Goodyear-Brown, P. (2022). *Big behaviors in small containers*. PESI.

Gordon, D. (2017). *Therapeutic metaphors: Helping others through the looking glass*.

Grant, R. J. (2017a). *AutPlay therapy for children and adolescents on the autism spectrum: A behavioral play-based approach*. Routledge.

Grant, R. J. (2017b). *Play-based interventions for autism spectrum disorder and other developmental disabilities*. Routledge.

Grant, R. J. (2023). *The AutPlay therapy handbook: Integrative family play therapy with neurodivergent children*. Routledge.

Gray, C. (2015). *The new social story book*. Future Horizons.

Green, E. (2009). Jungian analytical play therapy. In K. O'Connor & L. M. Braverman (Eds.), *Play therapy theory and practice: Comparing theories and techniques* (2nd ed., pp. 83–125). Wiley.

Green, E. (2010, March). Traversing the heroic journey: Jungian play therapy with children. *Counseling Today, 52*(9), 40–43.

Green, E. (2014). *The handbook of Jungian play therapy with children and adolescents*. Johns Hopkins University.

Green, E. J. (2005). Jungian play therapy: Bridging the theoretical to the practical. *VISTAS Online*, Article 15. https://www.counseling.

org/docs/default-source/vistas/vistas_2005_vistas05-art15.
pdf?sfvrsn=a56a4e95_12

Green, E. J. (2011). Jungian analytical play therapy. In C. E. Schaefer
(Ed.), *Foundations of play therapy* (pp. 61–84). Wiley.

Green, E. J., Crenshaw, D. A., & Langtiw, C. L. (2009). Play theme-based
research with children. *The Family Journal, 17*(4), 312–317. https://doi.
org/10.1177/1066480709347358

Green, E. J., & Myrick, A. C. (2014). Treating complex trauma in
adolescents: A phase-based, integrative approach for play therapists.
International Journal of Play Therapy, 23(3), 131–146. https://doi.
org/10.1037/a0036679

Griffiths, M. (2003). The therapeutic use of videogames in childhood and
adolescence. *Clinical Child Psychology and Psychiatry, 8*(4), 547–554.

Guerney, B. (1964). Filial therapy: Description and rationale. *Journal of
Consulting Psychology, 28,* 304–310.

Guerney, L. (1997). Filial therapy. In K. O'Connor & L. M. Braverman
(Eds.), *Play therapy theory and practice: A comparative presentation* (pp.
130–159). Wiley.

Guerney, L. (2001). Child-centered play therapy. *International Journal of
Play Therapy, 10*(2), 13–31. https://doi.org/10.1037/h0089477

Guerney, L. (2015). Filial therapy with children with anxiety disorders.
In D. A. Crenshaw & A. L. Stewart (Eds.), *Play therapy: A comprehensive
guide to theory and practice* (pp. 428–438). Guilford.

Guerney, L., & Ryan, V. (2013). *Group filial therapy: The complete guide
to teaching parents to play therapeutically with their children.* Jessica
Kingsley.

Hartwig, E. K. (2020). Puppet play therapy. In H. Kaduson & C. Schaefer
(Eds.), *Play therapy with children: Modalities for change* (pp. 107–124).
American Psychological Association.

Haas, S. C., & Ray, D. C. (2020). Child-centered play therapy with children
affected by adverse childhood experiences: A single-case design.
International Journal of Play Therapy, 29(4), 223–236. https://doi.
org/10.1037/pla0000135

Hambridge, G. (1955). Structured play therapy. *American Journal of
Orthopsychiatry, 25,* 304–310. https://doi.org/10.1111/j.1939-0025.1955.
tb00156.x

Hammel, S. (2019). *Handbook of therapeutic storytelling: Stories and metaphors in psychotherapy, child and family therapy, medical treatment, coaching and supervision.* Routledge.

Harvey, S. (2006). Dynamic play therapy. In C. Schaefer & H. Kaduson (Eds.), *Contemporary play therapy* (pp. 55–81). Guilford.

Harvey, S. (2016). Using drama in play therapy. In K. J. O'Connor, C. E. Schaefer, & L. D. Braverman (Eds.), *Handbook of play therapy* (2nd ed., pp. 289–308). Wiley.

Hashemi, M., Banijamali, S. S., & Khosravi, Z. (2018). The efficacy of short-term play therapy for children in reducing symptoms of ADHD. *World Family Medicine*, 17(4), 76–84. http://doi/10.5742/MEWFM.2018.93370

Helker, W., & Ray, D. (2009). Impact of child teacher relationship training on teachers' and aides' use of relationship-building skills and the effects on student classroom behavior. *International Journal of Play Therapy*, 18(2), 70–83. https://doi.org/10.1037/a0014456

Helker, W., Schottelkorb, A., & Ray, D. (2007). Helping students and teachers CONNECT: An intervention model for school counselors. *Journal of Professional Counseling, Practice, Theory, and Research, 35*, 31–45. https://doi.org/10.1080/15566382.2007.12033836

Henderson, D. A., & Thompson, C. L. (2015). *Counseling children.* Cengage Learning.

Herschell, A., & McNeil, C. (2005). Parent-child interaction therapy for children experiencing externalizing behavior problems. In L. Reddy, T. Files-Hall, & C. Schaefer (Eds.), *Empirically based play interventions for children* (pp. 169–190). American Psychological Association.

Herzog, J., Everson, R. B., & Taylor, J. (2015). The crisis of parental deployment in military service. In N. B. Webb (Ed.), *Play therapy with children and adolescents in crisis* (4th ed., pp. 218–238). Guilford.

Hillman, H. (2018). Child-centered play therapy as an intervention for children with autism: A literature review. *International Journal of Play Therapy*, 27(4), 198–204. https://doi.org/10.1037/pla0000083

Hillman, L. (2014). *Underlying constructs in play therapy themes: An exploratory factor analysis* [Doctoral dissertation, Baylor University]. http://hdl.handle.net/2104/9246

Hindman, M. L., Perryman, K. L., & Robinson, S. E. (2022). The adult public's perception of the utility of play therapy. *International*

Journal of Play Therapy, 31(1), 34–45. https://doi.org/10.1037/pla0000164

Hoffman, K., Cooper, G., Powell, B., & Benton, C. (2017). *Raising a secure child: How circle of security parenting can help you nurture your child's attachment, emotional reliance, and freedom to explore.* Guilford.

Holliman, R. (2021). Anatomy of a play theme: Helping supervisees work with themes in play therapy. In L. Fazio-Griffith & R. Marino (Eds.), *Techniques and interventions for play therapy and clinical supervision* (pp. 154–172). IGI Global.

Holmes, R. M., Gardner, B., Kohm, K., Bant, C., Ciminello, A., Moedt, K., & Romeo, L. (2019). The relationship between young children's language abilities, creativity, play, and storytelling. *Early Child Development and Care, 189*(2), 244–254. https://doi.org/10.1080/03004430.2017.1314274

Homeyer, L., & Bennett, M. M. (2023). *The guide to play therapy documentation and parent consultation.* Routledge.

Homeyer, L., & Lyles, M. (2022). *Advanced sandtray: Digging deeper into clinical practice.* Routledge.

Homeyer, L., & Sweeney, D. (2023). *Sandtray: A practical manual* (4th ed.). Routledge.

Hook, J. N., Davis, D., Owen, J., & DeBlaere, C. (2017). *Cultural humility: Engaging diverse identities in therapy.* American Psychological Association.

Hook, J. N., Farrell, J. E., Davis, D. E., DeBlaere, C., Van Tongeren, D. R., & Utsey, S. O. (2016). Cultural humility and racial microaggressions in counseling. *Journal of Counseling Psychology, 63*(3), 269–277. https://doi.org/10.1037/cou0000114

Hug-Hellmuth, H. (1921). On the technique of child analysis. *International Journal of Psychoanalysis, 2,* 287–305.

Hull, K. B. (2016). Technology in the playroom. In K. J. O'Connor, C. E. Schaefer, & L. D. Braverman (Eds.), *Handbook of play therapy* (2nd ed., pp. 613–627). Wiley.

Hull, K. B. (2020). Electronic game play therapy. In H. Kaduson & C. Schaefer (Eds.), *Play therapy with children: Modalities for change* (pp. 225–240). American Psychological Association.

Hutton, D. (2004). Margaret Lowenfeld's "World Technique." *Clinical Child Psychology and Psychiatry, 9*(4), 605–612. https://doi.org/10.1177/1359104504046164

Irwin, E. (2014). Drama therapy. In E. Green & A. Drewes (Eds.), *Integrating expressive arts and play therapy* (pp. 67–99). Wiley.

Jayne, K. M., Purswell, K. E., & Stulmaker, H. L. (2019). Facilitating congruence, empathy, and unconditional positive regard through therapeutic limit-setting: Attitudinal conditions limit-setting model (ACLM). *International Journal of Play Therapy, 28*(4), 238–249. https://doi.org/10.1037/pla0000101

Jayne, K.M., & Wehmeier, C.T.L. (2022). Cultural opportunities with LGBTQIA populations. In D. Ray, Y. Ogawa, & Y.-J. Cheng (Eds.) *Multicultural play therapy: Making the most of cultural opportunities with children* (pp. 65-87). Routledge.

Jernberg, A. (1979). *Theraplay: A new treatment using structured play for problem children and their families.* Jossey-Bass.

Jernberg, A., & Jernberg, E. (1993). Family Theraplay for the family tyrant. In T. Kottman & C. Schaefer (Eds.), *Play therapy in action: A casebook for practitioners* (pp. 45–96). Jason Aronson.

Jernberg, A. M., & Booth, P. B. (1999). *Theraplay: Helping parents and children build better relationships through attachment-based play* (2nd ed.). Jossey-Bass.

Jones, K. D., Casado, M., & Robinson, E. H., III. (2003). Structured play therapy: A model for choosing topics and activities. *International Journal of Play Therapy, 12*(1), 31–45. https://doi.org/10.1037/h0088870

Johnson, J. L. (2016). The history of play therapy. In K. J. O'Connor, C. E. Schaefer, & L. D. Braverman (Eds.), *Handbook of play therapy* (2nd ed., pp. 17–34). Wiley.

Jung, C. G. (1963). *Memories, dreams, reflections* (J. Jaffe, Ed.; R. Winston & C. Winston, Trans.). Vintage Books.

Kaduson, H. G. (2016). Play therapy across the life span: Infants, children, adolescents, and adults. In K. J. O'Connor, C. E. Schaefer & L. D. Braverman (Eds.), *Handbook of play therapy* (pp. 325–341). Wiley.

Kaduson, H., Cangelosi, D., & Schaefer, C. (2020). *Prescriptive play therapy: Tailoring interventions for specific childhood problems.* Guilford.

Kaduson, H. G., Cangelosi, D., & Schaefer, C. (Eds.). (1997). *The playing cure: Individual play therapy for specific childhood problems.* Jason Aronson.

Kaduson, H., & Schaefer, C. (Eds.). (2015). *Short-term play therapy for children* (3rd ed.). Guilford.

Kalff, D. (1971). *Sandplay: Mirror of a child's psyche*. Browser.

Kefir, N. (1981). Impasse/priority therapy. In R. Corsini (Ed.), *Handbook of innovative psychotherapies* (pp. 400–415). Wiley.

Kim, S. L. (2023). *Goodnight love: A bedtime meditation story*. Bala Kids.

Kissel, S. (1990). *Play therapy: A strategic approach. Charles C Thomas.*

Klein, M. (1932). *The psycho-analysis of children*. Hogarth Press.

Knell, S. (1993). *Cognitive-behavioral play therapy*. Jason Aronson.

Knell, S. (1994). Cognitive-behavioral play therapy. In K. O'Connor & C. Schaefer (Eds.), *Handbook of play therapy* (Vol. 2, pp. 111–142). Wiley.

Knell, S. (2003). Cognitive-behavioral play therapy. In C. Schaefer (Ed.), *Foundations of play therapy* (pp. 174–191). Wiley.

Knell, S. (2009a). Cognitive behavioral play therapy. In A. A. Drewes (Ed.), *Blending play therapy with cognitive behavior therapy: Evidence-based and other effective treatments and techniques* (pp. 117–134). Wiley.

Knell, S. (2009b). Cognitive-behavioral play therapy. In K. O'Connor & L. M. Braverman (Eds.), *Play therapy theory and practice: Comparing theories and techniques* (2nd ed., pp. 203–236). Wiley.

Knell, S. M. (2016). Cognitive-behavioral play therapy. In K. J. O'Connor, C. E. Schaefer, & L. D. Braverman (Eds.), *Handbook of play therapy* (2nd ed., pp. 119–134). Wiley.

Kohlhoff, J., Morgan, S., Briggs, N., Egan, R., & Niec, L. (2021). Parent-child interaction therapy with toddlers: A community-based randomized controlled trial with children aged 14–24 months. *Journal of Clinical Child & Adolescent Psychology, 50*(3), 411–426. https://doi.org/10.1080/15374416.2020.1723599

Kottman, T. (1993). The king of rock and roll. In T. Kottman & C. Schaefer (Eds.), *Play therapy in action: A casebook for practitioners* (pp. 133–167). Jason Aronson.

Kottman, T. (1994). Adlerian play therapy. In K. O'Connor & C. Schaefer (Eds.), *Handbook of play therapy* (Vol. 2, pp. 3–26). Wiley.

Kottman, T. (2014). Positive emotions. In C. Schaefer & A. Drewes (Eds.), *The therapeutic powers of play* (2nd ed.) (pp. 103-121). Wiley.

Kottman, T. (Ed.). (2020). *Bibliotherapy: Using books in play therapy*. Encouragement Zone.

Kottman, T. (2023a). *Familial encouraging connection therapy (FECT) facilitator's guide*. Encouragement Zone.

Kottman, T. (2023b) *Familial encouraging connection therapy (FECT) parent/ caregiver handouts*. Encouragement Zone.

Kottman, T. (2023c). *Teacher-child connection training (TCCT) facilitator's guide*. Encouragement Zone.

Kottman, T., & Ashby, J. (1999). Using Adlerian personality priorities to custom-design consultation with parents of play therapy clients. *International Journal of Play Therapy, 8*(2), 77–92. https://doi.org/10.1037/h0089432

Kottman, T., & Ashby, J. (2015). Adlerian play therapy. In D. A. Crenshaw & A. L. Stewart (Eds.), *Play therapy: A comprehensive guide to theory and practice* (pp. 32–47). Guilford.

Kottman, T., & Ashby, J. (in press). Adlerian play therapy. In D. A. Crenshaw & A. L. Stewart (Eds.), *Play therapy: A comprehensive guide to theory and practice* (2nd ed.). Guilford.

Kottman, T., & Meany-Walen, K. (2015). Adlerian family play therapy. In E. Green, J., Baggerly, & A. Myrick (Eds.), *Counseling families: Play-based treatment* (pp. 71-87). Rowman & Littlefield.

Kottman, T., & Meany-Walen, K. (2016). *Partners in play: An Adlerian approach to play therapy*. Wiley.

Kottman, T., & Meany-Walen, K. (2017). Adlerian play therapy: Practice and research. In R. L. Steen (Ed.), *Emerging research in play therapy, child counseling, and consultation* (pp. 100–111). IGI Global.

Kottman, T., & Meany-Walen, K. K. (2018). *Doing play therapy: From building the relationship to facilitating change*. Guilford.

Kottman, T., Meany-Walen, K., Parsons, M., & Dillman Taylor, D. (2021). *Treatment manual for Adlerian play therapy* [Unpublished manuscript].

Kottman, T., & Petersen, N. (2021). *How to talk so gamers will listen and listen so gamers will talk: Using the language of video games in play therapy and counseling*. Encouragement Zone.

Kottman, T., Petersen, N., Kottman, J., & Lavenz, B. (2018). *How to talk so gamers will listen and listen so gamers will talk: Using the language of video games in play therapy and counseling*. Encouragement Zone.

Kranz, P., Kottman, T., & Lund, N. (1998). Play therapists' opinions concerning the education, training, and practice of play therapists.

International Journal of Play Therapy, 7(1), 33–40. https://doi.
org/10.1037/h0089419

Lamb, R., & Etopio, E. (2021). Therapeutic extended reality. In H. G.
Kaduson & C. E. Schaefer (Eds.), *Play therapy with children: Modalities
for change* (pp. 241–257). American Psychological Association. https://
doi.org/10.1037/0000217-016

Landreth, G.L. (2002). Therapeutic limit setting in the play therapy
relationship. Professional Psychology: Research and Practice, 33(6),
pp. 529-535. https://doi.org/10.1037/0735-7028.33.6.529

Landreth, G. (2024). *Play therapy: The art of the relationship* (4th ed.).
Routledge.

Landreth, G. L., & Bratton, S. (2020). *Child-parent relationship therapy
(CPRT): An evidence-based 10-session filial therapy model* (2nd ed.).
Routledge.

Lankton, C., & Lankton, S. (1989). *Tales of enchantment: Goal-oriented
metaphors for adults and children in therapy.* Brunner/Mazel.

Leben, N. (2015). Directive group play therapy for children with
attention-deficit/hyperactivity disorder. In H. Kaduson & C. Schaefer
(Eds.), *Short-term play therapy for children* (3rd ed., pp. 325–352).
Guilford.

Leblanc, M., & Ritchie, M. (2001). A meta-analysis of play therapy
outcomes. *Counselling Psychology Quarterly, 14*(2), 149–163. https://doi.
org/10.1080/09515070110059142

Lee, A. (2009). Psychoanalytic play therapy. In K. O'Connor & L. M.
Braverman (Eds.), *Play therapy theory and practice: Comparing theories
and techniques* (2nd ed., pp. 25–82). Wiley.

Lee, E., Greenblatt, A., Hu, R., Johnstone, M., & Kourgiantakis, T. (2022).
Developing a model of broaching and bridging in cross-cultural
psychotherapy: Toward fostering epistemic and social justice.
American Journal of Orthopsychiatry, 92(3), 322–333. https://doi.
org/10.1037/ort0000611

LeFeber, M. (2014). Working with children using dance/movement. In E.
Green & A. Drewes (Eds.), *Integrating expressive arts and play therapy
with children and adolescents* (pp. 124–148). Wiley.

Leggett, E. S., & Boswell, J. N. (Eds.). (2016). *Directive play therapy: Theories
and techniques.* Springer Publishing.

Levy, D. (1938). Release therapy for young children. *Psychiatry, 1,*
387–389.

Lew, A., & Bettner, B. L. (2000). *A parent's guide to understanding and motivating children* (Rev. ed.). Connexions.

Li, L., & Tomasello, M. (2022). Disagreement, justification, and equitable moral judgments: A brief training study. *Journal of Experimental Child Psychology, 223,* Article 105494. https://doi.org/10.1016/j.jecp.2022.105494

Lieneman, C. C., Brabson, L. A., Highlander, A., Wallace, N. M., & McNeil, C. B. (2017). Parent-child interaction therapy: Current perspectives. *Psychology Research and Behavior Management, 10,* 239–256. https://doi.org/10.2147/PRBM.S91200

Lilly, J. P. (2015). Jungian analytic play therapy. In D. A. Crenshaw & A. L. Stewart (Eds.), *Play therapy: A comprehensive guide to theory and practice* (pp. 47–65). Guilford.

Lilly, J. P., & Heiko, R. (2019). Jungian analytic play therapy. *Play Therapy, 14*(3), 40–42.

Lin, Y. W., & Bratton, S. C. (2015). A meta-analytic review of child-centered play therapy approaches. *Journal of Counseling & Development, 93*(1), 45–58. https://doi.org/10.1002/j.1556-6676.2015.00180.x

Linn, S. (March/April 2009). Too much and too many: How commercialism and screen technology combine to rob children of creative play. *Exchange: The Early Childhood Leaders' Magazine Since 1978, 186,* 45–48.

Lindaman, S., & Hong, R. (Eds.). (2021). *Theraplay – Theory, applications and implementation.* Jessica Kingsley.

Liu, C. H., & Doan, S. N. (2020). Psychosocial stress cognition in children and families during the COVID-19 pandemic. *Clinical Pediatrics, 59,* 853–855. https://doi.org/10.1177/0009922820927044

Lloyd, J. (2018). *Whales in the desert: The use of metaphors in therapy.* Publish Nation.

Locatelli, M. G. (2020). Play therapy treatment of pediatric medical trauma: A retrospective case study of a preschool child. *International Journal of Play Therapy, 29*(1), 33–42. https://doi.org/10.1037/pla0000109

Loeb, D. F., Davis, E. S., & Lee, T. (2021). Collaboration between child play therapy and speech-language pathology: Case reports of a novel language and behavior intervention. *American Journal of*

Speech-Language Pathology, 30(6), 2414–2429. https://doi.org/10.23641/asha.16840459

Lolan, A. (2011). *Play therapists' practice patterns and perceptions of the factors that influence caregiver engagement in play therapy* (Publication No. 3501589) [Doctoral dissertation]. ProQuest Dissertations and Theses.

Long, D.W. (2023). *Great big breath: Mindfulness for kids made simple.*

Lowenfeld, M. (2008). *Play in childhood.* Sussex Academic Press. (Original work published 1935)

Lyles, M. (2021). Room for everyone: EMDR and family-based play therapy in the sand tray. In A. Beckley-Forest & A. Monaco (Eds.), *EMDR with children in the play therapy room: An integrated approach* (pp. 75–108). Springer Publishing.

Marschak, M. (1960). A method for evaluating child-parent interaction under controlled conditions. *Journal of Genetic Psychology, 97,* 3–22.

Marschall, A. (2023). *Clinical Documentation with Children and Adolescents: Treatment, Risks, and Ethics.* Taylor & Francis.

McNary, T., Mason, E., & Tobin, G. (2018). The unexpected purpose of technology in the playroom: Catharsis. *Play Therapy, 13*(3), 4–7.

McNeil, C., & Hembree-Kigin, T. (2010). *Parent-child interaction therapy* (2nd ed.). Springer.

McNeil-Haber, F. M. (2004). Ethical considerations in the use of nonerotic touch in psychotherapy with children. *Ethics & Behavior, 14*(2), 123–140. https://doi.org/10.1207/s15327019eb1402_3

McNicol, S., & Brewster, L. (2019). *Bibliotherapy.* Facet Publishing.

Meany-Walen, K. (2018). Adlerian play therapy with preadolescents. In E. Green, J. Baggerly, & A. Myrick (Eds.), *Play therapy with preteens* (pp. 49–66). Rowman & Littlefield.

Meany-Walen, K., Bratton, S., & Kottman, T. (2014). Effects of Adlerian play therapy on reducing students' disruptive behaviors. *Journal of Counseling & Development, 92*(1), 47–56. https://doi.org/10.1002/j.1556-6676.2014.00129.x

Meany-Walen, K. K., & Kottman, T. (2017). Adlerian play therapy: Practice and research. In R. L. Steen (Ed.), *Emerging research in play therapy, child counseling, and consultation* (pp. 100–111). IGI Global.

Medina, E. (2022). *I feel: A book about emotions.* Versify.

Meersand, P., & Gilmore, K. J. (2017). *Play therapy: a psychodynamic primer for the treatment of young children*. American Psychiatric Association.

Mellenthin, C. (2019). *Attachment centered play therapy*. Routledge.

Menassa, B. M. (2009). Theoretical orientation and play therapy: Examining therapist role, session structure, and therapeutic objectives. *Journal of Professional Counseling: Practice, Theory & Research, 37*(1), 13–26. https://doi.org/10.1080/15566382.2009.12033852

Milgrom, C. (2005). An introduction to play therapy with adolescents. In L. Gallo-Lopez & C. Schaefer (Eds.), *Play therapy with adolescents* (pp. 3–17). Jason Aronson.

Mills, J. (2015). StoryPlay: A narrative play therapy approach. In D. A. Crenshaw & A. L. Stewart (Eds.), *Play therapy: A comprehensive guide to theory and practice* (pp. 171–185). Guilford.

Mills, J., & Crowley, R. (2014). *Therapeutic metaphors for children and the child within* (2nd ed.). Brunner/Routledge.

Mirzaie, H., Mehraban, A. H., Hosseini, S. A., Fard, F. G., & Oori, M. J. (2019). Comparison of the effect of filial and Adlerian play therapy on attention and hyperactivity of children with attention deficit hyperactivity disorder: A randomized clinical trial. *Iranian Rehabilitation Journal, 17*(4), 341–350. https://doi.org/10.32598/irj.17.4.341

Money, R., Wilde, S., & Lawson, D. (2020). The effectiveness of Theraplay for children under 12: A systematic literature review. *Child and Adolescent Mental Health, 23*(3), 1–51. https://doi.org/10.1111/camh.12416

Mora, L., van Sebille, K., & Neill, L. (2018). An evaluation of play therapy for children and young people with intellectual disabilities. *Research and Practice in Intellectual and Developmental Disabilities, 5*, 178–191. https://doi.org/10.1080/23297018.2018.1442739

Mordock, J. B. (2015). Psychodynamic play therapy. In D. Crenshaw & A. Stewart (Eds.), *Play therapy: A comprehensive guide to theory and practice* (pp. 66–82). Guilford.

Morrison, M. (2006). *An early mental health intervention for disadvantaged preschool children with behavior problems: The effectiveness of training Head Start teachers in child-teacher relationship training (CTRT)* [Doctoral dissertation, University of North Texas]. http://digital.library.unt.edu/ark:/67531/metadc5311/

Morrison, M., & Bratton, C. (2010). Preliminary investigation of an early mental health intervention for Head Start programs: Effects of child-teacher relationship training on children's behavior problems. *Psychology in the Schools, 47*(10), 1003–1017. https://10.1002/pits.20520

Mortola, P. (2014). *Windowframes: Learning the art of Gestalt play therapy the Oaklander way.* Gestalt Press.

Mosher, D. K., Hook, J. N., Captari, L. E., Davis, D. E., DeBlaere, C., & Owen, J. (2017). Cultural humility: A therapeutic framework for engaging diverse clients. *Practice Innovations, 2*(4), 221–233. https://doi.org/10.1037/pri0000055

Moustakas, C. (1953). *Children in play therapy.* McGraw-Hill.

Moustakas, C. (1959). *Psychotherapy with children.* Harper & Row.

Moustakas, C. (1997). *Relationship play therapy.* Jason Aronson.

Müller, E., & Donley, C. (2019). Measuring the impact of a school-based, integrative approach to play therapy on students with autism and their classroom instructors. *International Journal of Play Therapy, 28*(3), 123–132. https://doi.org/10.1037/pla0000100

Murray, S. (2021). The therapeutic use of stories in play therapy. In H. Kaduson & C. Schaefer (Eds.), *Play therapy with children: Modalities for change* (pp. 93–106). American Psychological Association.

Myers, R. K. (2016). *Childhood witnessing of intimate partner violence (IPV) and early adulthood IPV among urban women.* Temple University.

Nalavany, B. A., Ryan, S. D., Gomory, T., & Lacasse, J. R. (2005). Mapping the characteristics of a "good" play therapist. *International Journal of Play Therapy, 14*, 27–50. https://doi.org/10.1037/h0088895

Nash, J. B. (2014). Social competence. In C. Schaefer & A. Drewes (Eds.), *The therapeutic powers of play: 20 core agents of change* (pp. 185–193). Wiley.

Nash, J. B., & Schaefer, C. E. (2011). Play therapy: Basic concepts and practices. In C. E. Schaefer (Ed.), *Foundations of play therapy* (2nd ed., pp. 3–13). John Wiley & Sons Inc.

National Association of Social Workers. (2021). Code of ethics of the National Association of Social Workers. https://www.socialworkers. org/About/Ethics/Code-of-Ethics/Code-of-Ethics-English

Nelson, J. (2006). *Positive discipline* (Rev. ed.). Ballantine.

Nelson, J., Bill, K., & Marchese, J. (2018). *Positive discipline for today's busy (and overwhelmed) parent: How to balance work, parenting, and self for lasting well-being*. Harmony.

Nelson, J., Erwin, C., & Duffy, R. (2019). *Positive discipline for preschoolers* (4th ed.). Harmony.

Nelson, J., Tamborski, M., & Ainge, B. (2016). *Positive discipline parenting tools: The 49 most effective methods to stop power struggles, build communication, and raise empowered, capable kids*. Harmony.

Neurospicy Creative. (2023). *Metaphors to mend the soul: Discover the power of healing through transformative imagery.*

Nhin, M. (2021). *Feelings ninja: A social, emotional children's book about emotions and feelings*. Grow Grit.

Niec, L. (Ed.). (2018). *Handbook of parent-child interaction therapy: Innovations and applications for research and practice*. Springer.

Nordling, W. J., & Guerney, L. (1999). Typical stages in the child-centered play therapy process. *Journal for the Professional Counselor, 14*, 17–23.

Norris, V., & Lender, D. (2020). *Theraplay – The practitioner's guide*. Jessica Kingsley.

Norris, V., & Rodwell, H. (2017). *Parenting with Theraplay: Understanding attachment and how to nurture a closer relationship with your child*. Jessica Kingsley.

Norton, C., & Norton, B. (2006). Experiential play therapy. In C. Schaefer & H. Kaduson (Eds.), *Contemporary play therapy: Theory, research, and practice* (pp. 28–54). Guilford.

Norton, C., & Norton, B. (2008). *Reaching children through play therapy: An experiential approach*. White Apple Press.

Oaklander, V. (1992). *Windows to our children: A Gestalt approach to children and adolescents*. Gestalt Journal Press. (Original work published 1978)

Oaklander, V. (1993). From meek to bold: A case study of Gestalt play therapy. In T. Kottman & C. Schaefer (Eds.), *Play therapy in action: A casebook for practitioners* (pp. 281–299). Jason Aronson.

Oaklander, V. (1994). Gestalt play therapy. In K. O'Connor & C. Schaefer (Eds.), *Handbook of play therapy* (Vol. 2, pp. 143–156). Wiley.

Oaklander, V. (2006). *Hidden treasure: A map to the child's inner self*. Karnac Books.

Oaklander, V. (2015). Short-term Gestalt play therapy for grieving children. In H. Kaduson & C. Schaefer (Eds.), *Short-term play therapy for children* (3rd ed., pp. 124–149). Guilford.

O'Connor, K. (1994). Ecosystemic play therapy. In K. O'Connor & C. Schaefer (Eds.), *Handbook of play therapy* (Vol. 2, pp. 61–84). Wiley.

O'Connor, K. (2000). *The play therapy primer* (2nd ed.). Wiley.

O'Connor, K. (2005). Addressing diversity issues in play therapy. *Professional Psychology, Research and Practice, 36*(5), 566–573. https://doi.org/10.1037/0735-7028.36.5.566

O'Connor, K. (2009). Ecosystemic play therapy. In K. O'Connor & L. M. Braverman (Eds.), *Play therapy theory and practice: Comparing theories and techniques* (2nd ed., pp. 367–450). Wiley.

O'Connor, K. J. (2016). Ecosystemic play therapy. In K. J. O'Connor, C. E. Schaefer, & L. D. Braverman (Eds.), *Handbook of play therapy* (2nd ed., pp. 195–226). Wiley.

O'Connor, K. J., & Ammen, S. (2013). *Play therapy treatment planning and interventions: The ecosystemic model and workbook* (2nd ed.). Academic Press.

O'Connor, K., & Vega, C. (2019). Ecosystemic play therapy. *Play Therapy, 14*(3), 32–34.

Ogawa, Y., Cheng, Y.-J., & Ray, D. C. (2022). Cultural opportunities and comfort in play therapy. In D. C. Ray, Y. Ogawa, & Y.-J. Cheng (Eds.) *Multicultural play therapy: Making the most of cultural opportunities with children* (pp. 29–43). Routledge.

Olson-Morrison, D. (2017). Integrative play therapy with adults with complex trauma: A developmentally-informed approach. *International Journal of Play Therapy, 26*(3), 172–183. https://doi.org/10.1037/pla0000036

Opiola, K. K., & Bratton, S. C. (2018). The efficacy of child-parent relationship therapy for adoptive families: A replication study. *Journal of Counseling & Development, 96*(2), 155–166. https://doi.org/10.1002/jcad.12189

Orth, U., & Robins, R. W. (2014). The development of self-esteem. *Current Directions in Psychological Science, 23*(5), 381–387. https://doi.org/10.1177/09637214145474

Owen, J., Drinane, J., Tao, K., Adelson, J., Hook, J., Davis, D., & Foo Kune, N. (2017). Racial-ethnic disparities in client unilateral termination:

The role of therapists' cultural comfort. *Psychotherapy Research, 27*(1), 102–111. https://doi.org/10.1080/10503307.2015.1078517

Owen, J., Drinane, J. M., Davis, D. E., Tao, K. W., Hook, J., & Kune, N. J. (2016). Client perceptions of therapists' multicultural orientation: Cultural (missed) opportunities and cultural humility. *Professional Psychology: Research and Practice, 47*, 30–37. https://doi.org/10.1037/pro0000046

Owen, J. J., Tao, K., Leach, M. M., & Rodolfa, E. (2011). Clients' perceptions of their psychotherapists' multicultural orientation. *Psychotherapy, 48*(3), 274–282. https://doi.org/10.1037/a0022065

Pardeck, J. (2013). *Using books in clinical social work practice: A guide to bibliotherapy.* Routledge.

Park, D.S. (2023). *Sleepy time nighty-night.* KDP.

Parker, M. M., Glickman, C. P., Smelser, Q., & DeRaedt, M. (2021). Therapeutic or traumatic: An exploratory study of play therapists' perceptions of toy guns and aggressive toys in the playroom. *International Journal of Play Therapy, 30*(1), 61–71. https://doi.org/10.1037/pla0000141

Patton, S. C., & Benedict, H. E. (2015). Object relations and attachment-based play therapy. In D. A. Crenshaw & A. L. Stewart (Eds.), *Play therapy: A comprehensive guide to theory and practice* (pp. 17–31). Guilford.

Peery, J. C. (2003). Jungian analytical play therapy. In C. E. Schaefer (Ed.), *Foundations of play therapy* (pp. 14–54). Wiley.

Perez, R., Ramirez, S., & Kranz, P. (2007). Adjusting limit setting in play therapy with first generation Mexican-American children. *Journal of Instructional Psychology,* 34(1), 22–27.

Pérez-Rojas, A. E., Bartholomew, T. T., Lockard, A. J., & González, J. M. (2019). Development and initial validation of the Therapist Cultural Comfort Scale. *Journal of Counseling Psychology, 66*(5), 534–549. https://doi.org/10.1037/cou0000344

Perls, F. (1973). *The Gestalt approach & eye witness to therapy.* Science and Behavior Books.

Petersen, N., & Kottman, T. (2022). Using tabletop games in play therapy. Encouragement Zone.

Pernicano, P. (2022). *Using trauma-focused therapy stories: Interventions for therapists, children, and their caregivers.* Routledge.

Perrow, S. (2012). *Therapeutic storytelling: 101 healing stories for children.* Hawthorne Publishing.

Perrow, S. (2017). *An A-Z collection of behaviour tales: From Angry Ant to Zestless Zebra.* Hawthorne Publishing.

Perryman, K. L., Christian, D. D., & Massengale, B. D. (2017). The impact of a two-day child parent relationship therapy training on attitude, knowledge, and skills. *International Journal of Play Therapy, 26*(4), 218–229. https://doi.org/10.1037/pla0000053

Phillips, R., & Landreth, G. (1995). Play therapists on play therapy: I. A report of methods, demographics, and professional/practice issues. *International Journal of Play Therapy, 4*(1), 1–27. https://doi.org/10.1037/ h0089404

Plastow, M. (2011). Hermine Hug-Hellmuth, the first child psychoanalyst: Legacy and dilemmas. *Australasian Psychiatry: Bulletin of Royal Australian and New Zealand College of Psychiatrists, 19*(3), 206–210. https://doi.org/10.3109/10398562.2010.526213

Pleines, K. E. (2019). An attachment-informed approach to trauma-focused cognitive behavioral therapy. *Clinical Social Work, 47,* 343–352. https://doi.org/10.1007/s10615-019-00701-7

Pope, K. S., Vasquez, M. J. T., Chavez-Dueñas, N. Y., Adames, H. Y. (2021). *Ethics in psychotherapy and counseling: A practical guide.* Jossey Bass.

Popkin, M. (2014). *Active parenting: A parent's guide to raising happy and successful children* (4th ed.). Active Parenting.

Post, P. B. (2014, August). Involving parents in child-centered play therapy. *Counseling Today.* https://ct.counseling.org/2014/08/ involving-parents-in-child-centered-play-therapy/

Post, P. B., Grybush, A. L., Elmadani, A., & Lockhart, C. E. (2020a). Fostering resilience in classrooms through child–teacher relationship training. *International Journal of Play Therapy, 29*(1), 9–19. https://doi.org/10.1037/pla0000107

Post, P. B., Grybush, A. L., Flowers, C., & Elmadani, A. (2020b). Impact of child–teacher relationship training on teacher attitudes and classroom behaviors. *International Journal of Play Therapy, 29*(3), 119–130. https://doi.org/10.1037/pla0000118

Post, P. B., Phipps, C. B., Camp, A. C., & Grybush, A. L. (2019). Effectiveness of child-centered play therapy among marginalized children. *International Journal of Play Therapy, 28,* 88–96. https://doi. org/10.1037/pla0000096

Post, P., & Tillman, K. S. (2015). Cultural issues in play therapy. In D. A. Crenshaw & A. L. Stewart (Eds.), *Play therapy: A comprehensive guide to theory and practice* (pp. 496–510). Guilford.

Punnett, A. F. (2016). Psychoanalytic and Jungian play therapy. In K. J. O'Connor, C. E. Schaefer, & L. D. Braverman (Eds.), *Handbook of play therapy* (2nd ed., pp. 63–92). Wiley.

Prue-Owens, K. (2021). Indigenous American Indians and Alaska Natives. In L. D. Purnell & E. A. Fenkl (Eds.), *Textbook for transcultural health care: A population approach: cultural competence concepts in nursing care* (pp. 151–185). Springer.

Purswell, K. E., Ayala-Carlson, A. K., & Spada, M. (2021). Play therapist qualities: A document analysis of current literature. *Journal of Professional Counseling: Practice, Theory & Research, 48*(1), 43–57. https://doi.org/10.1080/15566382.2020.1871258

Pykhtina, O. (2014, Fall). Computerized toys in play therapy: A barrier or an opportunity? *Playground,* 4–7.

Pykhtina, O., Balaam, M., Wood, G., Pattison, S., Kharrufa, A., & Olivier, P. (2012). Magic land: The design and evaluation of an interactive tabletop supporting therapeutic play with children. *Designing Interactive Systems Conference,* 136–145. https://doi.org/10.1145/2317956.2317978

Quetsch, L. B., Wallace, N., Norman, M., Travers, R., & McNeil, C. (2016). Parent-child interaction therapy with children with disruptive behavior disorders. In K. J. O'Connor, C. E. Schaefer, & L. D. Braverman (Eds.), *Handbook of play therapy* (2nd ed., pp. 343–356). Wiley.

Rank, O. (1936). *Will therapy.* Knopf.

Ray, D. (2011). *Advanced play therapy: Essential conditions, knowledge, and skills for child practice.* Taylor & Francis.

Ray, D. C. (2015). Research in play therapy: Empirical support for practice. In D. A. Crenshaw & A. L. Stewart (Eds.), *Play therapy: A comprehensive guide to theory and practice* (pp. 467–482). Guilford.

Ray, D. C., Burgin, E., Gutierrez, D., Ceballos, P., & Lindo, N. (2021). Child-centered play therapy and adverse childhood experiences: A randomized controlled trial. *Journal of Counseling & Development, 100,* 134–145. https://doi.org/10.1002/jcad.12412

Ray, D., & Landreth, G. (2015). Child-centered play therapy. In D. A. Crenshaw & A. L. Stewart (Eds.), *Play therapy: A comprehensive guide to theory and practice* (pp. 3–16). Guilford.

Ray, D. C., Ogawa, Y., & Cheng, Y.-J. (2022a). Cultural humility and the play therapist. In D. C. Ray, Y. Ogawa, & Y.-J. Cheng (Eds.) *Multicultural play therapy: Making the most of cultural opportunities with children* (pp. 13–28). Routledge.

Ray, D. C., Ogawa, Y., & Cheng, Y.-J. (Eds.). (2022b). *Multicultural play therapy: Making the most of cultural opportunities with children.* Routledge.

Razak, N. H. A., Johari, K. S. K., Mahmud, M. I., Zubir, N. M., & Johan, S. (2018). General review on cognitive behavior play therapy on children's psychology development. *International Journal of Academic Research in Progressive Education and Development, 7*(4), 134–147. https://doi.org/10.6007/IJARPED/v7-i4/4842

Reddy, L., Files-Hall, T., & Schaefer, C. (2005). Announcing empirically based play interventions for children. In L. Reddy, T. Files-Hall, & C. Schaefer (Eds.), *Empirically-based play interventions for children* (pp. 3–10). American Psychological Association.

Rezaee Rezvan, S., Karashki, H., Hajivosoogh, N. S., & Torabi, S. S. (2022). Developing a based-on-play cognitive-behavioral educational package and determining its effectiveness in improving the language disorders and social adjustment in bilingual children. *Journal of Research and Health, 12*(6), 377–388. https://doi.org/10.32598/JRH.12.6.1839.5

Ritzi, R., Ray, D., & Schumann, B. (2017). Intensive short-term child-centered play therapy and externalizing behavior in children. *International Journal of Play Therapy, 26*(1), 33–46. https://doi.org/10.1037/pla0000035

Riviere, S. (2015). Short-term play therapy for children with disruptive behavior disorders. In H. Kaduson & C. Schaefer (Eds.), *Short-term play therapy for children* (3rd ed., pp. 77–98). Guilford.

Robson, D. A., Allen, M. S., & Howard, S. J. (2020). Self-regulation in childhood as a predictor of future outcomes: A meta-analytic review. *Psychological Bulletin, 146*(4), 324–354. https://doi.org/10.1037/bul0000227

Rogers, C. (1951). *Client-centered therapy: Its current practice, implications, and theory.* Houghton Mifflin.

Rogers, C. (1957). The necessary and sufficient conditions of therapeutic personality change. *Journal of Consulting Psychology, 21*(2), 95–103.

Rubin, L. C (Ed.) (2020). *Using superheroes and villains in counseling and play therapy: A guide for mental health professionals.* Routledge.

Ryan, V., & Edge, A. (2012). The role of play themes in non-directive play therapy. *Clinical Child Psychology and Psychiatry, 17*(3), 354–369. https://doi.org/10.1177/1359104511414265

Salinas, C. L. (2021). Playing to heal: The impact of bereavement camp for children with grief. *International Journal of Play Therapy, 30*(1), 40–49. https://doi.org/10.1037/pla0000147

Sarah, B., Parson, J., Renshaw, K., & Stagnitti, K. (2021). Can children's play themes be assessed to inform play therapy practice? *Clinical Child Psychology and Psychiatry, 26*(1), 257–267. https://doi.org/10.1177/1359104520964510

Schaad, J., & Dion, L. (2021). Synergetic play therapy combined with EMDR therapy. In A. Beckley-Forest & A. Monaco (Eds.), *EMDR with children in the play therapy room: An integrated approach* (pp. 109–143). Springer.

Schafer, A. (2009). *Honey, I wrecked the kids: When yelling, screaming, threats, bribes, time-outs, sticker charts and removing privileges all don't work.* Wiley.

Schafer, A. (2011). *Ain't misbehaving: Tactics for tantrums, meltdowns, bedtime blues, and other perfectly normal kid behavior.* Wiley.

Schaefer, C. (Ed.). (1993). *The therapeutic powers of play.* Jason Aronson.

Schaefer, C. (1998). Play therapy: Critical issues for the next millennium. *Association for Play Therapy Newsletter, 17*(1), 1–5.

Schaefer, C. E. (2001). Prescriptive play therapy. *International Journal of Play Therapy, 10*(2), 57–73. https://doi.org/10.1037/h0089480

Schaefer, C. E. (Ed.). (2003). *Play therapy with adults.* Wiley.

Schaefer, C., & Drewes, A. A. (2009). The therapeutic powers of play and play therapy. In A. A. Drewes (Ed.), *Blending play therapy with cognitive behavioral therapy: Evidence-based and other effective treatment and techniques* (pp. 3–15). Wiley.

Schaefer, C., & Drewes, A. (2014). *The therapeutic powers of play: 20 core agents of change.* Wiley.

Schaefer, C. E., & Drewes, A. A. (2016). Prescriptive play therapy. In K. J. O'Connor, C. E. Schaefer, & L. D. Braverman (Eds.), *Handbook of play therapy* (2nd ed., pp. 227–240). Wiley.

Schaefer, C., Kelly-Zion, S., McCormick, J., & Ohnogi, A. (Eds.). (2008). *Play therapy for very young children*. Jason Aronson.

Schaefer, C., & Mattei, D. (2005). Catharsis: Effectiveness in children's aggression. *International Journal of Play Therapy, 14*(2), 103–109. https://doi.org/10.1037/h0088905

Schiffer, M. (1952). Permissiveness versus sanction in activity group therapy. *International Journal of Group Psychotherapy, 2*, 255–261.

Schottelkorb, A. A., Doumas, D. M., & Garcia, R. (2012). Treatment for childhood refugee trauma: A randomized, controlled trial. *International Journal of Play Therapy, 21*(2), 57–73. https://doi.org/10.1037/a0027430

Schottelkorb, A. A., Swan, K. L., & Ogawa, Y. (2015). Parent consultation in child-centered play therapy: A model for research and practice. *International Journal of Play Therapy, 24*(4), 221–233. https://doi.org/10.1037/a0039609

Schottelkorb, A. A., Swan, K. L., & Ogawa, Y. (2020). Intensive child-centered play therapy for children on the autism spectrum: A pilot study. *Journal of Counseling & Development, 98*(1), 63–73. https://doi.org/10.1002/jcad.12300

Schumann, B. (2010). Effectiveness of child-centered play therapy for children referred for aggression. In J. N. Baggerly, D. C. Ray, & S. C. Bratton (Eds.), *Child-centered play therapy research: The evidence base for effective practice* (pp. 193–208). Wiley.

Sears, H. (2023). *The magic in metaphor: Empowering children through healing stories*.

Seymour, J. W., & Rubin, L. (2006). Principles, principals, and process (P3): A model for play therapy ethics problem solving. *International Journal of Play Therapy, 15*, 101–123. https://doi.org/10.1037/h0088917

Shen, Y.-J. (2017). Play therapy with adolescents in schools: Counselors' firsthand experiences. *International Journal of Play Therapy, 26*(2), 84. https://doi.org/10.1037/pla0000037

Short, G. (2008). Developmental play therapy for very young children. In C. Schaefer, S. Kelly-Zion, J. McCormick, & A. Ohnogi (Eds.), *Play therapy for very young children* (pp. 367–377). Aronson.

Singh, J. P., & Ivory, M. (2015). Beneficence/nonmaleficence. *The Encyclopedia of Clinical Psychology*, 1–3. https://doi.org/10.1002/9781118625392.wbecp016

Skigen, D. (2008). Taking the sand tray high tech. In L.C. Rubin (Ed.), *Popular culture in counseling, psychotherapy, and play-based interventions* (pp. 165–180). Springer.

Slavson, S. R. (1943). *An introduction to group therapy*. Commonwealth Fund.

Sloves, R., & Peterlin, K. (1993). Where in the world is . . . my father? A time-limited play therapy. In T. Kottman & C. Schaefer (Eds.), *Play therapy in action: A casebook for practitioners* (pp. 301–346). Jason Aronson.

Sloves, R., & Peterlin, K. (1994). Time-limited play therapy. In K. O'Connor & C. Schaefer (Eds.), *Handbook of play therapy* (Vol. 2, pp. 27–59). Wiley.

Smith, M. L., & Glass, G. V. (1977). Meta-analysis of psychotherapy outcome studies. *American Psychologist, 32*(9), 752–760. https://doi.org/10.1037/0003-066X.32.9.752

Smith, T., Norton, A. M., & Marroquin, L. (2023). Virtual family play therapy: A clinician's guide to using directed family play therapy in telemental health. *Contemporary Family Therapy, 5*(1), 106–116. https://doi.org/10.1007/s10591-021-09612-7

Snow, M. S., Winburn, A., Crumrine, L., Jackson, E., & Killian, T. (2012). The iPad playroom: A therapeutic technique. *Play Therapy, 7*, 16–19.

Solomon, J. (1938). Active play therapy. *American Journal of Orthopsychiatry, 8*, 479–498. https://doi.org/10.1111/j.1939-0025.1938.tb06398.x

Spector, R. E. (2017). *Cultural diversity in health and illness* (9th ed.). Pearson.

Sperry, L., & Binensztok, V. (2019). *Learning and practicing Adlerian therapy*. Cognella.

Spooner, C. (2020). *Attachment-focused family play therapy: An intervention for children and adolescents after trauma*. Routledge.

Stauffer, S. (2018). Technology in play therapy: A collegial debate between seven veteran play therapists. *Play Therapy, 13*(3), 20–23.

Stagnitti, K. (2007). *Child-initiated pretend play assessment (ChIPPA) manual and kit*. Coordinates Publications.

Stammers, L. (2017). The neurobiology of touch: Developmental play therapy with a child diagnosed with sensory processing disorder. In J. Courtney & R. Nolan (Eds.), *Touch in child counseling and play therapy* (pp. 35–47). Routledge.

Steele, H. (2015). Commentary—Attachment in middle childhood: Looking back, forward, and within. In G. Bosmans & K. A. Kerns (Eds.), Attachment in middle childhood: Theoretical advances and new directions in an emerging field. *New Directions for Child and Adolescent Development, 148*, 99–104.

Stifter, C., Augustine, M., & Dollar, J. (2019). The role of positive emotions in child development: A developmental treatment of the broaden and build theory. *Journal of Positive Psychology, 15*(1), 89–94. https://doi.org/10.1080/17439760.2019.1695877

Stone, J. (2016). Board games in play therapy. In K. J. O'Connor, C. E. Schaefer, & L. D. Braverman (Eds.) *Handbook of play therapy* (2nd ed., pp. 309–323). Wiley.

Stone, J. (Ed.) (2019). *Integrating technology into modern therapies: A clinician's guide to developments and interventions*. Routledge.

Stone, J. (2022). *Digital play therapy: A clinician's guide to comfort and competence* (2nd ed.). Routledge.

Stone, J., & Schaefer, C. (2020). *Game play therapy: Therapeutic use of games with children and adolescents* (3rd ed.). Wiley.

Stulmaker, H. L., & Jayne, K. M. (201). Child-centered play therapy parent consultation model: Clinical implementation and implications. *Journal of Child and Adolescent Counseling, 4*(1), 3–19. https://doi.org/10.1080/23727810.2017.1344795

Stutey, D. M., Adeyiga, O., Luke-Browning, L. V., & Wubbolding, R. E. (2020). Group reality play therapy. *International Journal of Play Therapy, 29*(4), 237–248. https://doi.org/10.1037/pla0000132

Stutey, D. M., & Wubbolding, R. E. (2018). Reality play therapy: A case example. *International Journal of Play Therapy, 27*(1), 1–13. https://doi.org/10.1037/pla0000061

Sue, D. W., Arredondo, P., & McDavis, R. J. (1992). Multicultural counseling competencies and standards: A call to the profession. *Journal of Counseling & Development, 70*(4), 477–486. https://doi.org/10.1002/j.1556-6676.1992.tb01642.x

Summers, L. M., & Nelson, L. (Eds.). (2023). *Multicultural counseling: Responding with cultural humility, empathy, and advocacy.* Springer Publishing.

Swan, A. M., Bratton, S. C., Ceballos, P., & Laird, A. (2019). Effect of CPRT with adoptive parents of preadolescents: A pilot study. *International Journal of Play Therapy, 28*(2), 107–122. https://doi.org/10.1037/pla0000095

Swan, K., & Schottelkorb, A. (2022). Cultural opportunities with children with disabilities. In D. C. Ray, Y. Ogawa, & Y.-J. Cheng (Eds.) *Multicultural play therapy: Making the most of cultural opportunities with children* (pp. 109–127). Routledge.

Swank, J., & Weaver, J. (2020). Therapeutic use of board games with children. In H. Kaduson & C. Schaefer (Eds.), *Play therapy with children: Modalities for change* (pp. 209–224). American Psychological Association.

Sweeney, D. (2020). Sandtray therapy. In H. Kaduson & C. Schaefer (Eds.), *Play therapy with children: Modalities for change* (pp. 9–24). American Psychological Association.

Sweeney, D. (2021). Sandtray therapy. In H. G. Kaduson & C. Schaefer (Eds.), *Play therapy with children: Modalities for change* (pp. 9–24). American Psychological Association. https://doi.org/10.1037/0000217-002

Sweeney, T. (2019). *Adlerian counseling and psychotherapy: A practitioner's wellness approach* (6th ed.). Routledge.

Synergetic Play Therapy Institute. (n.d.). *What is synergetic play therapy?* https://synergeticplaytherapy.com/what-synergetic-play-therapy/

Tal, R., Tal, K., & Green, O. (2018). Child-parent relationship therapy with extra-familial abused children. *Journal of Child Sexual Abuse, 27*(4), 386–402. https://doi.org/10.1080/10538712.2018.1451420

Taft, J. (1933). *The dynamics of therapy in a controlled relationship.* Macmillan.

Tan, C. S., Tan, S. A., Hashim, I. H. M., Lee, M. L., Ong, A. W., & Yaacob, S. N. B. (2019). Problem-solving ability and stress mediate the relationship between creativity and happiness. *Creativity Research Journal, (31)*1, 15–25. https://doi.org/10.1080/10400419.2019.1568155

Tarroja, M. C. H., Catipon, M. A. A. D., Dey, M. L. T., & Garcia, W. C. (2013). Advocating for play therapy: A challenge for an empirically-based practice in the Philippines. *International Journal of Play Therapy, 22*(4), 207–218. https://doi.org/10.1037/a0034167

Taub, L. (2021). *Tales for the hidden mind.* Tikun Olam Books.

Taylor, E. (2019). *Solution-focused therapy with children and adolescents: Creative and play-based approaches.* Routledge.

Taylor, L., & Turner, K. (2022). Cultural opportunities with African American populations. In D. C. Ray, Y. Ogawa, & Y.-J. Cheng (Eds.), *Multicultural play therapy: Making the most of cultural opportunities with children* (pp. 147–163). Routledge.

Taylor, S. (2021). The use of music and movement in play therapy. In H. G. Kaduson & C. Schaefer (Eds.), *Play therapy with children: Modalities for change* (pp. 191–208). American Psychological Association. https://doi.org/10.1037/0000217-013

Terr, L. (1990). *Too scared to cry.* Harper & Row.

Thomas, D. A., & Morris, M. H. (2020). *Creative play therapy with adolescents and adults: Moving from helping to healing.* Routledge.

Thomas, R., Abell, B., Webb, H., Avdagic, E., & Zimmer-Gembeck, M. (2017). Parent-child interaction therapy: A meta-analysis. *Pediatrics, 140*(3), Article e20170352. https://doi.org/10.1542/peds.2017-0352

Trotter, K., Eshelman, D., & Landreth, G. (2003). A place for Bobo in play therapy. *International Journal of Play Therapy, 12*(1), 117–139. https://doi.org/10.1037/h0088875

Tucker, C., & Smith-Adcock, S. (2017). Theraplay: The evidence for trauma-focused treatment for children and families. In R. L. Steen (Ed.), *Emerging research in play therapy, child counseling, and consultation* (pp. 42–59). IGI Global. https://doi.org/10.4018/978-1-5225-2224-9.ch003

Turner, R., Schoeneberg, C., Ray, D., & Lin, Y.-W. (2020). Establishing play therapy competencies: A Delphi study. *International Journal of Play Therapy, 29*(4), 177–190. https://doi.org/10.1037/pla0000138

Umhoefer, J., Peabody, M. A., & Stewart, A. (2015). Play therapy with military-connected children and families. In D. A. Crenshaw & A. L. Stewart (Eds.), *Play therapy: A comprehensive guide to theory and practice* (pp. 385–399). Guilford.

VanFleet, R. (2009). Filial therapy. In K. O'Connor & L. M. Braverman (Eds.), *Play therapy theory and practice: Comparing theories and techniques* (2nd ed., pp. 163–202). Wiley.

VanFleet, R. (2013). *Filial therapy: Strengthening parent-child relationships through play* (3rd ed.). Professional Resource Press.

VanFleet, R. (2014). *Filial therapy: Strengthening parent-child relationships through play* (3rd ed.). Professional Resource Press.

VanFleet, R. (2015). Short-term play therapy for adoptive families: Facilitating adjustment and attachment with filial therapy. In H. Kaduson & C. Schaefer (Eds.), *Short-term play therapy for children* (3rd ed., pp. 290–324). Guilford.

VanFleet, R., Sywulak, A., & Sniscak, C. (2010). *Child-centered play therapy.* Guilford.

VanFleet, R., & Topham, G. L. (2016). Filial therapy. In K. J. O'Connor, C. E. Schaefer, & L. D. Braverman (Eds.), *Handbook of play therapy* (2nd ed., pp. 135–164). Wiley.

Van Hollander, T. (2022). *A resource of children's books & interventions for bibliotherapy.* Mainline Play Therapy.

Wade, M. E. (2015, September). Confidentiality concerns with minors. *Counseling Today, 58*(3), 11.

Waller, D. (Ed.). (2022). *The metaphor toolbox: Scripts and stories for hypnotherapists, counsellors and coaches.*

Ward, J., & Allred, N. (2023). *The librarian's guide to bibliotherapy.* ALA.

Wassenaar, E. (2023). Teacher-child connection training: An Adlerian play therapy approach to training preschool teachers. *Play Therapy, 18*(3), 4–9.

Watkins, C. E., Jr., Hook, J. N., Owen, J., DeBlaere, C., Davis, D. E., & Van Tongeren, D. R. (2019). Multicultural orientation in psychotherapy supervision: Cultural humility, cultural comfort, and cultural opportunities. *American Journal of Psychotherapy, 72*(2), 38–46. https://doi.org/10.1176/appi.psychotherapy.20180040 https://doi.org/10.1176/appi.psychotherapy.20180040

Webber, A., & Webber, J. (Eds.). (2023). *Using art, play, metaphor, and symbol with hard-to-reach young clients: Reach out to me.* Routledge.

West, S. R., & Sarosy, J. (2021). *How to tell stories to children.* Houghton Mifflin Harcourt.

International Centre for Children and Family Law. (2023). *Wheel of child development.* https://iccfl.training/courses/wheel-of-child-development/

White, J., & Wynne, L. (2009). Kinder training: An Adlerian-based model to enhance teacher-student relationships. In A. A. Drewes (Ed.), *Blending play therapy with cognitive behavioral therapy* (pp. 281–295). Wiley.

White, M. (2007). *Maps of narrative practice.* Norton.

White, M., & Epstein, D. (1990). *Narrative means to therapeutic ends.* Norton.

Williams, T. I. (2018). Modifying cognitions in the treatment of OCD in young people. In E. Storch, J. F. McGuire, & D. McKay (Eds.), *The clinician's guide to cognitive-behavioral therapy for childhood obsessive-compulsive disorder* (pp. 105–133). Academic Press.

Wilson, K., & Ryan, V. (2005). *Play therapy: A nondirective approach for children and adolescents* (2nd ed.). Elsevier.

Wilson, S. (2018). *My book about play therapy.*

Winburn, A., Perepiczka, M., Frankum, J., & Neal, S. (2020). Play therapists' empathy levels as a predictor of self-perceived advocacy competency. *International Journal of Play Therapy, 29*(3), 144–154. https://doi.org/10.1037/pla0000119

Winnicott, D. W. (1971). *Playing and reality.* Tavistock.

Winters, E. (2012). *When a donut goes to therapy.* Snowfall Publications.

Wohl, N., & Hightower, D. (2001). Primary Mental Health Project: A school-based prevention program. In A. A. Drewes, L. J. Carey, & C. E. Schaefer (Eds.), *School-based play therapy* (pp. 277–296). Wiley.

Wonders, L. L. (2020). Play therapy for children with selective mutism. In C. Schaefer, D. Cangelosi, & H. Kaduson (Eds.), *Prescriptive play therapy: Tailoring interventions for specific childhood disorders* (pp. 92–104). Guilford.

Wycoff, K. L. (2020). Consultation with a community-based organization serving urban youth: A case study. *Consulting Psychology Journal: Practice and Research, 73*(2), 163–180. http://doi.org/10. 1037/cpb0000190

Yaeger, M., & Yaeger, D. (2014). Self-regulation. In C. Schaefer & A. Drewes (Eds.), *The therapeutic powers of play: 20 core agents of change* (pp. 269–293). Wiley.

Yasenik, L., & Gardner, K. (Eds.). (2018). *Turning points in play therapy and the emergence of self: Applications of the play therapy dimensions model.* Jessica Kingsley.

Yasenik, L., & Gardner, K. (2024). *Play therapy dimensions model: A decision-making guide for integrative play therapists* (2nd ed.). Jessica Kingsley.

Yee, T., & Cheng, Y.-J. (2022). Racism in the playroom: Clinical errors that maintain racism. *Journal of Child and Adolescent Counseling, 8*(3), 128–143. https://doi.org/10.1080/23727810.2022.2113707

Zakershoshtari, M., & Bozorgi, Z. (2016). The effectiveness of play therapy on reduction of the symptoms of attention deficit hyperactivity disorder (ADHD) in children. *Asian Social Sciences, 12*(6), 188–192. https://doi.org/10.5539/ass.v12n6p188

Appendix A

Theory and Play Therapy Resources

The following is a list of additional resources we (Terry and Jeff) recommend should you want to learn more about play therapy theory and its applications (described in Chapter 3). While this is not a comprehensive list of the available resources, it does include some classic theoretical works and discussions of the theories and applications from experts in each area.

Adlerian Theory/Adlerian Play Therapy

Adlerian Theory

Adler, A. (1954). *Understanding human nature* (W. B. Wolf, Trans.). New York, NY: Fawcett Premier. (Original work published in 1927).

Adler, A. (1958). *What life should mean to you.* New York, NY: Capricorn. (Original work published in 1931).

Adler, A. (1956). *The Individual Psychology of Alfred Adler* (H. Ansbacher & R. Ansbacher, Eds.). Basic Books.

Carlson, J., & Englar-Carson, M. (2017). *Adlerian psychotherapy.* Washington, DC: American Psychological Association.

Dreikurs, R., & Soltz, V. (1964). *Children: The challenge.* Hawthorn/Dutton.

Maniacci, M. P., Sackett-Maniacci, L., & Mosak, H. H. (2014). Adlerian psychotherapy. In D. Wedding & R. Corsini (Eds.), *Current psychotherapies* (10th ed., pp. 55-94). Belmont.

Mosak. H., & Maniacci, M. (1999). *A primer of Adlerian psychology.* Brunner/Mazel.

Mosak. H., & Maniacci, M. (2010). The case of Roger. In D. Wedding & R. J. Corsini (Eds.), *Case studies in psychotherapy* (7th ed., pp. 12-31). Brooks/Cole.

Sperry, L., & Binensztok, V. (2019). *Learning and practicing Adlerian therapy*. Cognella.

Sweeney, T. (2105). *Adlerian counseling and psychotherapy* (5th ed.). Routledge.

Sweeney, T. (2019). *Adlerian counseling and psychotherapy: A practitioner's wellness approach* (6th ed.). Routledge. https://doi. org/10.4324/9781351038744

Watts, R. (2013). Adlerian counseling. In B. Irby, G. Brown, & S. Jackson (Eds.). *The handbook of educational theories for theoretical frameworks*. (pp. 459-472). Information Age.

Adlerian Play Therapy

Dillman Taylor, D., Thompson, K., & Kottman, T. (2022). Strengthening the efficacy of Adlerian play therapy through the measurement model. *International Journal of Play Therapy, 31*(3), 164-173. doi. org/10.1037/pla0000176

Kottman, T. (1993). The king of rock and roll. In T. Kottman & C. Schaefer (Eds.), *Play therapy in action: A casebook for practitioners* (pp. 133–167). Jason Aronson.

Kottman, T. (1994). Adlerian play therapy. In K. O'Connor & C. Schaefer (Eds.), *Handbook of play therapy* (Vol. 2, pp. 3–26). Wiley.

Kottman, T., & Ashby, J. (1999). Using Adlerian personality priorities to custom-design consultation with parents of play therapy clients. *International Journal of Play Therapy, 8*(2), 77–92.

Kottman, T., & Ashby, J. (in press). Adlerian play therapy. In D. A. Crenshaw & A. L. Stewart (Eds.), *Play therapy: A comprehensive guide to theory and practice* (2nd ed.) Guilford.

Kottman, T., & Meany-Walen, K. (2016). *Partners in play: An Adlerian approach to play therapy* (3rd ed.). American Counseling Association.

Kottman, T., & Meany-Walen, K. (2017). Adlerian play therapy: Practice and research. In R. L. Steen (Ed.), *Emerging research in play therapy, child counseling, and consultation* (pp. 100-111). IGI Global.

Kottman, T., Meany-Walen, K., Parsons, M., & Dillman Taylor, D. (2021). *Treatment manual for Adlerian play therapy*. [Unpublished manuscript].

Meany-Walen, K. (2018). Adlerian play therapy with preadolescents. In E. Green, J. Baggerly, &

A. Myrick (Eds.), *Play therapy with preteens* (pp. 49-66). Rowman and Littlefield.

Meany-Walen, K. K., & Kottman, T. (2017). Adlerian play therapy: Practice and research. In R. L. Steen (Ed.), *Emerging research in play therapy, child counseling, and consultation* (pp. 100–111). Information Science Reference/IGI Global. https://doi.org/10.4018/978-1- 5225-2224-9.ch006

Shen, S.-Y., Roller, K., & Kottman, T. (2021). Adlerian family play therapy: Healing the attachment trauma of divorce. *International Journal of Play Therapy, 30*(1), 28–39. https://doi.org/10.1037/pla0000146

Person-Centered Theory/Child-Centered Play Therapy

Person-Centered Theory

Raskin, N., Rogers, C., & Witty, M. (2014). Client-centered therapy. In D. Wedding & R. Corsini (Eds.), *Current psychotherapies* (10th ed., pp. 95-145). Brooks/Cole.

Rogers, C. (1951). *Client-centered therapy: Its current practice, implications, and theory.* Houghton Mifflin.

Rogers, C. (1957). The necessary and sufficient conditions of therapeutic personality change. *Journal of Consulting Psychology, 21*(2), 95-103.

Rogers, C. (1959). A theory of therapy, personality and interpersonal relationships as developed in the client-centered framework. In (ed.) S. Koch, *Psychology: A study of a science. Vol. 3: Formulations of the person and the social context.* McGraw Hill.

Rogers, C. R. (1961). *On becoming a person: A psychotherapist's view of psychotherapy.* Houghton Mifflin.

Rogers, C. R., Stevens, B., Gendlin, E. T., Shlien, J. M., & Van Dusen, W. (1967). *Person to person: The problem of being human: A new trend in psychology.* Real People Press.

Child-Centered Play Therapy

Axline, V. (1947). *Play therapy: The inner dynamics of childhood.* Houghton Mifflin.

Axline, V. (1969). *Play therapy* (Rev. ed.). Ballantine Books.

Axline, V. (1971). *Dibs: In search of self.* Ballantine Books.

Cochran, N., Nordling, W., & Cochran, J. (2022). *Child-centered play therapy* (2nd ed.). Routledge.

Glover, G., & Landreth, G. (2016). Child-centered play therapy. In K. O'Connor, C. Schaefer; & L. Braverman (Eds.), *Handbook of play therapy* (2nd ed., pp. 93-118). Wiley.

Guerney, L. (2001). Child-centered play therapy. *International Journal of Play Therapy, 10*(2), 13–31.

Landreth, G. L. (2024). *Play therapy: The art of the relationship* (4th ed.). Brunner-Routledge.

Landreth, G. L. & Bratton, S. (2020). *Child-Parent Relationship Therapy (CPRT): An evidence-based 10-session filial therapy model* (2nd ed.). Routledge.

Nordling, W. J., & Guerney, L. (1999). Typical stages in the child-centered play therapy process. *Journal for the Professional Counselor, 14,* 17-23.

Ray, D.C. (2011). *Advanced play therapy: Essential conditions, knowledge, and skills for child practice.* Routledge.

Ray, D., & Landreth, G. (2015). Child-centered play therapy. In D. A. Crenshaw & A. L. Stewart (Eds.), *Play therapy: A comprehensive guide to theory and practice* (pp. 3-16). Guilford.

VanFleet, R., Sywulak, A., & Sniscak, C. (2010). *Child-centered play therapy.* Guilford.

Cognitive-Behavioral Theory/Cognitive Behavioral Play Therapy

Cognitive-Behavioral Theory

Beck, A. (1976). *Cognitive therapy and the emotional disorders.* International Universities Press.

Beck, J. (1995). *Cognitive therapy: Basics and beyond.* Guilford.

Burns, D. (1999). *Feeling good: The new mood therapy.* New American Library.

Ellis, A. (2000). Rational emotive behavior therapy. In R. J. Corsini & D. Wedding (Eds.). *Current psychotherapies* (6th ed., pp. 168-204). Itasca, IL: F. E. Peacock.

Meichenbaum, D. (1986). Cognitive behavior modification. In F. H. Kanfer & A. P. Goldstein (Eds.), *Helping people change: A textbook of methods* (pp. 346-380). Pergamon Press.

Cognitive-Behavioral Play Therapy

Cavett, A. M. (2015). Cognitive-behavioral play therapy. In D. A. Crenshaw & A. L. Stewart (Eds.). *Play therapy: A comprehensive guide to theory and practice,* (pp. 83-98). Guildford.

Dasari, M., & Knell, S. (2015). Cognitive behavioral play therapy for children with anxiety and phobias. In H. Kaduson & C. Schaefer (Eds.), *Short-term play therapy for children* (3rd ed., pp. 25-52). Guilford.

Fazio-Griffith, L. (2018). Play therapy in middle schools: A cognitive-behavioral play therapy (CBPT) approach for preadolescent social skills development. In E. Green, J. Baggerly, & A. Myrick (Eds.), *Play therapy with preteens* (pp. 167-178). Rowman and Littlefield.

Knell, S. M. (1993). *Cognitive-behavioral play therapy.* Jason Aronson.

Knell, S. M. (1994). Cognitive-behavioral play therapy. In K. O'Connor & C. Schaefer (Eds.)., *Handbook of play therapy: Vol. 2. Advances and innovations* (pp. 111-142).

Knell, S. (2003). Cognitive–behavioral play therapy. In C. Schaefer (Ed.), *Foundations of play therapy* (pp.174–191). Wiley.

Knell, S. (2009a). Cognitive–behavioral play therapy. In K. O'Connor & L. M. Braverman (Eds.), *Play therapy theory and practice: Comparing theories and techniques* (2nd ed., pp. 203–236). Wiley.

Knell, S. (2009b). Cognitive behavioral play therapy. In A. Drewes (Ed.), *Blending play therapy with cognitive behavior therapy: Evidenced-based and other effective treatments and techniques* (pp. 117–134). Wiley.

Knell, S. (2016). Cognitive-behavioral play therapy. In K. O'Connor, C., Schaefer, and L.

Braverman, L. (Eds.) *Handbook of play therapy* (2nd ed., pp. 119-134). Wiley.

Razak, N. H. A., Johari, K. S. K., Mahmud, M. I., Zubir, N. M., & Johan, S. (2018). General Review on cognitive behavior play therapy on children's psychology development. *International Journal of Academic Research in Progressive Education and Development, 7*(4), 134–147

Ecosystemic Play Therapy

* Ecosystemic Play Therapy theory was created specifically for play therapy therapists and clients. It combines several theoretical approaches, but no recognized overarching ecosystemic theory exists.

O'Connor, K. (1993). Child, protector, confidant: Structured group exosystemic play therapy. In T. Kottman & S. Schaefer (Eds.), *Play therapy in action: A casebook for practitioners* (pp. 245-280). Jason Aronson.

O'Connor, K. (1994). Ecosystemic play therapy. In K. O'Connor & C. Schaefer (Eds.), *Handbook of play therapy* (vol. 2, pp. 61–84). Wiley.

O'Connor, K. (2009). Ecosystemic play therapy. In K. J. O'Connor & L. D. Braverman (Eds.), *Play therapy theory and practice: Comparing theories and techniques,* (2nd ed., pp. 367-450). Wiley.

O'Connor, K. (2011). Ecosystemic play therapy. In C. E. Schaefer (Ed.), *Foundations of play therapy* (2nd ed., pp. 253-272). Wiley.

O'Connor, K. (2016). Ecosystemic play therapy. In K. O'Connor, C., Schaefer, and L. Braverman, L. (Eds.) *Handbook of play therapy* (2nd ed., pp. 195-226). Wiley.

O'Connor, K. J., & Ammen, S. (2013). *Play therapy treatment planning and interventions: The ecosystemic model and workbook* (2nd ed.). Academic Press.

O'Connor, K., & Vega, C. (2019). Ecosystemic play therapy. *Play Therapy, 14*(3), 32-34.

Gestalt Theory/Gestalt Play Therapy

Gestalt Theory

Pearls, F. (1970). Four lectures. In J. Fagan & I. L. Shepherd (Eds.), *Gestalt therapy now* (pp. 14-38). Harper.

Perls, F., Hefferline, R. F., & Goodman, P. (1951). *Gestalt therapy: Excitement and growth in the human personality.* Crown.

Gestalt Play Therapy

Blom, R. (2006). *The handbook of Gestalt play therapy: Practical guidelines for child therapists.* Jessica Kingsley.

Carroll, F. (2009). Gestalt play therapy. In K. J. O'Connor & L. D. Braverman, *Play therapy theory and practice: Comparing theories and techniques* (2nd ed., pp. 283–314). Wiley.

Carroll, F., & Oaklander, V. (1997). Gestalt play therapy. In K. O'Connor & L. Braverman (Eds.), *Play therapy theory and practice: A comparative presentation* (pp. 184-203). Wiley.

Carroll, F., & Orozco, V. (2019). Gestalt play therapy. *Play Therapy, 14*(3), 36-38.

Oaklander, V. (1992). *Windows to our children: A Gestalt approach to children and adolescents.* Gestalt Journal Press. (Originally work published 1978)

Oaklander, V. (1994). Gestalt play therapy. In K. O'Connor & C. Schaefer (Eds.), *Handbook of play therapy* (Vol. 2, pp. 143–156). Wiley.

Oaklander, V. (2003). Gestalt play therapy. In C. Schaefer (Ed.), *Foundations of play therapy* (pp. 143-155). Hoboken, NJ: Wiley.

Oaklander, V. (1993). From meek to bold: A case study of Gestalt play therapy. In T. Kottman & C. Schaefer (Eds.), *Play therapy in action: A casebook for practitioners* (pp. 281–299). Jason Aronson.

Oaklander, V. (2006). *Hidden treasure: A map to the child's inner self.* Karnac Books.

Oaklander, V. (2011). Gestalt play therapy. *International Journal of Play Therapy, 10,* 45-55.

Oaklander, V. (2015). Short-term Gestalt play therapy for grieving children. In H. Kaduson & C.

Schaefer (Eds.), *Short-term play therapy for children* (3rd ed., pp. 124-149). Guilford.

Jungian Theory/Jungian Play Therapy

Jungian Theory

Douglas, C. (2008). Analytical Psychotherapy. In R. J. Corsini & D. Wedding (Eds.). *Current psychotherapies* (8th ed., pp. 107-140). Brooks/ Cole.

Jung, C. G. (1963). *Memories, dreams, reflections* (J. Jaffe, Ed.). Vantage.

Jung, C. G. (1969). Synchronicity: An acausal connecting principle. In G. Adler, M. Fordham, W. McGuire, & H. Read (Eds.), and R. F. C. Hull

(Trans.), *The collected works of C. F. Jung* (Vol. 8, pp. 419-519). Princeton University Press.

Jungian Play Therapy

Allan, J. (1988). *Inscapes of the child's world: Jungian counseling in schools and clinics.* Springer.

Allan, J. (1997). Jungian play psychotherapy. In K. J. O'Connor & L. M. Braverman (Eds.), *Play therapy: A comparative presentation,* (2nd ed., pp. 100-130). Wiley.

Allan, J., & Bertoia, J. (1992). *Written paths to healing: Education and Jungian child counseling.* Spring.

Allan, J., & Levin, S. (1993). "Born on my bum": Jungian play therapy. In T. Kottman & C. Schaefer (Eds.), *Play therapy in action: A casebook for practitioners* (pp. 209-244). Jason Aronson.

Green, E. J. (2005). Jungian play therapy: Bridging the theoretical to the practical. In G. R. Walz & R. K. Yep (Eds.), *VISTAS: Compelling perspectives on counseling, 2005* (pp. 75-78).   American Counseling Association.

Green, E. (2009). Jungian analytical play therapy. In K. O'Connor & L. M. Braverman (Eds.), *Play therapy theory and practice: Comparing theories and techniques* (2nd ed., pp. 83-122). Wiley.

Green, E. J. (2011). Jungian analytical play therapy. In C. E. Schaefer (Ed.), *Foundations of play therapy* (pp. 61–84). Wiley.

Green, E. (2014). *The handbook of Jungian play therapy with children and adolescents.* Johns Hopkins University.

Lily, J.P. (2015). Jungian analytic play therapy. In D. Crenshaw & A. Stewart (Eds.), *Play therapy: A comprehensive guide to theory and practice* (pp.48-65). Guilford.

Lily, J. P., & Heiko, R. (2019). Jungian analytic play therapy. *Play Therapy, 14*(3), 40-42.

Peery, J. C. (2003). Jungian analytical play therapy. In C. E. Schaefer (Ed.), *Foundations of play therapy* (pp. 14-54). Wiley.

Punnett, A. (2016). Psychoanalytic and Jungian play therapy. In K. O'Connor, C. Schaefer, & L. Braverman (Eds.), *Handbook of play therapy* (2nd ed., pp. 61-92). Hoboken, NJ: Wiley.

Narrative Theory/Narrative Play Therapy

Narrative theory

White, M. (2007). *Maps of narrative practice.* Norton

White, M., & Epston, D. (1990). *Narrative means to therapeutic ends.* New York, NY: W.W. Norton.

Zimmerman, J., & Dicerson, V. (1996). *If problems talked: Narrative therapy in action.* Guilford.

Narrative play therapy

Cattanach, A. (2006). Narrative play therapy. In C. Schaefer & H. Kaduson (Eds.),

Contemporary play therapy: Theory, research, and practice (pp. 82-99). Guilford.

Cattanach, A. (2008). *Narrative approaches tin play therapy with children.* Philadelphia, PA: Jessica Kingsley.

Mills, J. (2015). StoryPlay: A narrative play therapy approach. In D. Crenshaw & A. Stewart (Eds.), *Play therapy: A comprehensive guide to theory and practice* (pp.171-185). Guilford.

Mills, J., & Crowley, R. (2014). *Therapeutic metaphors for children and the child within* (2nd ed.). Routledge.

Taylor de Faoite, A. (2011). *Narrative play therapy: Theory and practice.* Jessica Kingsley.

Psychodynamic Theory/Psychodynamic Play Therapy

Psychodynamic Theory

Freud, S. (1938). *The basic writings of Sigmund Freud.* Modern Library.

Freud, A. (1946). *The psychoanalytic treatment of children.* Imago.

Freud, S. (1949). *An outline of psycho-analysis.* (J. Strachey, Trans.). Norton.

Freud, A. (1968). Indications and counter-indications for child analysis. *Psychoanalytic Study of the Child, 23,* 37–46.

Hug-Hellmuth, H. (1921). On the technique of child analysis. *International Journal of Psychoanalysis, 2*, 287–305.

Klein, M. (1932). *The psycho-analysis of children.* Hogarth Press.

Safran, J. D., & Kriss, A. (2014). Psychoanalytic psychotherapies. In D. Wedding & R. J. Corsini (Eds.), *Current psychotherapies* (10th ed., pp. 19-54). Brooks/Cole.

Winnicott, D. W. (1971). *Playing and reality.* Tavistock.

Psychodynamic Play Therapy

Benedict, H. (2006). Object relations play therapy. In C. Schaefer & H. Kaduson (Eds.),

Contemporary play therapy: Theory, research, and practice (pp. 3–27). Guilford.

Benedict, H., & Hastings, L. (2002). Object relations play therapy. In J. Magnavita (Ed.),

Comprehensive handbook of psychotherapy (Vol. 1, pp. 47-80). Wiley.

Cangelosi, D. (1993). Internal and external wars: Psychodynamic play therapy. In T. Kottman & C. Schaefer (Eds.), *Play therapy in action: A casebook for practitioners* (pp. 347-370). Jason Aronson.

Lee, A. (2009). Psychoanalytic play therapy. In K. O'Connor & L. M. Braverman (Eds.), *Play therapy theory and practice: Comparing theories and techniques* (2nd ed., pp. 25–82). Wiley.

Meersand, P., & Gilmore, K. (2017). Play therapy: A psychodynamic primer for the treatment of young children. American Psychiatric Association.

Mordock, J.B. (2015). Psychodynamic play therapy. In D. Crenshaw & A. Stewart (Eds.), *Play therapy: A comprehensive guide to theory and practice* (pp. 66-82). Guilford.

Patton, S. C., & Benedict, H. E. (2015). Object relations and attachment-based play therapy. In D. A. Crenshaw & A. L. Stewart (Eds.), *Play therapy: A comprehensive guide to theory and practice* (pp. 17–31). Guilford.

Punnett, A. (2016). Psychoanalytic and Jungian play therapy. In K. O'Connor, C. Schaefer, & L. Braverman (Eds.), *Handbook of play therapy* (2nd ed., pp. 61-92). Wiley.

Theraplay

* Theraplay is an approach to play therapy based on psychological theories of attachment. There is no independent Theraplay theory.

Theraplay

Booth, P., & Jernberg, A. (2010). *Theraplay: Helping parents and children build better relationships through attachment-based play* (3rd ed.). Jossey-Bass.

Booth, P., & Winstead, M. (2015). Theraplay: Repairing relationships, helping families heal. In D. Crenshaw & A. Stewart (Eds.), *Play therapy: A comprehensive guide to theory and practice* (pp. 141-155). Guilford.

Booth, P., & Winstead, M. (2016). Theraplay: Creating secure and joyful attachment relationships. In K. O'Connor, C. Schaefer, & L. Braverman (Eds.), *Handbook of play therapy* (2nd ed., pp. 164-194). Wiley.

Brody, V. (1978). Developmental play: A relationship-focused program for children. *Journal of Child Welfare, 57,* 591-599.

Brody, V. (1993).*The dialogue of touch: Developmental play therapy.* Treasure Island, FL: Developmental Play Training Associates.

Bundy-Myrow, S., & Booth, P. B. (2009). Theraplay: Supporting attachment relationships. In K. J. O'Connor & L. D. Braverman (Eds.). *Play therapy theory and practice: Comparing theories and techniques,* (2nd ed., 315-366). Wiley.

Jernberg, A. (1979). *Theraplay: A new treatment using structured play for problem children and their families.* Jossey-Bass.

Jernberg, A., & Jernberg, E. (1993). Family Theraplay for the family tyrant. In T. Kottman & C. Schaefer (Eds.), *Play therapy in action: A casebook for practitioners* (pp. 45–96). Jason Aronson.

Koller, T., & Booth, P. (1997). Fostering Attachment Through Family Theraplay. In K. O'Connor and L. M. Braverman (Eds.), *Play Therapy Theory and Application: A Comparative Presentation.* Wiley.

Lindaman, S., & Hong, R. (Eds.). (2021). Theraplay® – Theory, applications and Implementation. Jessica Kingsley.

Marschak, M. (1960). A method for evaluating child-parent interaction under controlled conditions. *Journal of Genetic Psychology, 97,* 3–22.

Munns, E. (2011). Theraplay: Attachment-enhancing play therapy. In C. Schaefer (Ed.), *Foundations of play therapy* (2nd ed., pp. 275-296). Wiley.

Norris, V., & Lender, D. (2020). *Theraplay: The practitioner's guide.* Jessica Kingsley.

Tucker, C., & Smith-Adcock, S. (2017). Theraplay: The evidence for trauma-focused treatment for children and families. In R. L. Steen (Ed.), *Emerging research in play therapy, child counseling, and consultation* (pp. 42–59). Information Science Reference/IGI Global. https://doi.org/10.4018/978-1-5225-2224-9.ch003

Integrative/Prescriptive Play Therapy

* Integrative/Prescriptive play therapy utilizes interventions from a variety of theoretical approaches. There is no independent integrative/prescriptive theory.

Gil, E., Konrath, E., Shaw, J., Goldin, M., & Bryan, H. (2015). Integrative approach to play therapy. In D. Crenshaw & A. Stewart (Eds.), *Play therapy: A comprehensive guide to theory and practice* (pp.99-113). Guilford.

Gil, E., & Shaw, J. (2009). Prescriptive play therapy. In K. O'Connor & L. M. Braverman (Eds.), *Play therapy theory and practice: Comparing theories and techniques* (2nd ed., pp. 451– 488). Wiley.

Kaduson, H., Cangelosi, D., & Schaefer, C. (Eds.). (1997). *The playing cure: Individualized play therapy for specific childhood problems.* Jason Aronson.

Kaduson, H., Cangelosi, D., & Schaefer, C. (Eds.) (2020). *Prescriptive play therapy: Tailoring interventions for specific childhood problems.* Guilford.

Kaduson, H., & Schaefer, C. (Eds.) (2015). *Short-term play therapy for children* (3rd ed.). Guilford.

Kaduson, H., Cangelosi, D., & Schaefer, C. (2020). *Prescriptive play therapy: Tailoring interventions for specific childhood problems.* Guilford.

Kaduson, H., Schaefer, C., & Cangelosi, D. (2020). Basic principles and core practices of prescriptive play therapy. In H. Kaduson, C. Schaefer, & D. Cangelosi (Eds.), *Prescriptive play therapy: Tailoring interventions for specific childhood problems* (pp. 3-13). Guilford.

Norcross, J. C. (2005). A primer on psychotherapy integration. In J. C. Norcross & M. R. Goldfried (Eds.), *Handbook of psychotherapy integration (2nd ed., pp. 3-23)*. University Press.

Schaefer, C. (2001). Prescriptive play therapy. *International Journal of Play Therapy, 10*(2), 57–73.

Schaefer, C. (2003). Prescriptive play therapy. In C. Schaefer (Ed.), *Foundations of play therapy* (pp. 306–320). Wiley.

Schaefer, C., & Drewes, A. (2016). Prescriptive play therapy. In K. O'Connor, C., Schaefer, and L. Braverman, L. (Eds.) *Handbook of play therapy* (2nd ed., pp. 227-240). Wiley.

Appendix B

Philosophical Assumptions Underlying Counseling and Play Therapy Theories

In response to the 12 questions Kottman and Meany-Walen (2018, pp. 40-42) proposed as essential for play therapists to consider, the tables below presents the philosophical assumptions of the ten historically significant approaches to play therapy identified by the Association for Play Therapy (APT, 2023). We will list the questions first, followed by the responses.

1. What do you believe about the basic nature of people? Are people inherently good (positive, self-actualizing, etc.), bad (negative, irrational, evil, etc.), neutral, or some combination of these? If you believe people are some combination of good, bad, and neutral, how would you describe the configuration of these factors?

2. How are personalities formed/constructed?

    a. What factors influence the formation of personality?

    b. What combination of heredity/environment influences the formation of personality?

    c. Which do you believe is more important in the development of personality: nature or nurture? If you had to designate a percentage of each of them, what would you decide?

    d. In relationship to what you believe about free will and determinism in the formation of personality, do you believe that people exercise free will in the formation of their personalities, or do you believe that personal qualities are determined by outside factors without input from the person? Or some combination of free will and determinism? If you believe it is a combination, can you assign a percentage to each?

    e. What is the relationship between thinking, feeling, and behaving? Is there a linear, causal relationship between thoughts, emotions, and behavior? If so, what causes this? If not, what is the relationship between these factors?

    f. What is the basic motivation for people's behavior?

    g. What are the basic elements of a person's personality?

3. What is your stance on perception of reality—is it subjective or objective?

4. What do you believe is the role of the therapeutic relationship in counseling? Do you believe the therapeutic relationship is necessary and sufficient (as in, it is the primary and only factor in clients moving toward healthy functioning)? Do you believe the therapeutic relationship is necessary and serves as the foundation for helping clients through the creation of opportunities to entertain alternative perspectives, to learn new coping skills, learn and practice socially appropriate behaviors, to let go of destructive patterns, and so forth?

5. In counseling, do you think you need to help clients extensively explore the past, look at their current issues in the context of their past, or focus only on the here-and-now without considering anything about the past?

6. Do you believe it is important to help clients become more aware of their own motivation and patterns by helping them gain insight/become more conscious? Or do you believe clients will improve if they learn better coping skills without becoming more aware of their motivation and patterns? Or do you believe clients will improve if they experience certain conditions that activate their own self-actualizing tendencies without additional information, practice, or insight?

7. What do you believe should be the primary focus of counseling—creating a relationship with the client or helping the client make changes in personality, feelings, behaviors, attitudes, or thoughts? If you believe it is important to help clients make changes, do you believe it is important to help clients make changes in only one of these factors or in some combination of these factors? If so, which would be the "firing order" you would prioritize?

8. How do you define psychological maladjustment?

9. What do you think should be the goals of counseling?

10. How can you tell if your clients are getting "better"? How will you judge whether clients are making progress?

11. Do you imagine your role as a counselor to be more directive or nondirective in your play therapy sessions?

    a. Would you prefer to create the space for the client to grow without making suggestions for in-session activities or homework (allowing the client to play without therapist intervention in play therapy)? Or are you more comfortable intervening by inviting clients to participate in structured techniques and assigning homework?

    b. How comfortable with participating in active interactions with the client are you? Do you believe it is never appropriate to play with the client in a session? Do you believe it is only appropriate to play with a client at the client's invitation? Do you believe it is acceptable to initiate playing with a client? If a client invites you to play something, do you think you must play even when you are not comfortable with what the client wants you to play?

12. If you are working with a child client, what is your stance on working with parents? Teachers? Do you believe it is always necessary to involve parents and/or teachers? Do you believe it is not necessary to include these adults in counseling? If you believe it's necessary, to what degree do you think they should be included?

Table B1

Question 2a

Theory	Basic Nature of People	Factors That Influence Formation of Personality
Adlerian	Positive and self-actualizing	Family, school, community, culture, temperament.
Child-Centered	Positive and self-actualizing	Born with "organismic valuing" (awareness of sensory and visceral experiencing of their environment) to determine whether things are good for them or not or "real self". Gradually develop "conditions of worth," ideas about who they should be and how they should act in order to be worthy of acceptance and love or "ideal self."
Cognitive-Behavioral	Potential to be rational or irrational	Development of the patterns of thinking (either rational or irrational); begin with cognitive patterns modeled by parents.
Ecosystemic	Neutral	Personality as the "sum of intra- and interpersonal characteristics, attributes, cognitions, beliefs, values, and so forth that make a person unique." Nested systems, including family, school, peer, culture, legal, medical, and others.

Theory	Basic Nature of People	Factors That Influence Formation of Personality
Gestalt	Neutral	Striving toward need fulfillment and self-regulation, the individual's relationship with their environment and development of contact boundary disturbances (including faulty introjects from their parents), and the movement toward awareness of the environment and self-awareness.
Jungian	Neutral	1. Children's relationships with their parents and their perception of whether they are getting their needs met by their parents. 2. Psychological ego defenses, such as repression, projection, hallucinations, and the splitting of "good" and "bad." 3. Normal pressures of life can combine with the less-than-ideal responses from others (especially their parents) to these pressures, can result in children's ego fragmenting. 4. The process by which children and their parents deal with this fragmentation ("de-integration and re-integration") leads to the development of attachment patterns and adjustment or maladjustment in children. 5. Archetypes, which are the form the basic structural matrix of the human personality.
Psychodynamic	Negative	Moving through psychosexual development stages and dealing with conflicts and fixations at each stage.
Theraplay	Does not take a stand on this	Early interactions between parent and child.
Prescriptive	Dependent	Dependent upon treatment plan chosen.

Table B2

Question 2c

Theory	Nature/Nurture
Adlerian	60% nature and 40% nurture.
Child-Centered	Born with a tendency to self-actualize and with organismic valuing, depending on messages from parents and others, may develop "conditions of worth" 50% nature and 50% nurture.
Cognitive-Behavioral	Born with a potential for being rational or irrational and a predisposition toward happiness, love, communion with others and growth 20% nature and 80% nurture.
Ecosystemic	30% nature and 70% nurture.
Gestalt	Personality is believed to be constructed from the combination of biology and environmental influences. All experiences contribute to the development of the personality. Each individual has a unique set of genetic blueprints that help to form how experiences are perceived and differentiated in the personality. 40% nature and 60% nurture.
Jungian	Born with innate structures, like the psyche, which consists of the ego and the Self. The relationship between children and their parent(s) shapes the differentiation of the ego from other psyche structures. 50% nature and 50% nurture.
Psychodynamic	Nature is the innate drive toward sexual gratification and aggression; nurture is childhood experiences and the passage through the psychosexual stages. 70% nature and 30% nurture.
Theraplay	Not directly addressed. People are born with the need to connect, and there is such a strong emphasis on the idea that people are shaped by getting or not getting the attuned, responsive care for caregivers they need to develop in healthy ways. 25% nature and 75% nurture.
Prescriptive	Dependent upon treatment plan chosen.

Table B3
Question 2d

Theory	Free Will/Determinism
Adlerian	Free will; one goal of therapy is to increase clients' awareness they have a choice.
Child-Centered	Mostly free will. 80% free will and 20% determinism.
Cognitive-Behavioral	Always have a choice in how they interpret the events that happen and that interpretation determines how they react to those events.100% free will.
Ecosystemic	Free will. Experiences and interactions with other people influence, but do not determine, the choices they make and the path they take through life.
Gestalt	Free will. Individuals are responsible for their actions and the choices that they make.
Jungian	Both/neither. Capable of making their own conscious decisions and are influenced by the personal unconscious and collective unconscious.
Psychodynamic	Deterministic. Direct cause and effect relationship between biological drives and childhood experiences, and current behavior, without the mitigation of choice.
Theraplay	Not addressed. Choice is stressed as being important.
Prescriptive	Dependent upon treatment plan chosen.

Table B4
Question 2e

Theory	Relationship Between Thinking, Feeling, and Behaving
Adlerian	Circular/non-linear. All three of these elements influence one another: thinking has an impact on feeling and behaving; feeling has an impact on thinking and behaving; behaving has an impact on feeling and thinking.
Child-Centered	Relationship among thinking, feeling, and behaving was never a central focus; thinking about getting needs met comes first.

Theory	Relationship Between Thinking, Feeling, and Behaving
Cognitive-Behavioral	Linear causal relationship between thinking, feeling, and behaving with thinking leading to feeling and behaving.
Ecosystemic	Thinking influences feeling, behaving, and interpersonal relating; intervention starts with thinking.
Gestalt	Focus more on senses, the body, and the emotions and less on the intellect.
Jungian	Relationship is not linear. Feelings can be attributed to persons' experiences or the archetypes with which they identify. These feelings contribute to how they think about themselves. Behavior is in response to unfinished struggles of parents (in childhood and adulthood) or themselves.
Psychodynamic	Not addressed in this theory; not considered important.
Theraplay	Not addressed in this theory; interventions focus on behavior rather than affect or cognition.
Prescriptive	Dependent upon treatment plan chosen.

Table B5

Question 2f

Theory	Basic Motivation for Behavior
Adlerian	Increase a sense of belonging and connection; overcoming feelings of inferiority.
Child-Centered	Attempt to satisfy the needs of the organism. Trying to move toward ideal self as a way to satisfy conditions of worth.
Cognitive-Behavioral	Maximize survival and pleasure.
Ecosystemic	Meet needs and avoiding punishment and pain.
Gestalt	Reach a homeostatic balance in one's life by meetings one's needs; avoid rejection and abandonment and gain approval from others.

Theory	Basic Motivation for Behavior
Jungian	Seek individuation. Comes from the unconscious—either the collective unconscious (the archetypal patterns that have evolved over time and across cultures) or the personal unconscious (repressed memories and instinctual drives.
Psychodynamic	Increase pleasure and avoid pain.
Theraplay	Basic motivation for behavior is explained in terms of parent-infant relationships, which are supported by two innate drives: the drive to stay close in order to be safe and the drive to share meaning and companionship.
Prescriptive	Dependent upon treatment plan chosen.

Table B6

Question 2g

Theory	Basic Components of Personality
Adlerian	Personality not divided into basic components. Important elements: assets; functioning at life tasks (work, love/family, friendship, spirituality/meaning of existence, and self); goals of misbehavior (gaining attention, power, revenge, and proving inadequacy); the Crucial Cs (courage, capable, connect, and count); and personality priorities (pleasing, comfort, superiority, and control).
Child-Centered	Personality not divided into basic components. Organismic valuing and conditions of worth, which form the basis of the real self and the ideal self.
Cognitive-Behavioral	Do not posit elements of personality—not a personality theory, per se.
Ecosystemic	Not a theory of personality. Borrows from a variety of personality theories: depends on which theory you choose to be the foundation of your work with clients.

Theory	Basic Components of Personality
Gestalt	No components of personality. Organismic self-regulation (a balance between good health and need fulfillment), development of a strong sense of self (one that is separate from other people, refuse responsibility for other people's behavior or feelings, and recognition of needs and how to get them met—even through the use of appropriate aggression), healthy contact boundaries (when all of the senses are engaged in the present, resulting in healthy mind, body, intellect, and a sense of security), and holism (whole greater than sum of parts and all aspects of the individual are important and worthy of consideration and support).
Jungian	The psyche is made up of three parts: ego, the personal unconscious, and the collective unconscious.
Psychodynamic	The id, the ego, and the super-ego. The id, the sole component of the personality that is present from birth, is the source of instinctual drives, particularly sexual and aggressive drives. The id moves people to act according to the pleasure principle, the instinct to avoid pain and maximize pleasure. The ego is the organized component of the personality that includes defensive, perceptual, intellectual-cognitive, and executive functions. It is the part of the personality that makes sense of the world—makes realistic assessments about which of the id's demands and passions can be met with minimal negative impact on the person. The super-ego is the internalization of the rules set by society—usually taught to children by parents and family, then reinforced by schools.
Theraplay	Not addressed.
Prescriptive	Dependent upon treatment plan chosen.

Table B7

Question 3

Theory	Perception of Reality—Objective or Subjective
Adlerian	Reality is perceived subjectively; what people make of what happens in their lives is more important than what actually happens.
Child-Centered	Subjectively. Rogers coined the word "subceive," as a conglomerate of subjectively and perceive.
Cognitive-Behavioral	Perception of reality is always subjective.
Ecosystemic	Subjective.
Gestalt	Subjective—therapist's job is to step into client's unique perspective.
Jungian	Individuals perceive reality subjectively- not a significant concept in Jungian theory.
Psychodynamic	Subjective.
Theraplay	Not an important concept in this approach; subjective.
Prescriptive	Dependent upon treatment plan chosen.

Table B8

Question 4

Theory	Role of Therapeutic Relationship
Adlerian	The relationship serves as the foundation for everything else that follows in the therapeutic process; relationship is a collaborative partnership where the therapist and client share power and responsibility.
Child-Centered	The relationship is the therapy; it is not the preparation for therapy or behavioral change. Clients grow in a positive direction if they experience unconditional positive regard, genuineness, and empathy in relationships.
Cognitive-Behavioral	Depends on the type of CBT. Play Therapists usually say the relationship should be based on positive regard, empathy, and genuineness; however, this relationship is not sufficient to lead to change.

Theory	Role of Therapeutic Relationship
Ecosystemic	Therapeutic relationship is a vehicle for helping clients engage in problem-solving, which ultimately leads to behavior changes and getting needs met in socially appropriate ways.
Gestalt	Establish a collaborative relationship with the client--an I-Thou relationship in which two people meet, are equal in power and entitlement, and are willing to bring their full selves to the relationship.
Jungian	Therapeutic relationship through authenticity, trust, and equality. Therapist's job is to create a space of temanos: "the sacred place where transformation can occur because it is safe."
Psychodynamic	The therapist is a participant-observer who assumes responsibility forguidance and interpretation—uses empathy, intuition, and introspection in creating a space free of anxiety so clients can access and freely express their unconscious—avoiding self-disclosure, which would interfere with client's transference.
Theraplay	The focus is on the relationship between the caregiver and the child (or adolescent), with both the caregiver and the child participating in sessions. The parent or caregiver's therapeutic relationship with the child is critical, so the Theraplay therapist builds an attuned, supportive relationship with both the adult caregiver and the child, models expectations, and as a way to support parents/caretakers learn how to interact with the child in ways that are filled with play, joy, safety, and security.
Prescriptive	Dependent upon treatment plan chosen.

Table B9

Question 5

Theory	Focus on Past, Present, or Present in the Context of the Past
Adlerian	Explores the past, often using early recollections with clients. It is always in service of helping clients understand what is happening in their thinking, feeling, and behaving in the here-and-now.

Theory	Focus on Past, Present, or Present in the Context of the Past
Child-Centered	Almost exclusively on the present, not the past.
Cognitive-Behavioral	Present.
Ecosystemic	The past and the present are important, with the past providing clues for functioning in the here-and-now.
Gestalt	Present, in the context of the past. Past interactions and experiences and self-acceptance influences how someone feels, thinks, and behaves in the present. Focus in many therapy sessions is on the senses and the body in the present, without reference to the past.
Jungian	Past could influence the future; future aspirations can shape behavior. Focus in therapy on the present.
Psychodynamic	Focus is on the past.
Theraplay	Present only.
Prescriptive	Dependent upon treatment plan chosen.

Table B10

Question 6

Theory	Insight/Increased Consciousness Needed for Change to Occur
Adlerian	Gaining insight is one of the key components of change.
Child-Centered	Increasing consciousness is not a direct goal of therapy.
Cognitive-Behavioral	Insight in cognitive-behavioral therapy and play therapy is defined as an increased awareness of irrational beliefs and a willingness to shift to more rational beliefs—this is necessary for change. Other types of insight not valued.
Ecosystemic	In some cases, it is important with certain clients to help them become more aware of their own motivation and patterns by using interpretation and feedback. With other clients, clients will get better if they learn better coping skills without becoming more aware of their motivation and patterns.

Theory	Insight/Increased Consciousness Needed for Change to Occur
Gestalt	Emphasis is on awareness of the environment, of personal process and feelings, of personal needs, of boundaries, and of the self—not on a cognitive understanding. Awareness is a holistic experience that involves the mind, the body, the emotions, and the senses.
Jungian	Increase in consciousness is necessary for healing.
Psychodynamic	Necessary for change to occur—becoming more aware of unconscious processes is essential.
Theraplay	No need for the child to gain insight for change to occur.
Prescriptive	Dependent upon treatment plan chosen.

Table B11

Question 7

Theory	Primary Focus in Counseling
Adlerian	Help people make changes in how they are living their lives; depends on the phase.
Child-Centered	The therapeutic relationship between the therapist and the client.
Cognitive-Behavioral	Goals are based on changing thinking and behaving to help reduce symptoms and improve functioning; identify and modify potentially maladaptive beliefs and use play combined with behavior strategies to address issues of control, mastery, and responsibility for behavior change.
Ecosystemic	Help the client maximize their ability to get their needs met effectively without interfering with the ability of others to get their needs met.
Gestalt	The present moment so client gains awareness of the environment and self-awareness, which helps client learn to appropriately fulfill needs and allows client to move toward optimal positive potential in their feelings and bodily sensations.

Theory	Primary Focus in Counseling
Jungian	Help the client develop their unique identity, overcome or come to terms with losses, and adapt to demands of family, school, and society; activate the individuation process; develop the ego; improve communication between the conscious and the unconscious; help clients develop flexible defense mechanisms; and activate the self-healing mechanism so that reintegration of the personality can occur.
Psychodynamic	Help children find better ways to express pent-up feelings and to develop more mature defenses against anxiety; strengthen the ego and help children accomplish developmental reorganization; address conflicts and defenses; to make way for the emergence of the self.
Theraplay	Improve the interaction between parent/caregiver and child.
Prescriptive	Dependent upon treatment plan chosen.

Table B12

Question 8

Theory	Definition of Psychological Maladjustment
Adlerian	Discouragement —Discouraged clients are "acting as if" their self-defeating mistaken beliefs about self, others, and the world are true. They are stuck in feelings of inferiority.
Child-Centered	Incongruence between the real self and the ideal self.
Cognitive-Behavioral	Exaggerated and persistent inappropriate response to stimuli based on faulty reasoning.
Ecosystemic	(a) Unable to get their needs met without interfering with the rights of others; (b)suffer from factors such as severe medical conditions, developmental delays, or mental health issues; and/or (c) are "embedded in problematic systems or interpersonal relationships.

Theory	Definition of Psychological Maladjustment
Gestalt	Contact boundary violations (which usually involve the inability to appropriately distinguish oneself from others and the environment, and a weak sense of self), faulty introjections from parents or society (which are almost always negative beliefs about the self), or the inability to meet one's own needs.
Jungian	Occurs when disturbances in the ego-Self axis interfere with individuation process. Not enough ego strength to deal with disturbing materials or experiences leads to difficulty with reintegration.
Psychodynamic	Conflicts between the ego, the id, and the super-ego. Fixations in specific psychosexual stages, lack of resolution of the Oedipal or Electra complex, and overuse or misuse of defense mechanisms.
Theraplay	Outcome of early and/or on-going unresponsive, neglectful, or abusive care--child views self as unlovable, views others as uncaring and untrust-worthy, and the world as unsafe.
Prescriptive	Dependent upon treatment plan chosen.

Table B13

Question 9

Theory	Goals of Counseling
Adlerian	Foster an increased sense of belonging and signifi-cance; help clients learn to deal with feelings of discouragement and inferiority in healthier ways; assist clients in changing their self-defeating beliefs, attitudes, and behaviors to more positive ones; help clients gain a sense of equality with others; and help people begin to make positive contributions to society and other people.

Theory	Goals of Counseling
Child-Centered	Create an environment in which there is psychological contact between client and the counselor. Through this process, clients' actualizing tendency is activated and they move toward more self-acceptance and healthy functioning; develop positive self-concepts and internal locus of evaluation; assume greater responsibility; become more self-directing, self-accepting, self-reliant, and self-trusting; engage in self-determined decision-making; and experiencing a greater sense of control.
Cognitive-Behavioral	Shift patterns of thinking, reduce negative ideation, and weaken the tendency toward irrational thoughts, which can lead to changes in emotions and behaviors.
Ecosystemic	Help client learn to get their needs met without interfering with others' ability to get needs met; to enhance attachment relationships and develop resources for reducing psychopathology and coping with interpersonal problems. Bring cognitive, emotional, and interpersonal developmental levels to as close as possible chronological age and for the levels of these domains to be relatively equal.
Gestalt	Restore the child to a healthy sense of self, to learn to accept parts of the self that have been previously rejected, to learn ways to fully support the self, and to be willing and able to experience pain and discomfort. Integration to fulfill needs or positive potential; reach a balance or feeling of congruence in life; learn to self-regulate; enhance self-awareness and self-acceptance; live in the here-and-now; and accept previously unaccepted parts of self.
Jungian	Activate the self-healing potential in psyche, strengthen the ego, stimulate and develop creativity and imagination, heal and transcend wounds, develop an interior life, foster development of a sense of competency and mastery, help develop skills to cope with future problems, and assist in gaining an understanding of the complexity of life and becoming open to change.

Theory	Goals of Counseling
Psychodynamic	Increase awareness of the internal unconscious conflicts underlying their self-defeating behavior and distressing feelings; give up overuse or misuse of primitive defense mechanisms and move toward mature defense mechanisms.
Theraplay	Fostering a positive and nurturing relationship between the caregiver and the child client; help the caregiver learn how to establish or reestablish secure attachment with the child; help the caregiver to attune to the child's needs; help the caregiver to learn to interact with the child in ways that change child's perceptions of caregiving from negative to positive; help the caregiver learn to provide structure, engagement, nurture, and challenge to the child—both in session and outside session; help the caregiver learn to reflect on his or her own emotional experiences and the child's emotional experiences in order to be able to coregulate with the child.
Prescriptive	Dependent upon treatment plan chosen.

Table B14

Question 10

Theory	Measuring Progress
Adlerian	Depends on the goals of therapy—measured by tracking whether clients are experiencing movement toward achieving these goals.
Child-Centered	Reduction in anxiety, confusion, defensiveness, and other self-defeating emotions; demonstration of positive self-concept; internal locus of evaluation; greater responsibility; more self-direction, self-acceptance, self-reliance, and self-trust; self-determined decision-making; and a greater sense of control in their lives. Observation of the child's behavior, the child's self-report, and reports from parents, teachers, and other significant adults.
Cognitive-Behavioral	Use observation, reports from parents and teachers, and (sometimes) formal assessments to assess movement toward goals.

Theory	Measuring Progress
Ecosystemic	Monitor clients' general goals related to learning to get needs met without interfering with others' ability to get their needs met, enhancing attachment relationships, developing resources for reducing psychopathology and coping with interpersonal problem, and increasing and equalizing functioning in the areas of cognition, emotion, and interpersonal relationships; checks in to make sure clients are moving toward attaining their personalized goals; may readminister psychometric instruments used in initial assessment.
Gestalt	Observation of the client to measure progress, with an occasional report from parents and teachers; decrease focus on the past and future and increased focus on the present moment; increase skills for fulfilling needs; increase willingness to experiment and try new things; increase client willingness to take responsibility for actions; and monitor for behavior that suggests client's development of appropriate aggressive energy, contact boundaries, self-acceptance and self-nurturance.
Jungian	Monitor progress toward achieving self-actualization and healing. More likely to display true self (e.g., shadow aspects, anima/animus balance) and more likely to have flexible defense structures.
Psychodynamic	From observation of the play and reports from caretakers, monitor progress with presenting problem; client's capacity for being appropriately aggressive, dependent, and adaptive; ability to deal with anxiety; uses mature defense mechanisms.
Theraplay	Observation and caregiver report concerning the improvement of the caregiver-child relationship and family interactions.
Prescriptive	Dependent upon treatment plan chosen.

Table 3.2
Question 11

Theory	Directive/Nondirective
Adlerian	Both—depends on phase of therapy, presenting problem, lifestyle of the client.

Theory	Directive/Nondirective
Child-Centered	Nondirective.
Cognitive-Behavioral	Directive.
Ecosystemic	Directive and therapist-driven.
Gestalt	Directive (at times) and nondirective (at other times), depending on the needs of client and the progression of therapy.
Jungian	Nondirective.
Psychodynamic	Mostly nondirective; occasionally directive.
Theraplay	Directive.
Prescriptive	Dependent upon treatment plan chosen.

Table 3.2

Question 11a

Theory	Creating Space/Using Structured Activities
Adlerian	Therapists combine nondirective interaction with directive intervention, depending on the phase of counseling and the needs of specific clients.
Child-Centered	Create space for child to move toward self-actualization; seldom, if ever, use structured or directive techniques.
Cognitive-Behavioral	Use activities to actively teach clients new ways of thinking, feeling, and behaving and providing opportunities for client to practice the more adaptive strategies for dealing with problems.
Ecosystemic	Use activities designed specifically to bring clients toward achieving their goals, all activities are planned by the therapist.
Gestalt	Create a safe and caring space is important; main focus is on the experiences and experiments introduced by therapist through strategies that include storytelling, music, art, dance/movement, photography.
Jungian	Create the space they call temenos, ask questions for clarification and soft interpretations; no structured activities.

Theory	Creating Space/Using Structured Activities
Psychodynamic	Create a space free from anxiety so clients can express themselves. Might use directed techniques to gather information about particular dynamics, help clients gain insight, and provide support for them to change their use of defense mechanisms.
Theraplay	Absolutely use structured activities.
Prescriptive	Dependent upon treatment plan chosen.

Table 3.2

Question 12

Theory	Play With Child
Adlerian	Play with the child—sometimes at the child's invitation and sometimes at the therapist's initiative.
Child-Centered	Rarely play with clients in sessions. Assiduously avoid leading client, relying on client to initiate interactions and take the lead in the play.
Cognitive-Behavioral	Play with client, both at client's initiative and at the therapist's invitation. Play can be directed by client or therapist.
Ecosystemic	Therapist usually participates in the experiences with the client.
Gestalt	Occasionally play with client (usually at client's behest); main function of therapist is developing and introducing specific exercises or "experiments" and scaffolding unfolding of the experience to facilitate client gaining increased awareness.
Jungian	Will play when invited by the client. The role of the therapist is participant-observer.
Psychodynamic	Not usually. Primary role is "participant-observer." If they choose to play, it will be for the purpose of gathering specific information or delivering an interpretation through a metaphor in the play.
Theraplay	Play with children mostly in service of modeling attuned caregiver behavior for parents/caregivers.
Prescriptive	Dependent upon treatment plan chosen.

Table 3.2

Question 12

Theory	Working With Parents
Adlerian	Integral part of the therapy.
Child-Centered	Occasional consultation sessions with parents, providing support, teaching skills, imparting knowledge, and monitoring parental perceptions of children's progress; filial therapy.
Cognitive-Behavioral	Therapist interviews parents to obtain information about child, the presenting problem, child's development, and parenting strategies. As the therapeutic process proceeds, therapist may conduct consultation sessions to help parents learn to modify their interactions with child, provide support to parents for reinforcing what child is doing in therapy, and provides information to them about child development and the presenting problem.
Ecosystemic	Yes.
Gestalt	Yes—provides education, encouragement, and referrals to counseling.
Jungian	Yes—provide instruction about parenting strategies, gather information about the child's struggles or progress, and provide parent support or refer for counseling elsewhere.
Psychodynamic	Ideally, treatment would be several times a week, and therapist would meet parents at least once a week, work with issues that have an impact on the emotional balance in the family and issues connected to the child—the goal is helping the parents develop a better understanding of child's internal conflicts and a clearer picture of their impact on the child.
Theraplay	Yes.
Prescriptive	Dependent upon treatment plan chosen.

Table 3.2

Question 12

Theory	Work With Teachers
Adlerian	Yes, if presenting problem is related to school and if the therapy takes place in a school setting.
Child-Centered	Occasionally consult; Child-Teacher Relationship Training.
Cognitive-Behavioral	Yes, if presenting problem is related to school.
Ecosystemic	Yes.
Gestalt	Yes.
Jungian	Not usually.
Psychodynamic	Not usually.
Theraplay	Not usually.
Prescriptive	Dependent upon treatment plan chosen.

Appendix C

Selected Sources for Information About Selected Play Therapy Techniques

Ashby, J., Kottman, T., & DeGraaf, D. (2008). *Active intervention for kids and teens*. American Counseling Association.

Curtis, E. (2022). *Art therapy activities for kids: 75 evidence-based art projects to improve behavior, build social skills, and boost emotional resilience.* Rockridge Press.

Damed Art. (2023). *ADHD emotion-regulation play therapy.* Author.

Epstein, S. (2019). *Creative interventions for challenging children and adolescents.* PESI.

Fazio-Griffith, L., & Marino, R. (Eds.) (2021). *Techniques and interventions for play therapy and clinical supervision.* IGI Global.

Goodyear-Brown, P. (2022). *Big behaviors in small containers: 131 trauma-informed play therapy interventions for disorders of dysregulation.* PESI.

Gruzewski, K. (2020). *Therapy games for teens: 101 activities to improve self-esteem, communication and coping skills.* Rockridge Press.

Gusman, L. (2020). *Essential art therapy exercises: Effective techniques to manage anxiety, depression, and PTSD.* Rockridge Press.

Kaduson, H., Cangelosi, D., & Schaefer, C. (Eds.) (2020). *Prescriptive play therapy: Tailoring interventions for specific childhood problems.* Guilford.

Kaduson, H., & Schaefer, C. (Eds.) (1997). *101 favorite play therapy techniques.* Jason Aronson.

Kaduson, H., & Schaefer, C. (Eds.) (2001). *101 more favorite play therapy techniques.* Jason Aronson.

Kaduson, H., & Schaefer, C. (Eds.). (2003). *101 favorite play therapy techniques* (Vol. III). Jason Aronson.

Kaduson, H., & Schaefer, C. (2021). *Play therapy with children: Modalities for change.* American Psychological Association.

Kottman, T. (Ed.). (2020). *Bibliotherapy: Using books in play therapy.* The Encouragement Zone.

Kottman, T. (Ed.). (2020). *Adlerian play therapy interventions for telehealth.* The Encouragement Zone.

Kottman, T., Petersen, N., Kottman, J., & Lavenz, E. (2021). *How to talk so gamers will listen and listen so gamers will talk: Using the language of video games in play therapy and counseling.* The Encouragement Zone.

Kottman, T., & Meany-Walen, K. (2016). *Partners in play: An Adlerian approach to play therapy* (3rd ed.). American Counseling Association.

Kottman, T., Ashby, J., & DeGraaf, D. (2001). *Adventures in guidance: How to integrate fun into your guidance program.* American Counseling Association.

LaVigne, M. (2020). *Play therapy activities: 101 play-based exercises to improve behavior and strengthen the parent-child connection.* Rockridge Press.

Leggett, E., & Boswell, J. (Eds.) (2016). *Directive play therapy: Theories and techniques.* Springer.

Mellenthin, C. (2018). *Play therapy: Engaging and powerful techniques for the treatment of childhood disorders.* PESI.

Petersen, N., & Kottman, T. (2022). *Using tabletop games in play therapy.* The Encouragement Zone.

Schaefer, C., & Cangelosi, D. (2016). *Essential play therapy techniques: Time-tested approaches.* Guilford.

Schaefer, C., & Cangelosi, D. (2002). *Play therapy techniques* (2nd ed.). Jason Aronson.

Turner-Bumberry, T. (2019). *2, 4, 6, 8 This is how we regulate: 75 play therapy activities to increase mindfulness in children.* PESI.

Index

101 stories for enhancing happiness and well-being (Burns, 2017), 271

A

Abreaction, 5, **8–9**, 36, 297, 303

Abuse and neglect, 24, 50, 75, 81, 316, 318, 321, 350, 352. *See also* Sexual abuse

Accelerated psychological development, 5, **18–19**

Acting-out behavior, 37, 40, 78

Active parenting: a parent's guide to raising happy and successful children (Popkin, 2014), 337

ACT procedure, 188–189, 338. *See also* Landreth

Adler, Alfred, 51

Adlerian play therapy, 29–30, **42–43**, 49, **50–57**, 177, 179, 189, 242, 282, 322, 329, 342
distinctive features, 56–57
goals of therapy, 55
parent/caregiver consultation models, 335–338
phases of the process, 53
role of the therapist, 53–54
theoretical constructs, 50–52
working with parents and teachers, 55–56

Advanced skills, 79, 243, **281–309**
co-telling a story, 295–296
metacommunication, 53, 165, 243, **281–288**
children's reactions to, 284–285
examples of, 285–288
phrasing and styles of, 283–284
purpose of, 283
mutual storytelling, 79, 281, **288–295**, 298
examples of, 292–295
how to use, 289–292
role playing and engaging in play, 296–301
examples of, 299–301
instant replay, 298–300
release therapy, 37, 298
role reversal, 296, 298–299, 301
teaching/practicing new behaviors, 300–301
whisper technique, 201, 203, 228, **296–300**

Adventure therapy. *See* Strategies

Ain't misbehavin': tactics for tantrums, meltdowns, bedtime blues and other perfectly normal kid behaviors (Schafer, 2011), 56, 337

Allan, John, 44, 80, 258

Allen, Frederick, 38

Altvater, R. A., 111, 362–363

Amaya's anger: a mindful understanding of strong emotions (Garcia, 2021), 20

American Counseling Association (ACA), 347, 353

American Psychological Association (APA), 326, 348, 353

Anger management, 11, 19, 25, 113, 128, 360–361

Anxiety. *See also* Stress
    in the child, 4, 10, 24, 50, 60, 63, 75, 85–86, 88–90, 123, 129–130, 160, 205–206, 311–313, **317–318**
    in the therapist, 186–187, 248

Archetypes, 80, 82, 85

Art activities. *See* Strategies

Ashby, Jeffrey S., 50

Association for Play Therapy (APT), 5, 49, 193, 326, 348–350, 352–353, 365–366

Attachment-based play therapy, 41–42

Attachment issues, 5, **13**, 68, 89–90
    reactive attachment disorder (RAD), 50
theories for working with, 41–42

Attention-deficit/hyperactivity disorder (ADHD), 15, 24–25, 46, 50, 99, 125, 196, 241, 304, 318

Autism, 24, 89

AutPlay Therapy, 49, 98, **99**

Axline, Virginia, 39, 57, 59, 124, 175

An A-Z collection of behaviour tales: from angry ant to zestless zebra (Perrow, 2017), 271

B

Baby talk, 321

Baggerly, Jennifer N., 360

Basic skills, 31, 87, 93, **133–229**
integration of, 235–248
deciding when to use, 235–243
    attitudes about cultural differences, 238–239
    context of child's life, 240–242
    course of play, 242
    individual child, 239–240
    intuition and experience, 237
    personal preference and personality, 238
    phase of therapy, 242–243
    theoretical orientation, 236
infusing skills, 243, 248–249
integrating skills, 243–248
    deciding which meld, 247
    mechanics of blending, 244

Beckley-Forest, A., 47

BE DIRECT skills, 333–334. *See also* PRIDE skills

Bellies to the sky: a bedtime breathwork book (Canning, 2021), 20

Benedict, Helen E., 41, 314

Bennett, M. M., 328

Bettner, B. L., 52

Bibliotherapy, 20, 61, 65, 67,
113, 164, 243, 271. *See also*
Metaphors
interactive, 271–272
reactive, 271–272

Bixler, R. H., 40, 175–176

Black, Indigenous, and people of
color (BIPOC), 224–225, 242,
256. *See also* Multicultural
orientation
African Americans, 187, 249,
305
Asian Americans, 187, 219, 232,
256
Mexican Americans/Latinx, 8,
188, 232
familismo, 188
personalismo 188
Native Americans, 10, 187

Books, 65, 113, 176, 236, 256,
270–272. *See also* Bibliotherapy
for adults, 31, 56, 271, 337,
415–427
on Adlerian theory/play
therapy, 415–417
on child-centered play
therapy, 417–418
on cognitive-behavioral
theory/play therapy,
418–419
on ecosystemic play
therapy, 420
on Gestalt theory/play
therapy, 420–421
on integrative/prescriptive
play therapy, 426–427
on Jungian theory/play
therapy, 421–422
on narrative play theory/
therapy, 423
on person-centered theory,
417
on play therapy
techniques, 451–452
on psychodynamic play
therapy, 424
on psychodynamic theory,
423–424
on Theraplay, 425–426
for children, 20, 119, 164, 271

Bradway, K., 44

Bratton, S. C., 24, 40, 331, 339

Bridging. *See* Broaching and
bridging

British Association of Play
Therapists, 21

Broaching and bridging, 262,
355–356, 358–359
examples of, 264

Brody, V., 41

Bullying, 262, 315–316, 320

C

Canadian Association for Play
Therapy, 366

Caregivers, working with. *See*
Parents

Carey, L. J., 44

Carmichael, K. D., 351

Carroll, Felicia, 79, 367

Cates, J., 328

Catharsis, 5, **7–8**, 37, 176, 297, 315

Cavett, A. M., 64

Cheng, Y.-J., 355–356, 360

Child-centered play therapy (CCPT), 24, 28, **39–40**, 46, 49, **57–63**, 111, 121, 176–177, 206, 221, 258, 313, 322, 329, 331, **338**, 341–342, 370
distinctive features, 63
goals of therapy, 61–62
phases of the process, 60
role of the therapist, 61
theoretical constructs, 58–60
working with parents, 62

Child Initiated Pretend Play Assessment (Stagnitti, 2007), 313

Child-Parent Relationship Therapy (CPRT). *See* Psychoeducational programs

Child-Teacher Relationship Training (CTRT), 341

Child-therapist relationship. *See* Therapeutic relationship

Circle of Security model, 339

Clients, appropriateness of, 23–26

Clinical depression. *See* Depression

Cochran, N. H., 57

Codes of ethics, 118, 347–348, 352–353. *See also* Legal and ethical issues

Cognitive-behavioral play therapy 28, **43**, 46, 49, **63–68**, 85, 206
distinctive features, 67–68
goals of therapy, 66
phases of the process, 64–65
role of the therapist, 65–66
theoretical constructs, 63–64
working with parents, 66–67

Communication, 5, 11, 17, 26–27, 31–32, 36, 67, 72, 133–134, 137, 147, 157, 163, 206, 240–242, 283–284, 314. *See also* Expression
direct, 134, 263, **320–321**
indirect, 136, 160
metaphoric, 28, 263, 283, 312, **320–321**. *See also* Metaphors
non-metaphoric, 259
nonverbal, 44, 63, 135–136, 160, 165, 186–187, 226, 229–230, 246, 282
verbal, 44, 63, 67, 135, 160, 226

Confidentiality, 117–118, 120–121, 328, 348–352

Consultation models. *See* Parent/caregiver consultation models

Control. *See* Power and control issues

Corrective experiences. *See* Alternative/corrective experiences

Courtney, Janet A., 99, 367

Covert reactions, 164, 283

COVID-19 pandemic, 8–9, 272

Creative problem-solving, 5, **15–16**, 72

Crucial Cs, 52–53, 55–57, 291,
336–337, 342

Cultural factors, 22, 110, 159, 225,
239–242, 259, 328. *See also*
Multicultural orientation
comfort, 239, 355
competence and humility, 22,
239, 347, **353–360**
considerations in limit-setting,
187–188
differences, attitudes and
beliefs about, 238–239
opportunities, 239–240, 242,
355, 359
symbolism, 313

D

Dance. *See* Strategies

Davis, D. E., 357

Depression, 10, 63, 75, 81, 85, 89,
250

Developmental play therapy,
41–42, 68

Dimensions model, **27–31**, 98
active utilization, 29
cofacilitation, 29
consciousness, 6, 27–30, 81, 86
conscious, 5, 29, 81, 86, 88,
147, 255, 322
preconscious, 86
subconscious, 36
unconscious, 5, **6–7**, 28–29,
36, 44, 54, 81–82, 85–86,
88–89, 238, 255
directiveness, 27–29
nonintrusive responding,
29–30
open discussion and
exploration, 29

Dion, Lisa, 100, 367

Direct teaching, 5, **6–7**, 53, 243,
320–321. *See also* Indirect
teaching

Divorce, 11, 24, 50, 63, 81, 169, 242,
250, 315, 349

Dramatic play, 45, 79, 83, 85, 113,
296

Dreikurs, R., 52

Drewes, Athena A., 5, 10, 47, 302,
353, 357, 361–362, 367–368

Drisko, J., 24

Dynamic play therapy, 45, 86

E

Ecosystemic play therapy, 28, **45**,
49, **68–75**, 110, 121, 147, 225
distinctive features, 74–75
Ecosystemic model, 69, 72
goals of therapy, 73
integrative metatheory, 68
fill elements, 68–69, 74
structure elements, 68–69,
74
personal theory, 69, 74
phases of the process, 70–71
role of the therapist, 71–72
theoretical constructs, 68–70
working with parents, 73–74

Edge, A., 313

Empathy, 5, 14
for the child, 12, 77, 130, 163,
189, 331, 338–339
in the child, **15**, 263, 298, 302

Encouragement, 31, 37, 202, 204, 207–213, 223, 227, 242, 246–247, 336, 342

Ending a session, 38, 107, **124–126**, 330. *See also* Termination of therapy
children who do not wish to leave, 126
cleaning the playroom, 53, 57, **124–126**
writing session reports, 107, 114, 117, **126–127**

Engaging in play, **296–301**, 330, 365. *See also* Advanced skills

Erickson, Erik, 313

Erickson, Milton, 100

Ethics. *See* Codes of Ethics. *See* Legal and ethical issues

Expanding feeling concepts, 17, 157, **165–166**. *See also* Vocabulary

Experiential play therapy, 28, 39, 258

Explaining the process, **114–122**, 364
personal application, 121–122
to children, 70, 87, 92, 107, **120–121**, 123–124
to parents and teachers, 25, 41, 91, 93–94, 107, **114–120**, 124, 327–328, 365–366
confidentiality, 117–118
explanation handout/ introductory book, 119
how long play therapy will take, 116–117
insurance and managed care, 120. *See also* Health insurance

personality priorities, 56–57, 115–116, 336
pitching play therapy, 115–116
reports about the session, 117
roles and responsibilities, 119
therapeutic goals, 119
what children should wear, 117
what play therapy is, 114–115

Expression, manner of, 7–8, 36, 45, 145, **159–161**, 303, 312, 363. *See also* Communication. *See also* Self-expression
affective tone, 159–161, 163, 259, 313
aggression, 175, 360–361
direct verbal, 44, 110, 159
emotional, 77–78, 80, 110, 128
implicit, 159–160, 202, **209–211**, 283
indirect, 159, 262
nonverbal, 44, 110, 159, 328
symbolic, 175

F

Familial Encouraging Connect Therapy (FECT). *See* Psychoeducational programs

Family play therapy, **45–46**, 124

Fears and phobias, 10, 63, 85, 112–113, 313, 363
counterconditioning, 5, **10**

Feedback from the child, 135–137, 146–147, 225, 240, 283. *See also* Communication. *See also* Expression
direct nonverbal, 147

direct verbal, 146
indirect nonverbal, 147
indirect verbal, 147

Feelings ninja: a social, emotional children's book about emotions and feelings (Nhin, 2021), 20, 164

Feeling words. *See* Vocabulary

Fetal alcohol syndrome, 24

Filial therapy. *See* Psychoeducational programs

FirstPlay, 49, 98, **99**

Flanagan, J. S., 267

Floor games (Wells, 1911), 36

Flynn, Jackie, 368

Freud, Anna, 36, 85–86, 88

Freud, Sigmund, 35–37, 85–86

G

Gameplay, 13, 17, 19, 72, 90, 94, 125, 227, 302–303, 358, 363. *See also* Toys
board games, 13, 17–18, 23, 111, 113, 303
therapeutic games, 17, 27
video games, 12, 111, 202, 256, 270, 289, 363–364

Gardner, J. E., 363

Gardner, Ken, 27, 29

Gardner, Ricardo A., 288

Gavin, S., 362

Gender-expansive children, 241

Gestalt play therapy, 28, 42, **43**, 46, 49, **75–80**, 85, 121, 179, 206, 258
distinctive features, 80
goals of therapy, 79–80
phases of the process, 77–78
role of the therapist, 79
theoretical constructs, 75–77
awareness and experience, 75, 77
contact-boundary disturbances, 75–77, 80
I-Thou relationship, 75, 77, 79–80
organismic self-regulation, 43, 75–77
working with parents, 80

Gil, E., 47, 95, 316, 353, 357

Ginott, H., 40, 175–176, 178–179

Goodnight love: a bedtime meditation story (Kim, 2023), 20

Goodyear-Brown, Paris, 100, 316, 339, 369

Grant, Robert Jason, 99, 369

Great Big Breath (Long, 2023), 20

Green, E. J., 84, 314, 360

Grief and loss, 24, 50, 75–76, 87, 90, 162, 184, 312–314

Guerney, Bernard, 39, 331

Guerney, Louise, 39, 60, 185, 331, 360, 369

The guide to play therapy documentation and parent consultation (Homeyer & Bennett, 2023), 126

H

Hambridge, Gove, 37–38

Harvey, S., 45

Health insurance, 107, 120, 126

Heiko, R., 81, 84

Hillman, L., 314

Hindman, M. L., 365

Holtz, Dana, 369

Homeyer, L., 113, 328

Honey, I wrecked the kids: when yelling, screaming, threats, bribes, time-outs, sticker charts and removing privileges all don't work (Schafer, 2009), 56, 337

Hook, J. N., 22, 238

How to tell stories to children (West & Sarosy, 2021), 271

Hug-Hellmuth, Hermine, 36

Hull, K. B., 111, 363

I

I feel: a book of emotions (Medina, 2022), 164

I'm happy-sad today: making sense of mixed-together feelings (Britain, 2019), 164

Indirect teaching, 5, **6–7**, 53, 243. *See also* Direct teaching. *See also* Metaphoric teaching

In-home therapy, 36, 112, 181

Initial session, 107, **121–124**, 137, 184, 335

Inspiring short stories for kids: motivational book about self-confidence, perseverance, gratitude, courage, and other values (AMghs Publishing, 2023), 271

Integrative play therapy, **47**, 96, 236. *See also* Prescriptive play therapy

Interpersonal and intrapersonal dynamics, 43, 229, 238, 243, 259, 303, 322, 327, 340

J

Jayne, K. M., 338

Jernberg, A. M., 41, 90

Johnson, J. L., 40

Jung, Carl G., 44, 80

Jungian analytical play therapy, 28, 42, **44**, 49, **80–85**, 111, 179, 206, 258, 314
distinctive features, 85
goals of therapy, 84
phases of the process, 82–83
role of the therapist, 83
theoretical constructs, 81–82
working with parents, 84

K

Kaduson, H. G., 47, 95–98

Kalff, D., 44

Kefir, N., 115

Kinder Training, 341–342

Kissel, S., 183

Klein, Melanie, 36

Knell, Susan M., 43, 63–64, 369

Kottman, Terry, 50, 52, 101, 110–111, 124, 176, 188–190, 268, 313, 316, 342; Kottman and Meany-Walen's method, **189–192**, 194. *See also* Limit setting

L

Labeling, 134–135

Landreth, Garry L., 39–40, 57, 61, 108–109, 177, 188–189, 219, 228, 237, 331, 360, 363; Landreth's method, **188–189**, 191–193. *See also* ACT procedure. *See also* Limit setting

Lankton, C., 266

Lankton, S., 266

Leading/not leading the child, 61, **148–152**, 165, 222, 227–229

Leblanc, M., 23–24, 339

Lee, A., 86

Legal and ethical issues, 21, 42, 118, 177, 193, 219, **347–353**, 366. *See also* Codes of ethics

Levy, D., 37

Lew, A., 52

Lilly, J. P., 81–82, 84, 258–259, 369

Limits, categories of, 176
absolute, 176, 178
clinical, 176, 178
reactionary, 176, 178
relative/negotiable, 176, 178–179, 184

Limit setting, **40, 175–177**, 241, 247. *See also* Adlerian play therapy
cultural considerations in, 187–188
in filial therapy, 330
practical considerations in, 185–187
styles of, 188
Landreth's method, 188–189, 191–194
Kottman and Meany-Whalen's method, 189–194
what to limit, 178
based on the individual child, 183–184
based on theoretical perspective, 178–180
based on therapist's personality, 181–183
based on the setting, 180–181
when to limit, 184–185

Linn, S., 363

Listening, 44, 115, 143, 242, 257, 338, 341
active, 328, 341, 356, 359
body posture, 144, 223
empathic, 62, 330, 339

Listening to my body (Garcia, 2017), 20

A little spot of anger (Alber, 2019), 20

Lolan, A., 326

Lowenfeld, Margaret, 36–37, 44

Lyles, M., 113

M

The magic in metaphor: empowering children through healing stories (Sears, 2023), 271

Maladaptive perfectionism, 24, 50, 318

Managed health care. *See* Health insurance

Marcy's having all the feels (Edwards, 2020), 164

Marschak, M., 91

Mattei, D., 361

McNary, T., 363

Meany-Walen, K., 52, 101, 110, 124, 176, 188–190, 268, 313, 316; Kottman and Meany-Walen's method, **189–192**, 194. *See also* Limit setting

Metacommunication. *See* Advanced skills

Metacompetency, 22

Metaphoric teaching, 7, 320–321. *See also* Indirect teaching. *See also* Metaphors

Metaphors. *See also* Bibliotherapy. *See also* Communication communicating through, 26, 28–30, 145, 229, 244, 255, **262–265**, 282–283, 311–313, **320–321**
child's reaction, 263–264
examples for communicating, 264–265
helping clients shift, 265–266, 302
importance of, 255–257
nonmetaphor kids, 259, 320
recognizing, 46, 85, **257–258**
therapeutic, 79, 88, **266–272**, 292, 298, 302
designing and delivering, 61, 236, 243, **267–272**
examples of therapeutic metaphors, 272–275
understanding the meaning of, 53, **258–262**
examples of possible meanings, 259–262
using the child's metaphor, 201–202, 210–211

Mills, Joyce, 100

Minimal encouragers, 201, 203, 206, 221, **223–224**
examples of, 208–213

Monaco, A., 47

Montessori, Maria, 36

Moral development, 5, **17**

Mosher, D. K., 354–355

Moustakas, Clark, 38, 60, 175

Movement, dance, and music. *See* Strategies

Multicultural orientation, 239, 353, 355–359. *See also* Cultural elements

Munns, Evangeline, 369–370

Music. *See* Strategies

Mutual storytelling. *See* Advanced skills

My book about play therapy (S. Wilson, 2018), 119

N

Nalavany, B. A., 21, 365

Narrative play therapy, 28, 42, **44**, 111, 121

National Association of Social Workers (NASW), 353

Neglect. *See* Abuse and neglect

The new social story book (Gray, 2015), 271

Nordling, William J., 60

Norton, B., 39, 176

Norton, C., 39, 176

O

Oaklander, Violet, 43, 370

Object relations theory, 41, **42**, 68

O'Connor, Kevin J., 45, 68–74, 356–357

Ogawa, Y., 239

Orozco, V., 79

Overt reactions, 164

P

P3 Model (Principles, Principals, Process), 352

Paper on touch: clinical, professional & ethical issues (Association for Play Therapy, 2022), 42, 351–352

Paradigm shifts, **26–27**, 31, 45, 339

Parent/caregiver consultation models, 335–339
Adlerian, 335–338
child-centered, 338
TraumaPlay, 339

Parent-Child Interaction Therapy (PCIT). *See* Psychoeducational programs

Parent-child relationships, 40–41, 62, 74, 90–91, 93–94, 96, 99, 330–331, 339. *See also* Psychoeducational programs
challenge in, 41, 90–91
engagement in, 41, 89–91
nurture in, 41, 90–91
structure in, 41, 90

Parents, working with, 13, 22, 39–40, 43, 49, 127, 129–130, **325–329**. *See also* Explaining the process. *See also* Psychoeducational programs
in Adlerian play therapy, 55–56
in child-centered play therapy, 62
in cognitive-behavioral play therapy, 63–67
in ecosystemic play therapy, 70, 73–74
in FirstPlay, 99
in Gestalt play therapy, 80
in Jungian analytical play therapy, 84

in prescriptive play therapy, 95–96
in psychodynamic play therapy, 86, 89
research support for, 339–340
in Theraplay, 89, 91–94
in TraumaPlay, 100

A parent's guide to understanding and motivating children (Lew & Bettner, 2000), 56, 337

Parker, M. M., 361

Passive voice, 189, 237

Patterns. *See* Themes and patterns

Peery, J. C., 84

Perez, R., 188

Perls, Fritz, 43

Personal qualities of a play therapist, 21–23
personal application, 121–123, 166, 180
personal style, 117, 162–163, 166, 229, 244, 248

Personal theory, 69

Peterlin, K., 46

Petersen, N., 111

Phenomenological field, 58, 258

Piaget, Jean, 36

Plausible deniability, 255

Play disruption, 164, 320

Playroom. *See* Setting up a space

Play Therapy Best Practices (Association for Play Therapy, 2022), 348, 350, 352–353

Play therapy dimensions model: new insights for integrative play therapists (Yasenik & Gardner, 2024), 31

Play therapy strategies. *See* Strategies

Pluralcentrism, 358

Positive discipline for preschoolers: for their early years—raising children who are responsible, respectful, and resourceful (Nelson, Erwin, & Duffy, 2019), 337

Positive discipline for today's busy (and overwhelmed) parent: how to balance work, parenting, and self for lasting well-being (Nelson, 2018), 56

Positive discipline: the classic guide to helping children develop self-discipline, responsibility, cooperation, and problem-solving skills (Nelson, 2006), 337

Positive emotion, 5, **9**, 19

Post, P. B., 325, 341

Posttraumatic play, 100, 297, 315–316

Posttraumatic stress disorder (PTSD), 46, 75

Power and control issues, 50, 125, 311–313, **319–320**

Prescriptive play therapy, 28, **47**, 49, 53, **95–98**, 111, 148, 206, 236
  basic tenets of, 95–96
    differential therapeutics, 95
    eclecticism, 96, 98
    integrative psychotherapy, 96
    prescriptive matching, 96
    individualized treatment, 96
  core practices of, 96–98
    comprehensive assessment, 96
    empirically supported treatments, 97
    monitoring of progress, 97
    role of the therapist, 97
    treatment selection, 97

PRIDE skills, 333. *See also* BE DIRECT skills

Professional issues, 177, **347–365**. *See also* Legal and ethical issues
  advice to beginners, 366–371
  cultural competence, 353–360
  inclusion of aggressive toys, 360–362. *See also* Toys
  professional identity, 364–366
  public awareness, 364–366
  technology in the playroom, 362–364

Psychoanalytic play therapy, **35–37**, 68, 88. *See also* Psychodynamic play therapy

Psychodynamic play therapy, 28, **35–37**, 49, **85–89**, 111, 182, 206, 221, 314, 330. *See also* Psychoanalytic play therapy
  distinctive features, 89
  goals of therapy, 88
  phases of the process, 86–87
  role of the therapist, 87–88
  theoretical constructs, 85–86
  working with parents, 89

Psychoeducational programs, 329–335, 337
  for teaching parents
    nondirective skills, 329–330
    Child-Parent Relationship Therapy (CPRT), 40, 329, **331–332**, 339–340
    Familial Encouraging Connect Therapy (FECT), 55, 329, **334–335**
    filial therapy, 39–40, 46, 62, 84, 129, 329, **330**, 331, 339, 341
    parent-child interaction therapy (PCIT), 329, **332–334**, 340

Psychopathology, 63–64, 70, 73–74, 117, 240

Psychosexual stages, 86

Psychosis, 50

Purswell, K. E., 22

Q

Questions, asking, 27, 53, 57, 87, 228, **229–230**, 236, 262
  child's reaction to, 282

Questions from children, 217–229
  nature of, 217–220
    dual-category questions, 220
    ongoing-process questions, 219–220
    personal questions, 218–219
    practical questions, 217

relationship questions, 219
responses to, 221–229, 236, 247
   answering the question,
      53, 221–223, 236
   answering with a question,
      228
   declining to answer,
      228–229
   guessing/interpreting,
      225–227
   ignoring the question, 223
   using minimal
      encouragers, 223–224.
      See also Minimal
      encouragers
   restating the question,
      224–225
   returning responsibility,
      227–228

R

Rank, O., 38

Ray, Dee C., 11, 57, 110, 238, 312,
   355, 357, 363, 370

Reality Play Therapy, 49, 68, 98, **99**

Recognition reflex, 220

Reflecting feelings, 22, 31, 126,
   157–166, 201, 203, 206, 236,
   241–243, 262,
   in different theoretical
      orientations, 40, 61, 94, 163,
      166, 247, 334, 342
   examples of, 166–169, 207–213
   expanding concepts, 165. *See
      also* Vocabulary
   how to reflect feelings, **158**, 296
   monitoring child's responses,
      164–165
   what to reflect, **159–164**, 322
      deeper feelings, 161–162

here-and-now versus
      patterns, 162–163
   manner of expression,
      159–161
   multiple feelings, 163–164

Registered Play Therapist (RPT)
   credentials, 349–350, 364, 366

Relationship play therapy, 38–39

Release therapy. *See* Advanced
   skills

Resiliency, 5, 16–17, 100, 312

Restating content, 31, **143–148**, 201,
   224–225, 238, 243
   in different theoretical
      orientations, 40, 60, 79, 87,
      93, **147–148**, 202–203, 206,
      236, 247, 296
   examples of, **148–152**,
      207–208, 212, 224–225
   focusing restatements,
      144–145
   how to restate, 143–144
   influencing by, 145–146
   monitoring reactions to,
      146–147, 242

Returning responsibility to the
   child, 16, 31, **199–206**, 221,
   237–238, **227–228**
   in different theoretical
      orientations, 53, 58, 61, 79,
      93–94, **206**, 236, 247, 296,
      319, 334
   examples of, **207–213**, 245, 264,
      287
   how to return responsibility,
      201–202, 262
      combined approach,
         203–204
      direct approach, 202
      indirect approach, 202–203

when not to return
    responsibility, 204–206
    child cannot take
       responsibility, 204–205
    current situation, 206
    history of child, 205
    regressive behavior, 205
when to return responsibility,
    200, 241–242

Ritchie, M., 23–24, 339

Rogers, Carl, 39, 59

Role playing, 62, 66–67, 203, 243, 281, **296–301**, 330. *See also* Advanced skills

Role reversal. *See* Advanced skills

Rubin, L. C., 272, 352

Ryan, Virginia, 57, 313

S

Sand tray therapy. *See* Strategies

Sarah, B., 313

Saviorism, 356

Schaefer, Charles E., 5, 10, 47, 302, 361, 364, 370

School-related issues, 45, 50, 55, 62, 67, 80, 84, 94, 128, 146, 206, 272–273, 315, 325–326, 328, 335, 338, 340–342, 361. *See also* Teachers

Schottelkorb, A. A., 338

Self-actualization, 58–59

Self-esteem, 5, **20**, 25, 40, 81, 89, 242, 249, 338, 341. *See also* Self-image

Self-expression, 5–6. *See also* Expression

Self-image, 50, 76, 282, 291. *See also* Self-esteem

Self-regulation, 5, 9, **19–20**, 94, 177, 184, 302, 339. *See also* Gestalt play therapy

Setting limits. *See* Limits. *See* Limit setting

Setting up a space, 26, 107, **108–109**, 112

Sexual abuse, 57, 81, 184, 218, 317

Seymour, J. W., 352

Shaw, J. A., 95

Short-term play therapy, **46**, 89, 91

Skills. *See* Advanced skills. *See* Basic skills

Sleepy time nighty-night (Park, 2023), 20

Sloves, R., 46

Snow, M. S., 111

Social competence, 5, **14**

Solomon, Joseph, 37

Soltz, V., 52

Solution-focused play therapy, 46

Stauffer, S., 362

Stone, J., 111, 363

StoryPlay, 49, 98, **100**

Storytelling. *See* Strategies

Strategies, 31, 281, **301–304**, 357
    adventure therapy, 31, 43, **302**
    art activities, 31, 44, 78–79, 93,
        113, 302–303, 313, 317
    movement, dance, and music
        experiences, 31, 43, 45, 78,
        113, 281, 302
    sand tray therapy, 4, 31, 43–44,
        85, 113, 192, 281, **303**
    storytelling and therapeutic
        metaphors, 7, 31, 43–44,
        53, 57, 78–79, 85, 93, 99–100,
        113, 258, 266, 270–271, 302,
        341. *See also* Advanced
        skills. *See also* Metaphors.
        See also Narrative play
        therapy
    structured play experiences,
        31, 43, 113, 302, **303–304**.
        See also Structured play
        therapy

Stress, 16. *See also* Anxiety. *See also*
    Posttraumatic stress disorder
    inoculation, 5, 11
    management, 5, 11–12

Structured play therapy, **37–38**,
    303–304

Stulmaker, H. L., 338

Stutey, Diane M., 99

Sweeney, Daniel, 113, 303, 360

Synergetic Play Therapy, 49, 98,
    100

T

Taft, Jessie, 38

Tales for the hidden mind (Taub,
    2021), 271

Taylor de Faoite, Aideen, 370

Taylor, S., 302

Teacher-Child Connection
    Training (TCCT), 341–342

Teachers. *See also* Parents
    explaining the process to, 107,
        114–122
    teacher-child relationship, 81,
        146, 226, 230, 319
    working with, 43, 49, 53, 55–56,
        62–63, 66, 96, 127–130, 314,
        322, 325, 329, 333, 337–338,
        340–342

Termination of therapy, 107,
    127–130, 326
    child reactions to, 65, 71, 87,
        129–130
    how to handle, 65, 129, 329,
        338, 348
    when to terminate, 38, 92,
        127–128
    who decides, 128–129

Themes and patterns, assessing,
    44, 118, 126–127, 137, 285, 290,
    311
    how the child plays out the
        problem, 314–321
    aggression and
        challenging authority,
        316
    anxiety level, 317–318
    communication, 320–321
    developmental issues, 321
    order and structure,
        318–319

overtly sexual play, 317
power and control, 319–320
repetitive play, 315–316
risk taking, 318
secrecy or privacy, 316–317
play themes, 87, 160, 239,
312–314
using your understanding of,
46, 322

Theoretical approaches, 22, 28,
49–50. *See also* Integrative play
therapy. *See also* Prescriptive
play therapy
based on theories for work
with adults, 42–44
choosing an orientation,
101–103
emerging, 49, **98–101**
integrating different theories,
44–47

Theoretical orientation, 35, 42,
49–50, 95–97, 120, 162–165,
235–236, 248, 281, 314
choosing an orientation or
approach, 101–103
in dealing with questions,
217, 223, 228–229. *See also*
Questions from children
tracking in different
orientations, 137. *See also*
Tracking
reflecting in different
orientations, 166. *See also*
Reflecting feelings
restating in different
orientations, 147–148. *See
also* Restating content
returning responsibility in
different orientations,
205–206. *See also* Returning
responsibility to the child

Therapeutic metaphors. *See*
Metaphors

Therapeutic powers of play, **5**, 96,
99–100, 302

Therapeutic relationship, 5–6, 9,
12, 38–39, 43–44, 51, 53, 55, 59,
72, 75, 80, 82, 89, 123–125, 137,
143, 148, 175, 177, 183, 193, 219,
226, 236, 240, 242–243, 336, 348,
350–351, 360

*Therapeutic storytelling: 101 healing
stories for children* (Perrow,
2012), 271

Theraplay, 28, **41**, 49, 68, **89–94**,
110, 121, 124, 129, 147, 236, 340
distinctive features, 94
goals of therapy, 93–94
phases of the process, 91–93
role of the therapist, 93
theoretical constructs, 90–91
working with parents, 94

Time-limited play therapy, 46

Tisdell, Timothy, 370

*Touch in child counseling and play
therapy: an ethical and clinical
guide* (Courtney & Nolan, 2017),
42

Toys, 5–6, 10, 26–27, 50, 67, 71,
123–127, 135, 160, 178–179, 313,
317. *See also* Gameplay
aggressive, 112–113, 316, 347,
356, **360–362**
choosing and arranging, 23,
36–37, 71, 87, **107–114**, 181,
319, 356–357, 363
expressive, 160–161, 229, 270,
289, 303
family/nurturing, 112
pretend/fantasy, 72, 112–114
scary, 112

Tracking, 31, **133–137**, 123, 148,
    201, 237–238
    in different theoretical
        orientations, 28, 40, 53, 61,
        79, 87, 93, **137**, 203, 206, 236,
        242, 247, 296, 330, 333–334,
        342
    examples of, **138–139**, 213, 245,
        364
    how to track, 133–135
    monitoring children's
        reactions to, 135–137

Transference, 46, 83, 86–89, 221

TraumaPlay, 49, 98, **100–101**, 329,
    339

Trotter, K., 360

Turner, R., 22, 365

*Turning points in play therapy
    and the emergence of self:
    applications of the play therapy
    dimensions model* (Yasenik &
    Gardner, 2018), 31

U

*Using art, play, metaphor, and
    symbol with hard-to-reach young
    clients* (Webber & Webber,
    2023), 271

*Using trauma-focused therapy
    stories: interventions for
    therapists, children, and their
    caregivers* (Pernicano, 2022),
    271

V

VanFleet, Risë, 46, 57, 62, 313,
    370–371

Vega, C., 68, 71

Vocabulary, 5, 87, 144, 157–158,
    165–166, 354
    feeling words, 166

W

Waller, Debbie, 255

Wells, H. G., 36

When a donut goes to therapy
    (Winters, 2021), 119

Whisper technique. *See* Advanced
    skills

White, JoAnna, 371

White, Michael, 44

Wilson, Kate, 57

World technique, 36, 44

Wubbolding, Robert E., 99

Y

Yee, T., 355–356, 360

Yasenik, Lorri, 27, 29

About the Authors

Terry Kottman developed Adlerian play therapy, an approach to work -ing with children and families that combines the ideas and techniques of Individual Psychology and play therapy. She founded the League of Extraordinary Adlerian Play Therapists and created a certification program for Adlerian play therapy. Terry is a presenter and author who regularly teaches classes and writes about play therapy. She is co-author (with Kristin Meany-Walen) of *Doing Play Therapy: From Building the Relationship to Facilitating Change* and *Partners in Play: An Adlerian Approach to Play Therapy* and several other books. In 2014, she was granted a Lifetime Achievement Award from the Association for Play Therapy; in 2017, she was given a Lifetime Achieve -ment Award from the Iowa Association for Play Therapy; and in 2020, she received a third Lifetime Achievement Award from the North American Society for Adlerian Psychology. In 2024, the National Board for Certified Counselors gave Terry the Innovation in Counseling: Practice and Clinical Service Award.

Jeffrey S. Ashby is a Professor of Counseling Psychology in the Department of Counseling and Psychological Services at Georgia State University. He is the Director of the Georgia State Play Therapy Training Institute, a Licensed Psychologist, and a Registered Play Therapist Supervisor. In addition, he is the Co-Director of Georgia State's Matheny Center for the Study of Stress, Trauma, and Resilience, a Diplomate of the American Board of Professional Psychology, a Fellow of the American Academy of Counseling Psychology, and a Fellow of the Georgia Psychological Association. Jeff has authored over 120 professional journal articles, numerous book chapters, and two books. Jeff lives in Atlanta with his wife Lucy and dog Zoey, with occasional visits from his four adult children (a constant adventure).